The
Modern Language
Review

APRIL 2015   VOLUME 110   PART 2

General Editor
PROFESSOR DEREK CONNON

English Editor
PROFESSOR ANDREW HISCOCK

French Editor
DR ALISON WILLIAMS

Italian Editor
PROFESSOR GUIDO BONSAVER

Hispanic Editor
PROFESSOR DEREK FLITTER

Germanic Editor
PROFESSOR ROBERT VILAIN

Slavonic Editor
DR KATHARINE HODGSON

Assistant Editor
DR JOHN WAŚ

MODERN HUMANITIES RESEARCH ASSOCIATION

The Modern Humanities Research Association

was founded in Cambridge in 1918 and has become an international organization with members in all parts of the world. It is a registered charity number 1064670, and a company limited by guarantee, registered in England number 3446016. Its main object is to encourage advanced study and research in modern and medieval European languages, literatures, and cultures by its publication of journals, book series, and its Style Guide.

Further information about the activities of the Association and individual membership may be obtained from the Membership Secretary, Dr Jessica Goodman, Clare College, Trinity Lane, Cambridge CB2 1TL, UK, email membership@mhra.org.uk, or from the website at www.mhra.org.uk

The Association's publications, including most back volumes, are available in print or electronically. Full details are available from www.mhra.org.uk

The Modern Language Review

The *Modern Language Review* is available to members of the Modern Humanities Research Association at a discounted rate. Membership is by application to the Membership Secretary; free membership is also available to postgraduates (subject to terms and conditions). Some other publications of the MHRA are available to members at special rates.

The *Modern Language Review* and other journals published by the MHRA may be ordered from JSTOR (http://about.jstor.org/csp).

ISSN 0026–7937 (Print)
ISSN 2222–4319 (Online)

DISCLAIMER

Statements of fact and opinion in the content of the *Modern Language Review* are those of the respective authors and contributors and not of the journal editors or of the Modern Humanities Research Association (MHRA). MHRA makes no representation, express or implied, in respect of the accuracy of the material in this journal and cannot accept any legal responsibility or liability for any errors or omissions that may be made.

TYPESET BY JOHN WAŚ, OXFORD

Guidelines for Contributors to *MLR*

The *Modern Language Review* publishes articles and book reviews in English on any aspect of modern and medieval European (including English and Latin American) languages, literatures, and cultures (including cinema). The journal does not publish correspondence. We are glad to receive general and comparative articles as well as those on language-specific topics. We encourage submissions from postgraduates. Articles should be submitted to the appropriate section editor in one typescript copy together with an identical electronic copy sent as an email attachment. Articles should conform precisely to the conventions of the *MHRA Style Guide*, 3rd edn, 2013 (ISBN 978-1-78188-009-8), obtainable from www.style.mhra.org.uk, price £6.50, US$13, €8; an online version of the *Guide* is also available from the same address. Authors should provide an abstract of their articles with keywords highlighted in bold type. This abstract should not exceed 100 words. At the end of articles and reviews contributors should include, in this order, their affiliation or location; name as it is to be printed; name and postal address for correspondence; and email address. Simple references should be incorporated into the text (see *MHRA Style Guide*, 10.2). Double spacing should be used throughout, including quotations and footnotes, which should be in the same large size of type as the rest of the article. Articles are typically about 8000 words in length including footnotes, but longer and shorter ones are also welcome. Quotations and references should be carefully checked. Quotations from languages covered by the journal, and from Latin and Greek, should be given in the original language. Latin and Greek passages should normally be translated or at least paraphrased; usually this is not required in the case of modern languages, though it may be helpful where dialects or early forms of the language are cited. However, since the journal has a broad readership, please provide translations or paraphrases of quotations within comparative or general articles (except for modern French). If in doubt, consult the appropriate section editor.

The *Modern Language Review* regrets that it must charge contributors for the cost of corrections in proof which the Editor in his or her discretion thinks excessive. Contributors should keep a copy of their typescript. Typescripts not accepted for publication will not normally be returned. If your article is accepted, you will be asked to supply a definitive version of it both in hard copy and as an email attachment. Authors should ensure that there is no discrepancy between the computer file and the printout.

It is a condition of publication in this journal that authors of articles and reviews assign copyright, including electronic copyright, to the MHRA. *Inter alia*, this allows the General Editor to deal efficiently and consistently with requests from third parties for permission to reproduce material. The journal has been published simultaneously in printed and electronic form since January 2001. Permission, without fee, for authors to use their own material in other publications, after a reasonable period of time has elapsed, is not normally withheld. Authors may republish contributions on a personal website or in an academic institution's digital repository without seeking further permission from the Association, but no earlier than 24 months after publication by the MHRA.

On publication of each issue of the journal authors will receive, by email, the finalized PDF of their contribution as it appears in the printed volume. Physical offprints are not supplied. Authors of articles will also receive a complimentary copy of the printed issue in which the article appears.

Articles and books for review should be sent to the Editor concerned:

General and Comparative. Professor Derek Connon, Department of French, Swansea University, Swansea, SA2 8PP (d.f.connon@swansea.ac.uk).

English and American. Professor Andrew Hiscock, School of English, Bangor University, Bangor, LL57 2DG (mhraassistant@bangor.ac.uk)

French. Dr Alison Williams, Department of French, Swansea University, Swansea, SA2 8PP (a.j.williams@swansea.ac.uk).

Italian. Professor Guido Bonsaver, Pembroke College, Oxford OX1 1DW (guido.bonsaver@pmb.ox.ac.uk).

Hispanic. Dr Duncan Wheeler, School of Modern Languages & Cultures, University of Leeds, Leeds LS2 9JT (d.wheeler@leeds.ac.uk).

German, Dutch, and Scandinavian. Professor Robert Vilain, School of Modern Languages, University of Bristol, 17 Woodland Road, Bristol, BS8 1TE (robert.vilain@bristol.ac.uk).

Slavonic and Eastern European. Dr Katharine Hodgson, School of Modern Languages, Queen's Building, University of Exeter, Exeter EX4 4QH (k.m.hodgson@exeter.ac.uk).

CONTENTS

Contents

Contents

Contents

SATIRICAL JOURNALS AND NEUTRALITY
IN THE FRANCO-PRUSSIAN WAR

In times of moral controversy or political conflict the position of the unaligned observer is seldom a comfortable one. Courted by opposing interests for their potential support or influence but at the same time despised for their perceived cowardice, selfishness, lack of principle, or hypocrisy, neutrals can find themselves under attack from all directions. This painful situation can become particularly acute in times of war, when the fabric of a nation and even its very identity may appear to be under threat.

By the outbreak of the Franco-Prussian War in July 1870 the number of journalistic outlets in the major European countries was increasing exponentially. Compared with the position in 1800 (when relatively few newspapers and journals existed) and in the totalitarian states of the twentieth century, in 1870 the print media offered a considerable diversity of opinion and analysis, although their expression was often necessarily muted.[1] Much of this diversity was to be found in the satirical and humorous journals that had begun to appear in a number of European cities following the establishment of Charles Philipon's *Le Charivari* in Paris in 1832.[2] Although a large number had sprung up in 1848–49, most of these had succumbed after a few months to the legal and political pressures of the counter-revolutionary period. But a small number survived, gradually augmented by the appearance of equally sturdy competitors,[3] a development which reached a peak in the mid-1860s. Such organs concentrated principally on local and national issues, but this changed almost immediately with the French declaration of war on Prussia. For the first time since they had become a significant force, satirical journals were confronted with an international event that produced resonances throughout Europe and beyond. This was an important watershed, raising questions affecting not only journals published in the combatant nations, but also those appearing in other jurisdictions. Would the critical spirit and sense of the ridiculous that most satirical journals had, in peacetime, brought to bear largely on domestic issues now be applied to international conflict? Where there were substantial political or philosophical differences between journals in a particular country,

---

[1] See Robert Justin Goldstein, *Political Censorship of the Arts and the Press in Nineteenth-Century Europe* (Basingstoke: Macmillan, 1989), and Roger Bellet, *Presse et journalisme sous le Second Empire* (Paris: Colin, 1967), pp. 11–44.

[2] See Hannes Haas, 'Die Wiener humoristisch-satirischen Blätter: Zur Produktionsgeschichte eines Zeitschriftentyps (1778–1933)', *Medien und Zeit*, 6 (1991), 3–8.

[3] See the comprehensive bibliographical survey in Goldstein, *Political Censorship*, pp. 210–11, n. 4.

Modern Language Review, 110 (2015), 317–38
© Modern Humanities Research Association 2015

would these be reflected in their responses to the war, or would the separate points of view converge, shaped by notions of patriotic solidarity? A comprehensive answer to these questions would go well beyond the confines of a single article, but what follows aims to shed some light on them by examining the response of satirical journals in four countries to a topic that at the time provoked extensive debate and not a little ill-will: the conduct of neutral states.

In contrast to the events of August 1914, the outbreak of war on 19 July 1870 was the result not of a concatenation of responses linked to legally binding treaties but of political (mis)calculation; once the conflict was under way most states were at pains to avoid becoming needlessly involved. Of those who adopted a neutral posture, the most significant in geo-political terms were Austria-Hungary and the United Kingdom. So this study will explore how the political and satirical journals of France and Prussia reacted to the behaviour and rhetoric of those uninvolved powers, how the equivalent organs in the neutral states responded to the unfolding events of the war, and how they regarded their own countries' stance in the conflict.

From the moment that hostilities began until after the Peace of Frankfurt, few of the leading French satirical journals paid significant attention to the conduct of the neutral states. The influential and well-established *Journal amusant*, for example, contrived in this period to ignore the issue completely. In its issue of 18 June 1871, the recently founded *Le Grelot* did devote a full front-page cartoon (Figure 1)[4] to a controversy centred on the United Kingdom, but only in order to ask whether 'Albion' would be 'perfidious' to itself by offering shelter to the leaders of the defeated Paris Commune.[5] Nor was there any developed discussion of the principle or practice of neutrality in *L'Éclipse*, a couple of peripheral items representing the sum of its attention to this area.[6] Because of the ultimately catastrophic military situation most of the journals involved were forced to suspend publication, often for many months, and so were unable to develop a comprehensive discourse involving (from their point of view) secondary topics such as the behaviour of uninvolved neighbouring countries. When they did appear, virtually their whole attention was taken up by much more immediate considerations: the early conduct of the war, the fall of the Bonapartist Empire, the siege of Paris, the peace conditions imposed by Germany, and the bloody conflict between the Versailles government and the Commune in Paris.

There was one remarkable exception, however. Even before war had become inevitable—or even probable—Paul Véron, editor-in-chief of *Le Cha-*

[4] The illustration may be viewed in full colour, and all of the figures can be examined in greater detail, in the online version of this article, available at www.jstor.org.

[5] 'Le mille-pattes international', *Le Grelot*, 18 June 1871, p. 1.

[6] 'Bavardages', *L'Éclipse*, 1 August 1870, p. 1; 'Chevrotines et menu plomb', *L'Éclipse*, 4 September 1870, p. 3.

FIG. 1. *Le Grelot*, 18 June 1871, p. 1 <http://digi.ub.uni-heidelberg.
de/diglit/grelot1871/0040> [accessed 26 November 2014].
Used with permission of Heidelberg University Library

rivari, had concluded that there was no point in counting on support from the United Kingdom in the current crisis. It would simply sit on its hands.[7] Four weeks later an unnamed writer ridiculed fears expressed elsewhere in the French press that Russia and the United Kingdom might intervene on the Prussian side. The final section of the article radiates confidence that this will not happen and that, in any case, France will assert herself without any foreign intervention on either side. France and Prussia should be left to fight the war out between them.[8]

Whether this position was shared by the journal's readers, many of them no doubt traumatized by the successive defeats at Wissembourg, Spicheren, and Wörth over the previous three days, is highly debatable. However, even any residues of editorial confidence seem to have drained away completely by 8 September, less than a week after the catastrophic surrender at Sedan, to be replaced by an accusation of betrayal on the part of the United Kingdom. On that day the magazine published an image showing a wounded French veteran with one arm in a sling, while a devilishly grinning British soldier excuses his inactivity: 'Oh! no! je pouvais rien faire pour vous.' The response is as contemptuous as it is bitter: 'On ne vous demande rien! Il me reste encore le bras qui vous a sauvé à Inkermann.'[9] In similar vein a cartoon two weeks later suggested strongly that not only Britain but also the other major non-aligned states were avoiding their responsibilities in the face of the calamity about to engulf France.[10] This represents one of the few occasions on which *Le Charivari* specifically addresses the behaviour of a plurality of neutral states. Perhaps because of its greater potential to intervene or mediate, almost all the journal's attention was focused on the United Kingdom; despite its obvious significance in European politics, Austria-Hungary features only rarely in this context.

This suggestion of culpable inactivity was reiterated over the following weeks and months, metamorphosing in the last days of the siege of Paris into an accusation of callous indolence on the part of the neutral powers. In late January 1871 the journal carried a cartoon showing Turkey, the United Kingdom, and Russia sitting in comfortable chairs, casually taking in the spectacle of an intensifying inferno caused by Prussian bombardment.[11] A few days later the city had surrendered, the bombardment had ceased, and—the British chargé d'affaires and his staff were about to return. This time the writer's acid comment unites the perceived cowardice of the embassy staff (regarded as typical of

---

[7] 'Bulletin politique', *Le Charivari*, 10 July 1870, p. 1.
[8] 'Bulletin politique', *Le Charivari*, 7 August 1870, p. 1.
[9] Untitled cartoon, *Le Charivari*, 8 September 1870, p. 3.
[10] 'Attendant qu'on vienne les égorger sur leurs sièges curules', *Le Charivari*, 26 September 1870, p. 3.
[11] 'La Galerie', *Le Charivari*, 27 January 1871, p. 3.

British attitudes in general) and the frustration of the French with expressions of sympathy made from across the Channel:

C'est juste. Il ne tombe plus de bombes. Voilà le moment de venir nous témoigner des sympathies sans danger.
Toute la politique anglaise est là.[12]

Three days later, Véron attempted to take stock of current relationships between France and the United Kingdom.[13] Noting that a 'Francophile move-ment' had sprung up in London, he muses sardonically on whether this might be seen as a token of 'remorse on the part of our neighbours' for their lack of action during the conflict. To be sure, he recognizes an obligation of gratitude for the relief aid provided by voluntary committees in the United Kingdom; but he then swiftly changes direction, recalling its disinclination to intervene at the outset of the war and, in effect, blaming the disaster that had since be-fallen France on British political apathy and moral cowardice. Long forgotten now are the self-confident statements from the same journal in August 1870 to the effect that third-party intervention was not desired and that the two principal antagonists should be left to fight things out between themselves. But holding the British accountable for France's current predicament is not the sole point of the article, for Véron goes on immediately to argue that this is not the proper time for recriminations. The French should turn their atten-tion to their internal affairs—'Elles sont assez enchevêtrées, hélas!'—and that is what Le Charivari went on to do. In the face of the uncertainty, tension, and, ultimately, chaos that increasingly characterized daily life in Paris in the first half of 1871, the journal turned its attention almost exclusively to domestic affairs. On 21 April it ceased publication temporarily as a protest against new restrictions on press freedom and because it felt that in the context of an increasingly bloody conflict between the Versailles government and the Paris Commune there was no place for a periodical which was 'required to be light-hearted'.[14] The attitudes and actions of rival powers, especially those with no direct stake in what was going on, commanded little interest under these circumstances.

But what of German responses? Clearly the state most directly involved from the outset was Prussia, where, among others, the Berlin-based journals *Kladderadatsch* (established in 1848) and the *Berliner Wespen* (renamed and moved from Hamburg in 1868) functioned relatively critically as mouthpieces for political liberalism. As far as the *Berliner Wespen* was concerned, Prussia was the victim of an unprovoked attack by the French Empire; the moral situation was clear; and all attempts to avoid involvement by invoking legal

[12] 'Échos', Le Charivari, 2 February 1871, p. 2.
[13] 'Bulletin politique', Le Charivari, 5 February 1871, p. 1.
[14] 'A nos abonnés', Le Charivari, 21 April 1871, p. 1.

neutrality were craven and hypocritical. In the poem 'Die Neutralen', published on 29 July and pointedly placed on the front page, the delicious sarcasm of the opening is followed by a stanza of ironic interior monologue:

> Der Würfel fällt! Mit ahnungsvollem Grauen
> Seh'n schon die Feinde uns're Waffen strahlen,
> Und ringsumher, dem Kampfspiel zuzuschauen,
> Gruppiren sich die freundlichen Neutralen.
>
> Sie wollen applaudiren nicht, nicht zischen,
> Sie wollen unpartheiisch und verträglich
> Vorläufig sich nicht in den Zweikampf mischen,
> Das heißt, so lang dies ihnen irgend möglich.[15]

The die is cast. The sight of our gleaming weapons is already filling our enemies with foreboding and horror. And the friendly neutrals are taking up position round about to observe the spectacle of the battle. They do not want to applaud or hiss. Good-natured and impartial, they do not want to get involved in the duel for the time being, which is to say for as long as possible.

The poem then focuses on five neutral states—Austria-Hungary, the United Kingdom, Russia, Denmark, and Italy—indicating that behind their fine words each has a selfish private agenda preventing it from siding with Prussia and thus keeping it out of the war. Their self-absorption and shiftiness are contrasted unfavourably with the focused reaction of the Prussians, captured in the final line: 'Mit unserm Erbfeind werden wir schon fertig' ('We'll soon sort out our old enemy').

The *Berliner Wespen* was not alone in its condemnation of those who had, as the journal saw it, failed to ally themselves with Prussia. On 4 September the editorial in the rival *Kladderadatsch* rehearsed the events leading up to the French declaration of war on 19 July, going on to imply a deviousness, not to say moral paralysis, on the part of the neutral states similar to that identified five weeks before in the competitor journal.[16] But, with rare exceptions, neither returned to the topic in this general way. Nor did they direct their attention to individual neutral states on the European mainland. Rather, as with *Le Charivari*, it is above all the behaviour of the United Kingdom that attracted the ire of the Prussian editors.

The first major shots in what was to be an extended verbal attack were fired on 7 August 1870, with the publication in *Kladderadatsch* of a six-stanza poem.[17] The contrast between the opening couplet of each stanza in *Sperrdruck* for emphasis (representing the public justification of the United Kingdom's neutrality) and the brusque second pair of lines (where the true

---

[15] 'Die Neutralen', *Berliner Wespen*, 29 July 1870, p. 1.
[16] 'Besinnen wir uns!', *Kladderadatsch*, 4 September 1870, p. 162.
[17] 'Englands neutrale Sympathien', *Kladderadatsch*, 7 August 1870, p. 143.

dynamic—commercial profit—becomes apparent) implies a hypocrisy unworthy of a great nation. The poem opens thus:

> *Ein Schrei des Abscheu's geht durch die Nationen,*
> *Wuth und Entrüstung füllt das Inselland—*
> Braucht ihr zufällig noch *Patronen,*
> Ich liefre sie, laut Preiscourant.

A cry of disgust goes through the nations; the island nation is filled with rage and indignation. Should you by any chance still require ammunition, I will supply it at current rates.

The balance, precision, and contrasts of tone maintained throughout make this one of the most memorable polemical poems of its time. Particularly telling are the stinging puns of the final couplet:

> *Und meine Wünsche, meine Friedensmühen*
> *Gerecht vertheilend, bleib ich* **so** *neutral:*
> Deutschland beziehe *bill'ge Sympathien,*
> Und Frankreich *theures Kriegsmaterial!*[18]

Here is how I remain neutral, justly dispensing my desires and my efforts for peace: let Germany receive cheap expressions of sympathy and France expensive war material.

In the months that followed, many sharply worded items testified to the fact that this poem (written by the co-editor Julius Lohmeyer) exemplifies a complaint frequently encountered in both *Kladderadatsch* and the *Berliner Wespen*, that in making substantial profits from selling ordnance to France while avoiding costly involvement by proclaiming military neutrality, the United Kingdom was guilty of gross hypocrisy and selfishness.[19] Occasionally, however, other reproaches surfaced. In a poem published on 26 February 1871, an unnamed writer takes both the United Kingdom and the United States to task for the sheer gall they have displayed in urging the victorious Germans to show generosity of spirit towards France.[20] Is this, like their neutrality, an expression of their humanity? Not at all; it is simply the result of cold calculation: if France became bankrupt, it would not be able to pay its bills of exchange to its neutral trading partners.

The following week the journal returned to the theme of magnanimity, rounding on the double standards of an imperial power that urged one way

---

[18] See also 'Eine kleine neutrale Erzählung', *Berliner Wespen*, 29 August 1870, p. 3, and 'Krämer-Politik', *Kladderadatsch*, 7 August 1870, p. 144.

[19] See, for example, 'Parlaments-Feuilleton', *Berliner Wespen*, 24 March 1871, p. 1; [untitled], *Berliner Wespen*, 19 May 1871, p. 3; [untitled], *Berliner Wespen*, 30 June 1871, p. 2; [untitled note beginning 'An Seine Excellenz'], *Kladderadatsch*, 12 March 1871, 2nd supplement, unpaginated; and 'Christlich-Anglikanisches Sendschreiben an die Witwen deutscher Landwehrleute', *Kladderadatsch*, 16 April 1871, p. 71.

[20] 'Den guten Rathgebern, unsern neutralen Englisch-Amerikanischen Freunden', *Kladderadatsch*, 26 February 1871, supplement, unpaginated.

of behaving on its neighbours but practised something entirely different in its own back yard. The poem 'Ermahnung zur Großmuth: Germania an Britannia' ('Exhortation to Magnanimity: Germania to Britannia') opens with an apparently self-deprecating gesture towards humane British principles; immediately thereafter, attention turns to what the author presents as the rapacious conduct of the British state in Ireland, India, New Zealand, southern Africa, and China as well as its behaviour towards the pauperized and exploited underclass within its own borders.[21] Compared with these telling strictures, the final accusation in the poem—that the United Kingdom is, in political terms, a toothless big-mouth—seems almost insignificant.

Perhaps the cleverest piece of writing directed at British neutrality is the poem 'Der liebe Vetter' ('Our Dear Cousin'), published in the same issue of *Kladderadatsch*[22] (Figure 2). The narrator, a British subject, moves constantly between phonetically and grammatically faulty German (in Fraktur) and surprisingly idiomatic educated English (in roman type). Sometimes either German words or words that exist in both languages have to be pronounced as English words (or at least as a monoglot English speaker might pronounce a German word) for the sake of the rhyme. The final stanza is a tour de force, suggesting sharply both the egotism and the moral self-deception involved in the kind of neutrality ascribed by the writer to political and business circles in the United Kingdom, and ending with a memorable punchline:

> Oh gallant France, indeed uihr sind
> Betrübt, wie Dir geschehen,
> Und würden gern mit guns and arms
> Noch weiter Dich versehen,
> Auch hatten uihr Dir beizustehn
> Most surely the intention,
> Wär' nicht our highest principle
> Always — non-intervention.

Oh gallant France, we are indeed distressed to see what has happened to you, and we would gladly continue to supply you with guns and arms. And we would most surely have the intention to stand by you if our highest principle were not always non-intervention.

It is clear that the view of British neutrality emerging from the pages of the two most prominent Prussian satirical journals differs fundamentally from that of their French equivalents. The main thrust of the Prussian censure was that Britain's economic relationship to France (as its major supplier of arms) breached the spirit, if perhaps not the letter, of its neutrality. In turn the perceived duplicity of this behaviour formed the basis for repeated moral denunciations. For obvious reasons, arguments such as these were unlikely

---

[21] 'Ermahnung zur Großmuth: Germania an Britannia', *Kladderadatsch*, 5 March 1871, p. 42.
[22] 'Der liebe Vetter', *Kladderadatsch*, 5 March 1871, p. 43.

43

Schultze. Run' mit 'n Kriegspanzer, und 'rin in 'n Civilkittel!

Müller. Zu welche friedliche Beschäftigung wirst du nu zurückkehren?

Schultze. Zu's Feldsackmähen. Damit wir im nächsten Kriege nicht wieder so blamirt werden!

Müller. Des is richtig. Der Mangel an Feldbeuteln, die in Versailles gefehlt haben, das is der einzige Vorwurf, den man Moltke machen kann, daß er daran nicht gedacht hat!

Müller. Was sagtst denn zu die vermuthliche sechswöchentliche Landestrauer?

Schultze. Wenn ich sagen könnte, was ich sagen möchte, so wollt' ich damit nur sagen, daß man sich doch eigentlich sagen müßte, wie lange wohl nach sechsmonatliche Geschäftsstille, durch noch fernere sechs Wochen Zulage die Verwundeten und Hinterbliebenen von den Milliarden Kriegskostenentschädigung — allgemeine Landestrauer haben könnten.

Noch kann nicht begreifen, wo diese Regierung die Aufführung eines Stückes wie diese „Hörmannsschlacht" von Kleist gestatten kann, da diese Römischen Legionen darin so schlecht wegkommen, und da im Deutschland gegenwärtig wieder so zahlreich weilenden Legionen von Gästen von Rom doch wohl einige Rücksicht verdienen.

Der bekannte Anti-Barbarus.

Der liebe Vetter.

Wir haben in the Times gelesen
Die Peace preliminaries:
Alsace and Metz, five milliards
Und Einzug gar in Paris.

Oh shocking! War denn Glory nicht
Für Deutschland ganz genügend?
Vergaßt ihr gänzlich Modesty,
Die alte deutsche Tugend?

Why? hat Old England nicht so oft
Gemahnt zur Moderation?
Und fürchtet ihr euch gar nicht mehr
Vor unsre Protestation?
Selbst Odo Russel konnte nicht
In that affair sich mischen,
Denn Bismarck (it was hardly fair),
Kept secret the condition.

Oh gallant France! Indeed uihr sind
Betrübt, wie Dir geschehen,
Und würden gern mit guns and arms
Noch weiter Dich versehen,
Auch hatten uihr Dir beizustehn
Most surely the intention,
Wär' nicht our highest principle
Always — non-intervention.

Die officiösen Tröster.

Heil uns! Der Friede ist möglich, denn er ist ehrenvoll. Wir behalten Belfort, jene formidable Riesenfestung des Elsaß.

Heil uns! Wir sind es los, jenes elende, traurige Felsennest im völlig französischen Theil des Elsaß, dessen strategische Bedeutung die des Berliner Kreuzbergs kaum überragen möchte; dessen Rückgabe längst beschlossene Sache war.

Wahrlich, ein großer Sieg unserer Diplomatie! Belfort bleibt uns erhalten, Belfort, das unüberwindliche Saragossa des Ostens, Belfort, das Metz des Elsaß, Belfort, das natürliche Ausfallthor gegen Deutschland. Sein Besitz wird uns Metz leicht verschmerzen lassen.

Immer deutlicher stellt sich die Herausgabe Belforts, als einer der

geschicktesten Schachzüge unserer Diplomatie heraus. Wahrhaftig, dieser offensiv und defensiv völlig belanglose Waffenplatz wäre für uns mehr eine Last, als ein Gewinn gewesen. Jede Schießscharte von Metz hat für Deutschland mehr Bedeutung als dieser Steinhaufe.

Was ist Elsaß? Was ist Metz? Was ist der Einzug in Paris? Was sind fünf Milliarden? Uns bleibt Belfort, Belfort, der Schlüssel des Westens, Belfort, der Fuß auf dem Nacken Deutschlands, Belfort, dessen unüberwindliche Mauern den Besitz des Rheines für Deutschland geradezu illusorisch machen. Wahrlich, ein für Deutschland schmachvollerer Frieden konnte nicht geschlossen werden! Frankreich ist gerettet! Ihm bleibt Belfort!!

Graf Nesselrode hat beantragt, daß zur Verhütung ansteckender Seuchen, die Schlachtfelder in Frankreich einer gründlichen Desinfection unterworfen werden.

Es ist das erste Mal, seit wir die Feder führen, daß wir uns mit einem russischen Diplomaten innigst einverstanden erklären müssen, da auch wir den Wunsch hegen, daß die Pest des Krieges auf immer von der Erde genommen werde.

Im Theater zu Bordeaux.
Die letzte Scene.

(Die todtkranke Republik wankt herein. Sie stützt sich auf beide Parteien. Man reicht ihr die Feder zum Unterschreiben des Friedens.)

Die Republik. Was soll ich thun?

Die Einen. Weh! Wenn du unterschreibst, Bist Du verloren. Denk', was du geschworen!

Die Andern. Du bist's, wenn du den Trotz noch weiter treibst!

Die Republik. In jedem Falle, also doch — verloren!
(Sie aufrichtend, nach Links gewendet)
Fluch euch, die ihr den bittren Dienst der Pflicht
Versagt, damit der Plebs euch nicht beschuldigt!
(nach Rechts gewendet)
Und Fluch auch euch! Denkt ihr, ich kenn' euch nicht,
Und wüßte nicht, warum ihr mich huldigt?
(Sie unterschreibt.)
Der Vorhang fällt.

Telegraphische Depeschen des Kladderadatsch.

Brüssel. [...]

Straßburg a. M. [...]

Cap Bismarck. [...]

Von der Schweizer Grenze. [...]

Rom. [...]

London. [...]

Benedig. [...]

Madrid. [...]

Versailles. [...]

Berlin. [...]

Paris. [...]

(Fortsetzung des Feuilletons im Beiblatt.)

Hierzu ein Beiblatt.

Wir bitten, das Beiblatt zu beachten.

FIG. 2. *Kladderadatsch*, 5 March 1871, p. 43 <http://digi.ub.
uni-heidelberg.de/diglit/kla1871/0085> [accessed 26 November
2014]. Used with permission of Heidelberg University Library

to appear anywhere in the French press, where the criticism centred on what was regarded as the United Kingdom's culpable disinclination to intervene actively in the conflict. But how were issues such as these presented in the British humorous press?

At the outbreak of the Franco-Prussian War the United Kingdom had a well-developed corpus of humorous periodicals, of which *Punch* (subtitled *The London Charivari*) was but the most prominent.[23] Despite its token of indebtedness to the Parisian journal, there was little overlap in the way the two organs saw the war and, in particular, the decision of Gladstone's government to remain neutral. From the beginning *Punch* attempted to claim the moral high ground, and the first issue following the declaration of war included two items that put distance between the combatants and the neutral onlooker. On 23 July the newly appointed editor, Charles Shirley Brooks, quoted Disraeli as having asserted that the causes of the war were purely diplomatic, adding (somewhat high-handedly in the circumstances) that neither power should have declared war before consulting the United Kingdom.[24] And in the same issue the finger was pointed with equal vigour at France and Prussia, an ironic poem reflecting on the 'fact' that as each side was as 'good' (or 'bad') as the other, neutrality was the only correct response for the United Kingdom.[25]

Punch was not alone in attempting to characterize the war as a conflict between two villains. The rival *Fun* (which, with a circulation of 20,000, was a serious competitor for *Punch* in the 1870s) stated baldly: 'There isn't a pin to choose between King and Emperor. Honest folks can feel no sympathy for a couple of area-sneaks who come to fisticuffs over the division of the "swag".'[26] The journal's suspicion towards both protagonists had been fuelled, at least in part, by the publication in *The Times* on 28 July of the draft of a supposed 'secret treaty' between Prussia and France from the late 1860s. According to this document, France would give Prussia a free hand in its relationship to the south German states, in return for which Prussia would assist the French to buy Luxembourg from the Netherlands and provide military support for any French invasion or annexation of Belgium.[27] Both parties attempted to wrest

[23] At this stage *Punch* had a circulation of 40,000 copies. Much useful information on it and its competitors is provided in Donald Gray, 'A List of Comic Periodicals in Great Britain, 1800–1900, with a Prefatory Essay', *Victorian Periodicals Newsletter*, 15 (1972), 2–39; J. Don Vann and Rosemary Van Arsdel, *Victorian Periodicals and Victorian Society* (Toronto: University of Toronto Press, 1994), 74–94; and M. H. Spielmann, 'The Rivals of *Punch*: A Glance at the Illustrated Comic Press of Half a Century', *National Review*, 25 (1895), 654–66.

[24] 'Punch's Essence of Parliament', *Punch*, 23 July 1870, p. 33.

[25] 'Prussian Pot and French Kettle', *Punch*, 23 July 1870, p. 36. Similar arguments were put in the issues of 30 July (pp. 43–44), 6 August (p. 62), 13 August (p. 66), and 20 August (p. 76).

[26] [Untitled leading article], *Fun*, 6 August 1870, p. 46. Like *Punch*, *Fun* appealed primarily to the educated middle classes, but remained steadfastly liberal while *Punch* moved steadily to the right.

[27] Dora Raymond offers a detailed review of the genesis and content of the 'treaty' and

political capital from the situation. The Prussian government (which had contrived the document's initial publication in the *Spener'sche Zeitung* of 27 July) was able to show that it was in the handwriting of the French Ambassador, Count Vincent Benedetti, and claimed that it represented French proposals to which Prussia had not agreed. They further asserted that the proposed treaty was just one of a number of secret overtures made by the French from 1864 onwards, none of which Prussia had accepted.[28] The French responded that the document was in Benedetti's hand as he had transcribed it at Bismarck's dictation during a private meeting, so that the 'treaty' was Prussian in origin. Furthermore, they insisted that secret negotiations in the 1860s had been initiated by the Prussians.[29] None of these arguments appears to have cut much ice with the satirical journals in the United Kingdom, which saw little to commend the position of either protagonist.[30] But the very existence of the proposed treaty raised acute concerns that the country might still be drawn into the conflict on the European mainland, as it had offered Belgium guarantees of its neutrality and independence and would have been honour-bound to respond militarily if its protégé had been invaded. But as neither France nor Prussia had any interest in needlessly attracting the hostile attention of third parties, a multilateral treaty guaranteeing the independence of Belgium and the Netherlands was hastily agreed. This calmed the tone of much of the British press, although on 27 August *Fun* reasserted its original position (reserving the right to intervene militarily in certain circumstances) in its leading article.[31]

The urge to remain neutral—albeit sometimes with qualifications related to national prestige or honour—characterizes the response of most British humorous journals in the early stages of the conflict. But perhaps the most noteworthy expression of this position is found in the Liverpool-based weekly *The Porcupine*, which insisted (using an argument remarkable for its time) that military intervention in the current—or, indeed, any other—conflict would be illegitimate because it would lack popular sanction:

A plebiscite, including every adult in Great Britain, male and female, would give us the national verdict of nine-tenths of the people,—strict neutrality in this Franco-German war, and non-interventions in foreign quarrels generally.[32]

This was not a commonly held view; nor did it find favour in government

of the effect of its publication in the United Kingdom: *British Policy and Opinion during the Franco-Prussian War* (New York: Columbia University Press, 1921), pp. 87–106.

[28] See *The Times*, 29 July 1870, p. 12.

[29] The original article to this effect in the *Journal officiel* on 30 July was quoted in *The Times* on 1 August 1870, p. 9.

[30] See *The Porcupine*, 30 July 1870, p. 176, and *Judy*, 3 August 1870, p. 151.

[31] [Untitled leading article], *Fun*, 27 August 1870, p. 76.

[32] 'Financial Reform Neutrality', *The Porcupine*, 17 September 1870, p. 241.

circles. But *The Porcupine* was at one with its competitors in insisting that neutrality was not the same as passivity. The United Kingdom was not to be seen as an unconcerned bystander, unaffected by the torment engulfing its neighbours. On the contrary, it was deeply involved in the struggle, both as an honest broker and as a provider of aid. It was doing its best to assist both parties, both of whom sometimes applied dubious standards of logic to their diplomatic manœuvrings.[33] Perhaps the neatest summary of this position is to be found in the Christmas Eve issue of *Punch*, where the British case is presented in lines more than a little reminiscent of Gilbert and Sullivan, themselves about to embark on twenty-five years of artistic collaboration:

> The nations, actuated by most selfish immorality,
> Hate us because we treat them all with just impartiality;
> They call it, in their spite, our 'egotistical neutrality.'[34]

The advocacy of neutrality in British satirical journals did not rest solely on moral or ethical criteria, however. Unsurprisingly, there was also a substantial element of pragmatism involved. On 13 August, in a poem addressed to Minister of War Edward Cardwell, *Punch* asked bluntly whether the United Kingdom would be ready if it were dragged into the war, a question posed again, in somewhat narrower terms, three weeks later.[35] By the beginning of October it had shifted its ground somewhat, arguing that Britain wanted to pursue peaceful neutrality but had to arm in case its neighbours attacked it,[36] a view also espoused, albeit much later, by *Fun*.[37] Why such arguments, having been given considerable prominence for several months, then largely disappear from the pages of British satirical journals, is a matter for conjecture. Perhaps the editors simply felt that they had made their point and that it was time to move on. No doubt they were also fully reassured by then that Gladstone's administration had no intention of becoming involved on one side or another and regarded the issue as closed.

While the majority of competitor journals shared *Punch*'s dismissive view of both protagonists in the war, they were by no means all as well disposed to the position of their own government or the perceived priorities of its

[33] See 'Our London Letter', *The Porcupine*, 27 August 1870), [following p. 220]. Also 'England's "Intervention"', *Punch*, 27 August 1870, p. 89; 'A Quarter of a Million', *Punch*, 22 October 1870, p. 171; 'Bull and Bullock to the Rescue' and 'The Cry of France and Germany—"To arms!" The Cry of England—"To alms!"', *Punch*, 12 November 1870, p. 199; 'A Truism of the Time', *Punch*, 1 October 1870, p. 143; 'Neutrality in a Nutshell', *Punch*, 22 October 1870, p. 168; [untitled leading article], *Fun*, 1 October 1870, p. 126.

[34] 'The Slang of the Stranger', *Punch*, 24 December 1870, p. 271.

[35] 'Is my Powder Dry?', *Punch*, 13 August 1870, p. 6. See also 'Reticence in Time of Row', *Punch*, 3 September 1870, p. 104; 'Mountebank Ministers', *The Tomahawk*, 13 August 1870, p. 55.

[36] 'Our Need of Armed Neutrality', *Punch*, 1 October 1870, p. 145.

[37] [Untitled leading article], *Fun*, 31 December 1870, p. 260. See also 'The Results of Intervention', *Punch*, 22 October 1870, p. 174.

people. In particular the conservative, outspokenly aristocratic *Tomahawk* argued consistently against the avarice and commercialism which, in its view, had corrupted the national spirit.[38] In the first days of the war, it presented an unmistakably contemptuous view of British society:

For the last fifteen years Britannia has had but one thought, but one ambition, a thought and an ambition bounded by the calf sides of her ledger. She has cared nothing for Glory, nothing for Renown—less even has she cared for Honour. To be rich has been her first care, to be respected her last consideration.[39]

A neutrality espoused solely for commercial reasons could command no respect, at home or abroad. And, having made clear its preference for a decisive French victory, *The Tomahawk* reiterated, at the close of an extended discussion, its despair at what it regarded as the ignominy at the heart of government policy and public opinion in the United Kingdom.[40] One week later the journal returned to its theme, once again lamenting the dominance of commercial considerations in the body politic, but this time offering an element of hope that national honour might still be upheld:

We say that we are 'a nation of shopkeepers' and laugh, but when our pride is touched we can shoulder our rifles and push home our bayonets with the best of them. In spite of our 'great love of peace', we have covered our flags with the names of victories by the score, *and, if necessary, we can and will repeat the operation.*[41]

An essay in the same issue, however, ends with completely different sentiments, which would not have been out of place in the pages of the much less bellicose *Punch*: 'The war having burst, the best thing we can do is to keep out of it, for times are changed sadly for the worse, and our going to war in the face of modern armaments would mean our humiliation and paralysis.'[42]

Following the publication of the 'secret treaty', however, *The Tomahawk* appeared again to harden its stance, condemning the 'utterly stupid and craven policy' of Foreign Secretary Lord Granville which had been adopted 'simply out of a regard for our pockets', and demanding that the United Kingdom should send an army of occupation to Belgium.[43] How its view might have developed over the course of the war we shall never know: on 27 August the journal ceased publication with no warning or explanation, and for reasons still unknown.

[38] Even before the war this was a well-rehearsed topic in *The Tomahawk*: see 'Canada to the Rescue', 11 June 1870, p. 225. *The Tomahawk*, founded in 1867, had already achieved a circulation of 50,000. Written almost exclusively by 'gentlemen', it was conservative politically, although sharply (and controversially) critical of individual members of the British royal family.

[39] 'The Little Difficulty', *The Tomahawk*, 23 July 1870, p. 25.

[40] Ibid., pp. 26–27.

[41] 'Down with Prussia!', *The Tomahawk*, 30 July 1870, p. 35 (emphasis added).

[42] 'Our Position in Europe', ibid., p. 37.

[43] '"A dignified and calm reserve"?', *The Tomahawk*, 6 August 1870, p. 45.

Meanwhile *The Porcupine* consistently upheld the very approach (grounded in financial and commercial considerations) that *The Tomahawk* had so despised. On 30 July it set out its first considered response to the outbreak of war.[44] In common with virtually every other journal it recognized the potential enormity of the conflict, but unlike most of its competitors did not discuss it in terms of right and wrong. It simply assumed that in the context of a war between two major powers on the European mainland neutrality was the correct posture for the United Kingdom. What the article does examine are the implications of the war for the economy if the United Kingdom remains neutral, suggesting that although the current conflict will 'produce much evil to England', it may eventually prove commercially beneficial, stimulating British manufacturing, iron production, and shipping.[45] With items such as this,[46] *The Porcupine* presented itself, no doubt unwittingly, as an example of attitudes which *Le Charivari* had mocked earlier in the year,[47] and which *The Tomahawk* had harshly condemned more recently.

Despite such differences, however, the attitudes struck by the major British humorous journals suggest at least a partial consensus. There were certainly diverging views on the nature of national prestige, the case for military intervention, the degree of preparedness for such a course of action, and the economic consequences of neutrality; but in every case the starting-point was, unsurprisingly, the national interest (albeit sometimes interpreted in different ways) and an assumption that the government's first duty was to protect that interest. Initially at least, most journals also offered a largely negative critique of the behaviour of both France and Prussia (these views diverging, however, as the Prussians laid siege to Paris for over four months). And throughout the conflict they were as one in allowing the United Kingdom to occupy the high moral ground, presenting it as a benevolent neighbour to both combatants, its involvement limited to humanitarian intervention. Although apparently self-evident in the United Kingdom, clearly this was not a stance represented or even understood in the satirical media of France or Prussia.[48]

If the position of the United Kingdom was hotly debated on both sides of the English Channel and the North Sea, the same can hardly be said of Austria-Hungary. In different circumstances it might, conceivably, have been party to the conflict, but from the outset its government pursued a policy, virtually unquestioned abroad, of non-involvement. But while Austrian neutrality was not a matter of international controversy, it certainly

---

[44] 'The Commercial Tornado', *The Porcupine*, 30 July 1870, 171–72.

[45] Ibid., p. 172.

[46] See also 'Neutrality', *The Porcupine*, 6 August 1870, p. 190.

[47] See 'A la buvette', *Le Charivari*, 14 January 1870, p. 2.

[48] For an overview of coverage of these issues in the mainstream British press see Raymond, *British Policy and Opinion*, pp. 67–81, 285–96, 304–06, and 310–12, and James Hawes, *Englanders and Huns* (London: Simon and Schuster, 2014), pp. 105–30.

generated considerable debate at home, with the various satirical journals developing markedly different agendas while all claiming to play the patriotic card.[49]

On the central issue they were all of one mind: Austria had to remain neutral, if only because, with its record of recent military disasters, the weak state of its finances and the major problems it was experiencing in attempting to hold together many ethnic and national groups within a single imperial state, it was in no position to wage war with anyone. On 31 July 1870 the widely read liberal journal *Der Floh* (founded only in January 1869 but already boasting a circulation of around 25,000) summarized the position with brutal clarity: 'Wir haben im eigenen Land' den Krieg' ('we are at war in our own country').[50] And the following week its well-established rival *Figaro* devoted a complex ten-stanza poem to the matter, offering intriguing comparisons between the attitudes, relationships, and political developments 'outside' (in the world of European power politics) and their equivalents in the domestic arena.[51] In this context by far the most significant part of the poem is the final section, which evokes not a parallel but a prophetic opposition: whichever of the current combatants is defeated will survive, however great its losses—but involvement in a major war might well mean the destruction of the Austro-Hungarian state.[52]

Much of the discussion of Austrian neutrality inevitably centred on or alluded to the question of national identity. For the German-speaking inhabitants of a multinational state whose capital had for centuries been the political and cultural epicentre of things German but which, since its military defeat in 1866, had been excluded from the process of political integration, this was a painful dilemma. Should they support the Prussians as fellow Germans or hope for some kind of vicarious revenge in the form of a French victory? Here there is a clear division of opinion among the Viennese journals.

The position of *Figaro* was made clear early on with the publication of a poem entitled 'Souvenir an 1813' ('Souvenir of 1813').[53] The very title, as well as the repetition of '1813' in the final line of each stanza, clearly implies that the national imperative of the wars of liberation has returned and that the current Emperor of the French has to be resisted just as his uncle had been.

[49] I am indebted to Dr Monika Lehner (University of Vienna) for much helpful information and advice concerning Viennese humorous and satirical journals.

[50] 'Rundschau', *Der Floh*, 31 July 1870, supplement, p. 1.

[51] 'Parallele', *Figaro*, 6 August 1870, p. 142. In the 1870s *Figaro* (which had been founded by Karl Sitter in 1857) positioned itself on the side of the 'little man' and had a history of attacking abuses of state power while generally avoiding party-political controversies.

[52] See also 'Neuestes', *Kikeriki!*, 1 August 1870, p. 1; 'Was profitiren wir bei dem gegenwärtigen Kriege?', *Hans-Jörgel von Gumpoldskirchen*, 1 October 1870, p. 2; 'Wochen-Lied von Hyppolit Schartenmayer: II', *Die Bombe*, 22 January 1871, p. 21.

[53] 'Souvenir an 1813', *Figaro*, 23 July 1870, p. 134.

The writer refers quite openly to the broken constitutional promises of 1813–15, surmises that a victory in the current conflict might well be followed by an equally grave betrayal, and demonstrates an awareness that certain elements in the population would even prefer a French victory. The French remain the enemy they have always been, and the final stanza makes it clear that the German people have now—perhaps—an opportunity to unite politically in freedom. But what is this 'Germany'? Clearly it is not the Kingdom of Prussia, against which France had declared war, but an entity ideally encompassing all German-speakers. Published in an Austrian journal and aimed at Austrian readers, the poem thus assumes that the Austrians remain German not only in terms of language but also of communal and even political allegiance. In this context (it suggests) it is right and proper to support the 'German' side in what was at that stage effectively still a war between France and Prussia. All Germans (including German-speaking Austrians) need to hold together to repulse the French invasion of German territory. With this poem *Figaro* appeals to a pan-Germanness to which the Prussians had decisively put an end in political terms four years earlier, yet in an epigram placed on the same page the journal not only censures the political ineptitude of successive Austrian administrations but also seems to suggest that the neutrality it appears to reject in the poem is, after all, the only sensible posture.[54]

While *Figaro* certainly accepted that the interests of Austria demanded a neutral stance in the war, its sympathies equally clearly seem to have lain with the Prussians and (latterly) their south German allies. Most of its competitors, however, developed a distinctly more guarded approach. The initial reaction of *Kikeriki!* to the outbreak of war was conveyed on the front page of the issue of 25 July[55] (Figure 3). A sombre poem, stressing the hunger, death, and destruction the war will bring, is juxtaposed with a cartoon showing Death standing in a field, wielding a scythe; on one side the heads of the corn are *Pickelhauben* (the spiked helmets worn by Prussian infantrymen), on the other French *képis*. Questions of guilt are not broached at this stage; all that is important is the universality of impending death.[56] Nevertheless, it was not long before the journal's instinctive resentment against Prussia emerged clearly. In a bitterly sarcastic poem entitled 'Preußenfreundliches Lied' ('Prussophile Song') it took issue openly with those Austrians who supported the Prussians on the basis that as fellow Germans they were, so to speak, members of the same family. After ten lines cataloguing a wide range of grievances against their northern neighbours, each stanza ends with the

---

[54] 'Nicht das Erstemal', ibid.

[55] 'Die Ernte in Deutschland', *Kikeriki!*, 25 July 1870, p. 1. *Kikeriki!*, founded in 1861, remained politically liberal until the 1880s.

[56] See also 'Kikeriki auf dem Schlachtfelde bei Wörth', *Kikeriki!*, 15 August 1870, p. 1, and 'Blut! Blut! Blut!', *Hans Jörgel von Gumpoldskirchen*, 20 August 1870, p. 1.

Die Ernte in Deutschland.

Wenn die Schnitter sonst erschienen
Zur erschnizten Erntezeit,
Welcher Frohsinn auf den Mienen,
Welch' ein Jubel weit und breit!
Welch' ein Chor von frohen Liedern,
Alt und Jung sie stimmten ein,
Tausend Echo's, sie erwiedern,
Was gesungen Groß und Klein!

Selbst die Sonne schien zu lächeln,
Weil ihr Segen Freude bringt,
Leise Abendwinde fächeln,
Wenn sie glanzumflossen sinkt;
Welch' ein zauberhaft Beginnen
Vor dem Eintritt düst'rer Nacht,
Wie mit halberwachten Sinnen
Hold ein Kinderauge lacht!

Nun erscheinen keine Schnitter,
Es ertönt kein Jubelsang,
Und ein drohend Ungewitter
Deckt den Sonnenuntergang.
Was des Landmanns Fleiß geschaffen,
Wird durch Rosses Huf zerstört,
Und im Klang der Kriegeswaffen
Wird kein Hülferuf gehört!

Doch, wenn tausend Schnitter trauern,
Die zu Bettlern sind gemacht,
Die man ohne viel Bedauern
Um ihr Stückchen Brod gebracht —
Kömmt nur erst der Kriegeslärm näher,
Wenn nur erst der Sturm recht saust,
Seht — es lacht sich doch ein Mäher
für Euch Alle in die Faust!

FIG. 3. *Kikeriki!*, 25 July 1870, p. 1 <http://anno.onb.ac.at/cgi-content/anno?aid=
kik&datum=18700725&seite=1&zoom=33> [accessed 26 November
2014]. Used with permission of the National Library of Austria

lines, 'Doch lasset das vergessen sein: | *Es sind ja uns're Brüder!*' ('But let that be forgotten—they are our brothers, after all!').[57]

A number of items published in the early stages of the war betray a desire to see the overweening Prussians taken down a peg, with a memorable piece of wishful thinking recorded in the final lines of a poem published on 8 August. Addressed 'denen von der Spree' ('to those people on the Spree'), it concludes:

> Ihr könnt's Eng jetzt schon 's Lachen spar'n,
> Ich sag' Euch heut nur Dös:
> 'Was uns de Hinterlader war'n
> Ist Euch die Mitrailleuse!'[58]

You can spare yourselves the trouble of laughing even now; all I am saying today is this: 'What the breech-loader was for us, the mitrailleuse will be for you!'

By the end of August *Kikeriki!* seemed to have settled on a view supportive of Austrian neutrality and equally dismissive of both sides. At a point when a German victory looked increasingly likely but had not yet been achieved, it published a double cartoon implying that even if the war meant the end of the Napoleonic dictatorship and of French dominance in Europe, there would be no real gain. In the first picture, Kikeriki is seen in the morning dancing with glee because Napoleon III is about to fall. The second picture shows him in the afternoon, sitting gloomily contemplating the dominance which Prussia will now enjoy on the European stage.[59] But only a week later it ran a piece which paid lip-service in the title to Austrian neutrality but in the body of the text pinned the blame for the war firmly on the King of Prussia.[60] Conveniently ignoring the circumstances of the 1866 war with Austria, it argued that the Prussians always preferred to fight with at least one ally against a single enemy. This was a bullying tactic no better than that of a group of schoolboys picking on a single boy in a fight.

Even before war had been declared, the normally avuncular but profoundly patriotic *Hans Jörgel von Gumpoldskirchen* (in its thirty-ninth year the doyen of the Viennese humorous and satirical journals) had taken a self-congratulatory moral stance, condemning scornfully the motivation of France and Prussia alike. This was a war which should not be happening; it was about to be triggered by a piece of foolishness on the part of the French and reflected the sulks and petty ambitions of two competing powers.[61] Elsewhere the

---

[57] 'Preußenfreundliches Lied', *Kikeriki!*, 8 August 1870, p. 1. See also 'Hoch', *Kikeriki!*, 15 August 1870, p. 2.

[58] 'Eingesendet', *Kikeriki!*, 8 August 1870, p. 3.

[59] 'Wie ich mir angesichts der preußischen Erfolge jetzt meine Zeit eintheile', *Kikeriki!*, 29 August 1870, p. 2. See also 'Europa's Zukunft', *Kikeriki!*, 29 August 1870, p. 1.

[60] 'Neutrale österreichische Ansichten über den neuesten Zivilisationskrieg', *Kikeriki!*, 5 September 1870, p. 2.

[61] 'Krieg oder Frieden?', *Hans Jörgel von Gumpoldskirchen*, 16 July 1870, p. 2.

journal took account of Austrian sensitivities, asserting that Prussia would re-gret its destruction of the German Confederation, as the French would never have attacked a united Germany which included Austria.[62] The following week it proclaimed its 'Neutralität bis an's Messer' ('neutrality right to the finish'), ironically a formulation calculated above all to discourage sympathy with the Prussian cause. France had declared war on Prussia, not on Germany. Austria could not be expected, particularly in the wake of Königgrätz, to kiss the hand of the Hohenzollerns.[63]

Hans Jörgel returned to the question of national sympathies a week later, shortly before the decisive series of German victories in Alsace.[64] In the course of an extended article it becomes clear that *Hans Jörgel*'s neutral stance was much more a question of dampening down potential pro-Prussian sympathies than it was of embracing an even-handed attitude towards both combatants. As a 'good German' he would deplore the consequences of a Prussian victory: a return of the reactionary aristocratic state re-established after the defeat of Napoleon. Defeat for the Prussians, on the other hand, would mean the (wel-come) triumph of constitutionalism in Germany. And as a 'good Austrian', his memory of recent Prussian double-dealing, aggression, and barefaced con-tempt is more than enough to prevent the flowering of any incipient sympathy towards his north German neighbours. By 13 August, however, reacting to the crushing German victories in Alsace, *Hans Jörgel* sounded a distinct note of caution, even of trepidation.[65] On the one hand, Königgrätz was no longer unique and could now be downgraded from a national humiliation to a mere disaster; but on the other, 'der schwarzweiße Hochmuth' ('the arrogance of the black-and-whites') might well decide to turn on Austria. Would the Prus-sians thank them for having remained neutral, or would they punish them? *Hans Jörgel* declared itself no friend of the French but argued that love of country led it to fear 'das *übermächtige* und deßhalb *übermüthige* Preußen' ('overmighty, and so overweening, Prussia'). The future was at best unclear.

Alone of the major Viennese journals, *Hans Jörgel* raises these uncom-fortable questions and, having aired them in a very direct manner, returns surprisingly quickly to its earlier preoccupations, among them the question of national sympathies. The clearest indication yet that legal neutrality could be assumed to coexist with emotional partiality is to be found in an item discuss-ing the French government's decision to expel all the Germans resident in its territory.[66] This measure was condemned throughout Europe, and *Hans Jörgel*

[62] A. L., 'Neues Rheinlied', ibid., p. 1.
[63] 'Neutralität bis an's Messer', *Hans Jörgel von Gumpoldskirchen*, 23 July 1870, p. 1.
[64] 'Preußisch oder französisch?', *Hans Jörgel von Gumpoldskirchen*, 30 July 1870, pp. 2–3.
[65] 'Was nun?', *Hans Jörgel von Gumpoldskirchen*, 13 August 1870, p. 2.
[66] 'Die Ausweisung der Deutschen aus Frankreich', *Hans Jörgel von Gumpoldskirchen*, 27 August 1870, p. 2.

denounces it without qualification as cruel, unnecessary, and idiotic. But the condemnation of this outrage cannot disguise the even greater antipathy felt towards the Prussians. In contrast to the revulsion he feels towards '*preußische Uebermacht* und *preußischen Uebermuth*' ('the arrogance and overmighty power of Prussia'), the writer insists that Austrians owe the French an enormous debt: for the revolution of 1789, which has secured the freedoms they now enjoy, and for those of 1830 and 1848, which have opened up the road to freedom. Given the panoply of repressive legislation which the Austrian press and population were subject to in 1870,[67] such formulations suggest at least a degree of understated irony. But even taking this into account there is no doubting that the writer's sympathies lie more with those who on this occasion were the aggressors than with the state to which most of the aggrieved expellees belonged.

Neither the continuing German advances nor the collapse of Napoleon III's government after the battle of Sedan brought about a loosening of *Hans Jörgel*'s attachment to its view of Austrian neutrality. On 1 October, when the outcome of the war, though still several months delayed, was clear to all, the journal reformulated its programme—in enlarged type on the front page: 'Nicht französisch, nicht preußisch, sondern "Gut österreichisch" ist der Bannerspruch der Volksschrift "Hans Jörgel" und diesem Spruche getreu hat unser Blatt in der letzten ereignißreichen Epoche ehrlich den Preußen wie den Franzosen *die Wahrheit* gesagt' ('The maxim by which the popular journal *Hans Jörgel* is known is not French or Prussian but 'loyally Austrian', and in accordance with this maxim our journal has, in this latest eventful period, told the honest truth to the Prussians as well as to the French').[68]

Hans Jörgel's final commentary on Austria's posture in the Franco-Prussian War came one week before the capitulation of Paris. In its leading article, the journal held to the position it had adopted throughout the conflict.[69] Chancellor Beust and Prime Minister Potocki had been right to insist on neutrality: the alliance offered by the Germans was Austria's best guarantee of peace; and if Bismarck did turn upon Austria, a reinvigorated France would enter the fray on the Austrian side, seeking vengeance. In the meantime, Austria should rejoice that its young men had not been slaughtered, its fields trampled, its villages burnt down, or its factories destroyed.[70]

For the leading Viennese journals, then, Austrian neutrality was a central

---

[67] See Goldstein, *Political Censorship*, pp. 37, 48, and 220.
[68] 'Nicht französisch, nicht preußisch', *Hans Jörgel von Gumpoldskirchen*, 1 October 1870, p. 1.
[69] 'Wie steht's denn mit uns Anno 71?', *Hans Jörgel von Gumpoldskirchen*, 21 January 1871, p. 2.
[70] See also 'Was profitiren wir bei dem gegenwärtigen Kriege?', *Hans Jörgel von Gumpoldskirchen*, 1 October 1870, p. 2, and 'Hans Jörgel-Stückeln', *Hans Jörgel von Gumpoldskirchen*, 31 December 1870, p. 3. Other journals were much more cautious in their responses to the proposed alliance with Germany. See, for example, 'Unglaublich, aber wahr!', *Kikeriki!*, 16 January 1871, p. 4; 'Zur preußisch-österreichischen Allianz', *Kikeriki!*, 23 January 1871, p. 1; 'Die neueste Freundschaft,

issue and the development of differing nuances in its understanding a matter of some moment. By contrast, any discussion of the other neutral powers is almost completely absent, only the behaviour of the United Kingdom attracting any significant attention, and then only in the pages of one journal: *Figaro*. In this context the Viennese journal replicates, at least in part, the view represented in the *Berliner Wespen* and *Kladderadatsch*, a cartoon in its Christmas Eve issue of 1870 bringing out the mercenary attitudes repeatedly highlighted in the Berlin journals.[71]

Throughout January the journal had carried 'reports' on British Foreign Secretary Lord Granville's attempts to convene an immediate peace conference, each time suggesting a degree of unacceptable vacillation on his part. That Granville's diplomatic ineffectiveness is linked to British commercial interests is not directly stated, but *Figaro* returned explicitly to such considerations in the final item it devoted to the United Kingdom's role in the war:

> Unterdessen ärgert sich
> *Bull* in *England* fürchterlich,
> Weil um ihn nicht mehr gefragt wird
> Und er auch daheim geplagt wird;
> Guck! — es ist sein altes Weh,
> *Irland* tritt ihm auf die Zeh'.[72]

Meanwhile John Bull in England is getting very annoyed because he is no longer in demand, and because he is also being pestered at home. Look! It is his old woe: Ireland is stepping on his toe.

The allegation of commercial avarice side by side with a gloating reference to the intractable nature of the 'Irish question' exemplifies the scanty but unmistakably negative picture of the United Kingdom that emerges from the pages of the Viennese satirical journals during and just after the Franco-Prussian War.

It is clear that the behaviour of neutral countries in the war of 1870–71 represented a significant topic for the satirical press of the major powers in western and central Europe. Understandably, it was particularly prominent in journals published in Austria and the United Kingdom, the only neutral states which could conceivably have influenced the course of events militarily, though in the leading Prussian journals the conduct of the British and American governments was also examined on a regular basis. Even in France, where more immediate concerns dominated from an early stage, *Le Charivari*, though shifting its ground considerably over time, devoted a measure of attention to discussion of the behaviour of its maritime neighbour.

die wir erst kriegt haben', *Kikeriki!*, 6 February 1871, p. 4; and untitled cartoon, *Figaro*, 1 January 1871, p. 4.

[71] Untitled cartoon, *Figaro*, 24 December 1870, [p. 233]. See also untitled cartoon, *Figaro*, 15 (1871), no. 4, p. 15.

[72] 'Guckindiewelt!', *Figaro*, 11 March 1871, p. 46.

At national level the range of opinion was widest in the United Kingdom and Austria. This was not an indication of the relative severity of press laws in force at the time, as the United Kingdom, alone of the major powers, had no system of press censorship, whereas the Austrian regime was one of the most restrictive in Europe. It simply reflected the fact that where individual journals had already developed distinctive political or social philosophies, those were applied to the question of neutrality, producing in both countries a varied response to the stance of their own government. (In neither case did the satirical press of one country show more than minimal interest in the attitudes or conduct of the other.) The situation in both France and Prussia was very different. There the responses to the behaviour of the neutral states were much more uniform, perhaps suggestive to some degree of a caution born of decades of restrictive legislation, but also reflecting the fact that in a war where national survival is thought to be at stake, and where each side regards the other as the aggressor, there is a natural tendency even for maverick satirical journals to champion the national cause.

This does not mean that there can never be a meeting of minds across national boundaries. As we have seen, journals in Austria, Prussia, France, and even the United Kingdom all denounced the perceived British obsession with commercial advantage to the exclusion of an ethical imperative. But such occasions are extremely rare. And although in legal terms neutrality is an objective, sharply defined concept with clear resonances of impartiality and disinterestedness, public discussion of the behaviour of neutral parties in a conflict is not necessarily characterized by these qualities, even when one uninvolved party is considering the behaviour or attitudes of another. In the context of the Franco-Prussian War there was seldom any agreement on the issue of neutrality; rather the discussion was characterized largely by the continuing assertion or insinuation of what were generally regarded at the time as irreconcilable differences.

University of Edinburgh   William Webster

INFLUENCE REVISITED: IRÈNE NÉMIROVSKY'S CREATIVE READING OF ENGLISH LITERATURE

The rediscovery of an important but forgotten novelist affords an opportunity to reflect on the literary-historical and critical strategies which can be used to (re)incorporate texts into established conceptions of a period, a genre, a national literature, or literature in general. More than ten years have passed since the rediscovery, thanks to the posthumous publication of the wartime novel *Suite française* in 2004, of the Russian-born French-language writer Irène Némirovsky, who perished in Auschwitz in 1942.[1] Since then, literary journalists, biographers, and academic critics—myself included—have attempted to situate Némirovsky's fiction in relation to diverse literary, historical, and political categories, such as inter-war French literature, popular realist literary fiction, literature about the Second World War and the Nazi occupation of France, literature and the Holocaust, and the memory of the war and the Holocaust in post-war and contemporary France and Europe. This article presents a critical reflection on the recourse to comparison in the processes of recuperation and analysis of Némirovsky's work. It argues that the frequent use of comparison in discussions of Némirovsky and her work in the twenty-first century is justified, and, in order further to demonstrate the fruitfulness of this approach, it pursues two related but contrasting lines of comparative enquiry. Its aims are twofold: to interrogate comparison as a critical strategy, and to use comparative criticism to extend our understanding of the work of a previously forgotten writer.

The Recourse to Comparison

In a recent contribution to the debate over the definition of comparative literature, Catherine Brown observes that comparison is a basic function of cognition and as such is 'involved in all thought', and that 'comparison in the strictest sense is involved in only a minority of literary criticism, whether described as comparative or otherwise'.[2] Leaving aside for the moment the issue of how rigorous commentators have been in their comparative methodologies, it is evident that the attempt to understand Némirovsky in the twenty-first century has taken an explicitly comparative form predicated on establishing sameness and difference. Which other writers is Némirovsky *like*? This question seeks to establish qualities such as recognizability, coherence, and relevance. Once they are established, another question arises: how is Némirovsky *distinct* from other writers? Does she have anything new

---

[1] Irène Némirovsky, *Suite française* (Paris: Denoël, 2004).
[2] 'What is "Comparative" Literature?', *Comparative Critical Studies*, 10 (2013), 67–88 (p. 67).

Modern Language Review, 110 (2015), 339–61
© Modern Humanities Research Association 2015

to tell us? Comparison is a means of attributing value, of demonstrating that Némirovsky is sufficiently *similar* to other writers to be meaningful (rather than just eccentric or bizarre and therefore justly forgotten) while also establishing that she is sufficiently *different* from them to be in some way original. It would be more difficult in the case of a newly rediscovered writer to attempt to attribute value solely on the basis of incomparability (uniqueness), as we do with established classics (such as Dante's *Divina commedia*, in Brown's example).[3] In the questions put to a rediscovered text, the two basic types of comparison evoked by Brown are at work—the fundamental perceptual requirement of distinguishing similarity and difference in the identification of distinct phenomena, and the comparative approach to literary criticism and history. In the immediate flood of journalistic appreciation of *Suite française* upon its publication in September 2004, Némirovsky was compared to (among others) Anne Frank,[4] Françoise Sagan,[5] Balzac, Sacha Guitry,[6] Vercors,[7] Flaubert,[8] André Maurois, Paul Nizan, and Roger Vailland.[9] These comparisons were more a matter of identification than of analysis, their aim being to help general readers recognize, situate, and evaluate an unfamiliar writer. This approach ran alongside a qualified discourse on 'uniqueness' which claimed that, while *Suite française* is not the *only* novel to have been written about the Occupation while the events were unfolding, it is a rare example of a contemporaneous account that is *aesthetically* successful.[10] Academic critics have in due course pursued what can more properly be termed comparative literary analyses, reading Némirovsky in relation to, for example, Carmen Conde,[11] Dostoevsky,[12] Tolstoy,[13] Jonathan

---

[3] Ibid., pp. 74–75.

[4] Olivier Le Naire, 'La Passion d'Irène', *L'Express*, 24 September 2004.

[5] Le Naire, 'La Passion d'Irène'; Claude Arnaud, 'Irène Némirovsky: le manuscrit retrouvé', *Le Point*, 30 September 2004.

[6] Arnaud, 'Irène Némirovsky'.

[7] Clémence Boulouque, 'Une émigrée dans la folie de la guerre', *Lire*, 1 October 2004; Annie Copperman, 'Renaudot: *Suite française* d'Irène Némirovsky', *Les Échos*, 9 November 2004; René de Ceccatty, 'Le "Guerre et paix d'Irène Némirovsky', *Le Monde*, 1 October 2004.

[8] de Ceccatty, 'Le "Guerre et paix" d'Irène Némirovsky'.

[9] Francois Nourissier, 'Némirovsky: équivoque, bouleversante, assassinée', *Le Figaro*, 23 October 2004.

[10] For example, in Le Naire, 'La Passion d'Irène': 'On peut en effet compter sur les doigts d'une main les témoignages d'une telle force écrits non a posteriori, mais bien durant la guerre. Oui, après Le *Journal* d'Anne Frank, cette *Suite française*, exceptionnelle du point de vue tant littéraire qu'historique, est un événement. Et un chef-d'œuvre.'

[11] Jean Andrews, 'Memorias de guerra, voces silenciadas: Carmen Conde e Irène Némirovsky', in *Mujer, literatura y esfera pública: España 1900–1940*, ed. by Pilar Nieva-de la Paz and others (Philadelphia: Society of Spanish and Spanish-American Studies, 2008), pp. 123–35.

[12] Stéphane Chaudier, 'Une humanité fantastique: Némirovsky et Dostoïevski', *Tagence*, 86 (2008), 67–88.

[13] Christian Donadille, '*David Golder*: un itinéraire de la dépossession et du rachat', *Roman 20–50*, 54 (2012), 7–18.

Littell,[14] Georges Bernarnos,[15] Natalie Sarraute,[16] Colette,[17] and Beckett.[18] In my own attempt to locate Némirovsky in the literary field of inter-war France, I compared her work with that of Hans Christian Andersen, Francis Carco, Joseph Kessel, Jean de Lacretelle, and François Mauriac.[19] The index of proper names in Olivier Philipponnat and Patrick Lienhardt's 2007 biography *La Vie d'Irène Némirovsky* indicates the extent to which they make reference to other writers in their presentation and explanation of Némirovsky's life and works.[20]

The recourse to comparison as a critical strategy with regard to Némirovsky's fiction is a matter of content as well as of context. In addition to the fact that a French-language writer bearing a Russian name immediately suggests the possibility of 'inter-national' and 'inter-lingual' readings,[21] several of Némirovsky's works themselves call explicitly for external comparison since they deal extensively with themes of emigration and foreignness (for example, *David Golder* (1929); *Le Bal* (1930); *Les Mouches d'automne* (1931); *Le Vin de solitude* (1935); *Les Chiens et les loups* (1940)). Further, a more specific type of external comparison is prompted by paratextual material. In the extracts from her working notes, included after the main text of *Suite française*, Némirovsky repeatedly refers to Tolstoy and *War and Peace*, which inevitably provoked literary journalists to compare these writers explicitly.[22] This comparison would doubtless have been made even without the benefit of extra-textual evidence, since the way in which Némirovsky uses the effect of historical events on fictional characters' lives to develop both plot and character in *Suite française* is clearly derived from the tradition of the historical novel, of which

[14] Richard J. Golsan and Susan Rubin Suleiman, 'Suite française and Les Bienveillantes, Two Literary "Exceptions": A Conversation', *Contemporary French and Francophone Studies*, 12 (2008), 321–30.

[15] Philippe Berthier, 'Sous le soulier de Satan', *Roman 20-50*, 54 (2012), 99–107.

[16] Alba Pessini, 'Ritratto di madri: Irène Némirovsky e Nathalie Sarraute', in *De claris mulieribus: figure e storie femminili nella tradizione europea*, ed. by Laura Bandiera and Diego Saglia (Parma: Monte Università Parma, 2011), pp. 329–46.

[17] Martina Stemberger, 'Selling Gender: An Alternative View of "Prostitution" in Three French Novels of the entre-deux-guerres', *Neophilologus*, 92 (2008), 601–15; Susan Rubin Suleiman, 'Famille, langue, identité: la venue à l'écriture dans *Le Vin de solitude*', *Roman 20-50*, 54 (2012), 57–74.

[18] Susan Rubin Suleiman, 'Choosing French: Language, Foreignness, and the Canon (Beckett/Némirovsky)', in *French Global: A New Approach to Literary History*, ed. by Christie McDonald and Susan Rubin Suleiman (New York: Columbia University Press, 2010), pp. 471–87.

[19] Angela Kershaw, *Before Auschwitz: Irène Némirovsky and the Cultural Landscape of Inter-War France* (New York and Abingdon: Routledge, 2010), pp. 56–57, 94–98, 131–34, 159.

[20] *La Vie d'Irène Némirovsky* (Paris: Grasset/Denoël, 2007).

[21] Brown, 'What is "Comparative" Literature?', p. 68.

[22] Némirovsky, *Suite française*, pp. 402–05. For example, the reviews cited above by Copperman, Arnaud, and de Ceccatty; see also Clémence Boulouque, 'Irène Némirovsky: échec à l'oubli', *Le Figaro*, 9 November 2004; Pascale Nivelle, 'Le Livre de ma mère', *Libération*, 29 October 2004; and many others since.

Tolstoy is one of the most important models. Tolstoy's *War and Peace* is only one—if the most commented—example of many cases of 'actual contact' or 'influence' in Némirovsky's œuvre.[23] In the various interviews Némirovsky gave to the inter-war literary press, when she was often asked who her favourite authors were, she mentions Huysmans, Maupassant, Oscar Wilde, Plato, Turgenev, Proust, Valéry Larbaud, Jacques Chardonne, Maurois, the Tharaud brothers, Tolstoy, Dostoevsky, Racine, Chateaubriand, Mérimée, Colette, Gerard d'Houville, Aldous Huxley . . .[24] Although these interviews show that Némirovsky was a voracious and international reader, they do not divulge how she incorporated her reading into her writing. Her manuscripts, on the other hand, reveal many instances of tangible 'influence', and these offer more scope for productive comparative analysis.[25] The novels also suggest evidence of their own to a particularly observant and well-informed close reader. For example, Susan Suleiman has recently offered a fascinating analysis of a textual connection between *Le Vin de solitude* and Colette's *La Vagabonde* in which she identifies an almost word-for-word similarity between key passages in the two novels which, she suggests, is more likely to be an unconscious reading memory than a case of conscious citation, and which is not documented in Némirovsky's manuscripts.[26] It is also worth noting that the 'suite' in the title of *Suite française*, as well as the presence of the theme of music in the novel, invites 'inter-artistic' analysis.[27] This is supported by a range of other musical references elsewhere in the manuscripts, as two further articles published in the same volume as Suleiman's have demonstrated.[28]

Such a wealth of textual and extra-textual evidence suggests that Némirovsky can fruitfully be approached as a literary 'nodal point' in the sense that Linda Hutcheon uses the term in her attempt 'to rethink the dominance of the national model of literary history'.[29] A 'nodal point', for Hutcheon, which may be, for example, a city, a writer, or a geographical feature, is a locus 'at which different cultures have met and merged'.[30] This article will demonstrate the extent to which this is an apt description of Némirovsky as a writer. Her active—and documented—engagement with

---

[23] Brown, 'What is "Comparative" Literature?', pp. 77–78.

[24] For a list of such interviews published in the inter-war press see Philipponnat and Lienhardt, *La Vie d'Irène Némirovsky*, pp. 476–77.

[25] These are conserved at the Institut Mémoires de l'édition contemporaine (IMEC), Caen.

[26] Suleiman, 'Famille, langue, identité', p. 71.

[27] Brown, 'What is "Comparative" Literature?', p. 68.

[28] Olivier Philipponnat, '"Un ordre différent, plus puissant et plus beau": Irène Némirovsky et le modèle symphonique', and Dominique Délas and Marie-Madeleine Castellani, 'Une symphonie inachevée: structure de *Suite française* d'Irène Némirovsky', *Roman 20-50*, 54 (2012), 75–86 and 87–97 respectively.

[29] 'Rethinking the National Model', in *Rethinking Literary History: A Dialogue on Theory*, ed. by Linda Hutcheon and Mario Valdés (Oxford: Oxford University Press, 2002), pp. 3–49 (pp. 3, 8).

[30] Ibid., p. 8.

such a sweep of French, European, Russian, and Soviet culture across a significant variety of genres suggests that it would be limiting—perhaps impossible—to read Némirovsky in a non-comparative manner.

Némirovsky as a Comparatist

The importance of comparison in Némirovsky's writing practice can plausibly be related to her educational background, since she had formal academic training in comparative literature. Having first studied Russian language and literature at the Sorbonne from 1920 to 1922, she obtained the *certificat d'études supérieures de littératures modernes comparées* in 1924.[31] In a small way, Némirovsky was part of an important moment in the history of comparative literature in France, having studied in the department established by Fernand Baldernsperger, Paul Hazard, and Paul van Tieghem. 1921 saw the launch of the *Revue de littérature comparée*, and Baldensperger's programmatic introduction to the first number defined the discipline as it was understood and taught at the Sorbonne.[32] In 1931 van Tieghem's concise volume *La Littérature comparée* outlined the principles and theories of the discipline for the French student and general reader.[33] Baldensperger and van Tieghem were interested in actual and provable literary interactions and influences. According to van Tieghem, 'Toute étude de littérature comparée [. . .] a pour but de décrire un *passage*, le fait que quelque chose de littéraire est transporté au-delà d'une frontière linguistique.'[34] Coincidence of theme or topic was not the domain of comparative literature; the term 'littérature générale' was reserved for the tracing of such literary developments across various literatures and cultures.[35]

Given Némirovsky's multilingual competence, international cultural heritage, and academic training, it is not surprising that she found occasional work as a critic of foreign literature. Her literary-critical texts provide further insight into her conceptions of transnational literary contact. In 1935 she was employed by the *Revue hebdomadaire* as the author of its 'Lettres étrangères' rubric and wrote three 'chroniques' in the series, presenting two American, two Soviet, and two English novels.[36] The first paragraph of her first contribu-

---

[31] Archives nationales AJ/16/4824; see Kershaw, *Before Auschwitz*, pp. 43–44, 69–70.
[32] 'Littérature comparée: le mot et la chose', *Revue de littérature comparée*, 1 (1921), 5–29.
[33] *La Littérature comparée* (Paris: Armand Colin, 1931).
[34] Ibid., p. 68 (van Tieghem's italics).
[35] Ibid., pp. 169–213.
[36] Irène Némirovsky, 'Deux romans américains: *La Mère*, par Pearl S. Buck, et *Le Facteur sonne toujours deux fois*, par James M. Cain'; 'Deux romans russes: *Complète remise à neuf* (*Kapitalny remont*), par L. Sobolev, et *Le Quartier allemand*, par Lew Nitobourg'; 'Deux romans anglais: *Voyage dans les ténèbres*, par J Rhys, et *Des étoiles étaient nées*, par Barbara Lucas', *Revue*

tion indicates her approach to the task of introducing foreign-language works to French readers:

Tout lecteur de romans étrangers poursuit un double but qui n'est contradictoire qu'en apparence. D'une part, il désire se dépayser, connaître d'autres mœurs, des habitudes de vie qui soient différentes des siennes, des paysages nouveaux, des âmes singulières ou surprenantes, mais, en même temps, il recherche à travers les pages du livre étranger l'image de cœurs fraternels.[37]

Némirovsky also claims here that great works which 'ne connaissent pas les frontières' are defined by the presence of a certain exoticism, or otherness, combined with themes pertaining to 'la commune humanité'.[38] This type of transnational reading, motivated by the dual attractions of difference and similarity, comes under the heading of what van Tieghem would have called *general literature*. While Némirovsky places Pearl Buck on a par with Tolstoy and George Eliot, these comparisons are not examples of actual contact between writers, but resemble those evoked by twenty-first-century critics of *Suite française*: they accrue familiarity and value to a text as yet unfamiliar to a new group of readers. The 'chroniques' reinforce the impression gained of Némirovsky from press interviews as someone for whom the experience of literature cannot be contained by national boundaries. They also suggest that for Némirovsky (as for traditional comparatists of the pre- and post-Second World War generations, and stretching on into our own) a proper appreciation of literature from another culture depends on foreign-language competence.[39] Némirovsky was suspicious of translation: she remarked that the brutal, violent, chaotic, and slang-ridden American of James M. Cain does not lend itself to translation, and recommended that non-anglophone readers should wait for the film adaptation![40] Nonetheless, when she came to preface the French translation of Cain's novel by Sabine Berritz a year later,

hebdomadaire, January 1935, pp. 490–97, February 1935, pp. 491–98, and May 1935, pp. 101–06 respectively.

[37] Némirovsky, 'Deux romans américains', p. 490.

[38] Ibid.

[39] Charles Bernheimer, like Harry Levin and Tom Greene before him, committed comparative literature as a discipline to maintaining foreign-language competence in his 1993 report to the American Comparative Literature Association; the issue is much debated in subsequent reports and responses. See *Comparative Literature in the Age of Multiculturalism*, ed. by Charles Bernheimer (Baltimore and London: Johns Hopkins University Press, 1995); *Comparative Literature in an Age of Globalization*, ed. by Haun Saussy (Baltimore: Johns Hopkins University Press, 2006); and for the most recent (2014–15) reports, <www.stateofthediscipline.acla.org>. Elizabeth Fox-Genovese divides the debate schematically, with appropriate caveats, into two camps: 'elitists' defend the reading of 'high' literature in its original language, and 'populists' advocate a more 'cultural studies' approach and support reading in translation ('Between Elitism and Populism: Whither Comparative Literature?', in *Comparative Literature*, ed. by Bernheimer, pp. 134–42 (p. 134)).

[40] Némirovsky, 'Deux romans américains', p. 497.

she admitted her initial scepticism but professed to have been won over by this translator's art.[41]

In 1931 Némirovsky had published a review, in Russian, in the Parisian émigré journal *Čisla*, of André Maurois's recent biography of Turgenev.[42] Here also, lack of knowledge of the relevant language and culture appears as a serious impediment to a true appreciation of foreign literature. According to Némirovsky, Maurois, the anglophone French novelist, essayist, and critic, cannot write effectively about Turgenev because he does not know Russian or Russia. His 'poetic' evocation of Moscow would not convince anyone who knows the real Moscow, and only a Russian reader will feel what 'Turgenevian'—a mixture of charm and purity, melancholy and tenderness—really means.[43] Némirovsky suggests that Maurois penetrates much more effectively into the soul of Dickens than into that of Turgenev, because he knows English, and England.[44] But Némirovsky's point about foreign-language competence is quite subtle. In her notebook she writes that 'Les Français, en général, n'aiment pas et ne comprennent pas T. [i.e. Turgenev] mais les Anglais l'aiment. C'est sans doute ce qui a fait faire ce livre à Maurois', and in the published review she remarks that Maurois looks at Turgenev from an English point of view.[45] Némirovsky's sensitivity to the way in which Maurois's engagement with Turgenev is mediated by his knowledge of English and English culture complicates the binary mode of comparatism initially implied by her criticism of Maurois, suggesting a critique of the binarism of Baldensperger and van Tieghem's approach. Némirovsky was clearly aware that comparative literature is a complex phenomenon involving more than the unidirectional passage of 'something literary' across a single linguistic border.

This is another reason why Némirovsky responds well to comparative approaches to literary history sympathetic to Linda Hutcheon's work on 'nodal points'. Drawing explicitly on Hutcheon's work to propose a new, global approach to French literary history, Christie McDonald and Susan Suleiman place 'negotiations with otherness and boundary crossings at the very centre of French literary history'.[46] Némirovsky's writing (both critical and fictional) supports McDonald and Suleiman's view that 'tensions between multiplicity

---

[41] Némirovsky, 'Préface', in James M. Cain, *Le Facteur sonne toujours deux fois* (1936) (Paris: Gallimard, 1948), p. 8.

[42] 'André Maurois. *Tourguénev*. Grasset 1931', *Čisla*, 5 (1931), 248–50. A French version of this text in Nemirovsky's hand appears in IMEC NMR 7.3 Notes pour 'La Vie amoureuse de Pushkin' et Notes de travail, headed 'Critique du Tourgéniev de Maurois'. I am very grateful to my colleague Jeremy Morris for translating the Russian text and for his generosity in discussing it with me at length.

[43] Némirovsky, 'André Maurois. *Tourguénev*. Grasset 1931', pp. 249, 250.

[44] Ibid., p. 249. André Maurois, *Un essai sur Dickens* (Paris: Grasset, 1927).

[45] IMEC NMR 7.3; Némirovsky, 'André Maurois. *Tourguénev*. Grasset 1931', p. 249.

[46] 'Introduction: The National and the Global', in *French Global*, ed. by McDonald and Suleiman, pp. ix–xxi (p. x).

and unity, between diversity and uniformity, between "same" and "other"'
and issues of migration and diaspora are crucial to understanding literature
written in the French language, and that emphasizing *international* 'points of
contact and multiple kinds of dialogue that found and inform literary space' is
a most productive reading strategy.[47] The instinctive recourse to comparison
on the part of journalistic critics and the more sustained attempts of academic
critics to locate Némirovsky in relation to her literary peers and predecessors
are exercises in this type of criticism. Through comparative studies of various types, Némirovsky is being (re)established as an important figure in the
history of European, as well as French, twentieth-century literature, and in
the process, her work is providing an opportunity to rethink French literary
history from a comparative perspective.

Creative Reception I: Némirovsky, Percy Lubbock, and E. M. Forster

An appreciation of Némirovsky's background, foreign-language competence,
educational experience, and critical interest in foreign literature is crucial
to a full understanding of the role sophisticated interaction between writers
from different linguistic backgrounds plays in her writing practice. The remainder of this article will be devoted to the analysis of two instances of
'actual contact' between Némirovsky and contemporaneous English literature. Why English literature? Firstly, because of the position from which I
approach the work of Némirovsky as an English reader writing largely for
an audience of English readers; secondly, because of the importance of 'the
third language' in comparative study. The most obvious axis of comparison
in the case of Némirovsky is France–Russia. However, as Brown points out,[48]
quoting Haun Saussy, attention to the 'third' language can reveal things that
remain obscured in binary analyses:

If a two-language pattern is adequate for formulating and answering most questions
of historical influence or typological similarity, the third language, like an uninvited
guest, points to the things that a two-language pattern leaves out. What is going on,
even in a dyadic relation, that a dyadic explanation leaves unaccounted for?[49]

In this section I approach Némirovsky's interest in Tolstoy through her explicit and sustained engagements with E. M. Forster's *Aspects of the Novel* and
Percy Lubbock's *The Craft of Fiction*.[50] In the following section I consider the
relationship between Némirovsky's fiction and that of Evelyn Waugh. These

---

[47] Ibid., pp. xi, xix.

[48] Brown, 'What is "Comparative" Literature?', p. 85. Némirovsky also read German, but the
use of English and references to English and American literature are considerably more frequent
in her texts and manuscripts.

[49] Haun Saussy, 'Comparative Literature?', *PMLA*, 118 (2003), 336–41 (p. 340).

[50] See also Angela Kershaw, 'Les Intertextes anglais de *Suite française*', in *Les Écrivains théo-*

two examples of comparative analysis differ in important respects. The first pertains to literary theory and the second to fiction. In the first, documentary evidence for the nature of the connection is extensive, permitting analysis of manuscript sources which reveal the genesis of Némirovsky's fiction. In the second, documentary evidence is also available, but is less specific in terms of the *nature* of the 'influence', and therefore an analysis of relationships between published novels is appropriate. Two different comparative methodologies will therefore be employed. The first is empirical and hermeneutic, while the second draws on the concept of 'radial' reading.[51]

The identification of 'actual contact' which subtends both these examples is now frequently dismissed as old-fashioned and obsolete. The study of 'influence', we are told, belongs to the history of comparative literature.[52] Susan Bassnett has humorously characterized the search for 'influences' as 'a kind of treasure hunt' and even 'a hopeless endeavour'.[53] Influence study was superseded by 'intertextuality'; those for whom intertextuality seems too radically decontextualized might be better advised to concentrate on the sorts of textual 'border crossings' identified by scholars of postcolonialism or cultural globalization.[54] Nonetheless, Brigitte Le Juez has recently suggested that the study of influence can (and should) be revived as 'creative reception', which she views as an 'essential phenomenon at the heart of all creative production', arguing that '[i]t is [. . .] the role of the comparatist to attempt a critical appraisal of such a fundamental, artistic phenomenon as the continuously innovative meeting of artistic minds'.[55] Bassnett is of course absolutely right to underline the fact that '[w]riters draw their inspiration from all kinds

---

riciens de la littérature (1920–1945), ed. by Bruno Curatolo and Julia Peslier (Besançon: Presses Universitaires de Franche-Comté, 2013), pp. 251–68, and Kershaw, *Before Auschwitz*, p. 178.

[51] Clive Scott, 'The Translation of Reading', *Translation Studies*, 4 (2011), 213–29 (pp. 221–22). Scott cites the term 'radial reading' from Jerome McGann, 'How to Read a Book', in *New Directions in Textual Studies*, ed. by David Oliphant and Robin Bradford (Austin: Harry Ransom Research Center and the University of Texas, 1990), pp. 12–37.

[52] Examples abound in the ACLA reports and responses. Peter Brooks typically associates influence study with the Sorbonne school of the 1920s in 'Must We Apologize?', in *Comparative Literature*, ed. by Bernheimer, pp. 97–106 (p. 97); Haun Saussy links influence to the rise of comparative literature in the era of nationalisms in the nineteenth century in 'Exquisite Cadavers Stitched from Fresh Nightmares: Of Memes, Hives and Selfish Genes', in *Comparative Literature*, ed. by Saussy, pp. 3–42 (p. 6); Jonathan Culler caricatures the usual accounts of the history of the discipline which relegate influence study to 'once upon a time' in 'Comparative Literature, at Last', in *Comparative Literature*, ed by Saussy, pp. 237–48 (p. 237).

[53] 'Influence and Intertextuality: A Reappraisal', *Forum for Modern Language Studies*, 43 (2007), 134–46 (pp. 137, 138).

[54] See Culler, 'Comparative Literature, at Last', p. 242.

[55] Brigitte Le Juez, 'Creative Reception: Reviving a Comparative Method' <http://stateofthediscipline.acla.org/entry/creative-reception-reviving-comparative-method> [accessed 28 April 2014], unpaginated. See also Geert Lernout, 'Comparative Literature in the Low Countries', *Comparative Critical Studies*, 3.1–2: *Comparative Literature at a Crossroads?* (February, June 2006), 37–46, for a defence of recent reincarnations of the archival approach.

of sources, some conscious, some unconscious, some acknowledged, some vehemently denied'.[56] The merit of the notion of *creative* reception of one writer by another is its capacity to contain both the conscious *and* the unconscious, the acknowledged *and* the denied. Le Juez's approach allows attention to empirical evidence and its meaning to be combined with a focus on the creative role played by the reader, which is what Bassnett recommends. The following analysis will therefore move from a consideration of the author as reader (Némirovsky as a reader of Forster, Lubbock, and Waugh) to embrace intertextual connections between the novels of Waugh and Némirovsky.

The extracts from Némirovsky's notebooks published in the annexes to *Suite française* contain several unidentified fragments in English. Among these are various quotations transcribed by Némirovsky from Percy Lubbock's *The Craft of Fiction* and E. M. Forster's *Aspects of the Novel*:

C'est peut-être an impression of ironic contrast, to receive the force of the contrast. The reader has only to see and hear.[57]

Méditer aussi: the famous 'impersonality' of Flaubert and his kind lies only in the greater fact [*sic*, for 'tact'] with which they express their feelings—dramatizing them, embodying them in living form, instead of stating them directly?[58]

All action is a battle, the only business [*sic*, for 'happiness'] is peace.[59]

There is also an explicit reference to Forster:

Je crois que ce qui donne à *Guerre et Paix* cette expansion dont parle Forster, c'est tout simplement le fait que dans l'esprit de Tolstoï, *Guerre et Paix* n'est qu'un premier volume qui devrait être suivi par *Les Décembristes*, mais ce qu'il a fait inconsciemment (peut-être, car naturellement je n'en sais rien, j'imagine), enfin ce qu'il a fait consciemment ou non est très important à faire dans un livre comme *Tempête*, etc., même si certains personnages arrivent à une conclusion, le livre lui-même doit donner l'impression de n'être qu'un épisode… ce qu'est réellement notre époque, comme toutes les époques bien sûr.[60]

Critics who related *War and Peace* to *Suite française* on its publication did not make the connection with *Aspects of the Novel*, but it is crucial, for while Némirovsky was inspired directly by the Russian classic, this influence was mediated through the theoretical works of two key contemporary literary critics of English modernism. As she was thinking through the narrative strategies she would employ in *Suite française*, Némirovsky was reading Tolstoy through

[56] Bassnett, 'Influence and Intertextuality', p. 138.

[57] Némirovsky, *Suite française*, p. 398; Percy Lubbock, *The Craft of Fiction* (London: Jonathan Cape, 1921), p. 71. The punctuation is transcribed incorrectly and should read: 'To receive the force of the contrast, the reader has only to see and hear.'

[58] Némirovsky, *Suite française*, p. 399; Lubbock, *The Craft of Fiction*, pp. 67–68.

[59] Némirovsky, *Suite française*, p. 404; E. M. Forster, *Aspects of the Novel* (London: Penguin, 2005), p. 136.

[60] Némirovsky, *Suite française*, p. 405.

Forster and Lubbock. Further examples of quotations transcribed from these sources occur in Némirovsky's notes for her 1935 novel *Le Vin de solitude* and in her notes relating to the 'chroniques' published in the *Revue hebdomadaire* in that year, as well as in her notes from the early 1940s relating to *Suite française*.[61] In addition to the notion of 'expansion', Némirovsky engages with Forster's concepts of 'flat' and 'round' characters,[62] and of 'story'. She concurs with Forster's view that the novel cannot abandon time, as the high modernist Gertrude Stein believed, but must, like all narratives since time immemorial, *tell a story*:

> Forster dit que la structure primitive du roman peut tenir en deux mots: 'Et après?'— les mots que disent le Sultan à Sheherazade, et que les conteurs de la primitive tribu humaine devaient entendre de leur public [. . .] on a tort de mépriser le 'Et après?'. C'est une grande qualité dans un roman. On l'a surestimé, mais maintenant on a, pour elle, un mépris immérité.[63]

The last part of this extract is particularly revelatory of Némirovsky's attempt to reconcile literary tradition and innovation. In the past—in Tolstoy's day?—novelists paid too much attention to satisfying the reader's desire 'to know what happens next'[64] but now—in the period of modernism—the pendulum has swung too far in the opposite direction. Némirovsky positions herself between the poles of (Russian) nineteenth-century realism and (English) twentieth-century modernism, taking what remains relevant from the former—such as the open-ended, 'expansive' character of Tolstoy's historical fiction—without adopting the excesses of formal experimentation that characterized the latter.

Némirovsky does not seem to have been interested in the more formalist 'aspects' Forster analyses, such as 'Pattern and Rhythm'. Careful examination of Némirovsky's use of Lubbock reveals a suspicion of excessive formalism, which Forster shares. Némirovsky's reading of Lubbock could be described as a misreading or—more positively—in Harold Bloom's terms, as misprision.[65] Most of the extracts she cites are taken from Lubbock's discussion of Tolstoy in Chapters III and IV of *The Craft of Fiction*. However, in these chapters Lubbock uses Tolstoy as a counter-example to illustrate the superiority of the

---

[61] IMEC NMR 13.9 *Le Vin de solitude*: brouillon et journal d'écriture (1/2); IMEC NMR 7.3; IMEC NMR 15.2 Nouvelles 1940, projets; IMEC NMR 2.15 *Suite française*: 'Captivité': manuscrit inachevé.

[62] In IMEC NMR 15.2 Némirovsky quotes from Forster's chapter on 'People': 'The test of a round character is whether it is capable of surprising in a convincing way. If it never surprises, it is flat. If it does not convince, it is flat pretending to be round' (Forster, *Aspects of the Novel*, p. 41).

[63] IMEC NMR 7.3; Forster, *Aspects of the Novel*, p. 41.

[64] Forster, *Aspects of the Novel*, p. 41.

[65] Harold Bloom, *The Anxiety of Influence: A Theory of Poetry* (New York: Oxford University Press, 1973).

formalist approach of modernist writers (of which he finds Henry James to be the best example). Némirovsky, by contrast, takes Tolstoy (via Forster) as a *positive* model for the integration of fiction and history in *Suite française*. Tolstoy divides Forster and Lubbock: Lubbock's formalism leads him to reject the Russian master, while for Forster the structural chaos of *War and Peace* incarnates the 'expansion' which he believes should define the modernist novel. Némirovsky quotes several passages from Chapter III which, taken out of context, appear to be positive comments on Tolstoy's techniques:

whatever his shifting panorama brings into view, he makes of it an image of beauty and truth that is final, complete, unqualified

It is true that Tolstoy's good instinct guides him ever and again away from the mere telling of the story on his own authority; at high moments he knows better than to tell it himself.

The business of the novelist is to create life, and here [i.e. in *War and Peace*] is life created indeed[66]

Némirovsky did not, however, note in her manuscripts that these arguments lead Lubbock to the conclusion that *War and Peace* is a formal *failure*:

In *War and Peace*, as it seems to me, the story suffers twice over for the imperfection of the form. It is damaged, in the first place, by the importation of another and an irrelevant story—damaged because it so loses the sharp and clear relief that it would have if it stood alone. Whether the story was to be the drama of youth and age, or the drama of war and peace, in either case it would have been incomparably more impressive if *all* the great wealth of the material had been used for its purpose, all brought into one design.[67]

It is on the question of 'design' that Némirovsky most seriously misunderstands—or most deliberately reinterprets—Lubbock:

But the meaning, the import, what I should like to call the moral of it all—what of that? [. . .] It is of the picture that we speak: its moral is in its design, and without design the scattered scenes will make no picture... oui, évidemment, c'est que je suis dedans et je ne peux pas le voir comme je vois la guerre de 14, qui était confuse et multiple, mais qui maintenant peut se dire en peu de mots: Comment la France a gagné la guerre? Mais ici, on est dans la matière. De quoi accouche-t-on? on ne sait pas. C'est ça qui gène.[68]

Lubbock's reference to 'design' helps Némirovsky conceptualize the central problem she faces in *Suite française*, namely that she is writing about events that are not yet over and whose 'design' cannot yet be perceived clearly. Forster's 'expansion' provides at least a partial solution, insofar as it validates

---

[66] IMEC NMR 2.15; IMEC NMR 15.2; Lubbock, *The Craft of Fiction*, pp. 27, 40, 41.
[67] Lubbock, *The Craft of Fiction*, pp. 40–41 (Lubbock's italics).
[68] IMEC NMR 2.15; Lubbock, *The Craft of Fiction*, p. 52.

open-endedness; Lubbock is not at all interested in the temporal relationship between the story and the historical events it narrates since for him, meaning is derived exclusively from form. This is not to say that Némirovsky neglected form altogether: she recognized that 'il *faut une composition*' and, as Olivier Philipponnat has recently demonstrated, the musical analogy—again informed by Forster—helped her to devise one for *Le Vin de solitude* as well as for *Suite française*.[69]

Paying attention to the contact between Némirovsky, Tolstoy, and two theorists of English modernism demonstrates, in a way that a binary study of Russian influences on her work cannot, the extent to which Némirovsky sought to reinvent the historical novel for her own era. As we have already seen in Némirovsky's comments about Maurois's study of Turgenev, in her theoretical understanding of literature, and in her own writing practice, 'influence' is not a binary relation but involves complex transactions between multiple writers and languages. It is also evident that 'influence' is a critical rather than a consensual relation. While Némirovsky's reading of Forster is sympathetic, if selective, her use of Lubbock is a dissenting one. These examples suggest that, considering its etymology, 'influence' is a misleading term. Contact between writers is not a straightforward 'flowing in' of matter from a single channel. Literature is the product of *in-fluence* only insofar as it is, in Haun Saussy's words, 'watered by many streams'.[70] Manuscript sources demonstrate that, while Némirovsky's writing practice is consonant with van Tieghem's conviction that the interest of literature lies in cross-national relationships, she did not restrict herself to binary literary relations or to simple appropriation.

Creative Reception II: Némirovsky and Evelyn Waugh

Like Némirovsky, Evelyn Waugh was suspicious of modernism's tendency towards abstraction. Neither Waugh nor Némirovsky believed form to be all: content and representation continued to matter.[71] Their approach to the modern novel was similar: never backward-looking stylistically, they sought to use modern literary techniques to convey the modern situation without abandoning the narrative traditions they believed remained serviceable in their time. Born in 1903, they were of the same generation. While the concept of generation in literary and intellectual history might be dismissed as imprecise, and coincidence of birth year is not necessarily significant, Némirovsky

---

[69] 'Irène Némirovsky et le modèle symphonique', p. 78; Forster, *Aspects of the Novel*, p. 149. See also Kershaw, *Before Auschwitz*, p. 89.

[70] 'Exquisite Cadavers', p. 5.

[71] Douglas Lane Patey, *The Life of Evelyn Waugh: A Critical Biography* (Oxford: Blackwell, 1998), pp. 12–13.

and Waugh can be located within a common 'generation unit' (Karl Mannheim's term) of European creative writers marked by their situation as young teenagers during the First World War and by their use of literature to respond to the upheavals wrought by the economic crisis and the redefinition of social and personal identities that characterized the 1920s and 1930s.[72] Each made their name with a best-selling novel depicting the malaise of the young post-war generation. Némirovsky's *David Golder* was published in Paris in December 1929, just a few weeks before Waugh's *Vile Bodies* appeared in London in January 1930. David Golder's daughter Joyce, a materialistic socialite, might plausibly be read as a French variation on the English theme of the Bright Young People. Joyce's life, like the lives of the characters in *Vile Bodies*, is a fast-paced sequence of parties and sexual encounters: she is part of what Waugh called 'this crazy and sterile generation', characterized by 'perverse and aimless dissipation'.[73] Némirovsky's *Le Pion sur l'échiquier* (1934) addresses the malaise of both the combatant generation (Christophe Bohun, aged 43 at the time of the action) and their sons (Philippe Bohun, aged 18).[74] *Vile Bodies'* Adam Fenwick-Symes, also a war veteran, might be seen as a younger incarnation of Christophe, who is a man who fails to find fulfilment in either work or relationships and cannot escape the all-pervasive materialism of his era. Philippe's indolence and inability to settle on a proper career are reminiscent of Waugh's characters: he appears at breakfast in his pyjamas, spends his time telephoning and socializing, and dabbles in cinema. These are commercially successful middlebrow novels which, though not aesthetically ground-breaking, have considerable stylistic integrity and value. Since Waugh's and Némirovsky's novels arise out of a common European situation, these *comparanda* are not strictly distinct. As K. Anthony Appiah remarks, it can be taken as read that European literatures are interconnected and 'make sense together'.[75] To compare Némirovsky and Waugh is to compare like with like, and it is obvious that reading them together illustrates the two fundamental premises of comparative studies Bernheimer identifies: that literature functions cross-culturally, and that 'the category of the literary' is constructed differently in different cultures.[76]

Némirovsky's reflections on her reading of Evelyn Waugh occur in the

---

[72] See Fiona Barclay and Cristina Johnston, 'Qu'est-ce qu'une génération?', *Modern & Contemporary France*, 22 (2014), 133–38.

[73] Waugh, 'The War and the Younger Generation', in Evelyn Waugh, *A Little Order: A Selection from his Journalism*, ed. by Donat Gallagher (London: Eyre Methuen, 1977), pp. 11–12. First published in *The Spectator*, 13 April 1929.

[74] In 'The War and the Younger Generation' Waugh distinguishes between 'the stunted and mutilated generation who fought' and 'the younger generation' (p. 11).

[75] 'Geist Stories', in *Comparative Literature*, ed. by Bernheimer, pp. 51–57 (p. 54).

[76] 'Introduction: The Anxieties of Comparison', in *Comparative Literature*, ed. by Bernheimer, pp. 1–17 (p. 10).

same manuscript source as her notes on Maurois's biography of Turgenev and for the *Revue hebdomadaire* articles.[77] The notebook contains quite detailed reflections on *Decline and Fall* (1928), *Vile Bodies* (1930), *Black Mischief* (1932), and *A Handful of Dust* (1934). The focus here will be primarily on *Vile Bodies*, though this does not of course discount the possibility of other readings teasing out further connections. In her notes Némirovsky identifies the main theme of *Vile Bodies* as 'le malaise de la jeune génération', the subject she had addressed in detail in her own fiction.[78] She makes three particularly interesting judgements about Waugh's take on the topic. Firstly, she finds it 'spécifiquement anglais'. *Vile Bodies* is populated by 'ces élégants chômeurs dont l'Angleterre semble être fleurie', and the characters' excessive drinking is surprising: 'quantité d'alcool ingurgité inusuelle pour un roman français'.[79] She reads the text in relation to the English vogue for fantasy, which 'garde dans son pays d'origine ses caractéristiques qui la font différer profondément du fantastique français'. She transcribed the passage from the 1930 Author's Note where Waugh states that 'the action of the book is laid in the near future', and she links this explicitly to Forster's discussion of fantasy in Max Beerbohm's *Zuleika Dobson*.[80] Secondly, Némirovsky judges *Vile Bodies* to be 'Trop intellectuel, trop "Soho" [she added 'Chelsea' in the margin], loin de la commune humanité'.[81] This vocabulary is significant. As we have seen, in her review of 'Deux romans américains' Némirovsky explicitly identified the presence of themes pertaining to 'la commune humanité' as a prerequisite for a border-crossing novel. The implication, therefore, is that Némirovsky believed Waugh would have difficulty in crossing the Channel.[82] Thirdly, the fact that she transcribed Arnold Bennett's critique of *Decline and Fall* as 'an uncompromising and brilliantly malicious satire' suggests she judged *Vile Bodies* to be an example of satire.[83] Douglas Lane Patey suggests that most critics, with the exception of Arnold Bennett, L. P. Hartley, and V. S. Pritchett,

---

[77] IMEC NMR 7.3. Némirovsky did not, however, publish reviews of Waugh in the *Revue hebdomadaire*.

[78] See Kershaw, *Before Auschwitz*, pp. 140–52, on the dominance of the theme of malaise in inter-war French fiction and in Némirovsky's writing.

[79] Nonetheless, she also found *Vile Bodies* reminiscent of Paul Morand's *France-la-Doulce* (1934), a profoundly anti-Semitic French novel whose Jewish film-maker protagonist resembles Waugh's Mr Isaacs (who is insulted by his leading lady as a 'Dirty Yid') (Evelyn Waugh, *Vile Bodies* (London: Penguin, 2000), p. 121).

[80] Waugh, *Vile Bodies*, p. xxxvii; Forster, *Aspects of the Novel*, pp. 109–11.

[81] IMEC NMR 7.3.

[82] *Vile Bodies* was not published in France until 1947, when it appeared as *Ces corps vils*, trans. by Louis Chantemèle (Paris: Table Ronde). Grasset published *Black Mischief* in 1938 as *Diablerie*, and *A Handful of Dust* in 1945 as *Une poignée de cendres*, both trans. by Marie Canavaggia. *Decline and Fall* was published in Brussels by Éditions universitaires in 1946 as *Conduite scandaleuse*, trans. by Franz Weyergans, and in Paris by Union Générale des Éditions in 1983 as *Grandeur et décadence*, trans. by Henri Evans.

[83] First published in the *Evening Standard*, 11 October 1928, p. 5, and reprinted in *Evelyn*

received *Decline and Fall* and *Vile Bodies* not as satire, but as mere comedy or farce, a response which Patey convincingly demonstrates to be erroneous.[84] Although Némirovsky did not like *Vile Bodies*—she writes that 'cela ne m'a pas beaucoup plu'—she apparently did not make this mistake.

Reading the novels of Waugh and Némirovsky together, we can begin better to understand these judgements. Let us take just two specific examples of themes which are treated repeatedly by both writers: the relationship between sex and money, and suicide. *David Golder* and *Vile Bodies* both present the sale of a woman to a marriage partner: Adam sells his 'share' in Nina to his rival Ginger, and Joyce sells herself to the ageing Fischl. In *Vile Bodies*, the situation is comically inappropriate, while in *David Golder* it is a dismal illustration of Joyce's materialism:

Il [Fischl] en veut pour son argent, lui, le vieux cochon, dit-elle tout à coup d'une voix qui tremblait de haine. Ah! Je voudrais le...[85]

> 'Lottie presented me with her bill.'
> 'Darling, what *did* you do?'
> 'Well, I did something rather extraordinary... My dear, I sold *you*.'
> 'Darling... *who to*?'[86]

Nina's incongruous 'Darling... *who to*?' humorously frustrates the reader's reasonable expectation that she will be horrified rather than curious, while her parting line 'But I think you're rather a cad' is a typical comic understatement. By contrast, Joyce's brutal 'Je voudrais le tuer' is emphasized by its delayed delivery and by a description of her pulling distractedly at her hair.[87] Suicide is tragically farcical under the pen of both writers. In *Le Pion sur l'échiquier* Christophe Bohun imagines committing suicide while shaving, but tells himself: 'Je joue, c'est un jeu de maniaque, je sais que je vais m'arrêter.' Then, provoked by a Linguaphone recording repeating absurd English, he presses the blade into his neck. His suicide is only partly intentional: as he passes out, he has 'le sentiment d'avoir connu une sottise sans nom'.[88] He recovers, but later dies of an infection. In *Vile Bodies* Simon Balcairn is also an incompetent suicide. He puts his head in the oven, but decides to start again when he realizes his head is resting on a newspaper article by one of his rival gossip columnists. He holds his breath, then tries sniffing, but then, like Christophe, loses control of the outcome: 'The sniff made him cough,

---

Waugh: The Critical Heritage, ed. by Martin Stannard (London: Routledge & Kegan Paul, 1984), p. 82; transcribed by Némirovsky in IMEC NMR 7.3.

[84] *The Life of Evelyn Waugh*, p. 58.

[85] Némirovsky, *David Golder*, in Irène Némirovsky, *Œuvres complètes*, 2 vols, ed. by Olivier Philipponnat (Paris: Librairie générale française, 2011), I, 408–549 (p. 523).

[86] Waugh, *Vile Bodies*, p. 166 (Waugh's italics).

[87] Némirovsky, *David Golder*, p. 523.

[88] Némirovsky, *Le Pion sur l'échiquier*, in Némirovsky, *Œuvres complètes*, I, 837–967 (p. 953).

and coughing made him breathe, and breathing made him feel very ill; but soon he fell into a coma and presently died.'[89] Waugh's succinctly balanced anadiplosis and his comically concise and anticlimactic 'and presently died' stand in stark contrast to the two pages of interior monologue which precede Christophe's death.[90]

Critics past and present have noted Waugh's use of exaggerated and often savage schoolboy humour in the service of satire, and its quasi-surrealist effect.[91] As Patey notes, to achieve this, Waugh replaces psychological verisimilitude with implausible caricature: 'Characters in Waugh's first novels seem empty, without psychological depth, because they have no depths to probe; an "external", un-subjective presentation accurately captures their modern selves.'[92] Némirovsky's novels remain bounded by psychological realism, and her characterization relies to a significant extent on interior monologue and narratorial exposition, though her satire is no less acute for this—one interwar critic likened her writing to the action of a scalpel.[93] Némirovsky satirizes the materialism of the *années folles*, while Waugh's 'maimed moderns'[94] lack any value system at all. Joyce's materialism makes her heartless and without compassion; Nina is simply vacuous. Yet Patey's reading of Waugh as a Christian, specifically Catholic, moralist shows that the implications of the vacuity of the Bright Young People are just as serious as the corrosion of humane values implied by the materialism of Némirovsky's characters. For Waugh, the rejection of a plausible moral framework, based on (Catholic) 'tradition', can result only in the disintegration of individual personality and in social fracture.[95] By contrast, *David Golder*, in common with much of Némirovsky's fiction, is 'une fable sans morale' and 'un roman de l'absurde', though no cathartic or productive possibility is ascribed to the recognition of meaninglessness here.[96] Némirovsky recognized in Waugh a fellow satirist; however, she did not identify with the 'fantastical' aspect of his fiction: his comic caricatures looked to her like intellectual posturing ('trop intellectuel, trop "Soho"') and disqualified him as a writer of works able to convey 'la commune humanité'. The relationship between Némirovsky and Waugh might therefore be expressed through the dual metaphor of the *foil*, which denotes both a reflective material and a fencing sword. There is reflection here, but also repulsion. Citing Oscar Wilde (another acknowledged influence

---

[89] Waugh, *Vile Bodies*, p. 90.

[90] Némirovsky, *Le Pion sur l'échiquier*, pp. 966–67.

[91] Selina Hastings, *Evelyn Waugh: A Biography* (London: Minerva, 1995), pp. 211, 259.

[92] *The Life of Evelyn Waugh*, p. 57.

[93] Nina Gourfinkel, review of *Le Bal*, in *Nouvelle revue juive*, September/October 1930, in IMEC FSQ315 *Le Bal*.

[94] Patey, *The Life of Evelyn Waugh*, p. 57.

[95] Ibid., p. 56.

[96] Philipponnat, '*David Golder*: Notice', in Némirovsky, *Œuvres complètes*, I, 402, 403.

on Némirovsky), Le Juez argues that 'influence' contains recognition: 'Setting aside the prose and poetry of Greek and Latin authors, the only writers who have influenced me [writes Wilde] are Keats, Flaubert and Walter Pater, and before I came across them I had already gone more than half way to meet them. Style must be in one's soul before one can recognize it in others.'[97] 'Influence' is not straightforwardly prospective; it also implies a connection or similarity which *pre-dates* 'actual contact'. But neither is 'influence' a synonym of 'approbation', as we saw in Némirovsky's reading of Lubbock.

The empirically verifiable and hermeneutically comprehensible connection between Némirovsky and Waugh begs the question of the possible influence of English literature in general and Waugh in particular on Némirovsky's later work. *La Proie* (1938) and *Deux* (1939) also deal with the malaise of the young inter-war generation. Based on the same generational configuration as *Le Pion sur l'échiquier*, *La Proie* recounts the failed attempt of Jean-Luc Daguerne, the son of a First World War veteran and aged 23 at the start of the action in 1932, to make a life for himself without family money in a situation of European financial crisis. *Deux*, which according to Némirovsky herself was 'le premier livre optimiste que j'écrirai',[98] recounts the lives of a group of young veterans and their friends from the immediate aftermath of the war through into the 1930s. Both these novels contain significant English intertextual references. *La Proie* cites Oscar Wilde's maxim 'La tragédie de la vieillesse n'est pas que l'on devient vieux, mais que l'on reste jeune' (Chapter 19 of *The Picture of Dorian Gray*: 'The tragedy of old age is not that one is old, but that one is young'), which retrospectively could apply to Christophe's father James Bohun in *Le Pion sur l'échiquier*, who, despite his aged body, still thinks like a young businessman, as it could prospectively to *Deux*, where it is uttered in a slightly reworked form by Marianne's father and later by her lover Dominique.[99] *Deux* bears a quotation from Kipling's *The Second Voyage* as an epigraph: 'We seek no more the tempest for delight, | We skirt no more the indraught and the shoal— | We ask no more of any day or night | Than to come with least adventure to our goal...'.[100] *Deux* is peppered with references to England and English.[101] Both these novels' themes chime with

---

[97] Le Juez, 'Creative Reception'.

[98] Olivier Philipponnat, '*La Proie*: Notice', in Némirovsky, *Œuvres complètes*, II, 14.

[99] Némirovsky, *La Proie*, in Némirovsky, *Œuvres complètes*, I, 1649–1821 (p. 1779); Némirovsky, *Le Pion sur l'échiquier*, pp. 862–64; Némirovsky, *Deux*, in Némirovsky, *Œuvres complètes*, II, 15–200 (pp. 57–58, 187).

[100] Némirovsky, *Deux*, p. 15.

[101] Régine, who eventually opens an antiques shop in London (*Deux*, p. 128), had hoped to marry Lord Sendham (p. 49), who, like a character from a Waugh novel, has a title but no money (p. 57) and whose marriage to '*The Right Honourable So and So*' the narrator imagines being reported in *Tatler* magazine (p. 64); Antoine and Evelyne go to New York via England (p. 130), and the tragic culmination of this trip (Evelyne's suicide) depends, plot-wise, on the *pension* of an English governess (pp. 134, 135–36, 144); Dominique meets his future wife in England (pp. 161,

those of Waugh's early fiction, such as the gender politics of the new sexual freedom;[102] the disappointing reality of sex for women;[103] the emotional pull of the family house for the male protagonist;[104] the sham of marriage;[105] divorce, and exile.[106] However, since Saussy contends that the identification of common motifs is '[a]n enabling hypothesis at best' and 'cannot serve as a conclusion',[107] I offer instead an example of 'radial' reading, as defined by Jerome McGann.[108] Radial reading is a reciprocal communicative exchange which 'puts one in a position to respond actively to the text's own (secret) discursive acts'.[109] It is then a form of what Le Juez calls 'creative reception'. In Scott's words, radial reading involves

reading out onto, and incorporating, other acts of reading and reference, ancillary texts and contexts, marginal notes, glosses, intertextual materials, such that the constructing of texts is intimately part of an autobiography of reading and associating, a process without end.[110]

The advantage of this term over 'intertextuality' for the present analysis is that it prioritizes reception over textuality. I offer here one brief example—others could be envisaged—from my own 'autobiography of reading', as a reader of Némirovsky and Waugh. In *Vile Bodies* Waugh (tongue doubtless firmly in cheek) suggests that motor cars provide 'a very happy illustration of the metaphysical distinction between being and becoming'. Ordinary cars 'have definite being' and maintain 'their essential identity' while racing cars, which are constantly being modified and rebuilt, 'are in perpetual flux; a vortex of combining and disintegrating units; like the confluence of traffic at some spot

183) and their daughter, Rosette, looks like an English portrait (p. 188); English vocabulary is used repeatedly in the novel, for example 'fair play' (p. 61), 'le clan' and 'le gang' (p. 93), 'love' (p. 115).

[102] Both Adam Fenwick-Symes and Tony (*A Handful of Dust*) are victims of women's sexual freedom, as Jean-Luc believes himself to be (*La Proie*, p. 1669); *Deux* by contrast presents women as victims of free sexuality through the story of Solange's near-fatal abortion.

[103] Compare Marianne's 'déception' (*La Proie*, p. 46) at her brutal deflowering with Nina's 'I don't think that this is at all divine' and 'It's given me a pain' (*Vile Bodies*, pp. 67–68).

[104] Tony's obsession with Hetton is present in reverse in Jean-Luc's hatred of Le Vésinet (*La Proie*, p. 1692) and Antoine's hatred of Saint-Elme (*Deux*, p. 87); Marianne's family's lake house is a symbol of their bohemianism (*Deux*, pp. 108–09).

[105] Marianne and Antoine's marriage, rather like Tony and Brenda's, is described as a lie, a mask, and as acting (*Deux*, pp. 159 138, 135). This novel could be read as a direct inversion of *A Handful of Dust*—where Waugh depicts a marriage that destroys individuals, Némirovsky described *Deux* as 'l'histoire de deux êtres, de nature folle, mauvaise, instable, que la vie, l'amour, le mariage perfectionnent' (Philipponnat, '*Deux*: Notice', in Némirovsky, *Œuvres complètes*, II, 13).

[106] Marie Bellanger needs her husband to take the blame for their divorce in order to receive financial assistance (*La Proie*, p. 1670), which is exactly what Tony ultimately refuses to do for Brenda in *A Handful of Dust*; Marie's lover, like Tony, departs for South America.

[107] 'Exquisite Cadavers', p. 14.

[108] 'How to Read a Book', p. 27.

[109] Ibid., pp. 28, 31.

[110] 'The Translation of Reading', p. 221.

where many roads meet, streams of mechanism come together, mingle and separate again'.[111] Typically for Waugh, in *Vile Bodies* satire turns to shocking disaster when an inebriated Agatha Runcible crashes her borrowed car during a motor race, a calamity that has been ironically foregrounded by frequent allusions to the crowd's seemingly exclusive fascination with potential deaths at dangerous corners.[112] In an ironic reversal of the idea of building and rebuilding, when Agatha's racing car is discovered after the crash, it is fragmented.[113] Adam casually reports her funeral as an afterthought, remarking that 'There was practically no one there'.[114] A reader of Némirovsky might *read out onto* this iconic episode of English modernist fiction: the common motif of the car crash in Némirovsky and Waugh enables the hypothesis that a car crash which occurs on the last page of *Deux* is overdetermined as a signifier of the malaise of modernity. In *David Golder* the first mention of Joyce driving a car (borrowed, like Agatha's) suggests the possibility of its destruction when its owner exhorts: 'Ne la démolis pas.'[115] Joyce is repeatedly warned about the speed of her driving: 'tu te tueras une nuit sur ces routes'; 'Tu vas te casser ta jolie petite gueule, ma Joy'.[116] Driving represents nihilistic pleasure for Christophe, as for Joyce, although he is middle-aged and drives slowly and it is his son Philippe who speeds past in a racing car.[117] Christophe and his wife watch a news report about the death of a competitor in a motor race: 'Sur un autodrome de Los Angeles, une auto capotait, prenait feu; un nuage de fumée, d'étincelles, un homme que l'on emporte à la hâte, qui va mourir quelque part, que l'on oublie', recalling the end of the race in *Vile Bodies* when '[t]he motor ambulances began a final round of the track to pick up survivors'.[118] On the concluding page of *Deux*, Marianne and Antoine witness a car crash from their taxi:

A l'angle du rond-point et de l'avenue des Champs-Élysées, une auto qui venait de passer devant eux dérapa et heurta rudement un réverbère. Ils entendirent un bruit de vitres cassées et les coups de sifflet des agents, mais ne virent rien d'autre que la foule accourue.

Ils se sont joliment amochés, dit le chauffeur, avec une sorte de cordiale férocité.

— C'est vite fait, murmura Marianne.

Oui, c'est vite fait... Quand Antoine était plus jeune, il trouvait la vie brève et la mort l'épouvantait. Maintenant, il n'y pensait jamais...[119]

[111] Waugh, *Vile Bodies*, pp. 133–34.
[112] Ibid., pp. 133, 137, 137–38, 139.
[113] Ibid., p. 152.
[114] Ibid., p. 174.
[115] *David Golder*, p. 454.
[116] Ibid., pp. 454, 476.
[117] *Le Pion sur l'échiquier*, pp. 879, 880, 992.
[118] Ibid., p. 876; Waugh, *Vile Bodies*, p. 149.
[119] *Deux*, p. 200.

As a conclusion to *Deux*, this crash signifies the acceptance of death in the context of the main protagonists' more general embracing of the reality and the mundanity of their marriage: as in the Kipling quotation which serves as the novel's epigraph, they 'seek no more the tempest for delight' but hope instead 'to come with least adventure' to the end of their lives. As such, the crash and the characters' brief reflections on it provide structural and thematic closure. However, reading radially, it becomes what McGann calls a *secret discursive act*: the episode opens out again onto much wider networks of signification, established in Némirovsky's previous work and common to European modernist fiction, in which cars and speed function as signifiers of, for example, nihilism and pleasure (Agatha, Joyce, Christophe), affluence and destructiveness (the races in *Vile Bodies* and *Le Pion sur l'échiquier*), and a carelessness which slides into callousness (the racing driver 'que l'on oublie'; Agatha's funeral). Perhaps there is a hint of such signifieds in the taxi driver's 'cordiale férocité'. It is, however, the textual reciprocity of radial reading that allows these meanings to resonate in the reader's mind. The reader who allows herself to be creatively influenced by a writer who may or may not have directly influenced Némirovsky is thus led to question the authorially proclaimed optimism of Némirovsky's last inter-war novel. The tempest may no longer be a source of delight, but it is still raging; the malaise of modernity is not a natural disaster but a result of the economic, social, technological, and ontological realities of inter-war Europe, of which the motor car is such a potent symbol.

Cui bono?

'French, eh?' he said. 'I guessed as much, and pretty dirty, too, I shouldn't wonder. Now just you wait while I look up these here *books*'—how he said it!—'in my list. Particularly against books the Home Secretary is. If we can't stamp out literature in the country, we can at least stop its being brought in from outside. That's what he said the other day in Parliament, and I says "Hear, hear..."'.[120]

So responds the customs official to the foreign books in Adam's luggage when he arrives in Dover from France in the second chapter of *Vile Bodies*. The final chapter returns to France, and Waugh's comedic satire of English literary parochialism receives a dystopian echo as Adam sits '[o]n a splintered tree stump in the biggest battlefield in the history of the world'.[121] Cross-Channel traffic, of culture or soldiers, is part of English history, whether the Home Secretary likes it or not. The novel's conclusion is of course Waugh's futuristic evocation of the war that would end Némirovsky's life. Great claims have

---

[120] Waugh, *Vile Bodies*, p. 20 (Waugh's italics).
[121] Ibid., p. 186.

been made for the ethical and political power of comparative literature as a discipline. Baldensperger saw French comparative literature as rooted in the urgent need for international understanding and a sharing of common values in the wake of the First World War,[122] and, as Tobin Siebers notes in his concluding contribution to Bernheimer's volume, 'comparative literature represented the spirit of peace, sincerity, reasonableness, and hope' after the Second World War.[123] But for Siebers, 'the theoretical assumption that literary works, if studied cross-culturally, will produce better world citizens' is 'the most dubious claim of the discipline'.[124] Indeed, viewed at the macro level, this looks unreasonable. And yet, at the micro level—at the level of specific examples—comparative literature is able to generate progressive readings which affirm literary 'hospitality' and thereby contest essentialist forms of cultural nationalism. More optimistically than Siebers, Mary Louise Pratt contends that comparative literature should be viewed as 'an especially hospitable space for the cultivation of multilingualism and polyglossia, the arts of cultural mediation, deep intercultural understanding, and genuinely global consciousness'.[125] Djelal Kadir states even more strongly the political import of comparability:

Incomparability is the dynamic, not of criticism, or of comparatistic counterpoint, but a handmaiden of terror. Terror thrives on unbreachable difference, on exceptionalism, on the cultural and political monads that lie beyond the plausibility of dissensus and outside the possibility of the negotiable consensus [. . .] 'Same', much like the unbreachable different, the indifferent, and the exceptional, is as inimical to comparative literature as it is nurturing and abetting of terrorism. Exception has historically functioned as the path to, and as the cover for, genocide.[126]

The Otto lists of banned books under the Nazi occupation of France during the Second World War, as well as the infamous book burnings of the Third Reich, are examples pertinent to the genocide of which Némirovsky was a victim. The destruction of Adam's manuscript by the customs official is certainly of a different scale, but not necessarily of a different order. Though Waugh's writing is seen, with good reason, as archetypally English, and Némirovsky's literary goal was full acceptance as a French novelist, neither writer can be accused of cultural monadism. Némirovsky's tragically misplaced faith in French hospitality to immigrants finds a strong echo, perhaps even a justification, in her own hospitality towards the literary traditions of other countries. If the reinstatement of Némirovsky as a significant writer

---

[122] Baldensperger, 'Littérature comparée', p. 29.

[123] 'Sincerely Yours', in *Comparative Literature*, ed. by Bernheimer, pp. 195–203 (p. 195).

[124] Ibid., p. 197.

[125] 'Comparative Literature and Global Citizenship', in *Comparative Literature*, ed. by Bernheimer, pp. 58–65 (p. 62).

[126] 'Comparative Literature in an Age of Terrorism', in *Comparative Literature*, ed. by Saussy, pp. 68–77 (p. 74).

is to be more than a cynical manipulation of the 'devoir de mémoire'—the recycling of French war guilt in order to sell books on the basis of a tragic biographical backstory[127]—then attention must surely be paid to the broader hospitality of her writing practice. Linda Hutcheon equates 'comparative' with 'inclusive':[128] Némirovsky's hospitable Frenchness can best be understood in the global perspective proposed by McDonald and Suleiman. Her rediscovery is appropriate in an age that seeks—and still needs—to question monolithic identity politics and essentialized, racist conceptions of the national.

Why compare? *Cui bono*?[129] Using the metaphor of landline as opposed to Wi-Fi technology, Saussy suggests that the '"space of comparison", rather than requiring that different works or traditions be deliberately wired up to communicate, sees them as always already connected; the question is just how'.[130] Case studies like this one contribute to answering the 'just how' question. Literatures are always already in contact, but there is work to do to show, empirically and hermeneutically, how those connections were made and functioned, and to explore the creative possibilities generated by literary contact. The concept of 'creative reception' offers a way of understanding 'influence' that is less restrictive than traditional models. The aim of this examination of Némirovsky's relationships with Forster, Lubbock, and Waugh has been to demonstrate and explore the cross-cultural hospitality of Némirovsky's writing practice. Addressing the perennial questions of the definition and purpose of comparison, Roland Greene suggests: 'One might say that when comparatists ask the sorts of questions they usually do, the ability to move among different languages and literatures will almost always be visible in their work as a condition.'[131] Beginning from the questions to be answered rather than from the methodology to be adopted, Greene sees comparative literature as a discipline asking questions that can only be answered comparatively. The question 'Why is Némirovsky an important writer?' is a comparative one because it cannot be answered by reference to French literature alone.

UNIVERSITY OF BIRMINGHAM   ANGELA KERSHAW

[127] See Josyane Savigneau, 'Renaudot, Goncourt et marketing littéraire', *Le Monde*, 12 November 2004.

[128] 'Rethinking the National Model', p. 3.

[129] Brown, 'What is "Comparative" Literature?', p. 83.

[130] 'Exquisite Cadavers', p. 31.

[131] 'Their Generation', in *Comparative Literature*, ed. by Bernheimer, pp. 143–54 (p. 145).

UNDER THE MAGNIFYING GLASS: INVESTIGATING THE FIRST WORLD WAR IN RECENT CRIME NOVELS BY BEN ELTON, AND JAN EIK AND HORST BOSETZKY

'This war is . . . stupid', declaims Douglas Kingsley from the dock in the opening chapters of Ben Elton's 2005 novel *The First Casualty*. 'It offends my sense of logic. It offends my sense of my scale.'[1] It is a stance with which the modern anglophone reader, schooled on a diet of Sassoon and Owen, might all too readily agree. But as Kingsley faces trial as a conscientious objector in 1917, his principled stand against the war is complicated by the fact that he is operating, not only as a private citizen, but as a senior police inspector, celebrated detective, and uniformed representative of the very moral code that sent Britain to war in the first place. The trial leads to a national scandal. Inspector Hermann Kappe, protagonist of Jan Eik and Horst Bosetzky's *Nach Verdun* (*After Verdun*, 2008), is considerably more covert regarding his scruples about the war, but he too battles with his conscience as he finds himself going through the motions of upholding law and justice in a wartime Berlin where such easy pre-war concepts are rapidly losing meaning. Contrasting in style, and markedly different in their negotiations with the generic conventions of the crime-fiction tradition, these novels nevertheless ask much the same questions of the role of the civilian detective in wartime. In both texts the surface story of a quest to solve a murder case is problematized by a second, more troubling narrative: that of an individual struggling to maintain his personal and professional integrity in a time of moral chaos. This struggle is the focus of the present article. Drawing on close readings of both texts, I will demonstrate how the process of sense-making traditionally associated with crime fiction takes on an extra layer of significance in the context of war. I will further argue that while twenty-first-century understandings of the 1914–18 conflict might lead the reader to expect these novels to take an unequivocally anti-war stance, the extent to which these expectations are actually met is determined by the narrative dynamics of the subgenres in question and the authors' willingness or otherwise to depart from them.

The First World War played a critical role in the historical evolution of the crime genre, though paradoxically its significance as a subject-matter lies, not in its prominence in the inter-war period, but rather in its virtual exclusion. With the notable exception of Dorothy L. Sayers and her veteran sleuth Lord Peter Wimsey, the bulk of the Golden Age writers remained deafeningly silent over the social and psychological trauma inflicted by the war. This is far from

I would like to acknowledge postdoctoral research funding from the Irish Research Council.

[1] Ben Elton, *The First Casualty* (London: Black Swan, 2006), p. 22. Further references will be given after quotations in the text identified by the abbreviation *FC*.

surprising when we consider that the function of Golden Age crime writing, in Britain at least, was largely escapist. With its taste for bucolic settings and unshakeable faith in the explaining away of violence and the restoration of order, the classic whodunnit of the 1920s and 1930s largely ignored the shattering impact of the war, allowing the reader—for the duration of the novel at least—to take comfort in the illusion of the continuity of once solid pre-war values of logic and rationalism . It may have been the upheaval of war that first brought Hercule Poirot to Britain—Christie introduces him in *The Mysterious Affair at Styles* (1920) as a Belgian refugee—but the great detective rarely sees cause to dwell on the traumatic circumstances of his uprooting. Across the channel, Simenon's Inspector Maigret, that other giant of the inter-war European crime scene, is similarly reticent about his experiences of the conflict. And yet it is precisely this socially and psychologically destructive aspect of the Great War—so traumatic for the crime writers and readers who lived through it—that has come to make it so attractive to the present generation. Since the mid-1980s writers such as Sébastien Japrisot and Didier Daeninckx (France), Andreas Pittler and Gerhard Loibelsberger (Austria), Charles Todd (USA), and Jacqueline Winspear, Rennie Airth, and Anne Perry (Britain) have all employed various facets of the crime genre to explore the shocks and legacies of the war. This surge of interest is a natural extension of the current international boom in historical crime fiction—the fastest-growing subset of the crime genre, according to Ray B. Browne[2]—as well as, in the British case at least, an inevitable market response to the international successes of the more consciously 'literary' war fiction of Pat Barker and Sebastian Faulks in the 1990s.

Nach Verdun and *The First Casualty* both reflect this generic trend and consciously depart from it. For despite the considerable formal and stylistic diversity very much in evidence in recent First World War crime writing, the overwhelming tendency for most of these authors has been to set their plots immediately after rather than during the war. There are a number of advantages to this approach. The work of the detective, based as it is on the interpretation of the past and the reconstruction of hidden stories, is understood by the reader to be essentially retrospective anyway; as is often the case with Second World War- or Holocaust-themed crime writing, a degree of temporal distance from the event itself arguably allows the fictional investigator to assess its relevance to the immediate criminal case more clinically. Both the post-war detective and the post-war criminal, meanwhile, are typically veterans of the conflict; unlike their Golden Age predecessors, they are open in their struggles with shell shock and social alienation, thus playing directly

---

[2] 'Historical Crime and Detection', in *A Companion to Crime Fiction*, ed. by Charles Rzepka and Lee Horsley (Oxford: Blackwell, 2005) pp. 222–32 (p. 223).

into modern crime fiction's fascination with psychological aberrance.[3] Above all, however, the tendency towards post-war positioning in the current wave of First World War crime writing comes down to plot logistics: who could be expected to care about a single murder in a time of mass slaughter? And how can a detective be expected to carry out a systematic investigation either at the fighting front, amid scarcely imaginable disorder and confusion, or even on a home front where the norms of civil society have been suspended?

Nach Verdun and *The First Casualty* not only meet these challenges on a practical plot level, but actually foreground them as thematic concerns. Despite the growing popularity of First World War crime fiction, these texts belong to a relatively small subset of works set during the conflict,[4] their plots unfolding alongside it, their protagonists facing the kind of moral and logistical obstacles for which no amount of peacetime training or experience could possibly have prepared them. This has several implications, not only for narrative structure, but for the position negotiated by the texts in relation to the crisis of war more generally. The wartime detective is a very different breed from his post-conflict counterpart. Experiencing the war in real time, he is denied the calming, cooling distance of retrospection; as a non-combatant, however, he retains a degree of detachment from the extremity of battle and an ability to view events in a broader perspective.

As seasoned career detectives, Kappe and Kingsley represent—or at the very least are expected to represent—logic, reason, and deduction, the traditional tools used by the investigator to impose order and extract meaning. In trying to make sense of the murder cases before them, the detectives cannot help but try to make sense of the war that produced them. This sense-making instinct is doubly significant in these texts because both Kappe and Kingsley, though different in personality, are very consciously modern figures, in many ways more recognizable as citizens of the twenty-first century than of the twentieth. Technically, of course, every detective in a historical crime novel written today, be they Roman lawyer or medieval nun, represents a modern viewpoint in the sense that they are products of a modern imagination and created for a modern popular readership. While some writers attempt to create the illusion of historical authenticity by investing their characters with

---

[3] First World War veteran detectives feature in, among others, Didier Daeninckx's *Le Der des Ders* (1984), Charles Todd's *A Test of Wills* (1996), Rennie Airth's *River of Darkness* (1999), and Bettina Balàka's *Eisflüstern* (*Ice Whispers*, 2006).

[4] The most commercially successful of these works has undoubtedly been Anne Perry's First World War series (2003–07), a sequence of five novels spanning the full duration of the conflict. Despite superficial thematic similarities, Perry's strategy of setting a series of small-scale detective plots against a grander espionage narrative places the texts somewhat apart from the works discussed here. Barbara Korte has analysed the ideological implications of this genre-blending in some detail. See Korte, 'Anne Perry: World War I as Period Mystery', *Clues: A Journal of Detection*, 28 (2010), 79–89.

what we might perceive to be the 'typical' values of their times, Kingsley and Kappe are deliberately anachronistic creations. They are out of step with their time, not only in their instinctive opposition to the war effort—more on which presently—but in their tendency towards self-doubt and cynicism, their rejection of nationalism, and their progressive views on women and minorities. In many ways, then, these detectives represents *us*, the modern reader, struggling to find ways to understand a conflict that popular memory generally interprets as a catastrophic exercise in futility.[5] In both cases, they undertake a double journey through the narrative: firstly, to solve a murder, and secondly, to try to square their conscience in relation to the conflict with the demands of their vocation. In so doing, they take on the role of moral avatars, the eyes and ears of a twenty-first-century consciousness itself still trying to make sense of the war.

With its focus on resolution and restoration and its reluctance to question the legitimacy of state-imposed moral codes, crime fiction has traditionally been labelled by critics as a socially conservative genre.[6] In recent decades, however, this assumption has become increasingly untenable, not least because of the global success of Scandinavian noir, and the impact of writers such as Henning Mankell and Stieg Larsson employing the genre towards unapologetically political ends. Historical crime writing has also demonstrated its potential in this regard, as illustrated by the debates unleashed in France by the publication of Didier Daeninckx's *Meurtres pour mémoire* in 1984, a shocking *néo-polar* which served, not only to expose some of the uglier moments in twentieth-century French history, but actually to force the retrial of former chief of police Maurice Papon for war crimes.[7] Before even starting to examine the content of either *Nach Verdun* or *The First Casualty*, then, it is important to consider them in relation to this tradition of politically engaged crime writing. Each of the authors of these works has, at various stages of his career, demonstrated a belief in the sociocritical possibilities of popular writing. Jan Eik grew up in the former East Germany and was a founding member of the crime-fiction section of the GDR's Writers' Union in the 1980s. In his case, social criticism is embedded, not so much in the content

---

[5] While Samuel Hynes has argued that feelings of waste and pointlessness have long been prevalent in First World War poetry and literary fiction (*A War Imagined* (London: Bodley Head, 1990), p. x), more recent work by Dan Todman suggests these myths have come to dominate virtually every sphere of popular culture in Britain today (*The Great War: Myth and Memory* (London: Hambledon and London, 2005), p. 222). Popular memory of the war in Germany is considerably harder to gauge owing to the relative scarcity of literary and artistic responses to the conflict in the post-memory period.

[6] Dennis Porter, *The Pursuit of Crime: Art and Ideology in Detective Fiction* (New Haven: Yale University Press, 1981), p. 1; Stephen Knight, *Form and Ideology in Crime Fiction* (London: Macmillan, 1980), p. 2.

[7] Claire Gorrara, 'Reflections on Crime and Punishment: Memories of the Holocaust in Recent French Crime Fiction', *Yale French Studies*, 108 (2005), 133–45 (p. 140).

of his writing, but in the fact that he came to write crime fiction at all under a regime that considered the genre deeply suspect from an ideological stand-point. His co-author Horst Bosetzky, meanwhile, is generally credited with having popularized the *Soziokrimi* subgenre in the 1970s, experimenting with various conventions of the American hard-boiled tradition in order to analyse West German society during a particularly stormy period in its history.

The case of Ben Elton is particularly interesting. Better known for his comedy and television work than for his crime writing (*The First Casualty* was only his second foray into the genre), Elton through his regular attacks on the Thatcher administration and involvement in the Red Wedge collective became established as something of a darling of the British Left in the 1980s. This reputation has since been tarnished,[8] but Elton's place in popular culture is assured by his co-authorship of two of the most influential sitcoms in British television history: *The Young Ones* (1982–84) and *Blackadder* (1983–89). The impact of the latter series is particularly relevant here. *Blackadder Goes Forth*, the fourth and final installation of the satirical series, is entirely set in the trenches of Flanders in 1917. It depicts the military operation as an unmitigated shambles, the worst-planned war 'since Olaf the Hairy, High Chief of all the Vikings, accidentally ordered eighty thousand battle helmets with the horns on the *inside*' (episode 3), and has come to be regarded both as a classic of the genre and as a modern cornerstone of British popular memory of the Great War. *Blackadder Goes Forth* articulates in the loudest terms the perceptions of waste and futility currently dominant in British war memory, and today enjoys the status (or fate) of a go-to classroom resource for teaching the Great War in schools.[9] In January 2014, a century after the assassination at Sarajevo and a quarter-century after the series was first broadcast, its makers found themselves accused of distorting and manipulating popular understanding of the British war effort of 1914–18. Writing in the *Daily Mail*, the then Education Secretary Michael Gove defended the military leadership of what was 'plainly a just war' fought by honourable patriots 'committed to defending the western liberal order'. He furthermore complained that:

[o]ur understanding of the war has been overlaid by misunderstandings, and misrepresentations which reflect an, at best, ambiguous attitude to this country and, at worst, an unhappy compulsion on the part of some to denigrate virtues such as patriotism, honour and courage. The conflict has, for many, been seen through the fictional prisms

---

[8] Elton's apparent abandonment of political satire and embracing of more populist—and lucrative—projects such as rock musicals have led many of his former fans to denounce him as a sell-out. See Brendan O'Neill, 'Ben Elton Has Always Been a Middle Englander', *Daily Telegraph* online edition, 25 April 2013 <http://www.telegraph.co.uk/culture/comedy/10017963/Ben-Elton-has-always-been-a-Middle-Englander.html>, and Brian Logan, 'Ben Elton: Selling Out More than Venues?', *Guardian* theatre blog, 16 May 2007 <http://www.theguardian.com/stage/theatreblog/2007/may/16/beneltonsellingoutmoretha> [both accessed 17 December 2013].

[9] Todman, *The Great War*, p. 172.

of dramas such as Oh! What a Lovely War, The Monocled Mutineer and Blackadder, as a misbegotten shambles—a series of catastrophic mistakes perpetrated by an out-of-touch elite. Even to this day there are Left-wing academics all too happy to feed these myths.[10]

The 'Left-wing academics' in question were quick to respond, among them the Cambridge historian Richard Evans, the shadow Education Secretary Tristram Hunt, and the former *Blackadder* actor turned amateur historian, Tony Robinson. In the so-called 'history wars' that raged across the British media in the ensuing weeks, the television series and its ideological objectives remained a constant focal point.

Given the common subject-matter, it is difficult for any reader familiar with *Blackadder* to read *The First Casualty* without the caustic anti-war message of the series in mind. This naturally sets up certain expectations; indeed, the immediate strategy in both novels here of using detectives with pronounced anti-war sympathies invites certain expectations. But can the narrative demands of the crime genre live up to these expectations? Do the two very different subgenres adapted by these texts offer the appropriate tools with which to shape an anti-war narrative, or are they in fact structurally programmed to resist such an undertaking?

'Nach Verdun' (2008)

Nach Verdun is the fourth instalment in the 'Es geschah in Berlin' ('It Happened in Berlin') series, a multi-authored chain of historical crime novels (twenty-one to date) featuring Inspector Hermann Kappe and running from 1910 up into the early 1950s. The preceding book, authored by Eik, saw Kappe racing to catch a killer in the restless hot summer of 1914, grimly aware of the fact that imminent mass mobilization will both jeopardize his case and change his own life for ever. In this novel, set in 1916, we learn that Kappe has actually been released from military duty because of a diagnosis of narcolepsy, while his sidekick Galgenberg has had the good fortune to be sent home injured. As the Allied sea blockade intensifies and the city slowly starves, the pair are called upon to investigate the apparently connected deaths of a grocer and an invalided officer, each murdered with a hand grenade. Early suspects include a well-known anarchist, eventually released due to lack of evidence, and subsequently the trade unionist and factory worker Karl Nassmacher, who confesses to both murders and is lauded by the flourishing anti-war movement as a hero of the people and nemesis of the profiteer and of the

[10] Michael Gove, 'Why Does the Left Insist on Belittling True British Heroes?', *Daily Mail* online edition, 2 January 2014 <http://www.dailymail.co.uk/debate/article-2532930/MICHAEL-GOVE-Why-does-Left-insist-belittling-true-British-heroes.html> [accessed 3 February 2014].

warmongering officer class. As the threat of class war bubbles and Berlin's newspapers furiously debate the legitimacy or otherwise of political murder, the discovery of a dead woman's diary leads Kappe to realize that it was she, and not Nassmacher, who murdered the profiteering grocer out of revenge for his refusing to help her feed her dying baby. Confronted with this evidence, Nassmacher withdraws his confession and glumly relinquishes his status as a political hero. Meanwhile, the murderer of the officer remains at large; a chance comment from an old mentor leads Kappe to track down survivors of the victim's regiment. Here he learns of the man's arrogance and cruelty towards his men, and of his fateful decision to send out a platoon of men on a suicide mission at the height of the Battle of Verdun. He further learns of the officer's particularly brutal treatment of one Heinrich Pietsch—but also that that same Pietsch was blown up in battle. When another survivor claims to have seen Pietsch in Berlin, albeit with hideous facial injuries, Kappe uncovers a case of mistaken identities and finally collars his man.

The novel's condemnation of the war and of those driving it might seem to a British readership to represent a very familiar view—indeed, were it available in translation, *Nach Verdun* might easily be assumed to articulate the very 'lions led by donkeys' thesis so fervently rejected by Michael Gove and others. Yet such assumptions are misleading. Memory of the First World War is configured very differently in Germany from France or Britain. Basic assumptions about the war, as Jay Winter and Antoine Prost point out,[11] vary considerably from nation to nation, and what might seem obvious to a British readership is very far from obvious to both readers and writers of German popular fiction, operating in a national culture in which collective memory of the First World War remains overshadowed by the Second. Indeed, German commentators frequently appear somewhat mystified by the British obsession with the Great War. The *Süddeutsche Zeitung*'s report on Gove's 'history wars' in 2014 is distinctly bemused in tone,[12] while Klaus Harprecht, reviewing the German translation of Pat Barker's Booker Prize-winning *The Ghost Road* in *Die Zeit* in 2000, pointedly wonders why the British author, born at the height of the carnage of the Second World War, should choose to devote so much of her literary output to the First.[13] Despite evidence of a recent surge of interest in 1914–18 in Germany—Alan Kramer points to a growing volume of scholarly works, television documentaries, and museum exhibitions since

---

[11] Winter and Prost, *The Great War in History: Debates and Controversies, 1914 to the Present* (Cambridge: Cambridge University Press, 2005), p. vii.

[12] Alexander Menden, 'Ein bisschen Remmidemmi in Sarajevo', *Süddeutsche Zeitung* on-line edition, 10 January 2014 <http://www.sueddeutsche.de/politik/grossbritannien-und-der-erste-weltkrieg-ein-bisschen-remmidemmi-in-sarajevo-1.1859712> [accessed 19 November 2014].

[13] 'Hier begann Auschwitz', *Die Zeit* online edition, 31 August 2000 <http://www.zeit.de/2000/36/Hier_begann_Auschwitz> [accessed 19 July 2014].

the 1990s,[14] while several academic studies of the origins of the conflict featured prominently in the non-fiction best-seller lists in 2013 and 2014[15]—this scholarly interest has yet to spill over into public discourse to anything like the same extent as it has in Britain. Most notably, it has yet to produce any quantifiable impact on contemporary film and literary production. Novels such as *Nach Verdun* that seek to buck this trend remain conspicuously rare.[16]

In seeking to locate *Nach Verdun* within the broader picture of First World War memory, then, it is important to bear in mind that the authors, unlike their British counterparts, are not writing for a readership already saturated with constant public debate over the meaning of the conflict and how it should be commemorated. Arguably, they use this relative unfamiliarity to their advantage: the fact that the First World War plays such a modest role in German collective memory in a sense releases the authors from any pressure to engage with contemporary historiographical debate on the conflict, the complexities of which are unlikely to be familiar to its target readers. This is a critical point, because the question that has dominated German First World War historiography since the Fischer controversy in the 1960s—the extent to which Germany must shoulder full responsibility for the war[17]—poses the kind of large-scale representational challenges that the novel is ill-equipped to meet. And so *Nach Verdun* sidesteps this debate completely. Its foregrounding of the civilian experience of the conflict, the challenges faced by returning soldiers and the deterioration of economic conditions on the home front, reflects, not a specifically German perspective on the war, but a more general turn in European historiography in the 1960s and 1970s towards social history

[14] 'The First World War and German Memory', in *Untold War: New Perspectives in First World War Studies*, ed. by Heather Jones and others (Leiden: Brill, 2008), pp. 385–411 (p. 411).

[15] Jeevan Vasagar, 'Best-Seller List Reveals German Desire to Reassess Great War', *Financial Times* online edition, 17 January 2014 <http://www.ft.com/intl/cms/s/0/5fdf9fba-7f57-11e3-b6a7-00144feabdco.html#axzz3Aq2nfOMQ> [accessed 23 July 2014].

[16] It is striking that crime fiction is one of the few areas in contemporary German and Austrian literature to tackle the subject of the First World War. Recent examples include Gerhard Loibelsberger's *Todeswalzer* (*Death Waltz*, 2013), which is set in the summer and autumn of 1914, and Andreas Pittler's *Chuzpe* (*Chutzpah*, 2012), which deals with the end of the war and the chaotic early days of the First Austrian Republic. This (modest) trend might be at least partly explained by the current popularity of city-specific historical crime in the German-language market: both of these works, like *Nach Verdun*, are situated within much longer crime series that set out to span the first half of the twentieth century. In laying out such extensive historical parameters these series arguably have no choice but to address the period 1914–18. Interestingly, Bettina Balàka's *Eisflüstern* (2006), one of very few German literary novels about the First World War to be written in the post-memory period, also borrows elements of the crime genre in order to address the effects of shell shock.

[17] Fritz Fischer (1908–1999) caused uproar when he argued in his 1961 volume *Griff nach der Weltmacht* (Droste: Düsseldorf, 1961; published in English as *Germany's Aims in the First World War* (London: Chatto & Windus, 1967)) that Imperial Germany's aggressive foreign policy was solely to blame for the First World War. Fischer's thesis has been reappraised by many since, most recently Herfried Münkler in his best-selling 2013 study *Der Große Krieg* [*The Great War*] (Berlin: Rowohlt, 2013).

and 'history from below'.[18] Unsurprisingly, this approach to history meshes particularly well with the aims of the *Soziokrimi* form, which first surfaced in Germany at around the same time, with Bosetzky himself as one of its best-known progenitors.

Drawing on this legacy, *Nach Verdun* operates as a hybrid text, blending the socio-political concerns and the psychological depth of the *Soziokrimi* tradition with the pace and structure of the police procedural. Readers' responses to the text suggest that it is far from a classic of either form: comments posted on amazon.de indicate an appreciation for the novel's commitment to historical detail, but some disappointment with the management of the plot.[19] If we turn our attention away from the crime narrative, however, and onto Kappe's personal development within the time-frame of the novel, some points of interest emerge. As a protagonist, Kappe is something of an everyman. He is certainly not stupid or incompetent—he always gets the job done—but nor is he a cerebral heavyweight in the classic detective mould. The real importance of the murder investigation is not that it gives him the chance to showcase his investigative talents, but rather that it forces him out on a personal moral journey, hardening his political stance on the war and coming dangerously close to compromising his professional duties. Several structural elements facilitate this journey. The personal revenge stories driving both murders are, for much of the novel, concealed behind grand political narratives, as the detective explores the possibility that the deaths are the work of the forces of radical pacifism. This scenario allows the authors to drag Kappe into direct contact with trade unionists, anarchists, and Spartacists, and, though the lead turns out to be a false one, the impact on the detective is considerable. Despite taking a personal dislike to the suspect Karl Nassmacher, Kappe finds himself increasingly sympathetic to the movement that has canonized the young trade unionist as an anti-war martyr. He attends a Mayday march, theoretically in the line of duty, and silently agrees with the anti-war and internationalist slogans paraded around him. Shocked to learn that his only brother has been called to the front, he even finds himself murmuring these very slogans under his breath: 'Nieder mit der Regierung! Nieder mit dem Krieg!'[20] ('Down with the government! Down with the war!').

Kappe's gradual politicization is quite genuine but he keeps it almost entirely to himself. Only rarely does he articulate his feelings on the conflict, even to his trusted partner Galgenberg, and the reader knows that the likelihood of

---

[18] Winter and Prost, *The Great War in History*, pp. 18–19.

[19] Readers reviews posted at <http://www.amazon.de/geschah-Berlin-1916-Nach-Verdun/dp/3897735857> [accessed 23 December 2013].

[20] Horst Bosetzky and Jan Eik, *Nach Verdun: Kappes vierter Fall* [*After Verdun: Kappe's Fourth Case*] (Berlin: Jaron, 2008), p. 143. Further references will be given after quotations in the text identified by the abbreviation *NV*.

him ever actually mobilizing these sentiments and taking a stand against the war is negligible. Significantly, however, his shift towards pacifism is paralleled by a gradual loss of faith in his vocation. Early in the novel, Kappe baulks at the prospect of having to investigate the possible political dimensions to the murders, but then quickly reminds himself that 'Mörder war Mörder, und er hätte seinen eigenen Bruder, ohne zu zögern, der Justiz übergeben, wenn der einen anderen Menschen mit einer Handgranate getötet hätte' (*NV*, p. 33: 'Murder was murder, and he would have brought his own brother to justice without missing a beat if he had killed someone with a hand grenade'). As the case progesses, however, this belief, both in the very idea of justice and in his own calling to pursue it, is severely shaken. The further the case progresses, the more Kappe struggles to summon up any kind of sympathy for the murder victims. The profiteer and the army officer emerge through his investigations as irredeemably odious individuals, between them representing the ugliest aspects of German commerce and militarism. The murderers, on the other hand, a bereaved mother in one case and a traumatized, hideously mutilated soldier in the other, have had their lives destroyed by the war and their attempts at revenge seem entirely justified. As Kappe reflects to himself that 'Tyranny darf man aber umbringen' (*NV*, p. 186: 'after all, you can kill tyrants'), the familiar categories of 'victim' and 'culprit' dissolve to such a point that the pursuit of so-called 'justice' seems pointless.

This breakdown of traditional moral values in the novel is reinforced by an equally disconcerting undermining of human agency: the star detective, the very figure we might expect to champion the power of the individual mind to triumph over chaos, is forced to consider his own powerlessness. *Nach Verdun* does indeed conform to the model of the conventional crime novel to the extent that the crimes are solved; whether it is in fact the detective himself who does the solving, however, is questionable. As the novel opens, Kappe is shown to have a sound professional reputation and a string of high-profile success stories to his name. He is admirably methodical in his conducting of the investigation: crime scenes are combed for clues; bodies are autopsied; witnesses questioned; leads followed. None of these strategies, however, actually leads to the solving of the crimes. Much of the crucial evidence comes to Kappe not through skill but almost entirely by chance. It is the anarchist Ernst Bergmann, entirely unprompted, who first suggests to Kappe that Nassmacher's confession does not stand up. Several chapters later, the grocer's widow voluntarily presents herself at police headquarters with the story of her husband's argument with the mother of a starving baby; again, Kappe would never have established this connection through police work alone. The murderer of the officer, meanwhile, is identified only after Kappe's old mentor insists he focus his attention on the victim's old regiment, plunging the detective into a crisis of self-doubt as he realizes 'wie viel ihm noch fehlte, um wirklich ein herausragender Kriminaler zu sein' (*NV*, p. 181: 'how far he had yet to go to become a really outstanding investigator'). Kappe would never have made this critical breakthrough on his own initiative, and he knows it.

Unlike in the classic whodunnit, then, where the cerebral agility of the detective strikes a victory for logic, reason, and the power of the individual human mind, Kappe's progress through this case is bounced unevenly along by a combination of lucky breaks and chance encounters. This is itself somewhat unsettling: does the fact that the murders are solved really amount to anything at all if this resolution is reached, not through the traditional forces of human agency, but in spite of them? Moreover, if the intellect cannot be relied upon to clear the fog and impose some sense of order in times of crisis, then what can? The detective's ultimate sense of powerlessness is further reinforced by the narrative structure of the novel. Told from the viewpoints of multiple characters, the text splits the perspective of the reader from that of the detective, almost to the point of having them follow two separate investigations. A prologue presenting an officer maltreating his men on the Western Front should alert any seasoned crime reader to the likelihood of a causal connection to any subsequent murder cases. We are thus encouraged to suspect a revenge narrative from the very beginning; it takes Kappe most of the novel, and the critical intervention of his mentor, to reach the same conclusion. Similarly, and in line with the psychological dimensions of the *Soziokrimi* tradition, the reader is granted access to the thoughts of the increasingly desperate Frieda Hermann, allowing us to identify her as the killer of the profiteering grocer pages and pages before the investigator does. This structural strategy of privileging the perspective of the reader over that of Kappe, forcing him into a perpetual game of catch-up, pointedly undermines his status as detective.

These moral, professional, and epistemological crises come crashing together in the novel's conclusion. The mystery may have been solved and the murderer of the officer apprehended, but the question remains as to what, if anything, has actually been achieved here. Galgenberg's triumphant closing line—'wir ham endlich unsan Handgranatenmörder!' (*NV*, p. 206: 'we have 'im at last, our hand grenade murderer!')—presents a parody of neat narrative closure while actually calling attention to its very impossibility. Kappe's silence here underscores this failure. He has seen enough to realize that it is the murderer who is deserving of our pity, and not his putative victim. The case may be closed, but too many difficult questions have been dragged into the light for the detective to enjoy any sense of moral victory. What kind of society chooses to punish tragic figures like this one who have had their lives destroyed by forces far beyond their control? The omission from the story of the trial and sentencing of the murderer is itself significant. Classic detective fiction can afford to end this way because the legitimacy of the legal system is taken for granted and we know that the murderer will get his just desserts.[21] A modern readership, however, particularly one with an interest in war and the effects of shell shock, will hold out hope that such mitigating factors will be taken into account. We are denied this, however, cut off without ever knowing what becomes of the real victim in this story, and this is unsettling. Furthermore, and again in keeping with Bosetzky's long-standing championing of the *Soziokrimi*, the solving of the 'crimes' in *Nach Verdun* highlights the persistence of the broader social factors that brought them about in the first place. The sadistic militarism personified by Oberleutnant von Zabelsdorff lives on. Women and children continue to starve as profiteering shopkeepers continue to take advantage of food shortages; innocent young men like the unfortunate Heinrich Pietsch continue to suffer horrific injuries in a war that has nothing to do with them.

The final outcome of the investigation, then, is that Kappe has undertaken a personal moral journey shaped by his encounters with dreadful suffering and victimhood (starving children; shattered veterans; bereaved parents), with radical pacifism, and with increasingly empty warmongering. His road to enlightenment (from the modern reader's perspective, at least) is not extended into the novel's conclusion, which is deeply pessimistic. The solving of the crimes fails to mark any kind of triumph. Instead, the narrative importance traditionally placed by the genre on the final discovery of the truth is dwarfed when measured up against the grim social and political forces driving the war, forces against which the detective is powerless. Kappe's 'victory' here is meaningless. In ending with such an abrupt open–shut conclusion, so generically familiar and yet so obviously inappropriate in the circumstances, the novel points towards its own inability to restore and reassure, and to the genre's inability to represent satisfactorily the complications of crime and punishment in times of crisis. This admission of failure, however, itself communicates a powerful condemnation of war.

'The First Casualty' (2005)

What if Kappe had not been quite so modest and conscientious? What if he had in fact decided to put his professional duties to one side and take a principled stand against the war? Ben Elton's Inspector Kingsley does exactly this, yet paradoxically finds himself dragged closer to the war itself than Kappe might ever have imagined. Incarcerated in Wormwood Scrubs because of his

---

[21] Porter, *The Pursuit of Crime*, p. 121.

refusal to serve, Kingsley is kidnapped by the Secret Intelligence Service, who fake his death, give him a new identity, and send him off into the heat of the third Battle of Ypres to investigate the unexplained death of the celebrated officer poet Alan Abercrombie. Posing as military police officer Christopher Marlowe (!), Kingsley wastes no time in proving that the initial suspect, a Bolshevik agitator, has been framed. His apparently indefatigable sleuthing instincts drive him to chase witnesses and possible murder weapons right into the trenches and ultimately over the top: to his horror, he finds himself participating in the Battle of Ypres and inadvertently killing several Germans. Close questioning of Abercrombie's junior officer and former lover, meanwhile, reveals that the poet, famous for his patriotic doggerel, had grown completely disillusioned with the war in the months before his death and had been threatening to 'do a Sassoon' (*FC*, p. 152) by publishing his latest anti-war verse in the London papers. As the clues finally slot together, Kingsley is able to prove that it was the Secret Serviceman Captain Shannon, his own immediate superior, who murdered Abercrombie in an attempt to prevent the emergence of an influential pacifist voice that might swing British public opinion against the war effort. Shannon dies, his corpse dumped in no man's land so as to avert a national scandal; all ends tied up, Kingsley is released from his mission and allowed home to his wife and son.

In many ways *The First Casualty* is an ideal text through which to examine the possibilities and contradictions of pacifism, as it is opposition to the war, rather than the war itself, that drives the plot forward. Abercrombie is murdered because of his decision to come out publicly against the war; Kingsley is imprisoned, kidnapped, and set on the case because of his refusal to serve. The detective considers himself a thinking man as well as a career policeman, and spends much of the novel debating the causes, morals, and effects of the war in great detail. What, then, does the text itself ultimately conclude about the morality of the conflict and of those who take a stand against it? The immediate outcome of the murder plot appears at first to communicate a reasonably clear anti-war message: the murderer represents the barbarism of the national war effort and is clearly an unmitigated villain; the victim's embracing of pacifism is natural and laudable, and he did not deserve to die. As with *Nach Verdun*, however, focusing on the detective's individual journey through the text calls attention to a series of complications. Both Kingsley and Kappe learn about the nature of war through their investigations, and both are fundamentally changed by it. Owing to a number of structural factors, however, these processes of change unfold in considerably different ways.

Whereas *Nach Verdun*, with its emphasis on teamwork, protocol, and stark urban realism, is instantly recognizable as a police procedural, *The First Casualty* is initially harder to locate on the crime-fiction spectrum. The novel combines crime, comedy, and romance in a fusion of styles and genres that is not to all critical tastes: 'the effect is that of a Barbara Cartland story re-written by a dirty-minded schoolboy during a monotonous history lesson', as the *Independent* reviewer crisply put it.[22] Kingsley's abduction and deploy-ment to Flanders by the SIS initially seems straight out of a spy thriller, but once his investigation starts in earnest the text immediately begins to enact a very plausible impersonation of a whodunnit. This, in many respects, seems an unlikely choice for a novel set in the trenches. The classic whodunnit fa-vours comfortable, socially stable environments in which to locate its murder narratives, preferably rural, ideally isolated in some way (the locked room; the snowbound train; the cut-off hotel). Elton inverts this spectacularly by pitching his detective into the most terrifying and unpredictable setting ima-ginable: the Western Front. Not only are the surroundings considerably less comfortable than, for example, St Mary Mead, but the range of potential sus-pects, motives, and murder weapons seems, initially at least, virtually infinite. And yet, when we peel away the horror, the sex, and the politics, so many of the essential components of the whodunnit—the celebration of deduction and interpretation; the emphasis on the intellectual process of decoding of the puzzle; the clean, satisfying conclusion—are firmly in place. Crucially, Kingsley himself is an instantly recognizable detective hero in the Golden Age mode. He is, as we are told at various stages of the text, recognized as the finest detective in Britain. As we follow him through the case, we are treated to numerous examples of his thoroughness, his exceptional eye for detail, and his crucial imaginative leaps. Though wearing a uniform and acting on the orders of the crown, Kingsley enjoys the intellectual freedom of working alone, thus placing him considerably closer to the lone amateur sleuths of the Golden Age than to the harried, bureaucracy-bound policeman Hermann Kappe. Most importantly of all, and again in marked contrast to the unfor-tunate Kappe, Kingsley loves being a detective. Like his literary predecessors Holmes and Poirot, Kingsley is arrogant and vain, and revels in his public status as detective prince. He suffers from none of Kappe's disillusionment and professional self-doubt; the satisfaction he derives from detecting sparks an almost chemical response in him ('his blood was up' (*FC*, p. 320); 'the hunt was on' (*FC*, p. 346); 'some unanswerable compulsion drove him on' (*FC*, p. 347)).

The force of Kingsley's talents for and innate love of the art of detecting is what binds this novel closest to the whodunnit model, but it is also what shapes its stance on the war. Kingsley's obsession with logic, the very trait that makes him such an exceptional detective, is what drives him to object

[22] Jane Jakeman, 'Floundering in Flanders Fields', *Independent* online edition, 11 Novem-ber 2005 <http://www.independent.co.uk/arts-entertainment/books/reviews/the-first-casualty-by-ben-elton-326180.html> [accessed 17 December 2013].

to the conflict. He tells a hostile courtroom that his objections are not moral or religious but intellectual, that the British response to the German military threat is out of all proportion and that his conscience will not allow him to take part in something so fundamentally illogical:

[W]hatever his faults, the Kaiser leads an industrialized, imperial Christian nation! Just as does his first cousin, His Majesty King George. It is true that we are a democracy and Germany is an oligarchy but it is not for that reason that we fight. Indeed, our ally Russia was until recently every bit the absolute monarchy that Germany is. I can see no reason why all these most similar European nations have pronounced the death sentence upon one another's populations. (*FC*, p. 18)

In championing logic as his central guiding principle, Kingsley cannot but allow his intellect to dictate his conscience. As the novel progresses, however, this position is gradually revealed to be untenable. Firstly, it is pointed out to Kingsley by a series of different characters that his principled stand has already been compromised by the fact that he has spent years happily working for a British establishment guilty of the morally indefensible and entirely 'illogical' oppression of trade unionists, suffragettes, Fenians, and homosexuals. Secondly, in retrieving evidence the detective not only (accidentally) participates in battle but kills a dozen Germans, rescues a British officer, and is hailed a hero. Worst of all is Kingsley's final realization that he, the conscientious objector, actually enjoys combat. Conditioned to approaching life calmly and rationally, he finds the front-line experience of animal terror and survival strangely thrilling. While Kingsley never for one minute loses faith in his professional ability to solve the case, his faith in himself as a thinking, moral being is shaken:

[T]he perverted irony of his position filled him with horror [. . .] try as he might, he could not argue that his conscience was clear. Looking at it from whatever angle, he still emerged as a hypocrite. Having lost everything on a point of principle he had then tossed that principle aside in his desire to be a good detective, and probably also to prove his own courage to himself. (*FC*, p. 333)

Kappe's moments of crisis, as we have seen, send him down a road of self-doubt and disillusionment, scuppering any hope of a satisfactory narrative outcome. The whodunnit detective is made of sterner stuff, however, and Kingsley is able both to recognize his moral qualms and to find ways of accommodating them. As the case draws to a close, his language changes, and 'justice' subtly replaces 'logic' as his credo. Anything he does to further the investigation, he reasons, is morally justifiable: the investigation must be completed 'because justice must be done. The concept that there *was* such a thing as right and wrong had to be maintained' (*FC*, p. 421, Elton's italics). This argument is hardly very convincing, especially to Kingsley himself, but it underlines a critical turning-point in his understanding of himself as a detective. Kingsley's personal journey through the war teaches him that his vocation is stronger than his opposition to the conflict, and that in order to maintain his sanity and self-worth he must separate his moral self from his detecting self. He does this by uncoupling his fixation with logic from his conscience and concentrating it entirely on his professional talents instead. Hermann Kappe never manages to make this separation, with the result that his moral stance on the war and his moral doubts about his vocation become ever more entangled as the text progresses. Kingsley, on the other hand, simply realigns his priorities and gets on with the case. Politics and principles cease to count for very much once the narrative dynamics of the whodunnit start gaining momentum. Caught up in the thrill of the chase, all that matters to the detective is to find his man, and all that matters to us, the reader, is to enjoy his triumph as he does so. Defying the reader's (and his own) initial expectations, Kingsley abandons his principles and gradually learns to accept the war. This places him very obviously out of step with the anti-war narratives that currently dominate popular British war memory, narratives Elton himself helped to shape through the influence of *Blackadder*.

Despite this, however, and despite the fact that the author makes no effort to conceal or excuse what is essentially a full-blown moral sell-out, Kingsley's final cornering of the murderer is presented as a triumph for two reasons. Firstly, despite the growing diversification of the genre and the rise of challenging, deliberately unsettling crime novels in recent decades, the clean resolution of the traditional whodunnit still generates an unmistakably pleasurable thrill. And secondly, in the middle of a mechanized war in which millions of men had been stripped of any sense of control over how they lived and died, this conclusion rehabilitates the possibility of individual agency and marks a victory for logic and intellect over confusion and chaos.

Conclusion

Crime fiction set in a time of war, as Margaret Anne-Hutton has recently observed, has the potential to affect both how we see that war and how we understand the workings of the genre itself.[23] *Nach Verdun* and *The First Casualty* are structured around the crises and identity struggles experienced by their respective protagonists over the course of their investigations, and as a result they draw particular attention to the problems faced by the thinking individual—by any individual—trying to negotiate a moral position on war. In choosing to make these concerns so central to the narrative, meanwhile, these texts differ radically from the crime fiction of the immediate post-1918 period, whose response to the trauma of the war was to carry on almost as if

[23] *French Crime Fiction 1945–2005: Investigating World War II* (Farnham: Ashgate, 2013), p. 10.

it had never happened. Nevertheless, a comparison of the generic frameworks adapted by these texts in representing the war suggests that this shift may not be quite as pronounced as it seems. *Nach Verdun*, operating as a cross-breed between the *Soziokrimi* and the police procedural, lays bare the inability of traditional concepts of justice, and the failure of traditional modes of crime writing, to match up to the extraordinary moral crises thrown up by the war. The result is an unremittingly bleak anti-war narrative. *The First Casualty*, however, despite its exceptionally self-aware protagonist, demonstrates that the 'good clean fun' of the classic whodunnit narrative, the thrill of the chase, and the satisfaction of the grand reveal are ultimately enough to quell any moral anxieties lingering behind them. The uplifting, soothing function of plot, long associated with the Golden Age, is reactivated to package up the war for a new generation, as both detective and text surrender to narrative dynamics and gradually relinquish their conscientious objections.

Trinity College Dublin   Nóra de Buiteléir

EMBEDDED EXTEMPORE VERSE IN THE INTIMATE
LETTERS OF JOHN, LORD HERVEY (1696–1743)

Early in her book *Eighteenth-Century Letters and British Culture*, Clare Brant declares that 'the genre of letters' was 'the most important kind of writing in the eighteenth century'.[1] Although her concern is with prose letters, the same period was also the heyday of the verse epistle, so letters in verse are part of the same cultural-historical phenomenon.[2] This essay is about a kind of hybrid: the prose letter that includes original verse by the letter-writer as part of its expressive fabric. It is not uncommon to find verse in the prose letters of both men and women in this period. Most often quoted from other sources, it can offer amusement or instruction, or display the letter-writer's wit and culture. Original verse is much rarer in letters of all periods, including the eighteenth century. Where it occurs, two kinds may be distinguished. One type is the set piece, written separately and fitted in at a suitable point, displayed rather than integrated, sometimes at or near the end. The other type is verse within prose letters that appears to be composed during the process of writing, that continues the matter of the letter but in a different mode of expression. It is this type that I am calling embedded extempore verse, because it is an immediate and integral part of the letter, unlike verse that has merely been inserted.[3]

Some illustrations will help clarify these distinctions. For instance, a representative example of verse quoted to display the correspondent's wit and culture occurs when, in a letter to George Montagu on 19 July 1759, Horace Walpole writes:

With English verdure, we have had an Italian summer, and

This essay was completed by Bill Overton before his death in September 2012; it was revised for publication by James McLaverty and Elaine Hobby.

[1] Clare Brant, *Eighteenth-Century Letters and British Culture* (Basingstoke: Palgrave Macmillan, 2006), p. 2.

[2] See Bill Overton, *The Eighteenth-Century British Verse Epistle* (Basingstoke: Palgrave Macmillan, 2007).

[3] Difficult questions attach themselves to verse that is published as extempore, such as Swift's 'Verses Spoken Extempore by Dean Swift on his Curate's Complaint of Hard Duty' (in *The Poems of Jonathan Swift*, ed. by Harold Williams, 2nd edn, 3 vols (Oxford: Clarendon Press, 1958), II, 674–75); Fielding's 'Written Extempore on a Halfpenny' (in *Miscellanies by Henry Fielding, Esq*, 3 vols, Wesleyan Edition of the Works of Henry Fielding (Oxford: Clarendon Press, 1972–97), I, ed. by Henry Knight Miller (1972), pp. 59–60); Burns's series of 'extempore' poems (in *The Poems and Songs of Robert Burns*, ed. by James Kinsley, 3 vols (Oxford: Clarendon Press, 1968), I, 24, 236–37, 297–99, 306, 328–30, 382; II, 578–79, 732); and, most famously, Wordsworth's 'Extempore Effusion upon the Death of James Hogg' (in *Last Poems, 1821–1850*, ed. by Jared Curtis, with Apryl Lea Denny-Ferris and Jillian Heydt-Stevenson, The Cornell Wordsworth (Ithaca, NY: Cornell University Press, 1999), pp. 305–07). From the point of view of this essay, these publications are perhaps best understood as reports of extempore verse.

Modern Language Review, 110 (2015), 379–98
© Modern Humanities Research Association 2015

> Whatever Sweets Sabean springs disclose,
> Our Indian Jasmine and the Persian Rose.[4]

As often in quotations of this type, Walpole is clearly quoting from memory, for, as the editors of his correspondence indicate, these lines from Dryden's play *Aureng-Zebe* should read:

> What Sweets soe'er *Sabean* springs disclose,
> Our *Indian* Jasmine, or the *Syrian* Rose.[5]

Hervey's own faith in the potential power of such quotations is evident from an anecdote in his *Memoirs*. When he found Walpole neglecting his duties, drawn away from court by his liaison with Mary Skerrit, he sent him an anonymous letter containing two lines adapted from Dryden's *All for Love*:

> Whilst in her arms at Capua he lay,
> The world fell mouldering from his hand each hour.

The result was dramatic: Walpole 'upon the receipt of this letter, came immediately to Richmond' and 'set everything right'. The couplet, which Hervey had skilfully adapted to his own purposes, had an irresistible force.[6]

While original verse inserted into a letter but not written during the process of composition is much less common than quotation from others, it often has a similar objective. For example, James How has argued that the correspondence between the Countesses of Hertford and Pomfret sought to promote an idea of cultural distinction against what they saw as a rising tide of commercialism.[7] To this end, they not only wrote as distinguished ladies might have been expected to write but gave examples of their accomplishment by quoting or translating verse, and by providing samples of their own ability to write it. Their correspondence includes two letters that are wholly in verse—in other words, that are verse epistles—but also a further two in which verse lines provide an ample filling in letters that are otherwise prose. As these fillings run to sixty-four lines in one case and fifty-four in the other, it is highly unlikely that they could have been composed during the letter-

---

[4] *Horace Walpole's Correspondence with George Montagu*, in *The Yale Edition of Horace Walpole's Correspondence*, ed. by W. S. Lewis, 48 vols (New Haven: Yale University Press; London: Oxford University Press, 1937–83), IX (1941), 240–42 (p. 241).

[5] John Dryden, *Aureng-Zebe*, IV. 1. 101–02, in *The Works of John Dryden*, 20 vols (Berkeley: University of California Press, 1956–2002), XII: *Plays: 'Amboyna', 'The State of Innocence', 'Aureng-Zebe'*, ed. by Vinton A. Dearing (1994), pp. 147–250 (p. 212).

[6] John, Lord Hervey, *Some Materials towards Memoirs of the Reign of King George II*, ed. by Romney Sedgwick, 3 vols (London: Eyre and Spottiswoode, 1931), I, 294–95; John Dryden, *All for Love*, II. 1. 295–96, in *The Works of John Dryden*, XIII: *Plays: 'All for Love', 'Oedipus', 'Troilus and Cressida'*, ed. by Maximillian E. Novak and George R. Guffey (1984), pp. 1–111 (p. 49). Roger Lonsdale kindly drew attention to this episode.

[7] James How, *Epistolary Spaces: English Letter-Writing from the Foundation of the Post Office to Richardson's 'Clarissa'* (Aldershot: Ashgate, 2003), p. 131.

writing process, especially as the published correspondence contains no other examples.[8]

Much more difficult to find are examples of verse that, the context suggests, were composed extempore while the letter was being written.[9] This is not just because relatively few people had the capacity to extemporize verse, even during a period when the ability to compose it was a valued social and cultural accomplishment for the aristocratic or genteel, irrespective of whether they had any aspirations to the name of a poet; it was also because some might find such shifts in register indecorous (Voiture, for instance, did not use them), or because writing verse came too close to the writer's 'trade', as Pope sometimes called it. Equally important as a barrier to the location of examples is the fact that few are likely to have been preserved, whether because they had their place in letters that have been destroyed or because, even where they are still extant, they have not come to light. Further archival work is needed to advance our knowledge of eighteenth-century letter-writing, and I am therefore especially indebted to the independent scholar Dr Michael Londry for providing me with an example of extempore verse. It occurs in a letter dated 2 September 1789 from Charlotte Elizabeth Sanders to her sister, a Mrs Buss, following some pointed comments on selfishness. In order to provide enough of the context to recognize what is at issue, I quote from the sentence that introduces the verse and the one that follows it:

you must when you seriously consider, think you are wrong to expect one that is mewd up in the woods and fields to be capable of writing a long letter, when you, who are constantly, seeing, or hearing, something new, will not fill a quarter of a sheet to amuse your poor sister Bete

> Search through the world and if but one you find
> Free from all selfeshness, in life and mind
> I'll ask your pardon, own I've Judged amiss
> And freely blame myself for writeing this,

To make you relish the better, what I have said above, I will confess that I am at present actuated by the very principle which I may have appeared to you, to condemn as my readiness in complying with your desire, arises from a sincere wish that you would write very soon.

The quatrain gives every sign that it is an example of extempore embedded

---

[8] *Correspondence between Frances Countess of Hertford (Afterwards Duchess of Somerset) and Henrietta Louisa Countess of Pomfret*, 3 vols (London: for R. Philips, 1805; 2nd edn, 1806), I, 306–08; III, 69–71. Part of one such verse passage (I, 307–08) is reprinted in *Eighteenth-Century Women Poets: An Oxford Anthology*, ed. by Roger Lonsdale (Oxford: Oxford University Press, 1989), pp. 109–10; for further details see Overton, *The Eighteenth-Century British Verse Epistle*, pp. 54–55.

[9] Instruction on how to write such verse has not been found in the letter-writing manuals of the period, and no clear examples appear in the contemporary *Familiar Letters of Love, Gallantry, and Several Other Occasions: By the Wits of the Last and Present Age* (1724), an ever-growing collection published by Sam Briscoe.

verse (hereafter EEV). It arises from and returns to the immediate context, continuing and extending its content, and, so far as I have been able to determine, it does not appear to quote from or allude to any form of words that had been published previously, though its vocabulary and rhyme come from a common stock.[10] Although EEV may in principle be produced by any letter-writer, whether or not they have pretensions as verse-writers, it may be relevant that a Charlotte Elizabeth Sanders or Saunders appears as 'novelist, poet, and children's writer' in Janet Todd's *Dictionary of British and American Women Writers 1660–1800*,[11] though there is no entry for her in the *Oxford Dictionary of National Biography*.

Some of the eighteenth century's most distinguished writers toy with extempore verse, without deploying it in a consistent and serious way. Their letters show that the distinction between verse that merely appears to be extempore and that which is truly so can be difficult to make in practice. The writer's own verse, like the verse of others, might be held in mental reserve, ready to be called on or adapted when appropriate, or an entire letter, prose and verse, might be very deliberately composed, drafted in detail, and then written out fine, making the process of composition inaccessible. Such was evidently the practice in the case of Pope's letters to Henry Cromwell now in the Bodleian Library.[12] Like the Countesses, Pope might write a whole letter in verse or include substantial quotation in a prose context, but his vocation as a poet usually precludes any casual slipping from prose into verse. Sometimes he obscures the source of quotations in his letters: Henry Cromwell, for example, writes of his surprise at discovering that two French pieces that he had thought were Pope's own were actually by Voiture.[13] Often when Pope includes his own verse in his letters, it is poetry he has prepared earlier, and it could be introduced by the formula he uses in a letter to Swift: 'if I may quote myself'.[14]

Swift himself includes verse in his letters much more rarely, but once or twice he does so with an air of improvisation. When telling Esther Vanhomrigh how much he would like to be with her, he continues:

---

[10] Gale's *Eighteenth Century Collections Online* (ECCO) reveals parallels with 'Search through the world: How few, alas! we find, | Whose hoodwink'd reason not misleads the mind!' (*Poems on Several Occasions by H. G.*, 1748), and 'Search through the world, how few you'll find | To whom both Fate and Fortune have been kind!' (*Suicide: A Poem*, 1773). The availability of searchable full-text electronic databases such as *ECCO* has greatly facilitated the tracing of sources. See <http://www.jisc-content.ac.uk/node/64> [accessed August 2012].

[11] Janet Todd, *Dictionary of British and American Women Writers 1660–1800* (London: Methuen, 1987), p. 278.

[12] See Oxford, Bodleian, MS Rawl, Letters 90. Later letters show some revisions but they post-date the making of the initial fair copy.

[13] *The Correspondence of Alexander Pope*, ed. by George Sherburn, 5 vols (Oxford: Clarendon Press, 1956), I, 95 (3 August 1710).

[14] *The Correspondence of Alexander Pope*, II, 481 (23 March 1728).

> A fig for Partridges and Quails,
> Ye Daintyes, I know nothing of ye,
> But on the highest mount in Wales
> Would choose in Peace to drink my Coffee.[15]

But this passage constitutes a semi-comic summary rather than a continuance of the process of the letter. Similar use of verse, though this time wholly comic, is also found in a letter to Thomas Sheridan, while Sheridan's own letters sometimes contain casual comic verse that seems to be improvised but is displayed rather than integrated.[16]

Two writers from later in the century provide contrasting practices, without either showing a commitment to extempore verse. Johnson rarely includes verse in his published correspondence; his surviving letters are more business-like than Pope's or Swift's. He might quote Horace or Virgil, or adapt lines from Milton, but his only improvised lines are accompanied by an appropriate warning:

> My love to all
> Both great and small.

These verses I made myself, though perhaps they have been made before me.[17]

The absence of improvised verse from the letters is more striking because Johnson's ability to improvise is well documented.[18] Burns, by contrast, fills his letters with verse: his own poems, written out at length, and frequent quotation from, among others, Pope, Addison, Thomson, Milton, Blair, and Young. But, like Pope, Burns is too much the professional writer to improvise frequently. Every important letter was drafted before being written out fair and very little of his own verse goes unidentified by his editors as belonging to a published poem.[19] Some letters end with a comic envoi,[20] but the only serious integrated verse I have found that seems to be extempore is in a letter to Agnes M'Lehose:

---

[15] *The Correspondence of Jonathan Swift, D. D.*, ed. by David Woolley, 4 vols to date (Frankfurt a.M.: Peter Lang, 1999–), II (2001), 343 (12 August 1720).

[16] *The Correspondence of Jonathan Swift*, II, 559–60 (25 J[une] 1725). Scraps of comic verse, some of it in Anglo-Latin, some of the rhymes laid out as prose, are to be found in other letters (III (2003), 740; IV (2007), 181, 308–09, 313, 319–20, 327, 334), but they are part of a comic game rather than merged into an ordinary letter.

[17] *The Letters of Samuel Johnson*, ed. by Bruce Redford, 5 vols (Oxford: Clarendon Press, 1992), III, 414.

[18] In *The Poems of Samuel Johnson*, ed. by David Nichol Smith and Edward L. McAdam, 2nd edn (Oxford: Clarendon Press, 1974), twenty-four poems are recorded as impromptu, extempore, or dashed off for a particular purpose.

[19] *The Letters of Robert Burns*, ed. by J. De Lancey Ferguson, 2nd edn, ed. by G. Ross Roy, 2 vols (Oxford: Clarendon Press, 1985), p. xliv and passim.

[20] I, 46 (Letter 38), and I, 114 (Letter 105), for example.

I am, my lovely friend, much better this morning, on the whole; but I have a horrid languor on my spirits.—

> 'Sick of the world, and all its joy,
> 'My soul in pining sadness mourns:
> 'Dark scenes of woe my mind employ,
> 'The past and present in their turns.'[21]

This resort to verse to specify and intensify feeling is something to be found much more frequently in Hervey.

Hervey's letters present so many examples of extempore verse that they deserve to be ranked as a significant part of his achievement as a poet. That achievement is itself much more substantial than is usually recognized. Not only, out of a total of 130 poets, is Hervey among the twenty-nine with the largest contributions in the best-selling verse anthology of the period, Robert Dodsley's *Collection of Poems by Several Hands*, but some of his most distinctive verse has never been printed or does not appear there.[22] Like his parents, Hervey was also a prolific letter-writer. Hundreds of their letters and his survive, although those in his father's *Letter-Books* have been printed whereas most of Hervey's, whose letters are not represented there, have not.[23] There was, too, a tradition in the family of writing verse. This may have gone back as far as Hervey's great-uncle, Sir Thomas Hervey, who had known Abraham Cowley at Cambridge and who, dying young, was the subject of an elegy by him in 1642; it certainly extended to Hervey's father, to two of his brothers, and even, on a few rare occasions, to his mother.[24] Hervey's father, Lord Bristol, was a cultivated man. Not only was he an occasional poet himself, but he liked to stud his letters with verse. His *Letter-Books* contain a little over one hundred examples in English, and a much smaller number in Latin or French. The great majority, however, are direct or adapted quotations, mostly from

---

[21] I, 212 (Letter 182).

[22] *A Collection of Poems by Several Hands*, ed. by Robert Dodsley, repr. ed. by Michael F. Suarez, SJ, 6 vols (London: Routledge Thoemmes, 1997), I, 91; 116, n. 206. For details about several of Hervey's most interesting unpublished poems see Bill Overton, 'Lord Hervey, Poetic Voice and Gender', *Review of English Studies*, n.s., 62 (2011), 594–617.

[23] Lord Bristol's letter-books survive at the West Suffolk Record Office, Bury St Edmunds, and have been printed as *Letter-Books of John Hervey, First Earl of Bristol*, ed. by S[ydenham] H[enry] A[ugustus] H[ervey], 3 vols (Wells: E. Jackson, 1894). Many of Hervey's letters are preserved in the same archive, while others are in the British Library and the John Murray Archive in London, but only a relatively small selection is printed in *Lord Hervey and his Friends, 1726–38*, ed. by the Earl of Ilchester [Giles Stephen Holland Fox-Strangways] (London: John Murray, 1950). Hervey's three surviving letters to Charlotte Clayton, later Lady Sundon, are printed in A. T. Thomson, *Memoirs of Viscountess Sundon*, 2 vols (London: H. Colburn, 1847).

[24] Although Tom Hervey occasionally wrote verse, the brother who had greater pretensions as a poet was Henry. He angered his father and brother by proposing to publish a collection of his verse by subscription, a form of publication they considered below the family's dignity, but made some amends by writing an imitation in English verse of Hervey's Latin epitaph for Queen Caroline. See *Letter-Books*, III, 172–73, 195, 209. For details of verse by Lady Bristol, see below.

poets or dramatists of the Restoration, with Cowley as one of his favourites. There are only six examples that I have not been able to trace to other writers and that probably therefore constitute EEV, plus one eight-line verse epistle to his newly wed wife. All the other six examples consist of a single couplet, and only two occur in intimate letters, both to his wife.[25] This is a very small proportion of the verse he embedded in letters.

Although she appears to have produced little verse, it was Hervey's mother, not his father, who came closest to anticipating the kind of EEV that Hervey would write. There are only two instances, the first of which is no more than a couplet,[26] but the second is important enough to deserve quoting, along with its context, in full. It occurs in a letter from Bath, where she had gone for her health, dated 10 June 1723:

I really believe this sudden alteration for the better proceeds more from the time drawing near of my being to be happy again in your lovd society than from the waters or any other medicine,

> Since life's not worth the pain which I endure
> By being sent from you to seek my cure,
> Yet when I recollect how farr above
> The rest of mortals I am blest in love,
> By being possessd of all that heaven can give,
> I think it worth my while to strive to live;
> And by my care, if I prolong my days,
> Each added hour an age of pain repays.

I believe you will wonder at this piece of poetry; but what will not love inspire; yet such as I feel for you cannot be discribed either in verse or prose, but only in the heart of your faithfull E. B.[27]

It is not possible to determine whether Lady Bristol wrote these eight lines of endearment before inserting them in her letter or composed them during the process of writing, though the former seems more likely. If that is the case, it distinguishes them from most of the verse that her son put into prose letters. But, in that they constitute an endearment, the lines look forward to examples from her son to Stephen Fox and Francesco Algarotti; and they anticipate them, too, in their location virtually at the end of a letter. Her expectation that they will surprise her husband indicates that putting verse of her own into letters was scarcely habitual to her, although, as her letters to her husband are the only ones included in his letter-books, and as she had a wide circle of correspondents, it is not impossible that she did so in letters to others.

Before addressing the extempore verse that Hervey embedded in prose let-

[25] *Letter-Books*, I, 89 (to the uncle of his second wife), 167 (to his wife), 303 (to the Duke of Marlborough), 342 (to the Duke of Marlborough); II, 48 (to Delarivière Manley), 60 (to his wife); for the verse epistle see I, 96–97.

[26] *Letter-Books*, II, 127.

[27] *Letter-Books*, II, 314.

ters, a further comparison is instructive. Lady Mary Wortley Montagu was not only a poet of the period who was also a prolific letter-writer; she was one of Hervey's most important correspondents. Montagu included verse in letters for over fifty years, both quoted and original. Not counting her verse epistle 'Letter to Lord Hervey from Twict'nam wrote on the King's Birthday', clearly a set-piece because it has not only a title but an epigraph, Robert Halsband's edition of her *Complete Letters* has a total of seventy-nine examples in English.[28] Four of these, however, are literal translations by her of verse originally in Turkish; others include her epitaph on John Hughes and Sarah Drew, and eleven lines from her 'Letter from Mrs. Y[onge] to her Husband' (not published until long after).[29] But there are key differences between the verse that she included in letters and Hervey's. The most important is that the great majority of it is not original but is quoted or adapted from a previously published source. Fifteen items seem to be all or mostly by Montagu, but even two of these are in part adapted from previously published verse, and another is the passage from 'Letter from Mrs. Y[onge]' just mentioned. Of the remaining examples, four are literal translations by her from Turkish originals, while from those that remain I have been able to trace only eleven that lack one or more previously published sources and so can reasonably be regarded as original verse by her. This frequent resort to the verse of others is entirely consistent with her practice as a poet throughout her long career. As Isobel Grundy has pointed out, she 'regarded poetry as an unbroken tradition on which its latest practitioner could always draw', with the result that she 'often indulged in extensive borrowing, even of whole passages'.[30] One famous example will have to serve for many. In a letter to Francesco Algarotti of September 1736, she included the following lines:

> Why was my haughty Soul to Woman joyn'd?
> Why this soft sex impos'd upon my Mind?
> Even this extravagance which now I send
> Were meritorious in the name of Freind.
> Thee I might follow, thee my Lovely Guide,
> Charm'd with thy voice, and ever by thy side,
> Nor Land, nor sea, our common way divide.
> How much these golden Wishes are in vain!
> I dream to pleasure, but I wake to pain.[31]

[28] *The Complete Letters of Lady Mary Wortley Montagu*, ed. by Robert Halsband, 3 vols (Oxford: Clarendon Press, 1965–67).

[29] *Complete Letters*, I, 334–35, 336–37, 361, 388–89, 446; III, 219. 'Letter from Mrs. Y[onge] to her Husband' was first printed by Isobel Grundy in 1972; see *Lady Mary Wortley Montagu: Essays and Poems and 'Simplicity', a Comedy*, ed. by Robert Halsband and Isobel Grundy (Oxford: Clarendon Press, 1977; new edn, 1993), pp. 230–32.

[30] Isobel Grundy, 'The Verse of Lady Mary Wortley Montagu: A Critical Edition' (unpublished doctoral thesis, Oxford University, 1971), pp. 1, 89.

[31] *Complete Letters*, II, 106.

Grundy, who includes the nine lines as a complete poem in her D.Phil. edition of Montagu's verse, notes that line 7 is borrowed from Prior's 'Henry and Emma' and line 8 from Dryden's *Secret Love*; but the opening couplet, the most arresting of the whole piece, comes verbatim from a little-known early eighteenth-century tragedy, Charles Goring's *Irene; or, The Fair Greek*.[32] Montagu has used her reading and her excellent memory to produce a verse protest that hovers between her own thoughts and expressions and those of at least three other writers. Her letters contain many similar examples, though few as complex as this.

Because there is no edition of Hervey's letters in any way comparable to Halsband's for Montagu's, it is not possible to produce statistics concerning the verse that he included in them. What can be said is that there seem to have been two main reasons why he did so. The first he gave to his most intimate correspondent, Stephen Fox. Excusing a letter that has not been preserved and that appears to have been wholly in verse, he claimed: ''tis some days so much more natural to me to write in verse than prose, that I did it for my ease; and 'twas only want of time that hindered me putting it into a common epistolary form'.[33] The second reason is implicit in a similar remark eight years later to another intimate friend, Francesco Algarotti: 'as my thoughts, without any affectation, fall some Days so naturally into Rhyme, that I am forced to think twice to put them into Prose, and that I never constrain my Nature when I write or speak to you, forgive the Inconveniency of my Sincerity for the sake of that Affection which occasion's it'.[34] Hervey suggests here not only that he sometimes writes verse more easily than prose, but also that, for him, verse is the natural form for expressing affection. More generally, in the same way that shifts into verse in prose drama of the Restoration and earlier eighteenth century tend to suggest heightened emotion, he seems to have used verse in his letters to express feelings of particular force or complexity.

Part of the evidence for such a motive is that Hervey included EEV in letters only to a small number of correspondents. Among the 130-odd of his letters to Stephen Fox that have survived, 10 contain verse of this kind, including one that has two such passages, producing a total of 63 lines; among 46 letters to Montagu, 10 have passages of EEV, amounting to 100 lines; among 31 to Algarotti, 8, including one that has two such passages and amounting to 45

[32] 'Verse of Lady Mary Wortley Montagu', p. 576; *The Literary Works of Matthew Prior*, ed. by H. Bunker Wright and Monroe K. Spears, vol. I, 2nd edn (Oxford: Oxford University Press, 1971), 289, l. 395; *The Works of John Dryden*, IX, 154 (III. 1. 176); Charles Goring, *Irene; or, The Fair Greek* (London: for John Bayley, 1708), p. 4.

[33] Bury St Edmunds, Suffolk Record Office (SRO), 941/47/4, p. 73; *Lord Hervey and his Friends*, p. 26. In quoting from manuscripts I have lightly normalized spelling and orthography for ease of reading.

[34] John Murray Archive, Letter 5, fol. 4ʳ; copy in SRO, 941/47/4, p. 587; *Lord Hervey and his Friends*, p. 254.

lines; among 72 to Henry Fox, only one, amounting to a single couplet; and a further single couplet among the two extant letters to his doctor, George Cheyne. An additional example, written while Hervey was in Italy, has been preserved separately from the letter in which it was embedded, which does not survive; while another, in a letter to Frederick, Prince of Wales, has not been included among these statistics because it is in French.[35] The relative paucity of EEV in Hervey's letters to Stephen Fox, considering the length and intensity of their friendship, is explained by the fact that they spent as much time as possible together, especially during the period when they shared a house in London. On the other hand, the fact that there is so little in Hervey's letters to Henry Fox is explained by an apology early in their correspondence for having written to him in verse:

I won't reproach you with not having writ to me this fortnight, since I acknowledge it to have been my fault; for who would not (like you) rebuke an unconscionable Correspondent who, not content with persecuting you in prose, extends his Cruelty yet farther and inflicts himself upon you in Rhyme: however, he has will enough (which I fear you will have some Difficulty to believe) to take the Hint of your tacit reproof, good nature enough to give you his word, to offend no more, and honesty enough to keep it.[36]

The letter to which he refers seems no longer to be extant. All the same, 30 letters containing a total of 31 examples of EEV from a total of about 290 letters to these five correspondents—one of them averse to poetic flights, the other not one of his closest friends—plus a further item from the letter that has not survived, is a significant proportion. So is the total of over two hundred lines. As far as I know, no other letters by Hervey containing EEV have been preserved.

It is not, as I have argued, always easy to tell what should and should not be counted as EEV. By the term in this examination of Hervey's writing I do not mean verse written previously either by him or by another and fitted into the letter, but only verse composed by the letter-writer during the actual process of writing. Not only is it necessary to check whether the verse in question had been printed previously. A trickier matter is finding out whether or not it is, in effect, a self-quotation from Hervey himself. For example, in a few cases the verse Hervey put into letters includes lines from poems that had yet to be published. Thus two and a half lines in a letter of 1727 to Henry Fox found their way into his *A Satyr: In the Manner of Persius*, first printed in 1730; a couplet in the same year in a letter to Montagu also appears in his elegy on his sister Elizabeth, who had died two months earlier; and two couplets in a letter to Algarotti of 1736 occur in *The Difference between Verbal and Practical*

---

[35] 'Part of a letter written when I was ill at Naples—feb. 1729', SRO, 941/53/1, pp. 212, 214; 'Quant al Padrone', SRO, 941/47/4, pp. 268–69, printed in *Lord Hervey and his Friends*, p. 108.
[36] SRO, 941/47/4, p. 43 (15 June 1727).

Virtue, a satire printed six years later.[37] Although in the last case it seems unlikely that Hervey could have anticipated himself by a period of several years, I have erred on the side of caution by not counting it as an example of EEV. A trickier matter still is determining whether or not the verse was truly extempore. But useful evidence can be gained from autograph originals where these survive, such as crossings-out or other signs of continuous composition. Evidence of this kind is available from the great majority of those letters that survive in autograph form—all of Hervey's letters to Montagu and most of those to Algarotti. A simple example is that a mysterious note probably referring to Montagu's feelings for Algarotti ends with a triplet in the first line of which two words have been transposed; a few others are cited below.[38] Evidence from the large number of Hervey's letters that have been preserved only as autograph copies or copies by an amanuensis is more difficult to interpret. All the same, I have quoted remarks from letters to Algarotti and both Fox brothers saying that he was in the habit of segueing into verse, and there is further such evidence in another letter to Stephen Fox. Following three iambic pentameter quatrains, he remarks, with reference to the verse tragedy he was writing: 'Aceronia you see has made my thoughts so naturally jingle into Rhyme, that I find it is as Difficult to write a letter in plain Prose as a Dancing-Master does to walk into a Room; but as I have not time to ask my second thoughts, you must e'en take them hopping as they come at first.'[39] In several copies of his letters, too, lines set out as prose, either in his own hand or in that of an amanuensis, have been identified as verse by underlining or by deletion and reformatting. This may even suggest that, though verse they are, in the original document the lines were not set out as such at all.[40]

Another kind of evidence that the original verse embedded in over thirty of Hervey's letters was improvised is his skill at extempore composition. Not only

[37] Francesco Algarotti, *Il newtonianismo per le dame* (Naples: Giambatista Pasquali, 1739), n. p.; SRO, 941/47/4, p. 38 and *A Satyr: In the Manner of Persius* (London [i.e. Dublin]: [n. pub.], 1730), p. 6; 'Verses to the Memory of my dearest Sister the Lady Elizabeth Mansel' (SRO, 941/53/1, p. 214); 'Epitaph on Lady Betty Mansel, on her Tomb-Stone in Ickworth Church' (SRO, 941/53/1, p. 218, with 'zenith' for 'noon'); John Murray Archive, Letter 5, fol. 3^v, with copy in SRO, 941/47/4, p. 587, printed in *Lord Hervey and his Friends*, p. 254, and *The Difference between Verbal and Practical Virtue* (London: for J. Roberts, 1742), p. 7.

[38] 'Whose Meaning still in Riddles is express'd', 'still' and 'is' being the words transposed (SRO, 941/47/2, p. 15; letter dated 'Saturday 3. a' clock', probably in 1736).

[39] London, British Library (BL), Add. MS 513945, fols 77^v–78^r (25 June 1737), repr. in part in *Lord Hervey and his Friends*, p. 266. 'Aceronia' almost certainly refers to his verse tragedy *Agrippina*, which was never printed but survives in a single manuscript copy (BL, Egerton 3787, fols 13^r–49^v).

[40] 28 December 1728 to Stephen Fox (SRO, 941/47/4, p. 63); 20 June 1728 to Stephen Fox (SRO, 941/47/4, p. 78); 2 October 1731 to Stephen Fox (SRO, 941/47/4, p. 239); 30 October 1736 to Algarotti (SRO, 941/47/4, p. 582). Verse in the copied letters is usually written in a larger hand, suggesting that Hervey wished to call attention to it. As Lord Ilchester suggested, his purpose in keeping copies of his letters may have been to publish them in some form at a later date. See Ilchester, 'Preface', in *Lord Hervey and his Friends*, pp. ix–xviii (p. xiii).

are several of his poems that survive in manuscript marked as extempore,[41] but he was adept at producing verse to entertain those close to him. For example, in 1729 he wrote a verse letter of 229 lines to his wife about his travels in Italy that ends with the remark that, apart from the value it may have for its reader, it is only 'the poor offspring of a day, | Just to be read and thrown away'.[42] He also wrote two poems to entertain Frederick, Prince of Wales, one of them the example of EEV in French already mentioned, and two for Queen Caroline.[43] Such a practice was not unusual at a period when the ability to improvise verse was a valuable social and cultural accomplishment. Hervey and Montagu were unusually good at it, on one occasion producing an extempore verse dialogue of seventy-three lines.[44] Though not definitive evidence, such examples are consistent with an ability to produce verse in the process of writing prose letters. The rest of this article considers some examples, beginning with EEV in letters to Stephen Fox.

Most of this verse occurs during the earlier stages of the relationship, especially from late 1729, when the two returned from their stay in Italy, to late 1731, after which they were able to live together for a while. Most of it, too, consists of endearments. Two representative examples occur near the end of a letter dated 2 October 1731:

I write to You from the Dutchess of Richmond's; where I am to dine; she has a Belly up to her Chin and looks mighty well, his Grace is in great Anxiety for her Welfare and a Boy.[45] I am so for fear of any unforeseen Accident preventing our meeting on Friday.

[41] 'Written Impromptu to a Lady Stung by a Bee' (Bloomington, Lilly Library, Delany MS [1], item 9, transcribed by William Hervey as 'On Delia Stung by a Bee. extempore by Lord Hy.', SRO, 941/53/1, p. 208); 'To a Lady upon her asking the Author where he thought he should be that time twelve Month. Written off hand' (BL, Harley 7318, fol. 127ᵛ; another copy at the University of Leeds as 'an extempore Answer by Lord Hervey upon his Lady's asking him what He should be: that time twelvemonth' (Brotherton Library, LT q 20, fol. 82ʳ)); 'Translation of some lines in Ovid, El. 9. L. 3, Extempore by Ld. Hervey' (SRO, 941/53/1, p. 204). I gratefully acknowledge permission from the Lilly Library to cite a document in its care.

[42] BL, Add. MS 51345, fols 18ʳ–23ʳ.

[43] 'Quant al Padrone' and 'For if in Richmond-morning-walk' in a letter dated 6 November 1731 (SRO, 941/47/4, pp. 268–69; 270–71; printed in *Some Materials*, I, pp. xxxvii–xxxviii); 'To the Queen' and 'The Griff to the Queen' (*Some Materials*, II, 576–84; III, 804).

[44] Stafford, Sandon Hall, Harrowby MS 81, pp. 216–17; printed in Lady Mary Wortley Montagu, *Essays and Poems*, pp. 286–89. Hervey copied some of the lines in a letter to Montagu (SRO, 941/47/2, pp. 70–71); for discussion of a copy of lines 44–73 that casts light on how the dialogue was composed, see Isobel Grundy, '"New" Verse by Lady Mary Wortley Montagu', *Bodleian Library Record*, 10 (1981), 237–49.

[45] The Duke was to be disappointed in his second hope but not his first. The baby, born on 6 October, was to be Emilia Mary, later Duchess of Leinster (1731–1814) and political hostess (see *DNB* entry by Rosemary Richey). A son, Charles, had lived for only two months after his birth in the previous year. The couple already had one daughter, Georgiana Carolina, born in 1723; their wishes for a male heir were satisfied only in 1735. This son, also named Charles, succeeded his father as Duke in 1750 (G. E. C., *Complete Peerage of England, Scotland, Ireland, Great Britain and the United Kingdom*, 13 vols (London: St Catherine Press, 1910–59), X (1945), 838).

'Tis You alone my Fears and Wishes make,
From you my Thoughts their various Tincture take.
With every Good, whilst you are present, blest,
Of all, when you are absent, dispossessed.
Each hour at best a Blank; not one enjoyed;
A tedious Waking, or a sleeping Void.
And whilst the present I should strive to taste,
I wish the Future or I weep the past.

It is ridiculous to say one writes in a Hurry when one writes in Rhyme; but 'tis true; and you know I do not lie when I say I sometimes can write as fast in Verse as I can in prose. Adieu Dinner is on the Table. *Vendredi Viendra* and sure I am I would not change that Hour
For all the while once Fate has in its power.[46]

This passage not only shows how easily Hervey could slip into verse, but the manuscript, corrected by Hervey from the copy made by an amanuensis, underlines and partly offsets the closing couplet to show it is verse. The longer example of EEV also casts light on Hervey's ability to produce verse with such apparent ease. First, it is in iambic pentameter couplets, not only the stock form for serious verse at the period but also a metre relatively close in its typical rhythms to those of English prose. Second, it is simply but effectively organized according to a series of antitheses, providing a clear structure and line of development.

Two further letters also end with verse, and five others have verse near the end, so furnishing appropriate valedictions. An interesting example is an endearment sandwiched between two completely unconnected remarks, one about a pamphlet by Swift that Hervey is enclosing, the other about the recent death of Lady Abergavenny:

the enclosed, and the tale of a Tub are indisputably written with a vast deal of Spirit and vivacity, but I think he [Swift] deserves to be hanged for one, and to have his Gown pulled over his Ears for t' other. Adieu
My Heart's Delight in whom alone I find
All that at once improves and charms the Mind.
poor L. Ab. is brought to bed and there is a report today that she's dead.[47]

Hervey's endearments are not often in such incongruous company but his letters to Fox vary in the ardour they express. One of the earlier items cautions him about the dangers of a 'restless Mind', and one of the later reflects on those of an over-sensitive emotional state, remarking:

---

[46] SRO, 941/47/4, pp. 238–39, printed in part in *Lord Hervey and his Friends*, pp. 100–01.

[47] SRO, 941/47/4, p. 102 (25 November 1729), printed in part in *Lord Hervey and his Friends*, p. 40. The pamphlet may well have been *A Modest Proposal*, first printed in Dublin the previous month and then in London. For details of the printing and advertisement of the Dublin edition see James Ward, 'Bodies For Sale: Marketing *A Modest Proposal*', *Irish Studies Review*, 15 (2007), 283–94.

> For few or can, or wish to bring Relief
> And every touch we feel augment[s] our Grief.[48]

These are examples of Hervey's ability not only to express emotion in verse but to analyse it and to advise. After 1731, however, the fact that the two were able to spend more time together resulted in fewer letters, and several years later the relationship cooled, especially after Fox's marriage in 1736.[49] The last piece of verse embedded in one of the surviving letters to Fox occurs in the one already quoted in which Hervey remarked that he was finding it difficult to write in prose. In it he sought to analyse his own feelings, having surprised himself by enjoying what he called 'the common Pleasures' of a country life at the family seat in Suffolk. The middle stanza of three amounts to a kind of brief testament as he declares:

> I own, my Friend! my only pleasures lye
>   In human Creatures, and in Black and White;
> Whilst in my Conduct still I only try,
>   To reconcile what's pleasant with what's right.[50]

But this is not to be taken as evidence that his capacity for passionate feeling had moderated. On the contrary, he was about to become a fervent admirer of Francesco Algarotti, one of his two other favoured recipients of EEV.

Introduced to Hervey by a letter from Voltaire that he had brought with him, Algarotti (1712–1764) had come to London in March 1736 while he was writing *Il newtonianismo per le dame*.[51] Having entranced Montagu as well as Hervey by his intelligence, charm, and good looks, he left London on 6 September. Hervey's first three letters to him were written while staying with Stephen Fox in the country before Algarotti's departure. The letter is of particular interest because Algarotti used the six lines of EEV that it contains as one of the commendatory poems prefacing the second edition of his book, and because corrections in the manuscript show that they were composed in the process of writing the letter:

> When the gay Sun no more his Rays shall boast,
> And human Eyes their Faculty have lost:

---

[48] SRO, 941/47/4, p. 63 (28 December 1727); 330 (25 December 1731), printed in *Lord Hervey and his Friends*, p. 128. Hervey's lines echo 'Hear then, and let your song augment our grief, | Which is so great, as not to wish Relief' (Edmund Waller, 'Thyrsis, Galatea', in *The Poems of Edmund Waller*, ed. by G. Thorn Drury, 2 vols (London: Routledge; Boston: Dutton, 1905), I, 40–42 (ll. 13–14).

[49] For details of the marriage see Robert Halsband, *Lord Hervey: Eighteenth-Century Courtier* (Oxford: Clarendon Press), pp. 188–91.

[50] BL, Add. MS 513945, fols 77ᵛ–78ʳ (25 June 1737), printed in *Lord Hervey and his Friends*, p. 266.

[51] See Algarotti, sig. A6ʳ. The book was translated by Elizabeth Carter in 1741 as *Sir Isaac Newton's Philosophy Explain'd for the Use of the Ladies*, but the translation does not include any commendatory verses.

Then shall thy writings on those Subjects dye
Thy Wit and Learning in Oblivion lye,
England shall cease to boast her *Newton's* Head,
And Algarotti's Works no more be read.[52]

To give just one example out of the five manuscript corrections to the verse, lines 3–4 replace two previous attempts, both deleted and the first including a false second try at rephrasing: 'Then shall thy Colours too and thy Optics and thy Optics | Thy Colours and thy Optics too shall dye.' Two of the other examples of EEV to Algarotti are also compliments, but a further two are elegant but barbed gibes at Hervey's rival for Algarotti's affections, Lady Mary Wortley Montagu. This is the shorter, which occurs in a letter that also contains one of the items of EEV that compliment Algarotti:

In black and white whilst Chloris' Mind you trace,
With red and white whilst she adorns her Face;
'Tis true she trys by Nature and by Art,
Each way to force a Passage to your Heart;
But for her Vows compleat Success to find,
To make her Lover pleas'd, as well as kind,
She should be never mute, You always blind.[53]

Despite criticizing Montagu for her need to use cosmetics, the lines at least concede her wittiness and her skill with words. A year later, however, Hervey was able to recognize that warm friendship was the best for which he could hope from Algarotti. Only three of his subsequent letters contain EEV, one a revised version of a poem to be discussed below that he had included in a letter to Montagu, the other two wry reflections, each only a couplet in length, about his life as a courtier, and about the political propensities of the English respectively.[54]

Instead of Stephen Fox or Algarotti, it was Montagu who received most of Hervey's EEV in the last six years of his life. The ten examples, amounting to a total of 100 lines, show the greatest emotional complexity of all the extempore verse that he embedded in letters. They begin somewhat inauspiciously with a triplet referring tartly to Montagu's confused feelings about Algarotti shortly after he had left England in September 1736:

[52] John Murray Archive, Letter 2 (16 August 1736). I gratefully acknowledge permission from Mr and Mrs Murray to study and transcribe letters from Hervey to Algarotti. These lines owe something to the conclusion of *The Rape of the Lock*.

[53] John Murray Archive, Letter 4 (20 September 1736). The conclusion adapts Swift's 'Stella's Birth-Day': 'Oh, ne'er may fortune shew her Spight, | To make me *deaf*, and mend my *Sight*' (*The Poems of Jonathan Swift*, II, 758).

[54] SRO, 941/47/4, p. 610 (17/28 September 1737), printed in *Lord Hervey and his Friends*, p. 272; John Murray Archive, Letter 20 (7 October 1740).

> Whose Meaning still in Riddles is express'd, }
> May sometimes vainly try to show their Breast, }
> And when they wish it least perhaps, be guess'd.[55] }

The expression of the first line is Latinate and elliptical, a word such as 'someone' or a phrase such as 'a person' being implied before it. But, just as Hervey's tone to Algarotti changed once he had recognized that there were limits to the intimacy he could expect from his friend, so did that to Montagu following her decision to leave for Italy in an abortive attempt to join Algarotti there. It manifested itself in four passages of EEV, one bidding her farewell, two complimenting her, and the fourth wishing a second spring to one of her maturer admirers. All express a moving generosity of spirit, testifying to the strength of a friendship that had begun nearly twenty years earlier and that had survived all the tribulations of the emotional triangle involving Algarotti. Hervey's farewell is a good example:

> Since all the Pray'rs of weeping Friends were vain,
> To stay your hated Passage o'er the Main,
> Suffer at least our wishes to pursue }
> That charming Object which eludes our View, }
> And take from real Grief this fond Adieu. }
> Where'er you dwell, where'er you bend your way,
> Or fix'd by Land, or roving o'er the Sea,
> Be yours each Pleasure (more you can not find,)
> Which Those regret whom you have left behind:
> May all the Transports jealous Minds suggest
> Are tasted in a happy Rival's Breast,
> And all the Envious fancy we enjoy,
> Gild ev'ry Scene, and ev'ry Sense employ;
> May ev'ry Hour in gay Succession move,
> Your Days all Luxury, your Nights all Love.[56]

The passage is carefully constructed, not only showing Hervey's characteristic fluency at writing verse, but also suggesting that the emotions expressed are deep and sincere. In the opening five lines, this comes largely from several adjectives: 'hated' is surprisingly violent in a valediction, but highly effective for conveying strength of feeling, while 'charming' pays tribute to the pleasures that Hervey and others close to Montagu are losing, and 'real' and 'fond' have much more robust meanings than they have now. The remaining ten lines change the point of view to Montagu herself, not only acknowledging why she is leaving but also endorsing her motives and wishing her success in realizing them. In this there is not the least hint of reproach. Instead, Hervey both wishes Montagu the pleasures she gives to others and dissociates himself

---

[55] SRO, 941/47/2, p. 15, dated by Halsband 18 September 1736 (*Complete Letters*, ii, 108).

[56] SRO, 941/47/2, p. 75 (28 August 1739).

from envy. The chiasmus in 'Gild ev'ry Scene, and ev'ry Sense employ' is a telling example, but, considering his own strong feelings for Algarotti, the closing line is even more remarkable for what it wishes her: 'Your Days all Luxury, your Nights all Love'.

But not all of Hervey's EEV to Montagu strikes the same exalted note. During a period when he was experiencing not only political but also personal reverses and losses—the latter including the death in November 1737 of Queen Caroline as well as Montagu's move to Italy—it is scarcely surprising that three of the remaining examples are at the other end of the affective spectrum. All are acid protests at human folly, anticipated by his recognition, in one of the verse compliments he paid Montagu, that, 'sated with Ambition's grosser Fare', he finds his 'Luxury' only in correspondence with her.[57] The longest of the three runs to only eight lines:

> When the Philosophers attempt to scan
> The Motives of infatuated Man,
> Let them no more define, and judg by Rule,
> But solve each Riddle by that one Word Fool:
> And when by Chance (tho distant far) you hear
> Of all the Nothings that employ my Care,
> This one remaining Mark of Sense you'll see,
> I'll own you're just, when you cry Fool to Me.[58]

The lines reflect Hervey's characteristic scepticism about philosophy as well as his personal setbacks and disappointments. But it is also relevant that they were written towards the end of a life often troubled by poor health. This is reflected by some of the bitterest lines he ever wrote, stemming from his anger and frustration after an especially serious bout of illness:

> This world was made for Fools who can compound
> For a small crop on a hard-labor'd Ground
> I find the Growth of Pleasure is so small
> I long to tear my Lease and spurn it all.[59]

Only to a friend as close as Montagu could he express himself in such unqualified terms. It is significant that he chose to distil his feelings in EEV. Although there was probably no subject that the two regarded as beyond discussion between them, he may have felt emboldened in raising that of suicide by 'Addressed To ———', a poem written by Montagu either to him or to Algarotti during her despair following the latter's departure from England in 1736.[60] Different as the two poems are, especially in the greater length and

[57] SRO, 941/47/2, p. 87 (late June/early July 1740).
[58] SRO, 941/47/2, p. 105 (16 May 1741).
[59] SRO, 941/47/2, p. 121 (16 November 1741).
[60] *Essays and Poems*, pp. 290–91.

the philosophical turn Montagu gives hers, both express a wish, during a time of almost unbearable suffering, to be able to bid farewell to life and end it.

It was in the following year, however, that Hervey responded in a more considered way to the question of suicide. Again he chose to do so in EEV. His subject was the death of John Hedges, a colleague and friend of his at court, his pretext some rather conventionally elegiac lines that Montagu had written about it.[61] Echoing in prose the remark quoted above that he had made in verse to Stephen Fox, he wrote:

the news of poor Hedges's Death and your Comments upon it, enlarged *and raised my Imagination*, as you call it, more than any Leisure, or the reality of the finest Landskips Claude Lorain ever painted could do in seven years: nothing I own affects my Mind much, but human Creatures, and Black and White.

> Why dost thou ignorantly mourn his Fate,
> And wish his scanty Lease a longer Date?
> He's gone, his Honours green upon his Brow,
> The Lover's Myrtle, and the Poet's Bough;
> Unwasted yet to Ashes either Fire,
> Nor dwindled into Dotage from Desire:
> In the full Vigour of his Blood and Mind
> He drank of Life, and left the Dregs behind:
> Exempt from all th' Infirmities of Age,
> Nor doomed to totter on Life's latest Stage;
> (Where many breathe, though they no longer live,
> And all worth living for, despised survive:)
> Sure too the Record of his Fame to save,
> For Lady Mary writes upon his Grave.

This is a Subject that I really think inexhaustible, but luckily for you the Post will not allow me to say half what I could and would say upon it.[62]

These lines convey several different kinds of emotion. First, there is indignation at Montagu's expression of regret for Hedges' death (though most of her eight-and-a-half lines wish him Elysian bliss). Next there is satisfaction and relief, as the following eight lines pay tribute to Hedges' accomplishments and celebrate his good fortune in having died before his talents and pleasures could desert him. This leads to bitterness, in a parenthetical couplet scorning those who live on though their faculties have expired; and finally to a blend of

---

[61] What survives of the letter, the verse to which Hervey refers, is in Sandon Hall, Harrowby MS 256, Sandon Hall, Stafford, and is printed by Robert Halsband in *The Complete Letters of Lady Mary Wortley Montagu*, II, 112–13. Hedges (1688–1737) was MP for three Cornish constituencies successively from 1722 till his death, and Treasurer and Receiver General to the Prince of Wales. See *The History of Parliament: The House of Commons 1715–54*, ed. by Romney Sedgwick, 2 vols (London: HMSO, 1970), II, 125.

[62] SRO, 941/47/2, p. 57 (23 June 1737), printed in *Complete Letters*, II, 113. The letter in which Montagu used the phrase 'raised my Imagination' appears not to have survived. Hervey had already referred to it in a letter dated 18 June 1737 (SRO, 941/47/2, p. 54; printed in *Complete Letters*, II, 111–12 (p. 112)).

compliment and irony in the double-edged homage to Montagu as writer of Hedges' epitaph.[63] Hervey could also express himself pungently in prose, as two images that follow the verse lines indicate: 'let us meet as often as we can before we grow to be our own Ghosts, and become the walking Sepulchres of our own Merits and Pleasures'. But it was verse that seems best to have enabled him to put into words the complex feelings that the news of Hedges' death gave him, feelings that must have reminded him sharply of his own physical decline. So intensely did Hervey feel on the question that, in a letter to Algarotti about three months later, he expanded his response to Montagu into a poem of thirty-six lines, omitting the double-edged compliment and honouring his dead colleague at length.[64] It is not possible to say with certainty whether or not this too constitutes EEV, for the only copy that survives is in the hand of an amanuensis, but the poem is sufficiently different, and on a subject sufficiently emotive for Hervey, to make it likely. Near the end, for example, he expressed his sense of the bearing that Hedges' death had on him:

> So could I live, and so though early dye,
> Let none profane my Funerals with a Sigh,
> No ill-Judged fond Regret, no streaming Eye.

It is best regarded as one of Hervey's responses, in letters to two of his most intimate friends, to a topic that would not leave him alone.

This discussion of Hervey's EEV raises the questions of how seriously he took it, and how seriously it is to be taken. On the one hand, his letter-books suggest that he meant the letters they contain to be published, presumably after his death, especially because he took the trouble to annotate and correct them in his own hand. On the other, he did not keep copies of any of his letters to Montagu or most of those to Algarotti, and even his letters to the Fox brothers are incompletely represented, those of his letters that survive in autograph form having been passed on to his family after his death. To some extent, his attitude to the extempore verse that he embedded in letters probably reflects his attitude to his verse in general, as an aristocrat who did not write for money and to whom poetry came easily. But this does not mean it should not be taken seriously. Not only has his reception history hamstrung proper recognition of his merits as a poet, but extempore verse is itself rarely

---

[63] The final section here echoes the ideas, and a little of the vocabulary, in Hervey's 'Monimia to Philocles', first published in Dublin in 1726, and quoted here from Sandon Hall, Harrowby MS 255, pp. 79–88, probably transcribed by Montagu from a copy made available to her by Hervey. Monimia considers acting 'the Roman part':

> But coward-like irresolute I wait
> Time's tardy aid, nor dare to rush on fate;
> Perhaps may linger on life's latest stage,
> Survive thy cruelties, and fall by age.

[64] SRO, 941/47/4, p. 614 (28 September 1737).

taken seriously. More research is needed on the role played by verse in letters in general and by EEV in particular. Does the popularity of verse quotation in letters coincide with development of the letter as a publishable and collectable artefact? How is EEV related to gender, social class, and education? How typical is Hervey's use of EEV for intense relationships and emotions lying on the margins of respectability? Some of the interest of Hervey's EEV is biographical, but—and here its relation to his published verse is of positive value—it also has a literary dimension. I hope that this article will help establish EEV as a concept and stimulate the necessary archival research. I also hope it provides a clear idea of the range of extempore verse that Hervey embedded in letters, of its expressiveness, and of Hervey's value as a poet.

LOUGHBOROUGH UNIVERSITY   BILL OVERTON

TRANSCENDING TIME AND SPACE: BARRY MACSWEENEY'S EXPERIMENTAL ODES OF THE 1970s

Introduction

What you're getting in fact was the facets of a diamond, like the facets of a stone, like complete shape, like Gaudier-Brzeska's sculpture. They were dealing with shape directly. I'd never dealt with shape before, in fact what I'd dealt with was content, that was the actual shape. What you've got is not the background to the poem—in fact most poems are the background to what really should be said—what you've got is the high force energy, the compressed centre.[1]

When the British poet Barry MacSweeney made the above statement in 1978, he was referring to the poems of his collection *Odes: 1971–1978*.[2] By his own admission, in regard to its focus on 'shape', MacSweeney felt that this collection marked a distinct departure from his earlier writing. His allusion to the work of the sculptor Henri Gaudier-Brzeska, who, along with both Wyndham Lewis and Ezra Pound, was one of the founding members of the short-lived British Vorticist group, suggests a view of lyric poetry in which, to appropriate and extrapolate from Gaudier-Brzeska's own words, the emotional content is derived 'solely from the arrangement of surfaces'.[3] Moreover, MacSweeney's 'compressed centre' calls to mind Pound's notion of the poetic 'image' as being that 'which presents an intellectual and emotional complex in an instant of time', the complexity of which 'gives that sense of sudden liberation; that sense of freedom from time limits and space limits; that sense of sudden growth, which we experience in the presence of the greatest works of art'.[4] Through such comparisons, it is possible to situate MacSweeney's collection in the broad tradition of visual poetry of the twentieth century. However, on the back cover of the original Trigram edition of the *Odes* collection, MacSweeney reproduces a definition of the ode form from the fifth edition of *Webster's Collegiate Dictionary*, in which it is described as a 'poem suited to be set to music and sung or chanted'. In this manner, MacSweeney reveals a tension between the self-proclaimed visual orientation of his odes and the musical origins of the form. During the decade in which they were composed, the members of the British Poetry Revival movement, a loose group of experimental writers

---

[1] Barry MacSweeney, 'Interview with Eric Mottram', *Poetry Information*, 18, Interview Issue, ed. by Peter Hodgkiss (Winter/Spring 1977–78), 21–39 (p. 36).

[2] Barry MacSweeney, *Odes: 1971–1978* (London: Trigram Press, 1978).

[3] Henri Gaudier-Brzeska, 'Vortex (Written from the Trenches): July 1915', *Blast: Review of the Great English Vortex*, ed. by Wyndham Lewis, 2: War Number (July 1915), 33–34 (p. 34) (facsimile edn with foreword by Bradford Morrow (Santa Barbara: Black Sparrow Press, 1981)).

[4] Ezra Pound, 'A Retrospect', in *Literary Essays of Ezra Pound*, ed. by T. S. Eliot (London: Faber and Faber, 1954), pp. 3–14 (p. 4).

Modern Language Review, 110 (2015), 399–421
© Modern Humanities Research Association 2015

who came together during the 1960s and 1970s, actively sought to adopt and promote innovative forms of poetry in opposition to the more traditional forms espoused by the Movement group of the 1950s. As a member of this experimental movement, MacSweeney looked back to the inventive practices of both the Romantics and several earlier twentieth-century Modernist poets in order to create a form of ode-writing in which, Clive Bush believes, 'the deep history of the language' is explored.[5] Specifically, they reveal a shift in the nature of poetic form during the twentieth century that has seen poetry move away from its musical origins and towards a visual impetus. The first aim of this piece will be to discuss how the visual elements of both MacSweeney's 1978 *Odes* collection and a poetry poster entitled *Ode to Coal* that Mac-Sweeney designed in collaboration with the visual artist Michael Chaplin in 1978 are implicated within this twentieth-century reorientation.[6] Conversely, the second aim of this discussion will be to evaluate the lyrical nature of the poems and their connection to the historical evolution of the ode form in general. Ultimately, we shall see that though visual elements abound in the poems, MacSweeney never entirely abandons the musical origins of the ode form. Instead, he explores the interaction of these two material planes and achieves a form of poetic simultaneity: a moment in which G. E. Lessing's polarizing definitions of poetry as a temporal art form and of painting as a spatial one become inadequate.[7]

'facets of a diamond'

With regard to the visual alignment of MacSweeney's odes, his reference to the work of Gaudier-Brzeska in the opening quotation of this article is worth detailed analysis, primarily because of the difficulty of comprehending such an analogy between sculpture and poetic form and, secondly, due to the way in which such a comparison locates MacSweeney's odes in the wider tradition of early twentieth-century visual art. Gaudier-Brzeska was born on 4 October 1891 near Orléans, France. The son of a carpenter, the young Henri Gaudier (the appended 'Brzeska' was appropriated from his close friend Sophie Brzeska, whom he met in Paris in 1910) showed an early academic promise, gaining two scholarships to study first language and then business in Britain in 1906 and 1907 respectively. It was not until 1911, being partly inspired by what Roger Cole has described as 'the artistic opportunities which he antici-pated' occurring in the British capital, that Gaudier-Brzeska finally moved to

    [5] Clive Bush, *Out of Dissent: A Study of Five Contemporary British Poets* (London: Talus Editions, 1997), p. 373.
    [6] See Figure 6 below.
    [7] G. E. Lessing, 'Laokoon', in *Selected Prose Works of G. E. Lessing*, ed. by Edward Bell, trans. by E. C. Beasley and Helen Zimmern (London: George Bell and Sons, 1890), pp. 7–169 (pp. 19–33).

London on a permanent basis. In July 1914, after the commencement of the First World War, Gaudier-Brzeska left Britain to enlist in the French army. Less than a year later, on 5 June 1915, he was killed during a battle in the village of Neuville-Saint-Vaast.[8]

It was during the three years in which he lived in London that he came into contact with Pound and Lewis and helped to found the Vorticist movement. Of the group as a whole, William C. Wees has claimed that 'As a visual style, Vorticism can be pinned down to a particular way of juxtaposing abstract, geometrical shapes.'[9] In the work of Gaudier-Brzeska this is certainly a notable feature. Refering to his early charcoal drawings of human figures, Horace Brodsky claims that Gaudier-Brzeska 'resorts to the simple flat planes introduced by the Cubists' and that such 'studies have a chopped-out wooden effect, very fashionable in 1912'.[10] An example of such a figure can be seen in a letter that Gaudier-Brzeska sent to Sophie in 1911 (Figure 1).[11]

In another letter sent to Sophia in the following year, the artist describes this technique: 'instead of drawing the figure straight away [. . .] I draw square boxes altering the size, one for each plane, and then suddenly by drawing a few lines between the boxes [. . .] the statue appears'.[12] We can also see the influence of this practice in his wartime sketch *Machine-Gun in Action* (1915),[13] which owes something to both Jacob Epstein's *The Rock Drill* (1913) and perhaps Wyndham Lewis's cover for the second issue of *Blast* (1915).[14] Here, inorganic geometric shapes are no longer used as compositional guidelines, but represent the abstract contours of the figure in a manner which seems to fuse the body of the gunner with the machine he operates. In his *Self-Portrait* (c. 1913)[15] we can begin to see traces of what Pound called the 'soft bluntness' of Gaudier-Brzeska's sculpture.[16] The face is entirely composed of inorganic shapes whose bright colours seem to deny the influence of natural lighting, but the lines are not quite as harsh as they might be. Instead, they dissect the natural features of the face in a manner which is relatively sympathetic to its organic lines.

[8] Roger Cole, *Burning to Speak: The Life and Art of Henri Gaudier-Brzeska* (Oxford: Phaidon, 1978), p. 14.

[9] William C. Wees, *Vorticism and the English Avant-Garde* (Manchester: Manchester University Press, 1972), p. 6.

[10] Horace Brodzky, 'Introduction', in *Gaudier-Brzeska's Drawings*, ed. by Horace Brodzky (London: Faber and Faber, 1946), pp. 1–5 (p. 2).

[11] The illustrations may be viewed in full colour and in greater detail in the online version of this article, available at www.jstor.org.

[12] Gaudier-Brzeska, 'Letter to Sophie Brzeska', in *Sixty Drawings by Henri Gaudier-Brzeska 1891–1915* (London: Mercury Gallery, 1975), p. 16 (28 November 1912).

[13] Held in the collection of the Musée National d'Art Moderne, Paris.

[14] An image of the entire issue is available online at <http://library.brown.edu/pdfs/1144603354174257.pdf> [accessed 7 October 2014].

[15] Held in the collection of Southampton City Art Gallery.

[16] Ezra Pound, *Gaudier-Brzeska: A Memoir* (London: Clowes, 1939), p. 160.

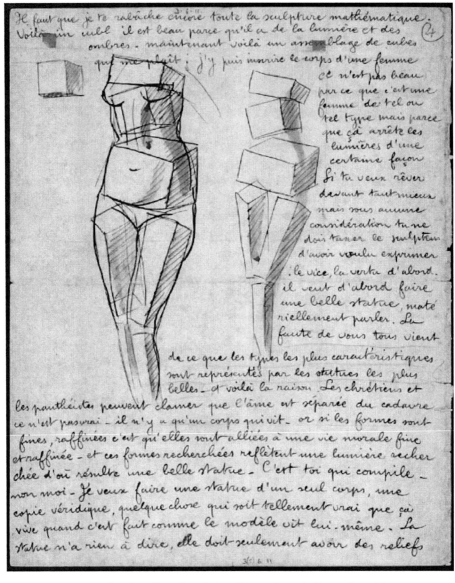

FIG. 1. Gaudier-Brzeska, *Cubist Figure* (1911). Reproduced by permission of the Albert Sloman Library, University of Essex

FIG. 2. Gaudier-Brzeska, *Bird Swallowing a Fish* (c. 1913–14).
Reproduced by permission of the Tate Gallery

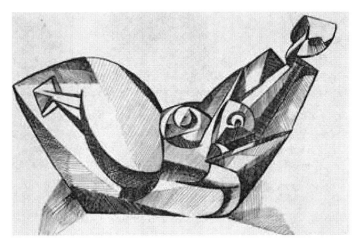

FIG. 3. Gaudier-Brzeska, sketch of
Bird Swallowing a Fish. Reproduced by permission
of Kettle's Yard, University of Cambridge

The impact of this technique can also be seen in Gaudier-Brzeska's sculptural work if we consider the relationship between his finished *Bird Swallowing a Fish* (c. 1913–14) and a preliminary drawing of the piece (Figures 2 and 3). In both we can once again see the sculptor juxtaposing geometrical shapes, but in the preliminary drawing the effect of this technique is more overt. Due to Gaudier-Brzeska's depiction of the influence of a light source shining down on the piece from the left of the drawing, the sketch of the sculpture reveals itself as being exclusively a composite of lines and shapes. The drawing

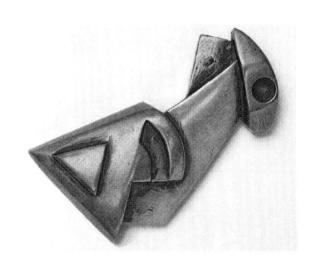

FIGS. 4 and 5. Gaudier-Brzeska, *Ornament* (1914) and *Fish* (1914). Both reproduced by permission of the Tate Gallery

actually more closely resembles a mineral deposit formed by natural geological processes—a multifaceted crystalline body—than the eponymous bird and fish. This effect is diminished in the final piece, which appears to be comprised of an even smaller number of shapes. To some extent the straight line seems to give way to the curve, and the overall effect is more obviously organic. Pound claims that, towards the end of his career, Gaudier-Brzeska came to the conclusion that 'combinations of abstract or inorganic forms exclusively, were more suitable for painting than for sculpture', partly because 'in painting one can have a much greater complexity, a much greater number of form units than in sculpture' and also because modern machinery has already 'used up so many of the fine combinations of three dimensional inorganic forms that there is little use in experimenting with them in sculpture'.[17]

This last point seems particularly pertinent when we look at such pieces as the totemic *Ornament* (1914) or the diminutive *Fish* (1914), both of which vaguely resemble the components of an industrial machine (Figures 4 and 5).

[17] Pound, *Gaudier-Brzeska*, p. 16.

A 'structureless matrix'

To begin to understand how the interplay of organic, natural lines and inorganic, industrial shapes in Gaudier-Brzeska's work is analogous to the form of MacSweeney's odes we should first consider the poetry poster that Mac-Sweeney designed in collaboration with the visual artist Mike Chaplin in 1978 (Figure 6). Both elements of the *Ode to Coal* poster, Chaplin's image and MacSweeney's poem, are evocative of Gaudier-Brzeska's work, though in different ways. The majority of the poster is dominated by Chaplin's image of a pithead at a colliery. In the foreground of the picture, which was based on a wax rubbing of an etching plate created by Chaplin in the early 1970s, nearly all of the compositional elements operate on a stringently vertical axis. Dark lines stretch from the bottom of the colliery—implying rather than demarcating the mechanical lines of the pithead—and reach up to the colliery crank wheels, which are composed of straight spokes that are not penned in by any circular circumference and which radiate from a central absence. They appear as twin suns rising, or falling, over the distant horizon of the piece. Over this perpendicular foundation is inscribed a second, more textural tier which resembles rough charcoal shading. Thick black vertical bands are disrupted by inverted arches and placed alongside beams of a grainy consistency. Within this layer, which dominates the central third of the poster, lines collide and intersect in a way that makes it difficult to discern architectural shape within this mass of texture. Amongst all this saturated space, the only clearly delineated shape is the pit lift and its shaft, which are both notable by their absence of texture. All this is contrasted with the simple, clean parabolas of the brown hills in the background of the image, which rise up above the more jagged and grainy foothills but never surpass the height of the pithead itself. Here we have an interaction between organic and inorganic lines, but the clearly incised facets that are characteristic of Gaudier-Brzeska's sculpture are absent.

However, as we follow the mineshaft's lift down into the subterranean depths of the piece, we discover MacSweeney's contribution to the composition depicted as a rich seam of words beneath the pithead. The poem appears as a series of disproportionate word clusters, or nodes, which form a rough horizontal wedge across the page. It is composed of various references to different types of coal ('lignite', 'anthracite', 'vitrain', 'cannel'), descriptions of coal's various physical characteristics ('lustrous | vitrain', 'conchoidal fracture | structure', 'burns well'), and statements about the atomic properties of carbon ('atomic number 6', 'valency of four'), which, partly due to a complete lack of punctuation, do not immediately indicate the order in which they should be read. One possible way to resolve this issue is by considering Chaplin's belief that MacSweeney used a graph that described the diminishing level of British coal production in the post-war period as a template for the poem.

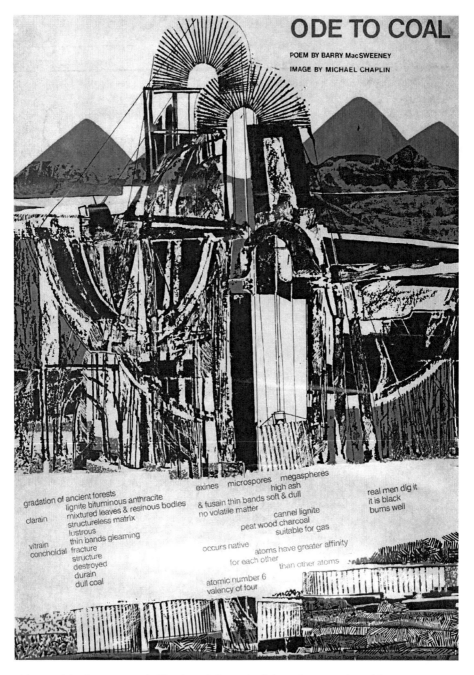

FIG. 6. MacSweeney and Chaplin, *Ode to Coal* (1978). Reproduced by permission of the MacSweeney estate and Mr Mike Chaplin (http://www.mikechaplin.com/)

This opinion, which Chaplin has shared with me in private correspondence, would suggest that the length of any given line in the poem corresponds to the level of coal output for a given year as depicted on MacSweeney's graph. Regrettably, Chaplin is unsure as to whether the graph that MacSweeney used related to the national annual output of coal or to that of a single pit, but as the poem is twenty-seven lines in length, we might draw the conclusion that each line of the poem represents a year of production between Clement Atlee's nationalization of the British coal industry in 1947 and the miner's strike of 1974. If we take each of the poem's three sections and rotate them to the left by ninety degrees we can see that the lines do form a graph that roughly correlates to the general decline in British coal production between the forties and the seventies. Without knowing the specific graph that MacSweeney used as his template for the poem, it is difficult to confirm whether or not this was what he intended; nonetheless, this view of the poem clearly implies at least one method of reading. If the length of the poem's lines are meant to represent a fall in coal production, then it is necessary for us to see the poem not as a series of nodes in a rough wedge shape that stretches across the bottom of the page, but rather as being comprised of three distinct stanzas whose size decreases from left to right. Only in this way can we rotate the three stanzas by ninety degrees and create the graph described above. Consequently, this would seem to suggest that we read the left stanza first, the middle stanza second, and the right stanza last. Furthermore, if we were to reorganize the poem to imply this reading scheme more overtly, we might stack the stanzas on top of one another—the left one on the top, the middle one beneath this, and then the right one at the bottom—and in so doing we would have created a poem that in its form strongly resembles many of the poems of the *Odes* collection.

Though this conclusion is convincing to some degree, it does raise the question of why, if this was MacSweeney's intention for the piece, he did not depict the poem in this manner in the final poster design. In the context of the rest of the poster, the nodal structure of the poem actually leads us away from this perception of its form. Instead, the presentation of the poem makes us view MacSweeney's words as the coal within the ground that Chaplin's pit-head seeks to mine. In this interpretation of the poem's form, the shapes and groupings of the words are not uniform because they seek to imitate the natural, unordered formation of coal. In this way, we can see that Macsweeney's poem operates in two distinct visual manners, both of which resemble several of Guillaume Apollinaire's poems from his collection *Calligrammes: Poems of Peace and War 1913–1916*. With this collection, Apollinaire began to create poems whose typeface and spatial arrangement on the page were reflective of their semantic content. For example, in the poem 'Il pleut' the five lines of the piece are set on a horizontal tangent so that they cascade, like the rain of the title, down to the next section of the poem.[18] Here the words of the poem become, like MacSweeney's *Ode to Coal* poem, visually dynamic. In the wake of the publication of Apollinaire's collection, 'calligramme' has now become a collective term for any poem that attempts to mimic this visual abandonment of linear structure, seeking instead what S. I. Lockerbie has described as 'a type of structure that would give the impression of a full and instant awareness within one moment of space-time'.[19]

Lockerbie's belief that visual poetry, such as the calligramme, can give the impression of one moment of space-time is predicated upon a refutation of what W. J. T. Mitchell has called Lessing's erroneous conclusion that poetry is solely 'an art in time, motion, and action' and that painting is 'an art of space, stasis, and arrested action'.[20] Joseph Frank clarifies Lessing's position in his 1945 essay 'Spatial Form in Modern Literature':

Form in the plastic arts, according to Lessing, is necessarily spatial, because the visible aspect of objects can best be presented juxtaposed in an instant of time. Literature, on the other hand, makes use of language, composed of a succession of words proceeding through time; and it follows that literary form, to harmonize with the essential quality of its medium, must be based primarily on some form of narrative sequence.[21]

Frank argues that the work of such Modernist writers as Eliot, Pound, and Joyce moved 'in the direction of spatial form' and goes on to say that 'the reader is intended to apprehend their work spatially, in a moment of time, rather than as a sequence'.[22] Such a notion seems to recall Pound's view that the poetic image gives the reader a 'sense of freedom from time limits and space limits', and the proliferation of 'spatial form' in Modernist literature is certainly notable. Apollinaire's calligrammes can, perhaps due to the influence of Cubism (itself a form of art that opposed Lessing's polarization), be seen as one result of this trend. In his essay on Stéphane Mallarmé, the nineteenth-century French Symbolist poet whose work would go on to inspire the practitioners of the Cubist, Futurist, and Vorticist styles, Jean Khalfa claims that 'With Mallarmé it had become clear that poetry had broken its essential link with time. Poetry now seems evidently linked with space, and

---

[18] Guillaume Apollinaire, 'Il pleut', in *Calligrammes: Poems of Peace and War 1913–1916*, ed. by S. I. Lockerbie, trans. by Anne Hyde Greet (Berkeley: University of California Press, 2004), pp. 100–01 (p. 100).

[19] S. I. Lockerbie, 'Introduction', in *Calligrammes: Poems of Peace and War 1913–1916*, pp. 1–20 (p. 3).

[20] W. J. T. Mitchell, 'Going Too Far with the Sister Arts', in *Space, Time, Image, Sign: Essays on Literature and the Visual Arts*, ed. by James A. W. Heffernan (New York: Peter Lang, 1987), pp. 1–18 (p. 1).

[21] Joseph Frank, 'Spatial Form in Modern Literature: An Essay in Two Parts', *Sewanee Review*, 53 (Spring 1945), 221–40 (p. 223).

[22] Ibid., p. 225.

rather than music, the companion art is now painting.' However, he is also quick to point out that the calligramme is only a simplistic manifestation of this shift:

At this point it is important to dispel an illusion, involuntarily created by Apollinaire with his famous calligrammes, poems whose visual appearance mimics the object they refer to, by a clever choice of words and line length and a special arrangement of lines on the page. Such games are ironical variations on the representative (or mimetic) idea of poetry, their semantic content often overflows the boundaries of their simple form and thus demonstrates the inadequacy of such a model.[23]

Our first interpretation of *Ode to Coal*'s form, referring to the graph of coal production, suggested that the true semantic content of the poem is a discussion of the degeneration of the British coal industry during the 1970s. However, this interpretation of the poem's form might, as Khalfa suggests, be seen as an ironical variation 'on the representative (or mimetic) idea of poetry'. On the other hand, if we were to accuse our second interpretation of the poem's form (in which the shape of the poem was thought to imitate a seam of coal) of the same level of irony, we would hit upon a problem. Khalfa claims that the appearance of a calligramme 'mimics the object' it refers to, and in the case of our second interpretation this opinion seriously impairs our ability to discern the true semantic content of the poem as revealed by our first interpretation. In our first interpretation, the shape of the poem mimics a graph that reveals a decline in coal production, but in our second interpretation the poem simply mimics coal. Without recourse to further contextual information, we would not necessarily be able to infer the meaning implied by the first interpretation from the form of the second. This would seem to support Khalfa's notion that the semantic content of calligrammes 'often overflows the boundaries of their simple form'. Though Khalfa is correct in this particular instance, it must also be acknowledged that the form of MacSweeney's poem actually attempts to offer us something more complex than a simple calligramme. This is because the referential object of the poem, the demise of the British coal industry, does not lie on the page. Each of the pieces of information MacSweeney includes about coal and carbon in the poem certainly has semantic content, but they do not individually, or even when taken together in the case of our second interpretation, reveal the meaning of the poem: they only contribute to that meaning. Now we can begin to see why MacSweeney drew an analogy between his poems and Gaudier-Brzeska's sculpture. For MacSweeney, the statements about coal in the poem are all comparable to the facets of a diamond because such incisions are made in order to optimize the play of light within gemstones. Light is

[23] Jean Khalfa, 'Art Speaking Volumes', in *The Dialogue between Painting and Poetry: Livres d'artistes 1874–1999*, ed. by Jean Khalfa (Cambridge: Black Apollo Press, 2001), pp. 11–36 (p. 28).

not a material property of such stones. In fact, the measurable brilliance of a given stone is achieved, as Gaudier-Brzeska said of his sculpture, through the 'arrangement of its surfaces'. The interaction between the form and the content of MacSweeney's poem, between its 'shape' and its 'compressed centre', seeks to imitate this relationship. The true semantic content of the poem is not materially present on the page. Instead, we are asked to infer its presence through the fragmentary glimpses we are given of it. The lines of the poem that read 'mixtured leaves & resinous bodies | structureless matrix' can be seen as an indication of this technique. In geology, a matrix is a mass of fine-grained rock in which crystals are embedded. More generally, it is an environment or material in which something develops. MacSweeney's words are the matrix in which the poem's meaning is embedded.

'Time is a jagged mark upon the wrist'

In order to understand the manner in which the poems of MacSweeney's 1978 *Odes* also utilize this same technique, let us look at the first 'Chatterton Ode' of the collection. Thomas Chatterton, an early Romantic poet and literary forger, was born in Bristol in 1752 and died at only eighteen years of age after drinking a fatal dose of arsenic. For the later Romantic poets, his premature death became a collective metaphor for wasted talent and poetic pathos.[24] Echoing this idea, Eric Mottram has suggested that the recurrence of Chatterton in MacSweeney's poetry points to both 'the possibility of curtailed talent' and a 'sacrificial society which wastes what it cannot consume'.[25] Mottram here defines the perceived semantic content of MacSweeney's first 'Chatterton Ode'. It remains for us to discuss how this content is revealed by the form of the poem. The poem comprises four word clusters which decrease in line length as they move down the page. It begins with the line: 'Time is a jagged mark upon the wrist'.[26] Expressed in this statement is a conception of temporal termination enacted through material inscription. In a manner that contradicts Lessing's view of poetry as a purely temporal form of art, this line seems to describe time not as a transitional sequence of moments but as a termination achieved through a pictorial metaphor. The 'jagged mark', which calls to mind suicide through a cutting of the wrist, reveals something of MacSweeney's view of the artist's life, which he sees as intrinsically linked with violent death. However, this line cannot be a direct reference to Chatterton

---

[24] Notable poems from the Romantic period that feature Chatterton include Samuel Taylor Coleridge's 'A Monody on the Death of Chatterton' (1796), William Wordsworth's 'Resolution and Independence' (1807), Percy Bysshe Shelley's 'Adonais' (1821), and John Keats's sonnet 'To Chatterton' (1848).

[25] Eric Mottram, 'Reading Barry MacSweeney's *Odes*', *Maxy's Journal*, 3 (1979), 28–39 (pp. 28–29).

[26] Barry McSweeney, 'Chatterton Ode', in *Odes*, p. 16.

because, as noted above, Chatterton died from a fatal overdose of arsenic. This lack of fidelity to the biographical details of the poem's proclaimed subject becomes more confusing when we consider the phrase that directly follows it: 'See | the child does not weep'. Because of the young age at which he died, Chatterton was often referred to as a 'child' or 'boy' by the later Romantics, so this would seem to be a reference to him. Moreover, the line in the second stanza in which MacSweeney writes that blood is held 'in | side an acorne-coppe' would appear to be an allusion to two lines in Chatterton's poem 'Ælla: A Tragycal Enterlude': 'Comme, wyth acorne-coppe and thorne, | Drayne mie hartys bloode awaie.'[27] Subsequently, the third stanza of MacSweeney's ode seems to continue this theme with a reference to the 'yellow buds' of acorns that are held in 'his making fingers'. The final stanza comprises two lines, each with only one word: 'Bread | Cyanide'. Once again, cyanide was not the poison that caused Chatterton's death, so this cannot be a direct reference to him. Instead, the juxtaposition of these two substances, bread that nurtures life and cyanide that destroys it, seems to offer a comment about literary immortality. Poison might destroy young talent, but in Chatterton's case his premature death has also granted him a level of immortality. The fact that all the constituent elements of the poem do not precisely recall the circumstances of Chatterton's life and death points to the conclusion that the subject of the ode is not truly Chatterton, or rather that Chatterton's life is but one illustration of the poem's real focus. Instead, just as Mottram suggests, the true focus of the poem is 'the possibility of curtailed talent'—a topic which, as will be discussed later in this article, recurs in MacSweeney's odes to Jim Morrison. Moreover, the 'jagged mark' of the poem, the cause of the poet's violent demise, is both a termination and, ironically, a means of achieving longevity. Death leads to life and inertia leads to continuation. In this way, MacSweeney's line plays with ideas both of life and death and of space and time. As with the *Ode to Coal* poem, the lack of shared thematic focus between the constituent lines—along with the inclusion of details that do not quite match the life of the poem's subject—pushes the poem beyond the particular in order to reveal a more universal theme.

As to how MacSweeney managed to achieve this effect in his odes, we should reflect on Basil Bunting's advice to young poets: 'Put your poem away till you forget it, then: [. . .] Cut out every word you dare. [. . .] Do it again a week later, and again. Never explain—your reader is as smart as you.'[28] Though the critic

---

[27] Thomas Chatterton, 'Ælla: A Tragycal Enterlude', ll. 1010–16, in *The Complete Works of Thomas Chatterton*, ed. by Donald S. Taylor and Benjamin B. Hoover (Oxford: Clarendon Press, 1971), pp. 174–228 (p. 211).

[28] Basil Bunting, 'Bunting's Advice to Young Poets', *Basil Bunting Poetry Centre* <http://www.dur.ac.uk/basil-bunting-poetry.centre/> [accessed 26 February 2013]. The text appears in the section entitled 'Some Bunting Quotes'.

Rebecca A. Smith has credibly questioned the level of Bunting's influence over MacSweeney, she has also pointed out that 'Bunting's advice on condensing the line was occasionally adopted' by him, and specifically makes reference to MacSweeney's *Brother Wolf* (1972) as an example of this.[29] *Brother Wolf*, which comprises a series of poems on the topic of Chatterton's life, was written around the same time that many of the odes were presumably started. Certainly, 'Flame Ode: for Elaine' (p. 13), 'Wing Ode' (p. 14), 'New Ode' (p. 15), the second 'Chatterton Ode' (p. 21), and 'Jim Morrison Ode' (p. 17) were all published as a collection by Transgravity in the same year,[30] while five more odes, including the 'Chatterton Ode' discussed above, were published the following year.[31] In her article, Smith also acknowledges MacSweeney's own brief description of Bunting's influence: 'Began job as reporter on local evening paper. Met Basil Bunting, poet [. . .]. Showed Bunting *Walk* poem, it came back sliced down to about 4 lines and a note: Start again from there. My first real lesson.'[32] Smith is right to question the level of Bunting's influence over MacSweeney, but, as evidenced by the condensed forms that recur in the *Odes* collection, I suspect MacSweeney does owe something to Bunting, and also perhaps, as Smith suggests, to his work as a journalist, in which brevity was a constant requirement. The manuscript copies of some of the odes, held in the Robinson Library's Special Collections in Newcastle, reveal the extent to which MacSweeney condensed his poems. For example, let us consider 'Torpedo'.[33] This poem has a similar shape to the 'Chatterton Ode' we have just discussed, though its meaning is not as easily understood. On an initial reading, the poem appears to demonstrate a preoccupation with phallic imagery: 'Make your naked pencil mine', 'Lavender torpedo', 'suck | seed'. The poem offers us little in the way of shared semantic content to explain why this should be so, but if we look at other drafts of the poem we can begin to make sense of it. Consider an early draft entitled 'Ode: Lead in Yr Pencil'.[34] For the most part, this draft is identical to the published version, but it does deviate in certain ways. The most significant of these deviations is the inclusion of two additional sections. The first reads:

> Blood of the poet
> on Eric Mottram's
> lips

[29] Rebecca A. Smith, 'Barry MacSweeney and the Bunting Influence: "A key figure in his literary universe"?', *Jacket Magazine*, 35 (2008) <http://jacketmagazine.com/35/index.shtml> [accessed 26 February 2013]. See Smith's third note for the discussion of *Brother Wolf*.

[30] Barry MacSweeney, *Five Odes* (London: Transgravity, 1972).

[31] Barry MacSweeney, *Six Odes* (London: [n. pub.], 1973).

[32] Barry MacSweeney, 'The Autobiography of Barry MacSweeney', in *The Boy from the Green Cabaret Tells of his Mother* (London: New Authors, 1968), pp. i–ii (p. i).

[33] Barry MacSweeney, 'Torpedo', in *Odes*, p. 39.

[34] Newcastle, Robinson Library, Special Collections, Barry MacSweeney Papers, fol. BM 1/4/3.

as he chews a
broken whisky glass.
He bleeds blood
of the poet.

Eric Mottram was a friend of MacSweeney's and, like MacSweeney, was a key figure in the British Poetry Revival. Both advocated experimental and Modernist forms of poetry over more traditional received forms, and both thought that the dominant trends in British poetry since the 1930s were not able to 'tolerate an art that went beyond a leisure-hours consumer inclination to rapid reading'. Moreover, both were part of a group of poets who in the early 1970s managed to gain control of the British Poetry Society. Mottram describes this situation in his article on the Revival:

The Poetry Society, which used to be considered the centre of reaction and tediously restricted conservatism, moved into the twentieth century in the early 1970s with a fresh and innovative organization voted into control by people deeply concerned with making it a centre of the Revival.[35]

This situation elicited a negative response from the more conservative elements of the Society. Mottram goes on to write that 'It was not long before the Arts Council moved in to quash this action, by threatening to withdraw funds unless its own unelected representatives were placed on the committee of management and certain members of the organization sacked' (Mottram, p. 20). One of the contributing factors that led to the schism between the Revivalists and their conservative counterparts was Mottram's inflammatory editorship of the Society's journal, *Poetry Review*, between 1971 and 1977. Peter Barry has examined this tense situation in his book, *Poetry Wars*. In particular, Barry refers to the cover of a Mottram edition of the *Poetry Review* that outraged many members of the Society:

The second Mottram issue (62:4, wrongly designated 61:4 on the title page) was for winter 1971–2 and had a cover which was described by Michelene Victor in *Time Out*, January 14–20 1972 as 'a phallic toad like cover by Jeff Nuttall which would make Kenneth Grahame blush with pleasure'. It did make some people blush, though (mostly) not with pleasure [. . .], for the complaining letters which were now being received often mentioned it.[36]

This cover features two figures, one on the front and one on the back. In his book Barry asserts that Bill Griffiths has identified the figure on the front cover as Mottram himself, owing to the fact that it wears the collegiate tie

[35] Eric Mottram 'The British Poetry Revival, 1960–75', in *New British Poetries: The Scope of the Possible*, ed. by Peter Barry and Robert Hampson (Manchester: Manchester University Press, 1993), pp. 15–50 (pp. 26 and 19–20).
[36] Peter Barry, *Poetry Wars: British Poetry of the 1970s and the Battle of Earls Court* (Cambridge: Salt, 2007), p. 24.

of King's College, where Mottram taught. The figure on the reverse, Griffiths also suggests, is meant to represent an opposing member of the Society.[37] Both phallic figures expel dark clouds of miasma into the air and ardently clutch loose manuscript sheets in their three-fingered hands. MacSweeney was a firm supporter of Mottram both as a poet and as editor of the *Poetry Review*. In his own 1979 article on the Revival, he wrote that in the history of the Poetry Society 'Mottram's editorship goes down as one of the most courageous and enterprising ever'.[38] In addition, Barry demonstrates with reference to an archival document that it was MacSweeney who instigated a mass resignation of the radical members of the Poetry Society in the wake of Mottram's dismissal from his position as editor.[39] Therefore, we can see that Mottram's presence in the draft of 'Ode: Lead in Yr Pencil' is built upon a relationship of close affinity between the two men. MacSweeney's opening line, 'make yr naked pencil mine', is a statement of solidarity and admiration. Moreover, the phallic imagery in the poem might be an ekphrastic allusion to the aforementioned cover of the *Poetry Review*. One reading of the poem might be that MacSweeney saw Mottram as the 'lavender torpedo', a violently masculine figure, aimed directly at the more conservative members of the Poetry Society.

However, the manuscript draft of the poem also discredits this interpretation to some degree. The second section that is included in the manuscript version, but which was ultimately cut from the final draft, comes directly after the section which refers to Mottram and reads:

> Oil is lubricant
>   friend.
> So are you,
>   slippier. Eels
> can't match the movement.
>
>   4lb breaking strain
>   is far too light
>   for you, Yorkshire
>   grayling.

We might easily see this as continuing the ideas of the previous section in that it seems to have been written in praise of Mottram. Yet, in addressing a 'Yorkshire | grayling', MacSweeney seems to contradict this, as Mottram was not from Yorkshire. Here, as with the 'Chatterton Ode' discussed above,

---

[37] Ibid.

[38] Barry MacSweeney, 'The British Poetry Revival 1965–1979', *South East Arts Review*, 9 (Spring 1979), 33–46 (p. 43).

[39] Peter Barry, 'Is There a Poet in This Archive?', *Archives: The Journal of the British Records Association*, 35.122, special issue on 'Literary Archives', ed. by Jennie Hill and Will Slocombe (April 2010), 58–64.

MacSweeney adds details which obstruct the possibility of the poem having a single, fixed referential object: a point that is further demonstrated by his omission of the Mottram stanzas in the final version. Instead of this, the true semantic content of MacSweeney's poem is a forceful refutation of received forms of poetry and a violent desire to oppose the proponents of such forms. Once again, this theme is insinuated rather than explained by the paratactic 'facets' of MacSweeney's compositional style.

The '(Clear swell | of | breath in | poems.)'

In the first three sections of this article, MacSweeney's experimental odes of the 1970s have been situated within the broad tradition of twentieth-century visual poetry, and their structural continuity with the sculptural work of Gaudier-Brzeska has been examined. One element of MacSweeney's poems that remains to be discussed is their musicality. Though it has been suggested that MacSweeney's poems are part of a wider twentieth-century reorientation of poetic form towards visual art, we must also acknowledge that in MacSweeney's case this reorientation is not achieved through the complete dissolution of the lyrical origins of the ode form. As will be discussed in this final section, in formal terms MacSweeney's poems do resist the internal poetic structure of the received metrical form of the ode; yet, in so doing, MacSweeney positions his work within a tradition of experimental writing that stretches back to the Romantics. In his article on the Revival, MacSweeney describes the key figures in this tradition:

A poetry revolution blossomed hand in hand with its industrial parent in the eighteenth century. As working people of Britain fought to wrest power away from owners, their poetry underwent a massive renaissance: starting with Thomas Chatterton in Bristol and William Blake in London, it went on via Shelley, Byron, Keats, Coleridge and Wordsworth. Our poetry then went into a steady decline, saved only in the first half of this century by the individual brilliance of Basil Bunting, Dylan Thomas, David Jones, Hugh MacDiarmid, and a handful of others.[40]

The first set of figures that MacSweeney refers to are of course the progenitors of the English Romantic tradition. To understand why MacSweeney believed his poetry to be a continuation of the revolutionary writing of these figures, we should consider what they understood the form of the ode to be. As a poetic structure, the ode can be traced back to the ancient Greeks and, later, the Romans. Utilizing a strict rhythmic and metrical structure, the classical ode, as epitomized by Pindar, was split into three distinct sections: strophe, antistrophe, and epode. Each section was chanted in a particular order by different groups of the chorus, who were, at least in the early Greek tradition,

---

[40] 'The British Poetry Revival', p. 33.

accompanied by a musical instrument called the *aulos*. By comparison, the ode in the English tradition has usually lacked such formal definition. In 1918, the critic Robert Shafer stated that 'the [formal] diversity amongst those English poems which have been called by their writers "odes" is bewildering'. Shafer then goes on to describe the ode as a lengthy 'lyrical poem, serious in tone and stately in its structure',[41] and in so doing foreshadows George N. Shuster's 1940 definition that elaborates upon the nature of the ode's 'stately structure': 'By the word "ode" I mean in general a lyric based either upon the model of some classic poem which bore that designation or upon other English poems which go back, directly or indirectly, to imitations of the bards of Greece or Rome.'[42] Moreover, in 1969 John Heath-Stubbs seems to reiterate Shuster's description when he writes: 'The term "ode", then, as used by English Poets, indicates a lyric of a special and formal kind, intended to reproduce the tone of classical Greek and Latin poetry.'[43] The two elements that seem to be echoed throughout these descriptions are the lyrical and mimetic facets of the ode form. Paul D. Sheats has suggested that, during the Romantic period, the ode's 'formal variants (the strict Pindaric, the stanzaic Horatian, and the irregular) had been mastered by Wordsworth, Coleridge, and others'.[44] Underlining this perceived perfecting of received forms by these earlier Romantic poets, John D. Jump has claimed that although 'the Greek themes never ceased to engage the imaginations of Percy Bysshe Shelley [. . .] and John Keats [. . .], both men achieved virtually complete independence of Classical traditions of [the ode] form'.[45] Shuster believes that Shelley was the first major poet to 'cut himself off from the classical humanist tradition', and that many of his odic models are uniquely Romantic, with forms so 'divorced from the basic Horatian quatrain that they survive not as moulds but as amorphous shapes which he sought to cut into patterns suited to his own lyric ideas'.[46] For Shuster, even in Shelley's 'Ode to Naples' and 'Ode to Liberty', which both closely mimic the structure of irregular Pindaric stanzas created by Abraham Cowley in the seventeenth century, such models are 'erroneously employed'.[47] Keats was perhaps even more overtly aberrational in his odic style. In his most famous odes, most of which appeared in a collection published in 1820,[48] Keats dismissed any

---

[41] Robert Shafer, *The English Ode to 1660: An Essay in Literary History* (London: Princeton University Press, 1918), pp. 1 and 3.

[42] George N. Shuster, *The English Ode from Milton to Keats* (New York: Columbia University Press, 1940), p. 6.

[43] John Heath Stubbs, *The Ode* (London: Oxford University Press, 1969), p. 1.

[44] Paul D. Sheats, 'Keats and the Ode', in *The Cambridge Companion to Keats*, ed. by Susan J. Wolfson (Cambridge: Cambridge University Press, 2004), pp. 86–101 (p. 86).

[45] John D. Jump, *The Ode* (London: Methuen, 1974), p. 44.

[46] Shuster, pp. 257–58.

[47] Ibid., p. 260.

[48] John Keats, *'Lamia', 'Isabella', 'The Eve of St. Agnes' and Other Poems* (London: Taylor and Hessey, 1820).

form of conventional odic rhyme structure in favour of a scheme of his own devising (ababcdecde) that may have been inspired by the form of the sonnet. However, what is certainly true is that for both poets the auditory insinuations of a poem (metre, rhyme, rhythm, etc.) were worthy of careful consideration.

The second group of poets that MacSweeney mentions above could roughly be described as Modernist writers, though that categorization is perhaps fraught with difficulties. While there are many similarities between these figures, there are also numerous ways in which they differ from one another. Jones, for instance, never wrote strictly lyrical poetry, whereas Bunting and Thomas often wrote in lyrical modes. Instead, Jones's work consisted of a combination of prose and free verse. However, he does at times reveal a preoccupation with the particular lyrical insinuations of the Welsh language in a manner that is at least partially reminiscent of MacDiarmid's poetic utilization of a 'synthetic Scots' dialect. Of his 1966 poem 'The Sleeping Lord', he says that 'it chances to be a piece that is essentially for the ear rather than the eye'.[49] Thus, even Jones at times displays an interest in the lyrical insinuations of poetry, but this interest never encouraged him to utilize received forms of lyrical verse. Bunting's interest in lyrical poetry is articulated in the first section of 'Bunting's Advice to Young Poets' (the second half of which was quoted above). In this piece Bunting writes: '1. Compose aloud; poetry is a sound. 2. Vary rhythm enough to stir the emotion you want but not so as to lose impetus. 3. Use spoken words and syntax.' Here Bunting inadvertently points to one of the problems of writing lyrical, Modernist poetry in free verse. Given the proliferation of free verse during the twentieth century, and a general lack of fidelity to the internal metrical structures of received forms of poetry, we are faced with the question of how one should judge the musicality of a poem that does not explicitly utilize such structures. Bunting's solution is to place an emphasis on rhythm and the sound of poetry when read aloud. The critic Jon Silkin has suggested that if we consider metre 'to be formalized rhythm, it may be possible to say that while metrical lines of verse have both metre and rhythm, free verse either mixes in, or has no metrical lines, and is rhythmic only'.[50] It is this, Silkin implies, that allows for the great diversity in the range of poetry that can be seen as free verse. MacSweeney's odes do not conform to the metrical patterns adopted by the Romantic writers, though they share something of the same experimental impetus; and MacSweeney himself seems to discredit the notion of a link between Bunting's advice regarding the musicality of poetry and his own collection when he writes: 'When I have read those poems I feel that in fact there's nothing going across,

[49] David Jones, 'Introduction to "The Sleeping Lord"', in 'The Sleeping Lord' and Other Fragments (London: Faber and Faber, 1974), pp. 70–96 (p. 70).
[50] Jon Silkin, 'The Healing Process: Metrical and Free Verse', in The Life of Metrical and Free Verse in Twentieth-Century Poetry (London: Macmillan, 1997), pp. 1–29 (p. 7).

because people are listening to completely new forms to which they've had no kind of introduction at all [. . .]. You can see the complete look of bewilderment.'[51] However, MacSweeney is not suggesting that the poems are devoid of musicality, rather that they are steeped in a music which is unfamiliar to the ear.

The collection's thematic engagement with music is perhaps its most significant acknowledgement of the musicality of the ode form. To explore this idea further, let us look at the most unusual poem of the *Odes* collection. 'Just 22 and I Don't Mind Dying: Official Poetical Biography of Jim Morrison' is the first poem of the sequence and is radically different in form from the rest of the poems in the collection. In fact, in regard to how it looks on the page, it has very little in common with the rest of MacSweeney's odes. Of his Morrison poems in general, MacSweeney writes:

Once I had written the Morrison poems, I was aware that I really could not go back to using the kind of forms I was using in BROTHER WOLF, that sort of more strung-out [. . .] [l]inear form. I couldn't do that. It seemed such a step forward in all sorts of ways—I'd learned to work in a different way. I don't think I've ever read a poem in the English language like Just 22 [. . .] it's very sharp. I knew I couldn't go back and start writing your little lyrical poems again, linear stuff.[52]

When MacSweeney claims that he does not think that he has 'ever read a poem in the English language like Just 22', he is ascribing to his work an experimental impetus that represents the break from the traditional forms of 'linear' and 'lyrical' poetry that has been discussed above. However, that is not to say that the poem does not have a thematic relationship with music. The poem begins with the lines:

> Rock litmus. Titration from Springfield, she
> wore no colour besides, unfashionable & mean, held
> such chemistry in high frond.
> Nothing else to commend her before she died.[53]

This dense, paratactic juxtaposition of cascading images, prefaced only by the poem's title and a dedication to the poet's brother, continues for seventeen stanzas and over four pages. If we attempt a narratological reading of even just this first stanza, we may instantly notice one obvious peculiarity. Despite the piece ostensibly being a biography of Jim Morrison, the first stanza invokes the name of another musician, Dusty Springfield. Between these two figures, MacSweeney intimates a continuum scale measured by the paraphernalia (litmus) and operations (titration) of chemical science. However, the two

---

[51] 'Interview with Eric Mottram', p. 37.

[52] Ibid.

[53] Barry MacSweeney, 'Just 22 and I Don't Mind Dying: Official Poetical Biography of Jim Morrison', in *Odes*, pp. 9–12 (p. 9).

musicians are not polarized on this scale. Springfield, in a description that references the supposed African American nuance of her vocal styling, wears 'no colour', is neither red nor blue, neither acid nor alkali. We are left to make our own decision in regard to Morrison's position on this scale, though surely his infamous lifestyle and early demise would situate him at one of the extremities. These themes do not continue into the next stanza, and in fact each typographical space between the stanzas appears to be a void through which narrative inference and continuity, like sound, cannot pass. What Mac-Sweeney's poem most closely resembles is the literary equivalent of one of Morrison's chemically fuelled nightmare excursions through the hedonistic world of celebrities such as 'Pete Townshend' (p. 10) and 'Keith Richards' (p. 12). A place where 'Palpitating spitfires' (p. 11) are used instead of micro-phones and gaudy 'Fabergé missiles' (p. 10) evoke images of both commercial decadence and incendiary creativity. Moreover, such a comparison is not simply analogical. In an interview with Eric Mottram in 1978, MacSweeney admitted that while writing the first Morrison ode he 'took about 45 Ben-zedrine that day in about 4 hours, with headphones on listening to the Doors records on the turntable'.[54] The result of this dalliance with illicit pharma-ceuticals is a poem which perpetually defers meaning. The poem's subject, as with the poems discussed above, is displaced from the page and we as readers are expected to follow in what appears to be his chaotic wake. Throughout the piece, we are meant to infer Morrison's presence rather than recognize it.

Despite the disparity of structure between 'Just 22 and I Don't Mind Dying' and the rest of the poems of the *Odes* collection, Morrison himself, like Chat-terton, recurs throughout. Like the majority of the poems of the collection, the second 'Jim Morrison Ode' takes the form of a series of disproportion-ate word clusters, or nodes, which decrease in size as they move down the page. It begins with the lines: 'Peristalsis writhes a sudden knot & | hangs himself.'[55] This reference to a violent act of self-destruction seems to recall the suicidal imagery of the first Chatterton ode. Once again, we have a return to the image of the young dead artist, though again we do not have biogra-phical fidelity, since Morrison did not hang himself but is believed to have overdosed on heroin. Peristalsis is the organic contraction of the muscles that line the oesophagus, and in the context of the poem it seems to represent a violent death cry that is anatomical, atonal, and without music: a constrained internal bodily function that cannot be externalized. Bunting once wrote that 'Poetry, like music, is to be heard. It deals in sound—long sounds and short sounds, heavy beats and light beats, the tone relation of vowels, the relations of consonants to one another which are like instrumental colour in music.'

[54] 'Interview with Eric Mottram', p. 36.
[55] Barry MacSweeney, 'Jim Morrison Ode', in *Odes*, p. 17.

He ultimately asserted that 'Poetry lies dead on the page, until some voice brings it to life.'[56] MacSweeney's line reflects on this notion. The music of the young Morrison is constrained by death and the musicality of MacSweeney's poem is hindered by its experimental form. As MacSweeney himself suggested above, all the poems of the *Odes* collection suffer from this same problem, demonstrated by the 'bewildered' looks MacSweeny received after reading the poems out loud.

In order to consider this problem further, let us look at 'Flame Ode'. As Bunting has suggested, this poem is certainly composed of 'long sounds and short sounds, heavy beats and light beats', but there are no continuous, or even measurable, metrical patterns. It is doubtful whether we could even divide it into comprehensible feet. An argument could be made for the rhythmic qualities of various lines, but a rhythmic pattern is not sustained throughout the poem. However, as with the Morrison poems, this piece displays a thematic interest in music. The final line of the poem reads: 'It is really distinct',[57] and in the poem we are given three clear alternatives as to what it is that is 'really distinct': the image of 'Two hawks and a plover', the music of the 'mountain spring', or the '(Clear swell | of | breath in | poems.)'. If we once again consider MacSweeney's technique of revealing the true semantic content of his odes through fragmentary, paratactical word clusters, which he believes to be analogous to both 'the facets of a diamond' and 'Gaudier-Brzeska's sculpture', we can begin to make sense of 'Flame Ode'. The majority of the poem is comprised of a series of pastoral images, the only exception being the parenthetical phrase quoted above. The critic John Lennard has suggested that such parentheses, or lunulae, often mark 'a boundary between two textual states', and that 'Poets use lunulae to register ontological disjuncture'.[58] In 'Flame Ode' this deliberate disjuncture is both overt and also especially pertinent, as a primary means by which we can glean the poem's true semantic content. The two distinct sets of images are linked by the idea of breath, which implies life and therefore resonates with the vitality of the rural images that MacSweeney describes. Moreover, this interaction is foreshadowed by the poem's title, as fire can both be metaphorically linked to life, and also kindled by breath. Here MacSweeney plays with Bunting's belief that 'Poetry lies dead on the page, until some voice brings it to life'. Breath is the means by which music is produced, but it can also limit it. Music, and therefore the reading aloud of poetry, is in essence the interplay of sound and silence mediated by the capacity and capabilities of one's breathing. MacSweeney's point is that silence and the breath are as important to poetry as Bunting's 'heavy beats and light

---

[56] Basil Bunting, *Collected Poems* (London: Fulcrum Press, 1968), rear inner cover.

[57] Barry MacSweeney, 'Flame Ode', in *Odes*, p. 13. Further references are to this page.

[58] John Lennard, *But I Digress: The Exploration of Parentheses in English Printed Verse* (Oxford: Clarendon Press, 1991), p. 242.

beats', and in this way the silence of poetry becomes a palpable force in his poem.

Conclusion

In his essay on the Revival, MacSweeney wrote: 'Literature does not exist in a vacuum. Writers have a definite social function like anyone else in society. The good ones keep language, alive, spirited.'[59] His experiments with the ode form during the 1970s are indicative of both elements of this statement. With their experimental form and lack of conformity to received odic models, MacSweeney's poems question the interaction of metrical and spatial elements within poetic composition, and constitute a literary manifestation of the personal and philosophical conflict between conservatism and experimentalism. Fundamentally, they attack the ways in which we read poetry and defy the concept of the poem as a capitalist recreational commodity that is intellectually and thematically transparent. This is MacSweeney's method of keeping both language and the ode form 'alive'. However, as discussed above, MacSweeney never entirely abandons the musical origins of the ode, and in this way he points to the experimental tradition of writing of which he is a part and which links him to the work of the Romantics. Because of their lack of traditional metrical consistency, the visual orientation of the odes does seem to represent the most compelling element of the poems in regard to their form, but their continual allusion to music creates poetry that is never quite content to remain silent.

ABERYSTWYTH UNIVERSITY   OLIVER BEVINGTON

[59] 'The British Poetry Revival 1965–1979', p. 34.

PLOTTING AND THE NOVEL: THE DUPLICITY OF ESPIONAGE IN BALZAC'S *UNE TÉNÉBREUSE AFFAIRE*

In March 1921 the young Marc Allégret wrote to inform André Gide that, in choosing which of Balzac's novels to read now that he had finished *Les Paysans* and *Le Cousin Pons*, he had been guided by Brunetière and had selected *Une ténébreuse affaire*, a work which Gide had, in fact, already singled out for his protégé's attention.[1] He added, by way of explanation of his enjoyment of the novel, as well as doubtless for the presumed enlightenment of his correspondent, who had professed not to have read it himself: 'C'est un de ses seuls romans où il y ait vraiment une intrigue.'[2] Such a statement might seem unexceptionable in respect of a novel that involves spying, kidnapping, an underground hiding-place, buried treasure, a trial (the outcome of which remains firmly in the balance), and the eventual putting to death of a model of moral rectitude, especially since these interwoven features occur in the context of machinations both personal and political, as well as a readiness for heroic self-sacrifice and a (largely 'off-stage') manipulation of events by Napoleon and, above all, Fouché.[3] The reader of *Une ténébreuse affaire* is, furthermore, placed in a position that necessitates a constant interpretation of fragmentary evidence, in an attempt to identify both the motivation behind the various actions of the numerous *intrigants* and the supposedly purposeful manner in which these actions are linked. The assumption that it is principally in terms of plot that Balzac's novel is structured has, moreover, been widespread, not least as a result of Régis Messac's claim, in his 1929 thesis devoted to the detective story (a work which has exerted unanticipated influence through the broad adoption of its findings by Walter Benjamin), that it constitutes the prototype of that genre,[4] with the characters engaged in a

---

[1] See André Gide and Marc Allégret, *Correspondance 1917–1949*, ed. by Jean Claude and Pierre Masson, Cahiers André Gide, 19 (Paris: Gallimard, 2005), pp. 402, 411, 413, 416. Brunetière, whom Gide pronounced a reliable guide, had written of *Une ténébreuse affaire*: 'Ce beau roman, dont je vois que certains biographes ou critiques de Balzac ne parlent qu'avec une espèce de moue dédaigneuse, n'en est pas moins, à mon sens, un de ses chefs-d'œuvre' (Ferdinand Brunetière, *Honoré de Balzac 1799-1850* (Paris: Nelson and Calmann-Lévy, [n.d.]), p. 100).

[2] Gide and Allégret, *Correspondance*, p. 416 (letter dated 13 March 1921). Gide had, in fact, read *Une ténébreuse affaire* in 1899 (see Gide, *Journal*, ed. by Éric Marty and Martine Sagaert, 2 vols (Paris: Gallimard, 1996), I, 290).

[3] The centrality of the Minister of Police is implied by the reference to 'le ténébreux génie de Fouché' (Balzac, *La Comédie humaine*, ed. by P.-G. Castex and others, 12 vols (Paris: Gallimard, 1976–81), VIII (1977), 553; all parenthetical references will be to this edition and volume). In the concluding section of the novel the narrator refers again to 'ce génie ténébreux, profond, extraordinaire, peu connu, mais qui avait bien certainement un génie égal à celui de Philippe II, à celui de Tibère et de Borgia' (p. 692). On Balzac and Fouché, see Jean Tulard, 'Fouché dans *La Comédie humaine*', *L'Année balzacienne* 1990, pp. 7–12.

[4] As Armine Kotin Mortimer notes approvingly, René Guise rejects the notion of *Une ténébreuse affaire* as a detective story, judging it instead to be 'le roman de la police' (see Mortimer, *For Love*

---

processing of clues in the manner of the *sauvages* of Fenimore Cooper.[5] Yet this is to ignore the question of the relative status attached to action and plot in the composition as a whole. It will be the purpose of this article to suggest that *Une ténébreuse affaire* is, in fact, constructed along significantly different lines, and in ways, moreover, that look forward to Gide's compositional technique in *Les Faux-Monnayeurs*.[6]

There can be little doubt that the composition of *Une ténébreuse affaire*, which was serialized in *Le Commerce* in January and February 1841, was encouraged by Balzac's reading of Cooper. He had not long since reviewed, favourably and at some length, *The Pathfinder* (translated by A. J. B. Defauconpret as *Le Lac Ontario*). As part of a sifting of the good and the bad in Cooper's work, he had expressed the view that *The Pathfinder*, a novel notable, *inter alia*, for its inclusion of a (French) spy, was, like the same author's *The Spy*, one of the American writer's finer achievements.[7] The keen observation, by Cooper's eponymous hero and his companions, of signs betraying the presence of hostile Indians as they make their way down the River Oswego is matched by an identical activity on the part of the enemy, and, as will be seen in more detail later, is paralleled in *Une ténébreuse affaire* by a repeated scenario of watching and being watched. More specifically, the fearful glance Dew of June casts at her husband in Cooper's novel[8] has its counterpart in the look of terror Marthe Michu gives her husband in the opening chapter of *Une ténébreuse affaire*, while the description of Michu engaged in observation of Malin de Gondreville is explicitly likened to 'la manière des Sauvages' (p. 523). Yet, in themselves, such allusions are little more than a tribute to Cooper, unless they

---

or for Money: Balzac's Rhetorical Realism (Columbus: Ohio State University Press, 2011), p. 47, n. 1).

[5] See Walter Benjamin, *Charles Baudelaire: un poète lyrique à l'apogée du capitalisme*, trans. by Jean Lacoste (Paris: Payot, 1982), pp. 64–65. It is, however, in the Parisian setting of *Splendeurs et misères des courtisanes* that Balzac himself draws the parallel with Cooper most explicitly (see Balzac, *La Comédie humaine*, VI, 673). See also Wells Chamberlin, 'Une ténébreuse affaire, roman policier', *Annales publiées par la Faculté des lettres de Toulouse: Littératures*, 6 (1958), 21–49; Gwen Thomas, 'The Case of the Missing Detective: Balzac's Une ténébreuse affaire', *French Studies*, 48 (1994), 285–98; Rayner Heppenstall, 'Balzac's Policemen', *Journal of Contemporary History*, 8 (1973), 47–56; Andrea Goulet, *Optiques: The Science of the Eye and the Birth of Modern French Fiction* (Philadelphia: University of Pennsylvania Press, 2006), p. 111; as well as Margaret Murray Gibb, *Le Roman de Bas-de-Cuir: étude sur Fenimore Cooper et son influence en France* (Paris: Champion, 1927). On Cooper as spy novelist see Brett F. Woods, *Neutral Ground: A Political History of Espionage Fiction* (New York: Algora, 2008).

[6] As will be seen, both works, in addition, proceed in terms of a focus on the counterfeit.

[7] See 'Lettres sur la littérature, le théâtre et les arts', I (July 1840), in *Œuvres complètes de Balzac*, ed. by Maurice Bardèche, 24 vols (Paris: Club de l'honnête homme, 1968–71), XXIV (1971), 82–113 (pp. 95–100).

[8] 'Sa petite femme, toujours patiente et soumise, et dont les grands et beaux yeux noirs ne se fixaient presque jamais sur son mari sans exprimer le respect, la crainte et l'amour...' (J. F. Cooper, *Œuvres*, trans. by A. J. B. Defauconpret, 30 vols (Paris: Furne and Jouvet, 1876–77), XVII (1877), 11).

are to be interpreted merely as an exploitation of the latter's popularity. Still more significantly, as again will be seen in due course, the primordial function of such activity in Balzac's novel is no longer confined to focusing attention on the narrative outcome. In Cooper, the observational activity of the characters is something on which their lives depend; they face a well-defined enemy and their courage and bravery in the face of that enemy inevitably casts them in a heroic role. Sympathetically portrayed, it is presumed that they will emerge victorious. The response invited from the reader is unambiguous—as Balzac himself said of *The Pathfinder*, 'C'est beau! c'est grand!'[9] In contrast, it will be seen that the emphasis on observational activity in *Une ténébreuse affaire* extends well beyond the confines of plot, and, moreover, beyond the exigencies of an extra-literary reflection on the function of espionage in relation to the subversion of law and order for political ends.

As for the view of *Une ténébreuse affaire* as a detective story, it is incontrovertibly the case that clues pointing in the right direction jostle for the reader's attention alongside signs that are eventually discovered to be false, with a calculated imbalance in favour of the latter. The capacity of the former to lead the reader to a correct understanding is all but annulled by the seemingly unanswerable facts that point in a different direction. It is only in retrospect that the reference to Marthe's pious upbringing by her mother is discovered to be crucial to the stance she adopts as an adult. As the daughter of a President of the Revolutionary Tribunal, her Republican credentials seem beyond question. There is nothing to suggest that her dislike of being dressed as an allegorical figure of Liberty is anything more than what it is said to have been, namely a child's objection to being put on display. Her husband certainly has no reason to suspect her anti-Republican sentiments. In his own case, we are surprised to see him praying, since this sits ill alongside his presentation as a Judas figure, which is the universal assumption made by all around him, including his wife, and also by the reader, who falls victim to the false authority exerted by the chapter title: 'Le Judas'. Balzac's regular readers would have been schooled, moreover, not to question the pertinence of Michu's head-and-shoulders resemblance to Judas Iscariot, especially given the linking of him to Revolutionary activity through the phrase 'apôtre de la Révolution' (p. 507). This very consensus discourages us from giving Michu's prayers a second thought. We experience a similar disinclination to attribute significance to a statement he makes with regard to his father-in-law's activity during the Revolution: 'Mon beau-père a sauvé bien des gens!' (pp. 509–10). Michu may display 'teintes mystérieuses' (p. 508), but the negative impression of him gained from his presentation is overwhelming. The potentially qua-

[9] According to an anecdote related in Léon Gozlan, *Balzac en pantoufles* (1856) (Villefranche-de-Rouergue: Société d'étude du livre français, 1981), p. 87.

lifying adverbial phrase in the reference to 'l'impression glaciale que Michu causait au premier abord' (p. 503) is unlikely to be taken as evidence that appearances in his case are deceptive, for it is swamped by the information that 'La terreur qu'il inspirait à sa femme, à sa belle-mère, à un petit domestique nommé Gaucher, et à une servante nommée Marianne, était partagée à dix lieues à la ronde' (p. 506). Marianne's name serves only to corroborate the impression that this is an exemplary Republican household. There are pointers to the true situation, in the form of references to 'les actes auxquels il était, pour son compte, parfaitement étranger' (p. 507) and to 'l'injustice de la foule' (p. 507), but they do not weigh heavily in the balance.

It will eventually emerge that, as Gwen Thomas has pinpointed, there are two distinct strands of action within *Une ténébreuse affaire*.[10] Several decades after the action that constitutes the diegesis, Henri de Marsay, in the *méta-récit* that forms an epilogue to the novel, invites Mme de Cadignan to enlighten Laurence de Saint-Cygne now that 'le secret de l'affaire' (p. 695) has been revealed. But if the motives of the central players become somewhat clearer, it is far from being the case that the conclusion removes all the uncertainties.[11] Thomas acknowledges the presence of elements of the detective story in Balzac's composition only to conclude, convincingly, that 'Long before the development of the classic detective novel, Balzac has revealed and "transgressed" the myths on which it is to be based.'[12] Although the misleading signs, the false assumptions, the red herrings, and the general ignorance that surround the plot are revealed as such, they are not replaced by a crystalline configuration of elements that were previously disparate and misleading, that is to say by an unambiguous, all-embracing truth. For this is not a simple story that is perversely disguised by the narrator and eventually accessed through a patient dismantling of the obstacles to understanding. No one, not even Fouché, Napoleon, or Corentin, and certainly not the reader, begins or ends with complete possession of the facts.[13] Characters are, at best, only incompletely aware of what exists beyond the motivation behind

[10] At a basic level, the reader is led to wonder: 'Will Corentin succeed in catching the conspirators red-handed, or will [. . .] Laurence [. . .] and [. . .] Michu succeed in concealing them?' (Thomas, 'The Case of the Missing Detective', p. 288).

[11] It is additionally the case, as Chantal Massol has observed, that the reader is left in the dark concerning the source of de Marsay's information (see *Une poétique de l'énigme: le récit herméneutique balzacien* (Geneva: Droz, 2006), pp. 196–97, n. 82).

[12] Thomas, 'The Case of the Missing Detective', p. 296. It is for this reason that *Une ténébreuse affaire* is not significantly weakened as a novel by the inconsistencies and improbabilities that H. J. Hunt legitimately identifies with reference to the outcome of Michu's trial (in the introduction to Balzac, *A Murky Business*, trans. by Herbert J. Hunt (Harmondsworth: Penguin, 1972), pp. 14–15). Thomas also notes that 'There is a super-sleuth, but no super-criminal' ('The Case of the Missing Detective', p. 293). As Massol puts it, 'le récit de détection se développe en l'absence d'énigme' (*Une poétique de l'énigme*, p. 70).

[13] 'No one has access to the whole truth' (Thomas, 'The Case of the Missing Detective', p. 292).

their own activity. As Alain observed of Balzac's title: 'jamais titre mieux choisi'.[14] In other words, although the reader is obliged to read in a manner that assumes that all will become clear in this notably difficult novel,[15] and that heed to the deceptive nature of appearances will be enough to ensure access to the truth, this is merely to postpone the discovery that the composition is not structured in such a reassuring manner. Instead, it gradually reveals to the doubtless initially recalcitrant reader a downgrading of plot that is, paradoxically, the result of a plurality of shadowy plots, both public and private, that constitute the matter of the novel's diegesis and become increasingly and inextricably entwined. The central organizing function of plot in the adventure-story format employed by Cooper is thus exploded in Balzac's novel. This phenomenon is reinforced by the universal emphasis on the difficulty of distinguishing between (in)fidelity and its semblance. An apparent ally can, in fact, be a foe, and vice versa. Among those more committed to the actual plotting (*complots*), allegiance and circumstances are shown to change, particularly in response to the perceived potential for self-advancement or personal gain. It is thus the defining essence of plot in general, rather than specific plots and their outcomes, that Balzac reveals so tellingly, together with its effects, for example the exponential growth of paranoia. As such, and to anticipate a later stage in our argument, this may be seen as the representation of a complex and shifting political reality that is characterized by a perceived need to contract contradictory alliances. It leads to the discovery that the powerful players in the novel are guided not by principles, but by a commitment to personal ambition that encourages them to position themselves in such a way as always to enable a change of tack.

The downgrading of plot in the wider sense is continued by the nature of the revelations of de Marsay. He informs those present in the epilogue that Corentin (whose ambiguous role as both investigator and instigator in the novel is embodied in the label 'l'agent principal' (p. 695)) had, in a scene previously witnessed by the reader in the form of a flashback, been humiliated by the young, whip-wielding Laurence on the occasion when he came to arrest the Simeuse twins, just as the future comte de Gondreville, in one of the many instances of doubling that occur in the novel, had been humiliated by

---

[14] Alain, *Balzac* (1937, entitled *Avec Balzac*), ed. by Robert Bourgne (Paris: Gallimard, 1999), p. 35. The difficulty of visual perception is reinforced in the novel by a contrast between the sharpness of the close-ups and the haziness of more distant panoramas that has significance beyond the realm of optics. As Françoise M. Taylor has noted: 'Fouché a les deux mêmes sèmes de caractérisation que Malin: l'invisibilité et la position, celle de l'araignée au centre de sa toile' ('Mythe des origines et société dans *Une ténébreuse affaire* de Balzac', *Nineteenth-Century French Studies*, 14 (1985–86), 1–18 (p. 5)).

[15] It was famously described by Alain as 'un des [romans de Balzac les] plus difficiles à lire' (*L'Œuvre de Balzac*, ed. by Albert Béguin and Jean A. Ducourneau (1949–53), 16 vols (Paris: Le Club français du livre, 1966), XI, 1307).

her earlier during the Revolution. In the context of 'high politics', this clearly ironizes the plot in relation to its presumed importance. The response can only be 'N'est-ce que ça?'. Such highlighting of petty motivation undermines the status of the activity and motivation that the reader has struggled to identify and understand. Our readiness to attribute prestige to action that is in due course shown to involve historical personages of note is, moreover, enhanced by its absence from view, just as the specific royalist plot centred on the prince de Condé is not portrayed directly. The essentially extra-diegetical nature of such activity, at least potentially, preserves its power and significance against the diminishment that would inevitably follow from recourse to the procedures of fictional representation. That said, the status of plot (*intrigue*) in *Une ténébreuse affaire* is undoubtedly affected, adversely, by the fact that the aristocrats' plot (*complot*) fails. (The duc d'Enghien is executed in 1804, and although the fact goes unmentioned in the novel, the Condé line will die out in the symbolic year of 1830.) Yet it is not just the aristocrats who fail. The plot against the First Consul hatched by some close to him is abandoned, just as the Jacobin plot against his life on Christmas Eve 1800 in the rue Saint-Nicaise, which is recalled in the course of Balzac's narrative, had failed to achieve its end. Most significant of all is the way the novel as a whole is suffused with an awareness of the ultimate failure of Napoleon some ten years hence.[16]

More generally, though without necessarily departing from the political perspective, the persistent emphasis on action in *Une ténébreuse affaire* serves only to reveal its futility. Action invariably ends up in denial of its presumption of purposefulness and of its ability to match in execution the degree of determination and vehemence of the protagonist's ambition. Indeed, in the case of the royalists, the greater their vehemence or intransigence, the more hamstrung they become with regard to their objectives.

In addition to operating a radical break from the adventure story with its privileging of plot, Balzac can be seen to have constructed in *Une ténébreuse affaire* a textual universe that is pervaded by an implicit reflection on the problematical nature of all attempts to identify and understand, rather than those narrowly related to an identification of the aims and motives of those on the other side of the political divide from Laurence de Cinq-Cygne, the Simeuse twins, and the Hauteserre brothers. The omnipresent misunderstandings in which the reader becomes embroiled are not concerned solely with the dimension of intrigue and plot. The reader's enquiry is not precisely consubstantial with that conducted by the policemen Corentin and Peyrade, not least because the latter are themselves the object of scrutiny. The 'true' picture to

---

[16] It is stated that 'l'amour-propre excessif de Napoléon est une des *mille* raisons de sa chute' (p. 553, emphasis added). See also p. 495.

which the reader gradually gains partial access is not merely the elucidation of an antagonistic structure that is initially cloaked in mystery, but that of a society characterized by denial of the possibility of anything like a complete or perfect understanding of others and thereby the absence of a basis on which even the most modest notion of community might be formed.[17] It is notable that in the imperfect communities featured, knowledge circulates in the form of gossip and the wrong assumptions that are invariably the latter's stock-in-trade. The prominence of words and phrases such as 'opinion' (passim), 'disait-on' (pp. 522, 554), 'un bruit public' (p. 613), 'le bruit courut' (p. 508), 'le caquet des campagnes' (p. 508), or 'Chacun avait attribué les courses [. . .] à' (p. 549) is testimony to the unreliability of information and assumptions alike. The reference, at one point, to the 'grand étonnement du pays' (p. 595) is evidence of the way events are invariably experienced. Initial assumptions, for example those that greet the low-born Marion's acquisition of the Gondreville estate, tend to be incorrect. The wise and sympathetically drawn priest reports with regard to Malin's arrival in Gondreville: 'l'on se perd en conjectures au sujet de ce voyage précipité' (p. 550). As important as the precise nature of these theories is the inevitability of the activity itself, its contradictory and apparently open-ended nature, and the difficulty of distinguishing between appearances and reality, of establishing the criteria for differentiating between truth and the merely plausible.

The author of *Une ténébreuse affaire* also plays hard and fast with the matter of the omniscience attributed to the narrative voice, in a manner that exceeds the requirement of recourse to narratorial red herrings in relation to the stance and motives of certain of the protagonists. There are clear indications that he is writing with the benefit of hindsight and, as the serialization of the novel in the press duly encourages, for an audience contemporary with its redaction. Notable references are made to subsequent moments in history, including the July Revolution and its aftermath. There is also the instance of proleptic reference to Michu's ultimate fate through the reference, on his introduction, to the way in which his neck seemed designed to invite severance by the guillotine. But although the narrator is, in such respects, allowed considerable knowledge of the situation, scenes are focalized through the participants, with an eye to the enhancement of their dramatic potential through an emphasis on the immediacy of the moment, which, in addition to privileging, as has been noted, first (misleading) impressions, calls for a suppression of omniscience on the narrator's part, to which attention is implicitly drawn through such nonetheless apparently authoritative phrases as

---

[17] I am grateful to one of the anonymous readers for *MLR* for the suggestion that there is a parallel here with the way in which in Balzac's *L'Envers de l'histoire contemporaine* (1846–48) 'understanding is reached only after a difficult process of moral purification'. This is undoubtedly worthy of being pursued in greater depth than is possible in the present discussion.

'sans aucune ironie apparente' (p. 516), 'une inexplicable rapidité' (p. 523), or 'pour le mieux surveiller peut-être' (p. 510). Also noteworthy in this respect is the controlled release of information, which is especially striking in relation to the identification of characters by name. It is not uncommon for characters to be introduced and described in advance of being named, the name being revealed, for example, in a subsequent direct address, as in the case of the Michu family, including their dog. As a result, the reader, instead of finding himself the recipient of information in the form of a detached ordering of information, is allowed the authentic experience of picking up on significant details as they appear. The narratorial perspective likewise oscillates between the view of Everyman ('Quiconque eût pu contempler cette scène' (p. 502)) and the specialized knowledge and understanding to which the reader believes himself to be entitled by the nature of his contract with the author, even if the author/narrator is in part concealed by the uncertain status of the observer whose role he assumes. The relative paucity of information vouchsafed by the curiously reticent (or selective) narrator is indeed striking, and reminiscent of the contemporary French short story.[18] Needless to say, what is in operation in this ambiguous narratorial stance is not genuine knowledge or ignorance on the part of the narrator. Instead the reader is treated here to a dimension of a playful narrative rhetoric that does not seem gratuitous precisely because it mirrors the way in which the reader makes sense of social and other situations outside literary and fictional representations.

Such a procedure, moreover, shows the author/narrator to engage in an activity of bluff and double bluff that mirrors the central activity of the diegesis, with its frequent emphasis on treachery and betrayal. It is, however, essentially in the service of a representation of a reality that is constantly shifting, with the individual's comprehension remaining elusive. It is indeed an affair that is *ténébreuse*, albeit one that also reflects Balzac's early attraction to the chiaroscuro of Rembrandt. What is important is not so much the truth unmasked as the instructive experience of being exposed to the insuperable difficulties of composing the picture, and, more generally, the dramatization of interpretation. In a work in which there is direct reference, for example, to Laurence de Cinq-Cygne's wily servant Gothard's 'langage [. . .] à la fois si faux et si vrai' (p. 572), reading must necessarily tread a difficult path between trust and scepticism. The reader does not merely observe the activities of characters who are at best only partially sighted with regard to the power struggles in which they find themselves embroiled, but also re-enacts this situation through the way he or she is imprisoned in an overlapping

---

[18] It is noteworthy that the editors of *Le Commerce* had invited Balzac to submit 'une nouvelle ou deux c'est-à-dire la valeur d'un volume in-8°' (Balzac, *Correspondance*, ed. by Roger Pierrot, 5 vols (Paris: Garnier, 1960–69), IV (1966), 210–11). The opening scene of *Une ténébreuse affaire* is indeed not unreminiscent of Mérimée's *Mateo Falcone*.

world of misleading appearances, We are, notably, implicated in the process of getting things wrong. The real and the counterfeit become indistinguishable in the absence of authoritative commentary and, as such, are linked to the widespread reference to the masquerade and, indeed, to the constant emphasis on costume that begins with the opening depiction of Michu as hunter.[19]

Balzac's approach to the novel in *Une ténébreuse affaire* is not, however, confined to a *mise en question* of the central function of plot or the self-conscious concern with interpretability that we have so far seen. In substitution for an organization in terms of plot, his composition is also tightly and self-reflexively constructed in respect of its restricted thematics. This is most evidently the case in respect of spying, with the novel developing out of a single, not to say obsessive, activity of observation. It is the predominant activity, one in which every character is more or less constantly engaged. There is constant emphasis on eyes, above all on eyes reading other eyes, though on occasion encountering impenetrability, and, in a characteristic reversal, on one occasion constituting a case of choosing not to see. (At Cinq-Cygne, Goulard the mayor closes his eyes when faced with portraits of Louis XVI, Marie-Antoinette, and other royalist figures (p. 551).) Espionage does not constitute a subject as such, or at least is not the main concern of Balzac's text. It loses its specificity in a universe that is characterized by constant suspicion and even incipient paranoia, and becomes the norm. Every character is on the 'qui vive' and is prone to be suspicious of everyone else, in the manner of Michu's dog Couraut, who possesses an evident etymological link to the sleuth Corentin. While obviously the stock-in-trade of the 'Parisian' policemen Corentin and Peyrade ('deux maîtres espions' (p. 563)), the activity of spying is subverted by the combination of its universality and the uncertainty that exists with regard to its purpose. Michu's gruff complaint or warning (albeit uttered to himself), 'des espions! le pays en fourmille' (p. 502), is far from being an overstatement. The narrator subsequently states 'On se sait espionné' (p. 512). Yet of Michu in turn, it is said 'il alla épier Marion' (p. 509). The peasant farmer Violette, who has nailed his colours to Malin's mast, spies on Michu and passes on the information to the police chief in Arcis, yet Michu is, in turn, aware where he keeps his money, though without having designs on it as such. Malin rewards Marion, but nonetheless has him placed under surveillance. Goulard the informer is, in Michu's mouth, 'cet espion-là' (p. 530), whereas of the endearing figure Gothard it is said: 'Toutes les ruses employées par les espions, il les pratiquait' (p. 539). (He conceals his admirable qualities 'sous la profonde ignorance et la torpeur des gens de

---

[19] On evocations of the masquerade in this work see Franc Schuerewegen, '*Une ténébreuse affaire* ou l'histoire et le jeu', *L'Année balzacienne 1990*, pp. 375–88.

la campagne' (p. 539).) Alongside the deployment of *espion*[20] and *espionner* in a technical sense, there thus exists a broadening of such terms and their association with a range of synonyms. The activity overlaps with what Max Andréoli legitimately terms 'le motif omniprésent de la chasse'.[21] In that connection, both Michu and Laurence de Cinq-Cygne are dressed as ostensible game hunters, while engaged in 'une chasse à l'homme', as is later echoed by the knowing question directed at Laurence by Mme d'Hauteserre: 'Quelle espèce de chasse avez-vous faite aujourd'hui?' (p. 633).

Thus rather than a world in which spies and the targets of espionage are clearly differentiated, spying is represented as a mutual activity, an example of the 'observer observed'. In the case of Michu and the spies, who is the hunter and who is the prey? The answer, of course, is that each figure is both, and not simply in Michu's case out of a devotion to self-preservation, as his ultimate fate (and, above all, his lack of dedication to his own defence) is there to show. There are two scenes in which this mutual observation is developed most fully. One of these is the cinematic scene[22] in the Hauteserre drawing room, in which, in a veritable tour de force, the confrontation of the various figures present is depicted almost exclusively in terms of their engagement in surreptitious observation of each other, the drama being intensified by the fact that no two viewpoints are precisely the same. The other is the opening scene, where the reader observes Marthe Michu and her mother, who are observing Michu, who is observing Couraut, who is on the look-out for strangers. Not only is the reader implicated in the same activity, but he is also assimilated to a putative observer 'caché dans un buisson' (p. 502), thereby accentuating the way observation in the novel is closely associated with a clandestine activity. In other words, the reader is, from the outset, cast in the role of 'spy', though, in contradistinction to the numerous 'spies' that constitute the dramatis personae, without being himself the object of suspicious scrutiny, except insofar as the writing induces a self-conscious awareness of, and critical detachment from, his role as reader. In this connection, it is significant that the initial perspective in the following chapter is not that of the two professional spies, the 'Parisian' outsiders. It is they who are spied upon in the first instance, becoming the objects of a detailed, external description that focuses on costume. Thus the reader's introduction to events is not from the perspective of the official mission of the law officers. Instead, the perspective is that of a patriarchal personage who, as a result of being billed as a Judas, can at this

---

[20] *Espion*, it might be noted, is more frequently employed in the plural in *Une ténébreuse affaire* than in the singular.

[21] Max Andréoli, 'Sur le début d'un roman de Balzac, *Une ténébreuse affaire*', *L'Année balzacienne 1975*, pp. 89–123 (p. 108).

[22] Balzac's own comparison is with a painting: 'un tableau vraiment digne du pinceau des peintres de genre' (p. 570).

stage only be assumed to be a figure of questionable moral and legal status. If the real, essentially sympathetic, Michu will gradually be revealed, these opening chapters deftly invite, through the absence of a strong authorial lead, speculation on the question of allegiance. In this activity of mutual espionage, allegiance emerges as a political choice. The question of which of the two sets of spies, if either, has justice on their side is all the more evident as a result of the answer being thwarted by the withholding of their true identity and motives. This serves as a highly appropriate introduction to a world in which, as will be discussed below, the consequences of uncompromising, albeit loyal, allegiance serve to call into question the very notion of ideological adherence.

Thus any impression of looseness the composition may present at the level of plot is offset by a remarkably tight reflexive network, in which a limited number of recurring figures and motifs are constantly in play, in what may be regarded as a *jeu de miroirs*. Faced with such a centripetal composition, in which the synchronic is privileged over the diachronic, the reader is obliged, not so much to process clues, as to reflect on the range of different positions represented in relation to a particular motif and to engage in a challenging attempt to differentiate between their positive and negative dimensions.

This dominant thematic network is nonetheless paralleled by Balzac's re-course to a frequent, and doubtless implausible, doubling of many of the characters,[23] who, incidentally, reinforce the impression of reflexivity through the author's inclination to endow them with names beginning with M or G. At the simplest level, the doubling takes the form of a second individual with parallel function or allegiances, as in the case of Michu being doubled in Laurence's equally loyal factotum Durieu. The diegesis itself also makes prominent use of *sosies*, with Corentin choosing five masked men possessed of a physical resemblance to Michu and the royalists. Talleyrand advises the marquis de Chargebœuf and his party to have recourse to *sosies* and to allow the latter to be arrested at Strasbourg in their place. Insofar as this form of doubling evokes a contrast between appearances and reality, the true and the counterfeit, an opposition highlighted at the trial, it is linked to the way the faithful servants Catherine and Gothard, on Michu's instructions, gallop in different directions to draw the *gendarmes* in pursuit, just as they act out a disguise to throw Corentin and Peyrade off the scent, which is paralleled by young François Michu's play-acting for the same purpose. The actual *sosies* are, however, also a means of alerting the reader to the function of doubles at a more important level, one that continues the activity instigated by the spectrum of references to spying, with the reader being led to engage in a reflection on the play of similarities and differences. Thus Michu, the false

---

[23] For some astute comments on the 'structure de dédoublement fonctionnel' in the context of 'une redistribution générale des places et des rôles', see Taylor, 'Mythe des origines et société dans *Une ténébreuse affaire* de Balzac', p. 2.

Judas, is contrasted with the real Judas, Violette.[24] The doubling is particularly pertinent when it operates in terms of what is already an example of coupling. In the context of the hand in marriage of Laurence, the Simeuse twins are thus duplicated in the Hauteserre brothers, who present a slightly greater degree of contrast. Such proliferation of doubling is a means by which the novelist advances in the direction of a sophistication denied by the stereotype. Each new instance introduces dimensions that the initial individual (or set of 'twins') is unable to accommodate, thereby taking the representation to a level that is inaccessible through the deployment of a single character. This is particularly effective in the case of the depiction of the different stances represented within the royalist camp, and, more generally, with regard to equating the real with a host of different points of view or opinions. Within simple couplings, the differentiation may be suitably unclear-cut. Commentators, most notably D. A. Miller,[25] have tended to reduce Corentin and Peyrade to a contrast between two approaches to police work: the modern and the traditional, with Corentin earning the designation of 'super-sleuth'.[26] Closer attention to their portrayal, however, reveals a much less precise differentiation.[27] Although Corentin's vision may be more extensive and although he embodies a greater ability to influence events, they work as a team: 'Il [Corentin] concevait, l'autre exécutait; il était l'idée, l'autre était la forme' (p. 514). Their eyes are complementary. Peyrade's are 'fureteurs et perspicaces' (p. 513), Corentin's 'impénétrables' (p. 514). Peyrade is by no means a straightforward illustration of an approach that is outmoded, and he is indeed described as 'l'homme aux belles traditions de l'ancienne police' (p. 552). Malin had earlier been made to describe him as 'un enfant de Lenoir [. . .] le seul qui ait les grandes traditions de la police' (p. 524). He has 'la prompte intelligence de l'espion' (p. 577).[28] It is he who states 'Nous n'avons pas affaire à des *gnioles*' (p. 560) and who works out that Michu is 'l'homme des Simeuese' (p. 577). It is perhaps not without significance that Balzac terms him 'celui qui *paraissait* être le subalterne' (p. 513, emphasis added).

The reflexivity is further enhanced by the oppositions that are contained within many of the more prominent individuals. Such representatives of intransigence as Napoleon and Laurence de Cinq-Cygne are led to act out of

---

[24] It may not be irrelevant to note that Napoleon had been nicknamed 'Le Père la Violette'.

[25] See D. A. Miller, *The Novel and the Police* (Berkeley: University of California Press, 1988), p. 22.

[26] The term is applied by Thomas, 'The Case of the Missing Detective', p. 287. The same critic dubs Peyrade 'his seedy side-kick' (ibid.).

[27] Chamberlin describes Peyrade as 'presque aussi rusé que son jeune supérieur' and concludes: 'Ensemble, ils forment une équipe redoutable, les talents de l'un complétant ceux de l'autre' ('*Une ténébreuse affaire*, roman policier', p. 25).

[28] It was recalled above that Michu talks readily of the two policemen as 'deux maîtres espions' (p. 563).

character, albeit temporarily, providing examples of the way a degree of mutual admiration can exist within a relationship of political opposition. But ambiguity of character is most evident in respect of gender. Françoise Taylor has brought out extremely well the androgynous nature of Laurence, observing that 'tous ceux qui gravitent autour d'elle sont atteints par cette androgynie', and commenting that this leads to castration in the form of 'indifférentiation sexuelle'.[29] In the text Laurence is explicitly Diana Vernon as well as Charlotte Corday and the biblical Judith. Reference is made to 'la virilité du caractère de Laurence' (p. 588). Her 'adresse à la chasse tenait du miracle' (p. 536). The point is hammered home in the statement: 'La virago se cachait sous la forme la plus féminine et la plus faible en apparence' (p. 537). The depiction of 'sexual non-differentiation', however, goes beyond the portrayal of Laurence as Amazon. The manner of speaking of the Simeuse twins is 'doux comme celui des femmes' (p. 601). The Cherubino figure Gothard (Laurence is, after all, a countess) is said to possess 'la ruse des femmes' (p. 539). The twins have androgynous Christian names: Paul-Marie and Marie-Paul. Michu cries whereas Laurence does not. The differentiation between Corentin and Peyrade sexualizes them as a couple. The latter is presented as a libertine, whereas Corentin is described, worryingly, as being 'sans passions et sans vices' (p. 514).

Such undermining of conventional oppositions leads, first and foremost at the level of the love element in the plot, to a sense of 'cela revient au même'. It is made clear that Laurence is indifferent to which twin or brother she marries. But this is part of a wider sense of futility, paralysis, fatigue, and sterility,[30] which, most importantly, has significance in relation to the representation of the royalists' endeavours.[31] Not only is it associated negatively with political intransigence, it is related to an implied advocation of compromise. The multiplication of points of view on the part of the otherwise tight-knit aristocrats allows the Hauteserre parents, for example, to be categorized as 'royalistes soumis' (p. 549). That there is no meaningful dialogue between the royalists in this respect is acknowledged by the sagacious marquis de Chargebœuf when he states: 'Mais le parler d'un vieillard est dans l'oreille des jeunes gens ce qu'est le parler des jeunes gens dans l'oreille des vieillards, un bruit dont le sens échappe' (p. 614). Yet the text, rather than advancing compromise as a guaranteed solution, reveals a spectrum of related positions that invites the reader to engage in an assessment of their positive and negative dimensions.

[29] Taylor, 'Mythe des origines et société dans *Une ténébreuse affaire* de Balzac', p. 14.

[30] The sterility in relation to the dynasty of which Laurence is part is rendered ambiguous rather than confirmed by the fact that the child she eventually has is a daughter, the reader being informed that 'par un privilège assez rare [. . .] le nom de Cinq-Cygne ne périssait point faute de mâles' (p. 508). In a striking scene, Laurence is depicted as 'étalée dans l'attitude que donne un accablement complet' (p. 542).

[31] Thomas refers to the 'sterility of the caste' ('The Case of the Missing Detective', p. 292).

On the positive front, reference has already been made to the momentary readiness to shift ground on the part of Napoleon and Laurence. (What a formidable couple they would have made!) Much of the attraction of the position of the abbé Goujet stems from an astute speech he makes to Corentin that contrasts the stance within the Hauteserre household with Laurence's fanatical opposition to Napoleon. (It is no surprise that he is raised to Bishop of Troyes.) But in the case of the unattractive Goulard, the policy becomes one of 'ménager la chèvre royaliste et le chou républicain' (p. 558). Opposition to intransigence may indeed lead to the questionable pursuit of *Realpolitik* (with Fouché and Talleyrand operating in the background). On the other hand, it is possible to detect a positive valency attached to the concept of alliance and a corresponding emphasis on the limitations of all individuals, Napoleon included. In this connection, it is significant that the card game played each evening in the Hauteserre household is *boston*, a game in which you do not play as an individual but forge alliances.[32] It is perhaps not fortuitous that Talleyrand's game is not *boston* but whist, and certainly not so when it is specified that Laurence 'ne sait pas tenir une carte'.[33]

That said, alliances are inevitably related to plots. When Malin reveals to his confidant, Grévin, the names of the leaders of the plot against the First Consul (Pichegru, Georges, Moreau, le duc d'Enghien, Polignac, and Rivière), the less than admiring reaction of the liberal party's oracle is 'Quel amalgame!' (p. 525). More widely, the relativism encouraged by a reality that is continually shifting is given additional resonance by the absence of a straightforward bipartisan politics. Unholy alliances are forged. Their 'unnatural' character is difficult for observers to accommodate within their established mindsets. It is said that the Hauteserre believe, like Fouché's opponents in history,[34] that the royalist attempt on Napoleon's life in the rue Saint-Nicaise was the work of Republicans. Moreover, the relativism that is the root of an invitation to the reader to engage in a perpetual consideration of the positive and negative dimensions of every aspect of the political picture is enhanced by a notable absence of the partisan on the part of the author. In broad terms, the perspective adopted can be considered sympathetic to the royalists, for it is their aspirations and dangers to which the reader is party, with them

[32] For a different view of the significance of the games of *boston*, see Schuerewegen, 'Une *ténébreuse affaire* ou l'histoire et le jeu', p. 379. In the language of chess, which possesses a specific function in the text of *Une ténébreuse affaire* (see Taylor, 'Mythe des origines et société dans *Une ténébreuse affaire* de Balzac', pp. 4–6), the almost inevitable outcome is 'stalemate'.

[33] Whist requires, in part, an ability to work out which cards have already been played and therefore the calculation of which have not. (I am indebted to one of *MLR*'s anonymous readers for pointing out in this connection that whist as 'a metaphor for politicking' features prominently in Stendhal's *La Chartreuse de Parme*, which Balzac had read in the summer of 1840.)

[34] See Marcel Le Clère, 'SAINT-NICAISE, attentat de la rue', in *Encyclopaedia universalis* <http://www.universalis.fr/encyclopedie/attentat-de-la-rue-saint-nicaise/> [accessed 27 September 2014].

also being seen as the objects of the devotion of their staff. Yet if it is clear where Balzac's sympathies lie, his focus is on the ways in which they are sorely tested. He astutely ensures that the heroic conduct of Laurence de Cinq-Cygne remains, for all that, questionable, and not merely as a result of her intransigence. Thomas has no hesitation in maintaining that the nobles, Laurence first among them, are, in part, 'stupid'.[35] It is therefore not solely as a result of her ambiguity in respect of such specific features as gender that causes uncertainty in the reader's response. We are torn between the arguably equal temptations to admire or to excoriate her. The decision, moreover, to bring her into a direct battle of wills with Napoleon is a clear indication of an unresolved tension within Balzac's historical and political consciousness.

But if the political dimension of Balzac's representation in *Une ténébreuse affaire* must be counted the most telling, the fact is that it shows him to have written a new kind of novel, one that would receive its textbook illustration in *Les Faux-Monnayeurs*.[36] The *rond-point* that features so insistently in the opening description of Gondreville constitutes, in anticipation of Gide's practice in his only 'roman', a *mise en abyme* of the compositional structure of the novel. Rather than a novel of action and plot, *Une ténébreuse affaire* is circular in nature, even if certain characters end up losing their lives or contracting a marriage. The characters, prodigious in number in this essentially panoramic text, display no development but are seized in respect of their particular position on a spectrum. They are situated with regard to the same, restricted number of thematic reference-points. The reader is thus presented with the need to distinguish between real and counterfeit and to identify through comparison the positive and negative implications of each example. It therefore comes as no surprise that Gide should have singled it out among the works of the *Comédie humaine* and then followed his own advice in reading it aloud ('avec émerveillement') to his wife in July 1921.[37] To Roger Martin du Gard, he described Balzac's 'habileté' in this particular novel as 'confondante'.[38] This, at a time when *Les Faux-Monnayeurs* was taking shape in his mind. Although it is Mérimée's *La Double Méprise* that Gide cites in the *Journal des Faux-Monnayeurs* as an example of 'le roman pur', the explicit concern with purity on a number of occasions in *Une ténébreuse affaire*, together with the obviously self-reflexive nature of the composition, would have provided

---

[35] Thomas, 'The Case of the Missing Detective', p. 289.

[36] In her introduction to the novel Suzanne J. Bérard notes: '*Une ténébreuse affaire*, à la date de sa publication (1841), fait entrer comme un courant d'air frais dans l'œuvre balzacienne' (p. 453).

[37] See Gide, *Journal*, I, 1131 (entry for 14 July 1921).

[38] André Gide and Roger Martin du Gard, *Correspondance*, ed. by Jean Delay, 2 vols (Paris: Gallimard, 1968), I, 169 (letter dated 19 July 1921). To Schlumberger he maintained '*Une Mystérieuse* [sic] *Affaire* [. . .] me décompose d'épatement' (André Gide and Jean Schlumberger, *Correspondance 1901–1950*, ed. by Pascal Mercier and Peter Fawcett (Paris: Gallimard, 1993), p. 742 (letter dated 20 July 1921)).

encouragement in the same direction. In some respects it would not be too much of an exaggeration to see Balzac's novel as an intertext for *Les Faux-Monnayeurs*, even in respect of certain apparently insignificant details.[39] In obvious imitation of the stereotypical decor of a realist novel, but operating as an example of a *mise en abyme* of the novel's tripartite construction,[40] the console table in the Profitendieu drawing room in *Les Faux-Monnayeurs*, for example, contains an 'encombrante pendule' flanked by 'deux candélabres de cristal'.[41] In the Cinq-Cygne drawing room, Laurence had stared at 'la vieille horloge de Boulle qui se trouvait sur le chambranle de la cheminée entre deux candélabres à fleurs' (p. 542).[42] Although it may be argued that Gide was doing no more than reproduce a 'textbook' example of realist bric-a-brac, it seems at least plausible to suggest that he was led to it by the highly self-reflexive nature of *Une ténébreuse affaire*. It should not surprise us to learn from Gide that *Une ténébreuse affaire* was held 'en particulière estime' by Paul Valéry,[43] or to discover that the poet had confided to Alain that the work's ending had left him with 'une impression de grand art'.[44] *Pace* the young Allégret, *Une ténébreuse affaire* really is a novel for those who are out of sympathy with the dependence of the genre on character and plot.

SELWYN COLLEGE, CAMBRIDGE   MICHAEL TILBY

[39] The parallel undoubtedly invites further investigation, not least with regard to the exemplary clarity of *Les Faux-Monnayeurs*, a work in which the apparent discontinuities are, in contradistinction to those of *Une ténébreuse affaire*, artfully constructed. In his *Journal*, Paul Claudel acknowledges 'les parentés indéniables' between *Une ténébreuse affaire* and his play *L'Otage* (1910), though he admits that the claim, made by a reviewer, had caused him surprise since he had read Balzac's novel 'quand j'étais tout jeune, 14 ans, et je n'y avais rien compris' (Claudel, *Journal*, ed. by François Varillon and Jacques Petit, 2 vols (Paris: Gallimard, 1968–69), I, 814). He assumes this to have been a case of 'mémoire subconsciente', a theory seemingly reinforced by the fact that he speaks of 'le conventionnel Merlin' and refers to 'une demoiselle de Cinq-Cygnes'. On the question of a parallel between the two works see Gérald Antoine, 'Balzac et Claudel', *Courrier balzacien*, 38 (1990), 3–13; and Antoinette Weber-Caflish, 'Cheminements de l'imagination claudélienne', *Bulletin de la Société Paul Claudel*, 189 (2008), 47–59.

[40] See Alain Goulet, 'Lire *Les Faux-Monnayeurs*', in *André Gide*, V: *Les Faux-Monnayeurs* (Paris: Minard, 1975), pp. 9–28 (p. 15).

[41] André Gide, *Les Faux-Monnayeurs* (Paris: Gallimard, 1972), p. 14.

[42] In the previous sentence there is a depiction of Laurence's gloves, hat, veil, and whip on a console table.

[43] Gide and Allégret, *Correspondance*, p. 411 (letter dated 10 March 1921).

[44] *L'Œuvre de Balzac*, XI, 1311.

QUEERING PHOTOGRAPHY: RACE, DEATH, AND SEXUALITY IN ROLAND BARTHES'S *LA CHAMBRE CLAIRE* AND *FRAGMENTS D'UN DISCOURS AMOUREUX*

> The photographic is maternal and the maternal is photographic.　　　(RUBY TAPIA)[1]

In his piece 'The Telephone and its Queerness', Ellis Hanson examines the extent to which the telephone functions as a device of sexual displacement and intimacy that renders the ear an eroticized *locus* during phone homosex.[2] Sharing similar qualities with the 'eroticized ear', the photograph may also function as a site where phenomenologies of sexual desire, race, and gender converge towards a phallogocentric singularity. For Roland Barthes, the photograph seemingly encapsulates his closeted homosexuality, queer desire, suicidal propensities, as well as a latent racial-political agenda. Such aspects of Barthes's private life can be uncovered through careful re-evaluations of *La Chambre claire: note sur la photographie* and of *Fragments d'un discours amoureux*.[3] Yet nowhere does Barthes overtly ascribe a homoerotics to both texts' narrations, whose diegetic narrator is deemed 'un homme naïf, non culturel, un peu sauvage qui ne cesserait de s'étonner de la photographie'.[4] Perhaps surprisingly, this evocation remains one of Barthes's least understood jokes, presumably delivered to shift the reader's focus away from the homoerotic subtext of *La Chambre claire* and *Fragments*.

In this context, the present article will reappraise key photographs in *La Chambre claire* and passages in *Fragments* to advance the hypothesis that Barthes's sexualized narrative queers the photographs and images that he includes or intimates: the images serve as indicators of the author-narrator's

My gratitude goes to Paul Anderson, Ruby Tapia, Jarrod Hayes, and Maria Fackler for their insightful comments throughout the various stages of this article.

[1] Ruby Tapia, *American Pietàs: Visions of Race, Death, and the Maternal* (Minneapolis: University of Minnesota Press, 2011), p. 30.

[2] Ellis Hanson, 'The Telephone and its Queerness', in *Cruising the Performative: Interventions into the Representation of Ethnicity, Nationality, and Sexuality*, ed. by Sue-Ellen Case and others (Bloomington: Indiana University Press, 1995), pp. 34–58.

[3] Roland Barthes, *La Chambre claire: note sur la photographie*, (Paris: Éditions de l'Étoile, Gallimard, Le Seuil, 1980); Roland Barthes, *Fragments d'un discours amoureux* (Paris: Éditions du Seuil, 1977). Subsequent citations from these works will be abridged as *La Chambre claire* and *Fragments* respectively.

[4] Roland Barthes, 'Entretiens 1980', in *Œuvres complètes*, ed. by Éric Marty, 5 vols (Paris: Seuil, 2002), v: *1977–1980*, pp. 929–51 (p. 934). This study suggests that, given the autobiographical elements in the trilogy *Roland Barthes par Roland Barthes*, *Fragments*, and *La Chambre claire*, the historic Barthes becomes inseparable from the textualized Barthesian voice. The autobiographical (or arguably autofictional) overlaps seen in this trilogy render the Barthesian narrator an avatar of the historical Barthes himself. See Douglas Crimp, 'Fassbinder, Franz, Fox, Elvira, Erwin, Armin, and All the Others', in *Queer Looks: Perspectives on Lesbian and Gay Film and Video*, ed. by Martha Gever and Pratibha Parmar (New York: Routledge, 1993), pp. 257–74 (pp. 260–62).

closeted subjectivity, of representations pertaining to racial politics, and/or of aberrant forms of sexuality. Queering the photograph connotes the bringing of content-related visual elements, framed by textual narration, into a homoerotic or counternormative relationship between the author-narrator, the diegetic subjects within *La Chambre claire* and *Fragments*, and the passive reader. This framing of 'queering' calls to mind David Halperin's definition of 'queer' as 'not a positivity but a positionality vis-à-vis the normative—a positionality that is not restricted to lesbians and gay men but is in fact available to anyone who is or who feels marginalized because of her or his sexual practices'.[5] As this article will demonstrate, Barthes's meditation on photography and the Maternal is characterized by his socially marginalized positionality as a closeted homosexual on the one hand, and by his epistemic engagements with castratory self-mutilation, suicide, and necrosexual fantasies on the other. The author-narrator sublimates these queer anti-positionalities into acceptable and seemingly hetero-narrative and hetero-visual forms. In so doing, Barthes strategically repositions himself and his writing towards the heteronormative, masking his and his works' queerness through rhetorical, performative processes of hetero-naivety.

Continuing within this framework, this study avers that the deceased Mother figure in *La Chambre claire*—the same character appearing in *Fragments*—functions as an anaclitic, epistemological surrogate of the author-narrator's desired yet unattainable virtualized homosexual male partner. After all, the author-narrator affirms that 'l'être que j'attends n'est pas réel'.[6] Both the Mother and homosexual Other figures are further racialized as 'coloured', and it is the epistemologically racialized Mother-*qua*-homosexual Other appearing in the famous *Photographie du Jardin d'hiver* with which the author-narrator affectively identifies and *not* uniquely his Caucasian mother Henriette Barthes.[7] Racialization in *La Chambre claire* and *Fragments* operates under the aegis of coloniality: Barthes's maternal grandfather Lieutenant Louis Gustave Binger, who claimed Côte d'Ivoire for France in 1887, tethers the semiotician to a racial-colonial context that has been problematically overlooked in critical Barthesian scholarship.[8] The colonial spectre of Binger and the lieutenant's maternal connections to Barthes complicate the

---

[5] David Halperin, *Saint Foucault: Towards a Gay Hagiography* (New York: Oxford University Press, 1995), p. 62.

[6] Barthes, *Fragments*, p. 49.

[7] This Mother-*qua*-homosexual Other figure is referred to as the 'M/Other'. In *Fragments*, the author-narrator conflates both beings into one body. This superposition will be further explored below.

[8] Barthes curiously reproduces a sketch of Binger in *Roland Barthes par Roland Barthes*, neither disclosing the French officer's name in a caption nor offering any genealogical connections between himself and Binger. See Roland Barthes, *Roland Barthes par Roland Barthes* (Paris: Éditions du Seuil, 1975), p. 14.

author-narrator's visualization of the M/Other by subjecting the Maternal to queering, racializing, and necrosexualizing constructs.[9] As this article seeks to demonstrate, *La Chambre claire* and *Fragments* should be interpreted as autofictional extensions of the author-narrator's earlier works, inseparable from the motivations and mediations inspired by his queer desire to reunite with the M/Other via registers of coloniality, racialization, and the post-mortem.

From Homoerotic Virtual Bodies to Death: Barthes's Prophecy

> Écrire sur soi peut paraître une idée pré-
> tentieuse; mais c'est aussi une idée simple:
> simple comme une idée de suicide.
> (ROLAND BARTHES)[10]

The author-narrator opens *La Chambre claire* using a hyper-sexualized rhetoric to suggest the creation of an 'erotic pact' between the photographed subject and its beholder:

Par nature, la Photographie [. . .] a quelque chose de tautologique: une pipe y est toujours une pipe. [. . .] On dirait que la Photographie emporte toujours son référent avec elle, tous deux frappés de la même immobilité amoureuse; [. . .] ils sont collés l'un à l'autre, membre par membre [. . .] unis par un coït éternel. (p. 17)

The secondary connotation of *pipe* as 'fellatio' becomes most apparent as the passage describes the photographed subject's engagement in an act of coitus with the beholding author-narrator. The positioning between the photographic subject and the author-narrator, as depicted in this passage, parallels that of two bodies mounting each other. Furthermore, defining *membre* as 'penis' is a possibility, given the ambiguous antecedent to which *unis* refers: The author-narrator formulates *unis* in the masculine plural ending, which would presumably refer to the male-gendered referent and to the author-narrator.[11] In addition, it is unclear whether the 'bodies' of the referent and the beholder are united in a virtual act of penetrative coitus or whether their virile members are simply frotting together 'membre par membre'. The referential ambiguity manifested in this sexualized rhetoric underwrites the

---

[9] Necrosexuality is here defined as an acted-out or fantasized (psycho)sexual engagement with corpses and undead beings. See Patricia MacCormack, 'Necrosexuality', in *Queering the Non/Human*, ed. by Noreen Giffney and Myra Hird (London: Ashgate, 2008), pp. 339–62.

[10] Barthes, *Roland Barthes par Roland Barthes*, p. 62.

[11] The same agreement applies if 'unis' is understood to refer to one male and one female subject, as is in fact the case grammatically here, where the agreement is triggered by the feminine noun 'photographie' and the masculine noun 'référent'. Nevertheless, the ambiguity of the grammatical agreement may also be used to imply a male–male link.

queerly prurient relationship between the photographic subject and its beholding author-narrator.

The photographic subject is further reified in corporal terms as the author-
narrator notes that 'le référent [est] l'objet désiré, le corps chéri' (p. 19). The
overarching genre of photography is also limned as pertaining to the body: 'La
photographie [. . .] est une science des corps désirables ou haïssables' (p. 36).
The author-narrator subsequently assesses his physical relationship with the
virtualized 'body' of the photographic genre: 'Qu'est-ce que mon corps sait de
la Photographie? J'observai qu'une photo peut être l'objet de trois pratiques
[. . .] de trois intentions: faire, subir, regarder' (p. 22). Given these three
objectifying intentions, the photograph occupies a passive agency that places
the author-narrator in an active position of power as its beholder. In this way
he is able to exercise control over the immobile photographed subject; but this
dominance is limited owing to its exclusively epistemic nature in the mind of
the author-narrator. The author-narrator thus sees this epistemological sexual
hegemony over the photograph as '[un] savoir photographique' existing in
'[le] plus pur Imaginaire' (pp. 22, 25).

The author-narrator's phallogocentric dominance over the photographic
subject becomes undermined the moment he sees himself photographed, revealing paranoia and a negative body image: 'Ah, si au moins la Photographie
pouvait me donner un corps neutre, anatomique, un corps qui ne signifie rien!'
(p. 27). This yearning for a normal body, far from being 'lourde, immobile,
entêtée', evokes Barthes's longing for physical homeostasis (p.27). After all,
Barthes offhandedly evokes his own struggles with pulmonary tuberculosis,
deeming the malady 'un véritable genre de vie, un mode d'existence, [. . .]
un choix'.[12] Barthes's tuberculosis indeed provokes permanent, lifelong lung
complications. The author-narrator sees the photograph as a site of his own
repression and health-related handicap, and his disabled subjectivity collapses
into the photograph's 'wounded' objectivity. He notes in this regard:

Je voulais [. . .] approfondir [la Photographie] comme une blessure. [. . .] C'est comme
si nous refoulions la folie profonde de la Photographie: elle ne rappelle son héritage
mythique que par ce léger malaise qui me prend lorsque je 'me' regarde sur un papier.
(p. 28)

This 'léger malaise', which translates as physical, emotive pain and melancholia, is indicative of the author-narrator's awareness of his own handi-
capped subjectivity as someone with physical debilities. Homoeroticizing the
photographic genre while ascertaining a body image far from homeostasis,

[12] Roland Barthes, *Le Grain de la voix* (Paris: Éditions du Seuil, 1981), p. 245. In the posthumous
text *L'Obvie et l'Obtus* Barthes underlines his apparent dislike for lungs. He explains thus: 'Le
poumon, organe stupide (le mou des chats!), se gonfle mais il ne bande pas' (Roland Barthes,
L'Obvie et l'Obtus: essais critiques III (Paris: Éditions du Seuil, 1982), p. 240).

the author-narrator contains his melancholic sentiments within an equally wounded entity—the photograph—to stabilize his debilitated subjectivity as queer and crip.

This pathological subjectivity exhibited by the author-narrator is what Anne Anlin Cheng qualifies as 'hypochondriacal': it is a way of melancholically 'perceiving the world and one's body with respect to social relations; [. . .] in the classic hypochondriac, [. . .] we see a person preoccupied with [. . .] the origins of [his or her body's] failure'.[13] Barthes's self-pathologization betokens an exclusionary, abjected distance from a normative, healthy body and operates 'within a melancholic structure [that] expresse[s] itself [. . .] in the language of hypochondria'.[14] In effect, Barthes's hypochondria is tempered and depathologized by regarding photography as an equally wounded entity. Barthes's pathological imaginations, rendering both the author-narrator and photograph hypochondriacal bodies, are defined by an anti-normative positionality, allowing his melancholia to interlink with the exclusionary nature of homosexuality and the abject nature of deathly illness.

The prophetic nature of *La Chambre claire*, Barthes's final work, published two months before his death, is revealed through the author-narrator's persistent *memento mori* fixations on his spectralization. The author-narrator speaks evocatively in this respect:

La photographie (celle dont j'ai l'intention) représente ce moment très subtil où, à vrai dire, je ne suis ni un sujet ni un objet, mais plutôt un sujet qui se sent devenir objet: je vis alors une micro-expérience de la mort (de la parenthèse): je deviens vraiment spectre. [. . .] Ce que je vise dans la photo qu'on prend de moi, [. . .] c'est la Mort: la Mort est l'*eïdos* de cette Photo-là. (pp. 30–32)

The author-narrator experiences these 'about-to-die' sentiments as he looks into the photograph that depicts himself, superimposing his photographed image onto what he sees as the reified phenomenology of death. The 'about-to-die' image that Barthes views in his self-photograph functions as a mediator between the extradiegetic author-narrator and death itself: in effect, the photograph becomes an intermediary through which the author-narrator epistemologically renders himself a spectre. Moreover, because Barthes considers that '[la] langue [. . .] c'est le phallus qui parle', his discourse fixated on death, synonymous with a truncation of life, *castrates* his narrative language-as-phallus, thereby suggesting Barthes's anatomical hypochondrialization via language.[15] If Barthesian narration functions as a form of corporal prosthesis, such a castratory self-mutilation epistemologically accords the author-narrator a phallus-lacking corporality anaclitically and affectively identifiable

---

[13] Anne Anlin Cheng, *Melancholy as Race: Psychoanalysis, Assimilation, and Hidden Grief* (New York: Oxford University Press, 2000), p. 69.

[14] Ibid.

[15] Barthes, *L'Obvie et l'Obtus*, p. 192.

with his mother's phallus-less body. In this regard, 'être déprimé', affirms Barthes, 'c'est *porter la figure de la Mère*'.[16]

The author-narrator's desire for the Maternal operates within a strictly epistemological realm, qualifiable as 'virtual', within which his body is free to self-associate affectively with the M/Other's. Brian Massumi describes affectivity and virtual corporeality in the following manner:

The virtual can perhaps best be imaged by superposing [. . .] deformational moments of repetition rather than sampling differences in form and content. [. . .] Imagination is the mode of thought most precisely suited to the differentiating vagueness of the virtual. [. . .] [It is] the mutual envelopment of thought and sensation, as they arrive together.[17]

Massumi accords particular import to the virtual, regarding it as a 'real but abstract' zone where the 'incorporeality of the body' is able to manifest itself.[18] Imagination becomes the means through which this bodily non-corporeality (or the body of a subject existing in an imagined, virtualized realm) is able to coexist with sensation. The author-narrator's anti-positional relationship with the virtual, and in particular with the virtual body of the Mother-*qua*-homosexual Other, is predicated on phantasmagoric, affective productions of his own imagination referred to as *l'imaginaire* or 'Image-repertoire'.[19]

The author-narrator's *male*-gendered discourse (the 'je narratif'), coupled with the corporal and affective self-identification with a *maternal* and phallus-less body, feminizes his subjectivity, thereby rendering him an intersexual of sorts. Thus, the author-narrator's male-gendered voice emanates from an imagined, castrated (and thus emasculated) body telescoped onto his mother's phallus-lacking body. Such a virtualized fusion of Barthes and his mother bespeaks an eroto-masochism, as the author-narrator makes clear:

Jamais solennelle — nullement par déclaration de rupture; cela vient sans prévenir, soit par l'effet d'une image insupportable, soit par brusque rejet sexuel: l'infantile — se voir abandonné de la Mère — *passe brutalement au génital.* [. . .] *Je cherche à me faire mal*, je m'expulse moi-même de mon paradis; [. . .] et la blessure ouverte, je l'entretiens, je l'alimente avec d'autres images. [. . .] L'idée de suicide, alors, me sauve; [. . .] je renais, [. . .] soit que je m'unisse fantasmatiquement à [l'objet aimé] dans la mort.[20]

The author-narrator's sentiment of feeling 'abandonné de la Mère' provokes a shift to the genitals such that his fantasy to reunite with his mother-*qua*-homosexual Other fuels an incestuous affect within the author-narrator,

---

[16] Barthes, *Fragments d'un discours amoureux*, p. 231 (emphasis added).

[17] Brian Massumi, *Parables for the Virtual: Movement, Affect, and Sensation* (Durham, NC: Duke University Press, 2002), pp. 133–34.

[18] Ibid., p. 21.

[19] Barthes affirms in an interview: '[*Fragments*] est le portrait d'un imaginaire, mon imaginaire' (Barthes, 'Entretiens 1980', p. 934).

[20] Barthes, *Fragments*, pp. 59, 95, 260 (emphasis added).

libidinally binding him to his absent mother. The transgressive, anti-positional nature of such an erotic affect finds its fruition within the equally transgressive realm of death and self-mutilation. This pathological, self-mutilating subjectivity (underscored by the above evocation 'Je cherche à me faire mal') underscores the author-narrator's hypochondriacal proclivities. Death via suicide and epistemic self-mutilation become the primary outlet through which the author-narrator can affectively reunite with his mother, thereby ridding him of his hypochondria.

Barthes continues to associate a masochistically inflicted wound with death: 'Mon identification est imparfaite: je suis une Mère [. . .] mais une Mère insuffisante. [. . .] Pour la moindre blessure, j'ai envie de me suicider.'[21] The author-narrator's desire to die crystallizes itself most clearly after his mother's death, after which his thirst for life diminishes:

Elle morte, je n'avais plus aucune raison de m'accorder à la marche du Vivant supérieur. [. . .] Je ne pouvais plus qu'attendre ma mort totale, indialectique. [. . .] C'est parce qu'il y a toujours en elle [la photographie] ce signe impérieux de ma mort future.[22]

The plausibility of reading these death-evoking passages as cryptic adumbrations of the author-narrator's planned suicide is available given the wealth of evidence supporting Barthes's unenthusiastic desire for life after his mother's passing.[23] Barthes's biographer Louis-Jean Calvet has revealed evidence found by the forensic surgeon in charge of the injured Barthes: the surgeon concludes that the actual cause of Barthes's death was linked to 'l'éclosion de complications pulmonaires chez un sujet particulièrement handicapé par un état d'insuffisance respiratoire chronique'.[24] A witness to Barthes's collision with a van remarks that the semiotician 'avait précisément regardé du côté d'où venait la camionnette'.[25] Barthes's botched suicide, perhaps precipitated by a desire to follow Michel Foucault's similar suicide attempts, consequently advances the aggravation of his already critical health complications.[26]

La Chambre claire includes a photograph that potentially foreshadows Barthes's death as suicide, and it can thus be suggested that this last major

---

[21] Ibid., pp. 69, 259.

[22] Barthes, *La Chambre claire*, pp. 113, 151.

[23] Louis-Jean Calvet, *Roland Barthes: 1950–1980* (Paris: Flammarion, 1990).

[24] Ibid., p. 300.

[25] Ibid., p. 296.

[26] In July 1978 Foucault encountered a near-death experience similar to Barthes's: under the influence of opium, Foucault was struck by a car while crossing rue de Vaugirard, a few miles from the Collège de France, where a van would ultimately hit Barthes less than two years later. Furthermore, Foucault made a botched suicide attempt in 1948, later extolling the 'simplest pleasures' of suicide in an essay published in 1979, the year before Barthes's death (Michel Foucault, 'Un plaisir si simple', in *Le Gai Pied 1* (Paris, 1979), pp. 1, 10). Suicide is curiously linked to photography in *L'Empire des signes* (1970), as Barthes reproduces two photographs of Funaki Kazuo, who attempts suicide in the very year of *L'Empire*'s publication (Roland Barthes, *L'Empire des signes*, in *Œuvres complètes*, ed. by Éric Marty, 5 vols (Paris: Seuil, 2002), III: *1968–1971*, pp. 347–444 (pp. 350, 438)).

work of Barthes's reads as a visual suicide letter whose would-be-alarming suicidal signals remain deliberately hidden to uphold the work's performative innocuousness and narrational naivety. In this regard, after the author-narrator evokes his 'mort future', he reproduces within the narration Alfred Stieglitz's photograph, *Le Terminus de la gare à chevaux* (*The Terminal*).[27] Barthes was struck while crossing rue des Écoles on 25 February 1980. Stieglitz's photograph, taken on 23 February 1893, depicts the busy southern end of a Harlem street; the photograph's street shot is framed by a street-crosser's viewpoint. This photograph's visualization of street-crossing constitutes a curious visual signalling whereby Barthes could have potentially envisioned the busy Parisian street where his suicide might transpire. After all, the author-narrator affirms that 'De Stieglitz ne m'enchante que sa photo la plus connue…'.[28] This trailing evocation offhandedly suggests that a fore-knowing Barthes may have been constructing his suicide while beholding Stieglitz's street-level photograph.

Yet, perhaps the most telling of all cryptic visual prophecies can be found at the beginning of *La Chambre claire*. Here, Barthes reproduces Daniel Boudinet's blue-coloured photograph *Polaroïd* (1979) but offers no commentary. Readers can ascertain that the veil's enclosing of the bed eerily resembles what hospital patients would see as they gaze outwardly towards the foot of their (death)bed. In effect, the absence of any body on the bed underscores the photograph's engagement with death and seclusion. Boudinet took *Polaroïd* in his apartment; and for Barthes, as he writes in *Journal de deuil*, the apartment space conjures up connotations of absence, sadness, and death itself. Beyond its literary denotations, Barthesian Death cannot be isolated from its familial context; for it also refers to Barthes's parents' passing. Remembering the death of his beloved mother, who passed away in their shared apartment, Barthes writes: 'Je pleure longtemps (rentré dans l'appartement insonore).'[29] It is plausible to suppose that Barthes may have imagined this kind of veiled hospital bed on which he would ultimately be laid to rest—a bed that would also be symbolic of his mother's deathbed. The photographed, veiled bed in Boudinet's apartment visualizes Barthes's imagination of death, allowing him to identify affectively with his dead mother. By placing Boudinet's caption-less photograph at the beginning of *La Chambre claire*, as well as Stieglitz's telling street-view image subsequently within his narration, the author-narrator foregrounds the spectral visuality of death, associating it with suicide and the Maternal.

[27] Barthes, *La Chambre claire*, p. 35.
[28] Ibid.
[29] Roland Barthes, *Journal de deuil: 26 octobre 1977–15 septembre 1979*, ed. by Nathalie Léger (Paris: Seuil, 1979), p. 47.

The Queer of Colour M/Other: Colonial and Necrosexual Considerations

> Sailors, soldiers, [...] Pimps, imps, shrimps,
> and all sorts of dirty fellows; [...] A progeny
> of all colors—an infernal motley crew.
> (COL. JAMES R. CREECY)[30]

Along with its representations of death, the photograph's repressive qualities also cryptically encapsulate the author-narrator's closeted subjectivity.
His desire towards men remains closeted by averting the reader's attention
from the latent homoeroticism underwriting the visual relations between
certain photographs featured in *La Chambre claire*. By specifically focusing on these photographs' innocuous, non-homoerotic visual elements, the
author-narrator underscores his performative naivety and heteronormativizing narration. This article will proceed to examine a representative selection
of *La Chambre claire*'s 'innocuous' photographs that maintain visual associations with homoeroticism and queer sexual potentialities: *Savorgnan de
Brazza* (1882) by Félix Nadar (Gaspard-Félix Tournachon); an unpublished,
archived family photograph of Barthes's grandfather, Lieutenant Binger; and
James Van der Zee's *Family Portrait* (1926).[31]

Assessing Nadar's *Savorgnan de Brazza*, in which two black French sailors
are found posing behind de Brazza, the author-narrator recognizes that the
sailor to the right 'bizarrement, a posé sa main sur la cuisse de Brazza; ce
geste incongru a tout pour fixer mon regard'.[32] The intimate proximity of de
Brazza and this sailor is such that their figures blend into each other. While
the author-narrator momentarily considers the image of this sailor's hand on
de Brazza's thigh—an image that betokens physical and emotional proximity,
particularly given de Brazza's inward positioning towards him—this gesture
surprisingly does not constitute the photographic *punctum* or arresting detail.
Rather, the author-narrator focuses on the innocuous 'les deux bras croisés du
second mousse' because he recognizes the queerness of the sailor's hand-on-
thigh gesture (p. 84). The author-narrator quickly qualifies this queer gesture
as 'farfelue' (p. 84).[33]

---

[30] James R. Creecy, 'A Duel in New Orleans, in 1829', in *Scenes in the South and Other
Miscellaneous Pieces* (Washington: McGill, 1860), pp. 275–79.

[31] Barthes, *La Chambre claire*, pp. 75, 85.

[32] Ibid., p. 84.

[33] Although one could qualify the 'touch' as representing colonial paternalism or as an amic-
able gesture, the associations of de Brazza and his colonial project in Africa largely point to a
little-known historical occurrence relating to homosexual, interracial interactions. This association
queers Nadar's reproduced photograph, making it a strong codifier of same-sex desire. Jeremy
Rich notes that two officials of de Brazza's third expedition to the Gabonese region of West
Africa were accused of having raped six African boys. This occurrence has been referred to as
the Faucher–D'Alexis Affair of 1884, named after the two offending officials under de Brazza's
command. See Jeremy Rich, 'Torture, Homosexuality, and Masculinities in French Central Africa:

Including Nadar's photograph constitutes a visual cue in which the author-narrator sees not only an epistemology of race, but also a deterritorialization of race: the figural blending occurring between the white de Brazza and the black sailor to the right represents the amalgamation of two coloured and racialized bodies into one. This homoerotic, spectacularizing visual super-position of two races fuses differing socio-political signifiers of coloniality onto one body, appearing as such by virtue of the touch. This effect flattens the stereotyped, hierarchical power-sex structures traditionally represented by the white and black body.[34] Both enmeshing bodies signify an interracial, biopolitical homogenization, as well as a latent homoerotism, thereby mark-ing both white and black bodies 'transgressive' or 'threatening' in the eyes of Barthes's white heterosexual audience. As Suzanne Schneider maintains:

The vision of the black male's ontological essence that has been passed down from this mid-nineteenth-century world may have been grounded in little less than something both as simple and as complex as one man's socially transgressive and class-crossing love for his male secretary. [. . .] Exposing *all* bodies (our own included) as marked (if only by the taint of desire), perhaps the body of the Other will cease to be the quintessential victim, the *ur-mark* of the vicissitudes of visuality.[35]

This racially and politically deterritorializing effect to which Schneider al-ludes, whereby both white and black bodies become unanimously queered, 'marked,' or transgressive, operates epistemically for the author-narrator. Given the displacement of colonial racial signifiers—as represented by the sailor to the right and by de Brazza's homoerotic visual bonding via the touch—Nadar's photograph posits a deterritorialized citizenry foregrounding homoerotic affect. The homogenization of race, as depicted in Nadar's pho-tograph, favourably equalizes the socio-political tensions between colonizer and colonized (or white and black, respectively). Such a racial homogenization not only establishes an idealized, neocolonial citizenry between Caucasians

The Faucher–d'Alexis Affair of 1884', *Historical Reflections*, 36 (2010), 7–23. The deployment of aberrant (homo)sexuality, as certain historians, including Robert Aldrich, have suggested, becomes synonymous with the colonial administration in Africa, suggesting that class and racial privileges allowed the colonizer to exercise sexual hegemony vis-à-vis the colonized in anti-normative forms that were (and have continued to be) deemed illegal in Africa (Robert Aldrich, 'Homosexuality in the French Colonies', in *Homosexuality in French History and Culture*, ed. by Jeffrey Merrick and Michael Sibalis (New York: Hawarth Press, 2001), pp. 201–18). Nadar's photograph of de Brazza was taken approximately in 1882, just two years before the incident. Nevertheless, it remains to be proved that de Brazza himself engaged in these acts, given that no historical record of the same-sex relations in this region of Africa exists to date beyond what is known of the Faucher–D'Alexis Affair.

[34] Barthes explicitly evokes this topos of flatness when he affirms: 'La Photographie est plate, dans tous les sens du mot' (Barthes, *La Chambre claire*, p. 164).

[35] Suzanne Schneider, 'Louis Agassiz and the American School of Ethnoeroticism: Polygenesis, Pornography, and Other "Perfidious Influences"', in *Pictures and Progress: Early Photography and the Making of African American Identity*, ed. by Maurice O. Wallace and Shawn Michelle Smith (Durham, NC: Duke University Press, 2012), pp. 211–43 (pp. 237–38).

and Africans, but also serves as a contract between the photograph and its beholder. Ariella Azoulay advances in this regard the view that 'whereas the nation-state is based on the principles of sovereignty and territorialization, the citizenry of photography, of which the civil contract of photography is the constitutional foundation, is based on an ethical duty, and on patterns of deterritorialization'.[36] By suggesting the dislodgement of molar institutions of sexual, political, and racial power, Azoulay disavows the hegemonic, hierarchical, and signifying qualities associated with oppressive social systems. The civil contract of photography allows for a reticulation of racial networks within a social space that rejects biopolitical hegemony.

Azoulay translates this kind of social space as 'a global form of [unified and rehabilitated] relation[s]' between and among the photographed subjects and beholder.[37] If the queering interracial interaction between the sailor to the right and de Brazza transcends the denotative rigidity of heteronormativizing socio-political and racial institutions, then queerness constitutes a critical element in establishing an epistemological citizenry of photography, at least in Barthes's photographic, colonial context. Thus, Barthes's queer social and sexual positionality vis-à-vis the heteronormative operates within the same realm as socially exclusionary homoerotic male, interracial interactions, as would perhaps be interpreted by Barthes's audience at the time. The space of the Barthesian photograph thus becomes the visual site where counternormative signifiers of homoeroticism undercut structural discourses of heterosocial normativity. What the author-narrator accomplishes by including Nadar's homoerotic photograph in *La Chambre claire* is to suggest the institutionalization of an idealistic, deterritorialized socio-political system extolling queer(ed) interracial interaction. Notwithstanding this idealization, Barthes suggests the non-attainability of this kind of deterritorialized social space; as he deflects the reader's attention from the revealing hand-on-knee touch between de Brazza and the sailor.

As T. J. Demos and Vincent Meessen have recently noted, Barthes's interest in the French colonialism of Africa stems from having a maternal grandfather who had claimed Côte d'Ivoire for France towards the end of the nineteenth century.[38] It is noteworthy that in his documentary on Barthes entitled *Vita Nova* (2009), Meessen reproduces an unpublished archival photograph in which Barthes's grandfather, Lieutenant Binger, appears seated

---

[36] Ariella Azoulay, *The Civil Contract of Photography* (New York: Zone Books, 2008), p. 128.

[37] Ibid., pp. 131–32, 146.

[38] T. J. Demos, *Return to the Postcolony: Specters of Colonialism in Contemporary Art* (Berlin: Sternberg, 2013), pp. 58–59. See also Vincent Meessen, *Vita Nova* (Brussels: Argos, 2009). Demos notes that Barthes's pro-colonialist position (as witnessed in *Mythologies*, for instance) progressively depoliticizes itself in his later works, as he turns from politically engaged writing to textual pleasure writing. However, as this article will demonstrate, colonial politics are certainly present and structure Barthesian desire within *Fragments* and *La Chambre claire*.

between two semi-nude Africans in a colonial camp. Binger's positioning between the African males strikingly echoes that of the queered de Brazza in Nadar's photograph.[39] A signifier of raciality and colonialism, Binger visually superposes himself onto the photographed de Brazza by virtue of his similar seated positioning between two African subjects. Consequently, given Barthes's direct familial relationship with Binger, the author-narrator could be led to identify vicariously with the superposed 'Binger/de Brazza' figure. Through this visual association and identification with both Binger and the queered de Brazza, Barthes becomes a bearer of colonial signifiers, harbouring a proximal, homoerotic connection with exposed African bodies.[40] Barthes's maternal lineage connecting him to Binger allows this homo-affective relationship to transpire; and as this article will shortly examine, the role of the Maternal thus plays an associative role in racializing queerness within the Barthesian photograph.

The narration continues in the second section of *La Chambre claire* and confers a notable importance on *La Photographie du Jardin d'Hiver* (1898), a non-reproduced photograph that allows the author-narrator to pine melancholically for his mother via involuntary memory.[41] Barthes, in a shift that embraces the Maternal, ascertains that the photograph's beholder establishes an affective relationship with the photographed subject through the phenomenologies of love and death, and not simply through pleasure or hedonistic motivations. The second section of *La Chambre claire* is particularly complex because it requires the reader to negotiate Barthes's rapport with his mother through a non-reproduced photograph on the one hand, and with the author's mother–son relationship outlined in his previous work *Fragments* on the other. As Tzvetan Todorov affirms while referencing Barthes's final three works *Roland Barthes par Roland Barthes*, *Fragments*, and *La Chambre claire*: 'Each voice [of Barthes] might appear authentic if we heard it in isolation; together, each stamps the others with the sign of borrowing (if not of theft).'[42] The *intra*textual qualities overlapping these three works should be read in relationship with one another; accordingly, defining the Mother in *La Chambre claire* is only possible by cross-examining the manner in which she is defined in Barthes's previous texts, most specifically in *Fragments*.

In *Fragments*, the closeted narrator strives to achieve reunification with his beloved object: the presumed heterosexual mother.[43] At the same time, the

[39] Demos, *Return to the Postcolony*, p. 50.

[40] For Barthes, the African body maintains homoerotic connotations: the semiotician's gay cruising episodes occur most notably in Morocco with young men from the area. See Ross Chambers, 'Pointless Stories, Storyless Points: Roland Barthes between "Soirées de Paris" and "Incidents"', *L'Esprit Créateur*, 34 (1994), 12–30.

[41] Barthes, *La Chambre claire*, p. 106.

[42] Tzvetan Todorov, 'The Last Barthes', *Critical Inquiry*, 7 (1981), 449–54 (p. 451).

[43] This reading of *Fragments* is informed by Kevin Kopelson's analysis treating the Barthesian

author-narrator undergoes paroxysmal fits of madness and contemplates his 'missing' *male* lover—a sort of Lacanian *objet petit a*—whom he conflates with his *mother*:[44]

Je souffre de ce qu'on me téléphone (pour la même raison); je m'affole de penser qu'à telle heure proche il faudra que je sorte, risquant ainsi de manquer l'appel bienfaisant, le retour de la Mère. (pp. 48–49)

Given the author-narrator's desire to imbricate the *homosexual* beloved male (*objet petit a*) onto his *heterosexual* mother, the mother and 'beloved gay Other' undergo a simultaneous queering. If readers treat the mother in *Fragments* as the same maternal figure appearing in *La Chambre claire*, it stands to reason that Barthes locates his desired, queered mother *and* his beloved gay Other in the *Photographie du Jardin d'hiver*. Barthes does not exclusively hallucinate seeing Henriette Barthes in the photograph but two bodies—female and male—virtually superimposed as one. The author-narrator's desire for his deceased mother, libidinally interlinked with the beloved gay Other, thus renders the dead-mother/living-son relationship not only queerly incestuous but also necrophilic. Perhaps it is for this reason that Barthes describes photography in the following terms:

Finalement ce qui me fascine dans la photo, et vraiment les photographies me fascinent, c'est quelque chose où la mort a son mot à dire, certainement. C'est peut-être une fascination un petit peu nécrophilique, pour dire les choses comme elles sont, une fascination de ce qui a été mort mais qui se représente comme voulant être vivant.[45]

The *Photographie du Jardin d'hiver* further prompts the author-narrator to fantasize deliriously about the inaccessible queer M/Other. He writes: 'La photographie devient alors pour moi un medium bizarre, une nouvelle forme d'hallucination.'[46] Hallucination, which blurs the Real with the Imaginary and neurosis with perversion, becomes a means through which the author-narrator epistemically 'accesses' the sodomitical phallus (of the queer Other) and the phallus-less corpse (of his mother). This intersexualized, 'undead' M/Other is equated with a 'sein [. . .] pour le nourrisson', which would superimpose the queer Other's phallus onto the Mother's breast.[47] It is this visualized epistemology of the M/Other with sexualized male and female

narrator as a stereotyped male homosexual. This queer narrator is the same as *La Chambre claire*'s. See Kevin Kopelson, *Love's Litany: The Writing of Modern Homoerotics* (Stanford: Stanford University Press, 1994), pp. 130–31.

[44] See Linda Kauffman, 'Dangerous Liaisons: Roland Barthes's *Fragments d'un discours amoureux* and Jacques Derrida's *The Post Card*', in *Special Delivery: Epistolary Models in Modern Fiction* (Chicago: University of Chicago Press, 1992), pp. 81–130 (p. 122).

[45] Calvet, *Roland Barthes*, pp. 263–64.

[46] Barthes, *La Chambre claire*, p. 177.

[47] Barthes, *Fragments*, p. 49. The author-narrator's mother-*qua*-homosexual Other is imagined as 'alive' in the hallucinating author-narrator's mind but additionally as 'dead': '[L]e sujet amoureux

sexual organs structured by the spectralized *Photographie du Jardin d'hiver* that the author-narrator desires and hallucinates; after all, the author-narrator reveals that 'je crée [cet être] et je le recrée sans cesse à partir de ma capacité d'aimer. [. . .] je l'hallucine'.[48]

This form of hallucination also allows the author-narrator to partake in antinormative sexual masquerades. If 'l'amoureux pourrait se définir [comme] *un enfant qui bande*', as the author-narrator evokes while suggesting 'je rêve que nous jouissons l'un de l'autre [l'être aimé] selon une appropriation absolue; c'est l'union fruitive [. . .] je jouis de cette union *dans la bouche*', the reader can further visualize an author-narrator—embodying a child—performing necrosexual cunnilingus onto the undead M/Other.[49] The author-narrator continues in perhaps the most revealing of formulations: 'Mon corps est un enfant entêté. [. . .] Il y a des trivialités subtiles, mobiles, qui passent rapidement sur le corps de l'autre: une façon brève (mais excessive) d'écarter les doigts, d'ouvrir les jambes, de remuer la masse charnue des lèvres en mangeant.'[50] The author-narrator's necrophilic desire to perform cunnilingus on the beloved perhaps stems from a plausible motivation to counteract his own hypochondria and prurience; but such an *imagined* act of coitus qualifies as an impossible eventuality preventing the author-narrator from accessing the maternal body. The imagination of cunnilingus /fellatio onto both the author-narrator's mother and his beloved is underwritten by the ultimate realization that reuniting anaclitically with the M/Other will not transpire. The affect of being emotively and sexually unfulfilled precipitates the narrator's melancholic hypochondria, which is as affirmed earlier a condition based on a lack of psychophysical homeostasis.

The author-narrator's hallucinatory realm in which he engages in child–adult necrosexuality additionally permits him to racialize the presumed Caucasian Mother-*qua*-homosexual Other as 'coloured'. The author-narrator describes the beloved's body as a 'sorte de figurine coloriée'.[51] The adjective 'coloriée', as opposed to the more usual 'colorée', refers to colour applications to *objects*. Barthes's consistent naming of the beloved Other as 'the loved Object' in *Fragments* is tethered to his fixation on photography's processes of objectifying, particularly as it involves his mother's photographic objectifica-

voit la vie de l'être aimé comme si de rien n'était' (Barthes, *Fragments*, p. 231). Similarly, the author-narrator evokes in *La Chambre claire*: 'Si la photographie devient alors horrible, c'est parce qu'elle certifie, si l'on peut dire, que le cadavre est vivant, en tant que cadavre: c'est l'image vivante d'une chose morte' (Barthes, *La Chambre claire*, p. 123).

[48] Barthes, *Fragments*, p. 49.
[49] Ibid., p. 267 (emphasis added).
[50] Ibid., pp. 54, 226.
[51] Ibid., p. 86. On Barthes's use of 'colorié(e)' in relation to exoticism see Lisa Lowe, *Critical Terrains: French and British Orientalisms* (Ithaca, NY: Cornell University Press, 1994), pp. 155, 167.

tion in *La Chambre claire*.[52] The author-narrator remarks in this regard: 'La Photographie [...] transforme le sujet en objet; [...] [ma mère] réussissait cette épreuve de se placer devant l'objectif. [...] J'observais [dans la *Photographie du Jardin d'hiver*] la petite fille et je retrouvai ma mère.'[53] By extension, this racialized construction of the 'coloured' homosexual Other would reracialize his mother from white to 'coloured-skin'. Barthes's personal homosexual relationships did occur with males of colour, albeit not exclusively.[54] Given Barthes's actual homosexual encounters with 'coloured' beloved objects of desire, specifically those experiences in North Africa described in his posthumous text *Incidents*, it stands to reason that the author-narrator frames the Mother-*qua*-homosexual Other in racialized and queer formulations.

Recalling Barthes's pro-colonial position in *Mythologies* that 'la France est un grand empire, que tous ses fils, sans distinction de couleur, servent fidèlement sous son drapeau', one can ascertain the author-narrator's familial connection with racialized colonial subjects.[55] Thus, through his maternal grandfather Lieutenant Binger, who was directly involved with Western African colonialism, Barthes is able to map racialized subjectivities onto the M/Other because certain photographs that he reproduces in *La Chambre claire* contain visual contiguities with a 'coloured' subject occupying a maternalized position. In this regard, Barthes reproduces a 1926 photograph by James Van der Zee in which an African American woman is seen standing in the background; she is referred to in maternal terms as a 'négresse nourricière'.[56]

The queer M/Other is racialized as 'coloured' by virtue of its visual associations with (1) the standing maternalized African American woman (or *négresse nourricière*) in Van der Zee's photograph, and (2) its politicized connection to Barthes's maternal lineage tying him to Lieutenant Binger's colonialist project in Africa. This project in turn becomes homoeroticized through its *visual* associations with Nadar's *Savorgnan de Brazza* photograph. Given Nadar's touchy-feely sailor and Van der Zee's coloured mother's right-standing position in both photographs (and the photographs' close sequential placement to each other in the narration), the narrator seemingly superimposes registers of coloniality, queerness, and maternity inherent within each aforementioned photograph to generate an overarching, synthesized visual imagery of a 'coloured' M/Other. *La Chambre claire* is truly a 'camera lucida' in this regard.[57] The *Photographie du Jardin d'hiver* is perhaps none other than

---

[52] Barthes, *Fragments*, pp. 85, 106, 156, 176, 188, 224.

[53] Barthes, *La Chambre claire*, pp. 28, 105.

[54] Roland Barthes, *Incidents* (Paris: Seuil, 1987), p. 30.

[55] Roland Barthes, *Mythologies* (Paris: Seuil, 1957), p. 189.

[56] Barthes, *La Chambre claire*, p. 73.

[57] The phrase is used in the title of the English translation of *La Chambre claire*. See Roland Barthes, *Camera Lucida: Reflections on Photography*, trans. by Richard Howard (New York: Hill and Wang, 1981).

Barthes's hallucination of Binger's, Nadar's, and Van der Zee's photographs superimposed onto each other to produce the 'coloured' M/Other with whom the author-narrator homoerotically identifies in the absent photograph. Visualized epistemology becomes Barthes's 'camera lucida' that performs this optical superposition, and the haunting absence of the *Photographie du Jardin d'hiver* only underscores the cruel optimism underwriting Barthes's phantasmagoria.

A queered visualization of coloniality represented by the archived photograph of Binger, by Nadar's photograph, and by Van der Zee's *négresse nourricière* structures the narrator's homoerotic affect by blending registers of racialization and sexuality into a narrative discourse that itself is corporealized as a homoerotically desired object. The narrator states in this respect: 'Le langage est une peau: je frotte mon langage contre l'autre.'[58] In *Fragments*, queer affect thus betokens a pathologized, anti-normative relationship between subjects engaging in the abject phenomenologies of necrophilia and incestuous desire, on the one hand, and in ontologizing processes of racialization, on the other. The masquerading author-narrator's relationship with abjection, racialization, necrosexuality through mediums of virtuality, visuality, and discourse renders his work transgressive in its own right; as the reader complacently becomes a spectator of these acts. Visualizing the grotesque as child–adult necrosexuality while following the author-narrator's abject phantasmagoria, readers submit themselves to the affects and effects of racialized necrophilia while engaging with *Fragments* and *La Chambre claire*.

The inextricability of race, death, sexuality, and the queered Maternal—all of which operate within the author-narrator's fantasy, producing epistemology and pathologizing imaginings—becomes a foundational element of the narrative of *Fragments* and *La Chambre claire*. This fetishistic 'fascination un petit peu nécrophilique', as evoked earlier, continually orients the author-narrator towards the abject, allowing for a paraphilic and affective engagement with the deceased. This abject relationship recalibrates the anti-normativity of 'queer' to make allowances for perhaps a new form of queer affect that transcends positionalities and intersectionalities, making way for a queer grotesque that subverts homonormative expectations of anti-normativity by embracing the most abject of abject queerness: queer necrosexuality. Indeed, recent scholarship in queer theory has extended the notion of the grotesque in terms of anti-positional sexualities. Justin Edwards and Rune Graulund have initially proposed the term 'queer grotesque', defined as that which 'subvert[s] the socially constructed "norms" of essentialist sexuality and seeks out new sites for same-sex desire through the sexual unease engendered by grotesquerie'.[59] Complicating Edwards and Graulund's conceptualization of

[58] Barthes, *Fragments*, p. 87.
[59] Justin Edwards and Rune Graulund, *The Grotesque* (New York: Routledge, 2013), p. 118.

the queer grotesque, readers can 'seek out new sites for same-sex desire' in an abject, post-mortem realm wherein incestuous queer affect operates not only between two familial subjects, but also between child and adult. The illicit affectivity underwriting this incestuous child-to-adult sex—which is in itself grotesque by virtue of its transgression and illegality—is accentuated by the sexual engagement with death itself.

Whether queer intersectionality also accounts for necrophilia is beyond this article's scope; however, an equally significant point to stress relates to necrosexuality's queerness as an anti-positional expression of libidinality with which the author-narrator of *Fragments* and *La Chambre claire* seemingly identifies. What is of import in the author-narrator's hypochondrialization and libidinal propensities towards necrosexuality is his insistence that he be regarded as a child, which further complicates his affective relationship with the undead, racialized M/Other, as well as the notion of the queer grotesque itself. A child engaging in familial necrosexuality is perhaps the most abject and taboo of all sexual disorders; but for the author-narrator, such an act is seemingly acceptable.[60] The anti-positional visuality of child–adult necrosexuality operating in a racialized context leads readers to recall the homoerotic pact between the photographic subject and its beholder, 'unis par un coït éternel', opening *La Chambre claire*. Queer visuality in the Barthesian universe, whether it connotes exteriorizations of necrosexuality or homoeroticism, bespeaks an anti-positionality that queers the readers by implicating them in the act of witnessing these aberrantly sexualized acts.[61]

The Message in a Bottle

> A small funerary monument, the photograph is a grave for the living dead. It tells their history—a history of ghosts and shadows—and it does so because it is this history.   (EDUARDO CADAVA)[62]

Were *Fragments* and *La Chambre claire* meant to be Barthes's last major works—forms of textual/visual suicide letters and phantasmagoric experimental writing? To what extent do queer sexuality, colonial considerations, and sublimated melancholia fuel the author-narrator's experiences with death; closeted homosexuality; and racialized, incestuous desire? These questions do

[60] Conversely, one could argue that a parent actively having necrosex with a child is equally abject. The most abject taboo here is linked to the presence of a child (whether dead or alive) participating in a context of sexual penetration involving at least one dead body.

[61] Barthes, *La Chambre claire*, p. 17.

[62] Eduardo Cadava, *Words of Light: Theses on the Photography of History* (Princeton: Princeton University Press, 1997), p. 10.

not have simple answers; but this article's reappraisal of *La Chambre claire*, framed largely by the narrational presence of *Fragments*, has tried to offer potential responses. Discourses treating the disavowal of authorial intent, with which Barthes most fully identifies in 'La Mort de l'auteur' (1968), become of particular significance in *La Chambre claire* and *Fragments*, as they lead readers to reconsider whether narrative intentionality is evacuated and indeed 'dead' in these autofictional works.[63] Perhaps an answer could be found in one of Barthes's earliest works *Mythologies* in which he reveals: 'Ce que je prétends, c'est de vivre pleinement la contradiction de mon temps, ce qui peut bien faire le sarcasme la condition de la vérité.'[64] Barthes affirms it himself: a patina of contradiction and irony cloaks his lifework; what seems fortuitous may in fact have been anticipated.

The 'naive' narrator, inseparable from the author holding the pen, presents readers with perhaps two of the most erotically intimate and Delphic of all his texts. *La Chambre claire*, when read in conjunction with *Fragments*, proposes associative signs that could potentially point towards an authorial intentionality that suffuses Barthes's reproduced texts and images. Was the semiotician's promulgation against authorial intentionality strategically destined to avert a reader's attention from latently queer communications in *La Chambre claire* and *Fragments* that, like a message in a bottle at sea, become discovered only decades after its launch? No answer is certain; but one observation cannot be denied: the maternal embrace awaiting Barthes sounded similar to the passing of a van.

UNIVERSITY OF MICHIGAN, ANN ARBOR   BENJAMIN HIRAMATSU IRELAND

[63] Roland Barthes, 'La Mort de l'auteur', *Manteia*, 5 (1968), 12–17.
[64] Barthes, *Mythologies*, p. 10.

EXEMPLARITY IN AND AROUND
THE *NOVELAS EJEMPLARES*

As Cervantes acknowledges in his title, the *Novelas ejemplares* stand between two brief narrative genres—exemplum and novella—which were seen as antithetical.[1] His teasing combination of novella and exemplum belongs in the tradition of brief narrative works which display or obscure the introductory statement of intention (the promythium) and the closing explication of meaning (the epimythium). This article will trace these elements in works before Cervantes's time, some of which he knew, some he probably knew, and some he almost certainly did not know; and in works inspired by the *Novelas ejemplares* and the *Decameron* after his time.[2]

Some salient points can be deduced from the bibliography of editions of novelle given in the Appendix below. First, Cervantes is almost right when he says he is the first to novelize in Spanish, as up till then the books available in Spanish were largely translations from the Italian.[3] Second, the *Novelas ejemplares* marked a watershed in Spain: few books of novelle were printed before 1613, and many after, with frequent reprints up to the end of the eighteenth century. Third, some works were much more popular than others: some sixty new books of novelle appeared between 1613 and 1700, but few were best-sellers. The most popular were indeed the *Novelas ejemplares* (twenty editions to 1700). The only other works to exceed three editions were: Pérez de Montalbán, *Sucesos y prodigios de amor en ocho novelas ejemplares* (twelve editions from 1626 to 1702) and his *Para todos* (eleven editions); Pedro de Castro y Añaya, *Auroras de Diana* (six editions); María de Zayas, whose two books of novelle, printed separately or together, attained eight editions to 1700 (with a further eleven editions in the eighteenth century). Cristóbal Lozano, *Soledades de la vida y desengaños del mundo: novelas y comedias ejemplares*

[1] Walter Pabst, *Novellentheorie und Novellendichtung* (Heidelberg: Winter, 1967), pp. 115–37. In this article I use *novella* (plural *novelle*) to indicate what Dr Johnson in 1755 called *novel*: 'a small tale, generally of love'; their authors I call novellists.

[2] Of the growing bibliography on short fiction in the Golden Age, see especially *Novelas amorosas de diversos ingenios del siglo XVII*, ed. by Evangelina Rodríguez Cuadros (Madrid: Castalia, 1986), pp. 9–87; Jean-Michel Laspéras, *La Nouvelle en Espagne au Siècle d'Or* (Montpellier: Éditions du Castillet, 1987); *Novela corta y teatro en el barroco español (1613-1685): studia in honorem Prof. Anthony Close*, ed. by Rafael Bonilla Cerezo and others (Madrid: Sial, 2012); *Los viajes de Pampinea: novella y novela española en los Siglos de Oro*, ed. by Isabel Colón Calderón and others (Madrid: Sial, 2013); *Ficciones en la ficción: poéticas de la narración inserta (siglos XV-XVII)*, ed. by Valentín Núñez Rivera (Bellaterra: Universitat Autònoma de Barcelona, Servei de Publicacions, 2013). For the European (or at least romance-language) context see Donatella Capaldi and Giovanni Ragone, 'La novella barocca: un percorso europeo', in *La novella barocca*, ed. by Lucinda Spera (Naples: Liguori, 2001), pp. 65–237.

[3] David González Ramírez, 'En el origen de la novela corta del Siglo de Oro: los *novellieri* en España', *Arbor*, 752 (2011), 1221–43; 'En el origen de la novela corta del Siglo de Oro: los *novellieri* desde sus paratextos', *Arbor*, 756 (2012), 813–28.

Modern Language Review, 110 (2015), 456–72
© Modern Humanities Research Association 2015

(1662), had sixteen editions in a hundred years. The pre-Cervantine novelle actually fared better overall: *Ysopete*, *Exemplario* (a version of the *Panchatantra*), *Decameron*, Trancoso, and Timoneda managed more than three editions. Of these, Castro and Lozano are barely studied.

Outside Spain the success of the Spanish novelle was largely in France in book form and in anthologies; they were never printed separately as chapbooks.[4] Another element of the bibliography of the genre in Spain is the ten-year period 1624–34 during which the printing of novelle and plays (*comedias*) was banned in Castile.[5] This was part of a campaign of moral rearmament, along with sumptuary laws, under Philip IV.[6] In the words of the ban: 'porque se ha reconocido el daño de imprimir libros de comedias, novelas ni otros deste género'.[7]

We may note the association of novelle and plays.[8] What they share is the possibility of entertainment and the fact that they could be read at home: the performance of plays was not affected by the printing ban.[9] The prohibition was secular. It concerned only Castile, which in this case includes the big printing centres of Andalusia such as Seville, and therefore the writ did not run in Aragon, including printing towns such as Barcelona, Valencia or Zaragoza. It was, furthermore, evaded: authors got their works printed in Aragon, or pretended that they were. They also avoided the word novella: Zayas, for instance, called her tales marvels, tragedies, *desengaños*, 'undeceivings'.[10] There were, however, some instances of the influence of censorship, notably the bowdlerizations made to a tale of incest by Pérez de Montalbán.[11] I shall

---

[4] José-Manuel Losada Goya, *Bibliographie critique de la littérature espagnole en France au XVIIe siècle: présence et influence* (Geneva: Droz, 1999).

[5] Jaime Moll, 'Diez años sin licencias para imprimir comedias y novelas en los reinos de Castilla, 1625–34', *Boletín de la Real Academia Española*, 54 (1974), 97–103.

[6] On his sumptuary laws, Juan Sempere y Guarinos comments 'En ningun tiempo se han dado en España providencias mas radicales para contener el luxo, que en el reynado de Felipe IV' (*Historia del luxo y de las leyes suntuarias en España*, 2 vols (Madrid: Imprenta Real, 1788), II, 117–32 (p. 117)).

[7] Moll, p. 98. The pragmatic of 1627 refers to 'libros no necessarios o convenientes, ni de materias que devan o puedan escusarse o no importe su lectura [. . .] y es bien que [. . .] no salga ni ocupe lo superfluo y de que no se espere fruto y provecho común' (p. 99).

[8] Mariano Baquero Goyanes, 'Comedia y novela en el s. XVII', in *Serta philologica F. Lázaro Carreter natalem diem sexagesimum celebranti dicata*, 2 vols (Madrid: Cátedra, 1983), II, 13–30; *Entre la rueca y la pluma: novela de mujeres en el Barroco*, ed. by Evangelina Rodríguez Cuadros and Marta Haro Cortés (Madrid: Biblioteca Nueva, 1999), p. 43. Alonso Fernández de Avellaneda, *El ingenioso hidalgo don Quijote de la Mancha*, ed. by Luis Gómez Canseco (Madrid: Biblioteca Nueva, 2000), called the *Novelas ejemplares* 'comedias en prosa' (p. 199).

[9] Carmen Sanz Ayán, 'Felipe IV y el teatro', in *Felipe IV: el hombre y el reinado*, ed. by José Alcalá-Zamora y Queipo de Llano (Madrid: Real Academia de la Historia, 2005), pp. 269–89 (p. 274).

[10] Anne Cayuela, 'La prosa de ficción entre 1625 y 1634: balance de diez años sin licencias para imprimir novelas en los reinos de Castilla', *Mélanges de la Casa de Velázquez*, 29 (1993), 51–76.

[11] Victor Dixon, '*La mayor confusión*', *Hispanófila*, 3 (1958), 17–26; *Novelas amorosas de diversos ingenios*, ed. by Rodríguez Cuadros, p. 51. The Spanish authors' negotiations with decency reflect

return to this when discussing extreme cases below. It is probable too that the slightly more salacious versions of the *Novelas ejemplares* in the Porras manuscript are authorial originals.[12] Moralizing pressure must explain the difference between the two novella collections of Tirso de Molina, alias the Mercedarian Gabriel Téllez. His first, *Cigarrales de Toledo* (1624), is amatory; eleven years later, his second, *Deleitar aprovechando* (1635), a title which wears its heart on its sleeve (to delight by/while benefiting), is essentially a collection of saints' Lives. We may recall here that saints' Lives were the recommended reading of the godly, often mentioned in opposition to *novelle* and plays.[13]

I turn now to Cervantes's own prologue to the *Novelas ejemplares*. His initial grumbles and jokes about his teeth show from the start that he is in playful mode: 'Quisiera yo, si fuera posible, lector amantísimo, escusarme de escribir este prólogo [. . .] los dientes ni menudos ni crecidos, porque no tiene sino seis, y ésos mal acondicionados y peor puestos, porque no tienen correspondencia los unos con los otros.' Rhetorically, it is I think important that his self-portrait is arranged in a series of extremes within which he positions himself: 'el cuerpo entre dos estremos, ni grande, ni pequeño, la color viva, antes blanca que morena; algo cargado de espaldas, y no muy ligero de pies'. This dual structure underlies the more literary content of his prologue. The opposed pair exemplum–novella is implicit there: '[a mis novelas] Heles dado nombre de *ejemplares*'. We are to understand that he is bringing together two things which are incompatible: the earnest moralizing classical or medieval exemplum, particularly associated with Roman heroism or Christian preaching; and the truant modern Boccaccian novella.[14] This combination of extremes is more explicit in the name which the work has in the various licences and which is taken to be the work's original title: *Novelas ejemplares, de honestísimo entretenimiento* (note also the chiasmus).[15]

---

the textual history of the older Italian *novelle*. For censorship of the *Decameron* and bowdlerized Spanish translations of Bandello see Laspéras, pp. 61–67; for Mondragón's bowdlerized Spanish translation (1588) of Guicciardini ibid., pp. 58–59; for the comments of French translators of Bandello ibid., pp. 59–61.

[12] *Novelas ejemplares*, ed. by Jorge García López (Barcelona: Crítica, 2001), pp. xliv, xcix–cii, and Jorge García López, 'Materiales para una edición crítica de las *Novelas ejemplares*', *Anales Cervantinos*, 42 (2010), 33–46.

[13] Pedro M. Cátedra and Anastasio Rojo, *Bibliotecas y lecturas de mujeres, siglo XVI* (Salamanca: Instituto de Historia del Libro y de la Lectura, 2004), pp. 147–48; Barry Taylor, 'Los libros de materia predicable: ¿obras de referencia o lectura privada?', *Revista de Poética Medieval*, 24 (2010), 211–24 (pp. 219–23).

[14] Henry Wheatland Litchfield, 'National *Exempla Virtutis* in Roman Literature', *Harvard Studies in Classical Philology*, 25 (1914), 1–71; Marc Van der Poel, 'The Use of *Exempla* in Roman Declamation', *Rhetorica*, 27 (2009), 332–53.

[15] *Novelas ejemplares*, ed. by García López, pp. xci, 8, 9, 11.

Earlier in the volume, in the *aprobación*, Fr. Juan Bautista recognizes this combination of pleasure and profit:

supuesto que es sentencia llana del angélico doctor Santo Tomás, que la eutropelia es virtud, la que consiste en un entretenimiento honesto, juzgo que la verdadera eutropelia está en estas novelas, porque entretienen con su novedad, enseñan con sus ejemplos a huir vicios y seguir virtudes, y el autor cumple con su intento, con que da honra a nuestra lengua castellana, y avisa a las repúblicas de los daños que de algunos vicios se siguen, con otras muchas comodidades; y así me parece se le puede y debe dar la licencia que pide. (pp. 5–6)

Dr Cetina echoes him: 'con semejantes argumentos nos pretende enseñar su autor cosas de importancia, y el cómo nos hemos de haber en ellas; y este fin tienen los que escriben novelas y fábulas' (p. 6), as does Fr. Diego de Hortigosa: 'hallo en él cosas de mucho entretenimiento para los curiosos lectores, y avisos y sentencias de mucho provecho' (p. 7).

This ought to remind us that this phraseology is as hackneyed as can be, inevitably to be found in the work of civil servants ticking boxes. All these statements are descendants of Horace's 'Omne tulit punctum qui miscuit utile dulci | lectorem delectando pariterque monendo' (*Ars poetica*, ll. 343–44: 'He who has mixed what is useful with what is pleasant has won every vote, delighting and advising the reader in equal measure'). Everybody says it—the censors and the authors in their prologues and titles—which is not to say that they do not mean it; but nor should it be taken as a statement of principle.[16]

Cervantes continues: 'si bien lo miras, no hay ninguna de quien no se pueda sacar algún ejemplo provechoso'. This is not adding anything. There is a precedent in the *Panchatantra* tradition which asks the reader to suspend judgement till he has read the book to the end.[17] And then: 'quizá [yo] te mostrara el sabroso y honesto fruto que se podría sacar'; he nods to the commonplace but just plays with it and teases the reader. 'Mi intento ha sido poner en la plaza de nuestra república una mesa de trucos': this image of the moderate and occasional pleasure of a game of skill is a modernization of the more common image of the bow; again, it is to be placed on a scale extending from full-time pleasure to full-time study.[18] His image of pleasure gardens

---

[16] Examples of 'exemplar' in titles include: Juan Pérez de Montalbán, *Sucesos y prodigios de amor en ocho novelas ejemplares* (1624); Baltasar Mateo Velázquez, *El filósofo del aldea, y sus conuersaciones familiares, y exemplares, por casos, y sucessos casuales* (1626); Luis Pacheco de Narváez, *Historia exemplar de las dos constantes mugeres españolas* (Madrid: Imprenta del Reyno, 1635); Alonso de Alcalá y Herrera, *Varios efectos de amor en cinco novelas ejemplares* (1641); María de Zayas y Sotomayor, *Novelas amorosas y ejemplares* (1637); Cristóbal Lozano, *Soledades de la vida y desengaños del mundo: novelas y comedias ejemplares* (1662); Isidro de Robles [publisher], *Varios efectos de amor en once novelas ejemplares* (1662). As all these post-date Cervantes's work, their titles very likely show his influence.

[17] *Exemplario contra los engaños y peligros del mundo*, ed. by Marta Haro Cortés and others (Valencia: Universitat, 2007), p. 64.

[18] On the image of the bow which proves the need for relaxation, see *Don Quixote*, I. 48; Tirso

is in the same tradition: 'Para este efeto se plantan las alamedas, se buscan las fuentes, se allanan las cuestas y se cultivan con curiosidad los jardines.' He boasts: 'yo soy el primero que he novelado en lengua castellana, que las muchas novelas que en ella andan impresas todas son traducidas de lenguas estranjeras, y éstas son mías propias, no imitadas ni hurtadas'. This is not actually true, as Timoneda had been there before him in 1567. But Cervantes is right to point out that most of the books on the market in Spain were translated from the Italian.[19]

He returns at the end of the prologue to the underlying value of his stories, previously called 'example' and 'fruit', and now 'mystery': 'Sólo esto quiero que consideres: que, pues yo he tenido osadía de dirigir estas novelas al gran Conde de Lemos, algún misterio tienen escondido que las levanta.' He brings together two commonplaces of the prologue: the underlying significance of the text and that the value of the work derives from the prestige of the patron. 'Mystery' suggests *sensus mysticus*, a term in exegesis, a type of allegory.[20]

So this much is clear: first and foremost, Cervantes does not want to be clear. This is an essential feature of his artistic make-up. This is what makes Riley's classic and much-admired *Cervantes's Theory of the Novel* such difficult reading.[21] Second, Cervantes shows he is aware of a literary idea which was

de Molina (cited in *Deleitar aprovechando*, ed. by Pilar Palomo and Isabel Prieto (Madrid: Turner, 1994), p. xii); Glending Olson, *Literature as Recreation in the Later Middle Ages* (Ithaca, NY: Cornell University Press, 1982), pp. 90–127; Alessandro Arcangeli, *Recreation in the Renaissance: Attitudes towards Leisure and Pastimes in European Culture, c. 1425-1675* (Basingstoke: Palgrave, 2003), pp. 12–14.

In the 1330s Don Juan Manuel opposed literature to dicing, a game of chance (*Libro infinido*, ed. by Carlos Mota (Madrid: Cátedra, 2003), p. 177); Cervantes likens literature to billiards (in contemporary English, *trucks*), a game of skill (on the distinction see Arcangeli, pp. 74, 115). See also Alexandra Walsham, 'Godly Recreation: The Problem of Leisure in Late Elizabethan and Early Stuart Society', in D. E. Kennedy, Diana Robertson, and Alexandra Walsham, *Grounds of Controversy: Three Studies in Late 16th and Early 17th Century English Polemics* (Melbourne: History Department, University of Melbourne, 1989), pp. 7–48, and John O'Neill, 'The *Novelas ejemplares* as a Forum for Cervantes's Socio-political Concerns', paper given at the conference of the Association of Hispanists of Great Britain and Ireland, Oxford, March 2013.

[19] On the history of the term 'novela' in Spanish before Cervantes, Laspéras (p. 21), among others, cites the use of 'novella' in the *Comedieta de Ponza* and in Cañizares's translation of the Seven Sages of Rome: neither text was printed till modern times. Critics have not apparently noticed that in the same manuscript in which Cañizares occurs, a subsection of Juan Rodríguez del Padrón, *Siervo libre de amor* (1439-41?), concludes a brief tragic tale of love in the Arthurian mode with the rubric 'aqui acaba la novella' (intro. by Antonio Prieto (Madrid: Castalia,1980), p. 107). In print, Laspéras (p. 21) notes the use of 'novela' in the *Exemplario contra los engaños* (1st edn 1493). Argote de Molina in his edition of *El conde Lucanor* (Sevilla: Hernando Díaz, 1575), sig. A4ᵛ, writes: 'Y si los libros de Novelas y Fabulas tienen lugar y aceptacion publica, los quales tienen un solo intento, que es entretener con apacible, y algunas veces dañoso gusto: mas justamente deue ser acetado este libro, pues demas de ser gustoso, tiene (como dicho tengo) tan buena parte de aprouechamiento.'

[20] For example, Henri de Lubac, *Medieval Exegesis: The Four Senses of Scripture*, 3 vols (Grand Rapids: Eerdmans, 1998–2009), II, trans. by E. M. Macierowski (2000), 107, 245, 246, 248, 252, etc.

[21] E. C. Riley, *Cervantes's Theory of the Novel* (Oxford: Clarendon Press, 1962).

common currency: the author of fiction must place himself somewhere on the scale which has teaching at one end and entertainment at the other. Third, fiction must have a point.[22] Critics bring together my first point (Cervantes's evasiveness) and my third (his acknowledgement of point) and commonly draw attention to the lack of the drawing of unambiguous morals in the *Novelas ejemplares*, and either strive to discern the message that the author would not tell us straight, or identify this imprecision as a mark of modernity.[23]

A distinctive quality of the *Novelas ejemplares* is that they do not do what their predecessors did. I shall therefore survey these predecessors to establish what constituted the norm from which Cervantes broke away. I shall also examine some Spanish novelle from after Cervantes's time and attempt to show that later authors were reluctant to follow his lead, and instead went back to the older ways. I shall argue also that 'exemplary' means no more or less than 'significant' or 'meaningful', and that there were many forms of fiction in and around Cervantes's time which are significant and therefore exemplary.

If we cannot understand a principle, we naturally ask 'Can you give me an example?' As Gregory the Great tells us, 'examples are more effective'.[24] Whether he was speaking of examples or exempla, later medieval authors, writing in the didactic tradition and often a religious one, took this as authority for the use of illustrative stories. The Horatian 'Omne tulit punctum' was little known in the Middle Ages, certainly not in Spain,[25] and instead the common image of the exemplum was digestive: parables and exempla are for the benefit of those who 'cannot chew theories', says the author of the *Speculum laicorum*.[26] What helped the medicine go down but a spoonful of sugar?[27] Medieval exempla were frequently comic, albeit in a grisly way.[28]

How can we know the point of a story? We might assume that a well-made tale needs no explanation. In antiquity illustrative stories, primarily

[22] B. W. Ife, *Reading and Fiction in Golden-Age Spain: A Platonist Critique and Some Picaresque Replies* (Cambridge: Cambridge University Press, 1985), p. 92.

[23] See, for example, among many, Paul Lewis-Smith, 'Free-Thinking in *El celoso extremeño*', in *A Companion to Cervantes's 'Novelas ejemplares'*, ed. by Stephen Boyd (Woodbridge: Tamesis, 2005), pp. 191–206.

[24] Barry Taylor, 'Some Complexities of the *Exemplum* in Ramon Llull's *Llibre de les bèsties*', *MLR*, 90 (1995), 646–58 (p. 646).

[25] Julian Weiss, *The Poet's Art: Literary Theory in Castile, c. 1400-60* (Oxford: Society for the Study of Medieval Languages and Literature, 1990), p. 231, detects little or no influence of Horace in fifteenth-century Spain. A search for 'tulit' on Corde (<http://corpus.rae.es/CORDENET.html> [accessed 3 March 2014]) suggests that the earliest citation of this Horatian tag is by Otálora, *Coloquios de Palatino y Pinciano*, c. 1550; see Jesús Gómez, 'Boccaccio y Otálora en los orígenes de la novela corta en España', *Nueva Revista de Filología Hispánica*, 46 (1998), 23–46.

[26] *Speculum laicorum*, cited by Taylor, 'Some Complexities of the *Exemplum*', p. 646.

[27] Barry Taylor, 'El hígado de don Juan Manuel: una imagen de placer y provecho en *El conde Lucanor*', in *Actes del VII Congrés de l'Associació Hispànica de Literatura Medieval, Castelló de la Plana, 1997*, 3 vols (Castelló: Universitat Jaume I, 1999), III, 447–58.

[28] *Le Rire du prédicateur: récits facétieux du Moyen Âge*, trans. by Albert Lecoy de la Marche; présentation, notes et annexes par Jacques Berlioz (Turnhout: Brepols, 1992).

animal fables, did not circulate without an introduction (the *promythium*) and conclusion (the *epimythium*). To quote Caxton's *Aesop*:[29]

He that is sure and wel garnyshed yet by fals counceyll may be betrayed/ wherof Esope telleth suche a fable/ ¶An Egle was somtyme vpon a tree whiche held with his bylle a nutte [. . .]/ ¶And thus many one ben deceyued thorughe fals counceylle and by the fals tongue of other[.][30]

Cervantes would have known the much-reprinted collection of Aesopic fables known as *Ysopete* or *Las fábulas del clarissimo y sabio fabulador Ysopo*.[31]

So prevalent was the packaging of fables and exempla that it is shocking when Ramon Llull (not so far as I know familiar to Cervantes) in the *Llibre de les bèsties* does not give an explicit explanation to his fables, in order to exercise the reader's wits. There is good reason to think that he owes this technique to his knowledge of Sufi tales.[32] This difficulty of course also has a precedent in the parables of Jesus: 'Qui habet aures audiendi . . .' (Mark 4. 9: 'He that hath ears to hear'); but I believe that the New Testament parables did not influence medieval and Renaissance literature beyond reinforcing the principle that ideas can or should be conveyed in material form.[33]

The epimythium normally brings out the meaning which is located in the end of the tale (subject to the complications described in the discussion of mismatches below). Although Erasmus is famous for his criticisms of the tales of the friars, his objection was not to the use of exempla but to extravagant fourfold allegorical glosses which read meaning into the stories. The strictures of Trent on the subject were in a similar vein.[34] The epimythium need not

---

[29] B. E. Perry, 'The Origin of the Epimythium', *Transactions and Proceedings of the American Philological Association*, 71 (1940), 391–419.

[30] *The Fables of Aesop as First Printed by William Caxton in 1484*, ed. by Joseph Jacobs, 2 vols (London: David Nutt, 1889), II, 20.

[31] Like Caxton, it is a translation of Steinhöwel. *Fábulas de Esopo: reproducción en facsímile de la primera edición de 1489*, ed. by Emilio Cotarelo y Mori (Madrid: Real Academia Española, 1929); see bibliography, pp. xx–xxxiii.

[32] Taylor, 'Some Complexities of the *Exemplum*', p. 654.

[33] '[. . .] procuré darles manera de doctrinal abscondida y solapada debajo de façías, fábulas, novelas y donaires [. . .] Este estilo y orden tuvieron en sus obras muchos sabios [. . .] como Ysopo y Catón, Aulo Gelio, Juan Bocacio, Juan Pogio florentín [. . .] Y Cristo enseñó con parábolas y exemplos al pueblo y a sus discípulos la doctrina celestial' (Cristóbal de Villalón, *El Crotalón*, ed. by Asunción Rallo (Madrid: Cátedra, 1990), pp. 83–84). Argote de Molina, in his edition of *El conde Lucanor* (Sevilla: Hernando Díaz, 1575), refers to the parables: 'Este mismo intento tuvo nuestro redemptor en toda la doctrina de sus parabolas' (sig. A4ᵛ). There is brief mention of the Old Testament fable of the trees in Judges 9. 8 in Baltasar Gracián, *Agudeza y arte de ingenio*, ed. by Evaristo Correa Calderón, 2 vols (Madrid: Castalia, 1969), discurso LVI (II, 206), and Sor Juana Inés de la Cruz (*Inundación castálida*, ed. by Georgina Sabat de Rivers (Madrid: Castalia, 1982), p. 372).

[34] José Aragüés, 'Humanismo y literatura ejemplar: del pretendido rechazo al exemplum en la obra de Vives, Erasmo y Melchor Cano', in *Juan Luis Vives: Actas del Simposio celebrado con motivo del V centenario del nacimiento (Valencia, del 5 al 9 de octubre de 1992)* (Madrid: Grugalma, 1993), pp. 121–47.

be improving. The fabliaux often make explicit the grubby immorality which they incarnate. In one tale the priest and the wood-carver's wife are lovers. The priest hides from the husband by stripping naked and posing on a wooden cross. The wood-carver is not deceived, says 'Oh look I've left his privities on', and chops them off.

> Cest essample nous montre bien
> que nul prestre, por nule rien,
> ne devroit autrui fame amer,
> n'a cele venir ni aler
> qui onques fust en chalengage,
> qu'i n'i laissast la coile en gage:
> si comme fist prestres Coustanz,
> qui i laissa les trois pendanz.[35]

> This exemplum shows us well
> that no priest, for any thing,
> should love another's wife,
> nor come and go to her,
> who was ever in a quarrel,
> at the risk of leaving his balls as surety:
> as did priest Courtanz,
> who left the three hanging there.

The other technique for glossing the meaning of tales was the narrative frame.[36] It does have a western European history, notably in Ovid's *Metamorphoses*; modern critics, however, quite rightly point out that it is a feature of oriental works such as the *Panchatantra*, known in Cervantes's Spain as the *Exemplario*. Here the promythium is pronounced not by the narrator but by a character in the frame. The promythium can be quite unsophisticated: the King says 'Tell me a tale of one who . . .'[37] The epimythium can be depersonalized, as in the fable of the fox and the eagle quoted above. Or it can be all too personal: in the *Panchatantra* the scheming jackals get rid of their political enemy by telling a tale of which the epimythium is 'therefore, O King, you should kill the Ox' (*Exemplario*, p. 110). In Zayas and *Cigarrales* the epimythium is very personal, as narrators choose stories with relevance to their own amatory situations.[38] This prescribing of topics for a novella is developed in the Renaissance in frames which allude to the academies, where the topic

---

[35] *Nouveau recueil complet des fabliaux* (*NRCF*), ed. by Willem Noomen and Nico van den Boogaard, 10 vols (Assen: Van Gorcum, 1983–98), IV (1989), 93–106. For a sample of explicit epimythia see IV, 12, 44, 106, 150, 216, 300.

[36] Barry Taylor, 'Frames Eastern and Western', in *D'Orient en Occident: les recueils de fables enchâssées avant les 'Mille et une Nuits' de Galland*, ed. by Marion Uhlig and Yasmina Foehr-Janssens, Cultural Encounters in Late Antiquity and the Middle Ages, 16 (Turnhout: Brepols, 2014), pp. 35–52.

[37] For example, *Exemplario*, p. 201.

[38] *Entre la rueca y la pluma*, ed. by Rodríguez Cuadros and Haro Cortés, p. 30.

forms the epimythium.[39] Tirso's frame for the *Cigarrales* is highly developed, and in the prologue he emphasizes the importance of framing: novelle should not be 'ensartadas unas tras otras como procesión de disciplinantes'.[40] This is sometimes thought to be a jibe at Cervantes, who famously has no frame.

For truant authors such as Chaucer or Juan Ruiz there are rich opportunities for interaction between frame and inner story. Chaucer's Wife of Bath, married five times, chooses to tell a tale on the subject 'What do women want?'. In Juan Ruiz the go-between Trotaconventos uses Aesopic fables—schoolboy reading—to seduce ladies for her master.[41] Another feature of the frame, from Petrus Alfonsi to Boccaccio, is audience reaction. In the *Decameron*, 'the ladies laughed although they knew they shouldn't':[42] further guidance to the reader as to how he should react.

History was traditionally a source of lessons, 'magistra vitae' (Cicero, *De oratore*, II. 9: 'the schoolmistress of life'), and this idea was still going strong in Cervantes's time.[43] Some collections of historical anecdotes were arranged under subjects on the model of Valerius Maximus, which we can take as promythia.[44] If the culmination of the anecdote is a saying, the genre is the apophthegm.

There is a long tradition of medieval authors of exempla claiming to have witnessed the tales they tell, or to have heard about them from witnesses.[45] Boccaccio never makes such a claim, but Marguerite de Navarre does, and she seems to have been a formative influence on many authors: it is agreed among her speakers that 'chacun dira quelque histoire qu'il aura veuë ou bien ouy dire à quelque homme digne de foy' ('each one shall tell some history which

[39] Willard F. King, *Prosa novelística y academias literarias en el siglo XVII* (Madrid: Real Academia Española, 1963).

[40] Tirso de Molina, *Cigarrales de Toledo*, ed. by Luis Vázquez Fernández (Madrid: Castalia, 1996), p. 108.

[41] Taylor, 'Frames Eastern and Western'; Cormac Ó Cuilleanáin comments of the *Decameron*: 'With the exception of the lewd Dioneo, there is no interaction between storyteller and story told. Here again Chaucer provides a striking contrast. Several of the Canterbury pilgrims tell their tales as a form of self-projection' (Giovanni Boccaccio, *Decameron*, trans. and ed. by Cormac Ó Cuilleanáin (Ware: Wordsworth, 2004), p. xix).

[42] VI. 8; see Olson, *Literature as Recreation in the Later Middle Ages*, pp. 205–06, on laughter among the listeners in the *Decameron*.

[43] It is quoted, for example, in *Historias tragicas exemplares sacadas de las obras del Bandello Verones; nueuamente traduzidas de las que en lengua francesa adornaron Pierre Bouistau y Francisco de Belleforest* (Salamanca: Pedro Lasso, 1589), sig. ¶3ʳ.

[44] José Aragüés, 'El modelo de Valerio Máximo y la configuración de las colecciones de *exempla* renacentistas', en *Actas del I Simposio sobre Humanismo y pervivencia del mundo clásico (Alcañiz, del 8 al 11 de mayo de 1990)*, ed. by J. M. Maestre Maestre and J. Pascual Barea (Cádiz: Servicio de Publicaciones de la Universidad de Cádiz–Instituto de Estudios Turolenses, 1993), pp. 267–82.

[45] See, for example, *The Exempla, or Illustrative Stories, from the 'Sermones vulgares' of Jacques de Vitry*, ed. by Thomas Frederick Crane (London: Folk-Lore Society, 1890), pp. 100–07: 'Audivi quod . . .'.

he will have seen or heard from some trustworthy man').[46] It was common for Spanish novellists to claim that 'names have been changed'.[47] Many of the Spanish novellists consider it important to place their stories in particular cities. Rhetorically the *laus urbis* is a regular feature,[48] though having stated the place they are not much interested in local colour, and Lugo has a rather abstract style;[49] some novellists, however, do name streets if they have sufficient insider first-hand knowledge.[50] Vázquez claims the characters in *Cigarrales* are historical (p. 58), and when Tirso wrote *Deleitar aprovechando*, he turned away from fiction that might have been historical to hagiography, in which all must be historically respectable.[51]

Carmen Rabell argues that the novella is informed by the genre of the *suasoria*, the invented legal case.[52] This partakes of some of the nature of history, as it must be verisimilar. *Suasoriae* lead us to extreme cases. Novelle often push at the limits of morality: we might recall Zayas's scene of a negro forced into degrading sex;[53] Pérez de Montalbán's blood-stained sheets as sign of defloration;[54] his tale of incest.[55] At a lesser level, men commonly gain access to their ladies' chambers;[56] there are knife-fights in the street;[57] and ghosts are at large.[58] Rabell comments on 'el deleite (a veces morboso) del lector' (p. 59). This might, as Rabell argues, reflect the legal mentality of the authors. In other cases the medieval preachers had been there before, telling tales of

---

[46] *L'Heptaméron des nouvelles*, ed. by Nicole Cazauran (Paris: Gallimard, 2000), p. 66. Cazauran (p. 29) sees this as a deliberate attempt by Marguerite to distinguish her work from Boccaccio's. Bandello too claims to be a reporter: *Tutte le opere*, ed. by Francesco Flora, 2 vols (Milan: Mondadori, 1934), I, 6, 321; similarly Tirso, *Deleitar*, p. xvii; and Zayas: 'que los que refiriesen fuesen casos verdaderos' (*Parte segunda del sarao y entretenimiento honesto (Desengaños amorosos)*, ed. by Alicia Yllera (Madrid: Cátedra, 1983), p. 118).

[47] Gonzalo de Céspedes, *Historias peregrinas y ejemplares*, ed. by Yves-René Fonquerne (Madrid: Castalia, 1970), p. 41; *Entre la rueca y la pluma*, ed. by Rodríguez Cuadros and Haro Cortés, p. 283, annotating Zayas, *Estragos*.

[48] *Entre la rueca y la pluma*, ed. by Rodríguez Cuadros and Haro Cortés, p. 167. This might explain the clumsy introduction of Zayas's *La fuerza del amor*, with its overuse of 'gallardo' (*Novelas amorosas y ejemplares*, p. 345). Céspedes is structured on a series of praises of cities.

[49] Francisco de Lugo y Dávila, *Teatro popular: novelas morales*, ed. by Emilio Cotarelo y Mori (Madrid: Viuda de Rico, 1906).

[50] Céspedes, *Historias peregrinas y ejemplares*, p. 42.

[51] On the critical debate around the question whether Zayas used real-life sources, see *Desengaños*, ed. by Yllera, pp. 40–43.

[52] Carmen R. Rabell, *Rewriting the Italian Novella in Counter-Reformation Spain* (Woodbridge: Tamesis, 2003).

[53] Zayas, *El prevenido engañado* (in *Novelas amorosas y ejemplares*).

[54] *Novelas amorosas de diversos ingenios*, ed. by Rodríguez Cuadros, pp. 52, 152.

[55] *La mayor confusión*.

[56] Lugo y Dávila, *Teatro popular*.

[57] *Novelas amorosas de diversos ingenios*, ed. by Rodríguez Cuadros, p. 136.

[58] Céspedes, *Historias peregrinas y ejemplares*, p. 45. I have not seen María Aranda, *Le Spectre en son miroir: essais sur le texte fantastique au Siècle d'Or* (Madrid: Casa de Velázquez, 2011).

ghosts or incest for the express edification of their audience.[59] Trancoso tells of a mother who instructs her daughter to demonstrate her spinning so as to impress a suitor. She disobeys, and cooks some potatoes instead. Mother, 'tentada do demónio', makes her a poisoned cake which Daughter eats greedily and dies. Trancoso concludes: 'Este conto se escreveu para exemplo das filhas que sejam obedientes a suas mães e virtuosas.'[60] This is the equal of the cautionary horrors recounted by preachers such as Jacques de Vitry.[61] Some novellists of course have no frame, epimythium, or promythium, a notable example being Poggio, who states in his prologue that his purpose is merely entertainment.[62]

The ending is the locus of exemplarity. Where there is an epimythium, it often glosses the end of the story, while exemplarity need not be morally improving: for every wise improving apophthegm there is a wisecrack. Poggio and the jokebooks have endings but not epimythia. Gracián Dantisco advised the courtier how to tell stories: 'Porque allí se debe tener más tiento, y ser la maraña del tal cuento clara, y con tal artificio que vaya cevando el gusto, hasta que, con el remate y paradero de la novela, queden [los oyentes] satisfechos.'[63] Similarly Zabaleta praises 'la dependencia del cuento, porque en esta lectura el principio hace gana casi incorregible de llegar al fin'.[64]

Exemplarity can be broad in meaning: an exemplary tale need only be significant. Exemplarity can approximate to tragedy: we see this in the titles of Bandello, *Historias trágicas ejemplares*, and Luis de Guevara, *Sucesos trágicos*.[65] Rodríguez Cuadros points to sadistic elements which should be understood as tragic,[66] while nobody doubted that tragedies were exemplary.[67] When in 1614 Avellaneda said the *Novelas ejemplares* were more properly satirical than

---

[59] Frederic C. Tubach, *Index exemplorum: A Handbook of Medieval Religious Tales* (Helsinki: Suomalainen Tiedeakatemia, 1969), pp. 451–52, 461.

[60] Gonçalo Fernandes Trancoso, *Contos e histórias de proveito & exemplo*, ed. by João Palma-Ferreira (Lisbon: Imprensa Nacional-Casa da Moeda, 1974), pp. 6–9.

[61] *The Exempla*, ed. by Crane, index, pp. 273–93, lists among others: Hermit cured of love by stench of putrefying remains; Nun, chaste but proud and talkative, burned after death from waist up; Nun tears out eyes because prince has fallen in love with them; Physician removes black mark from woman's face and skin; Shears, sign of, made by woman, after her tongue was cut out; Son on way to gallows bites father's lip because he did not reprove him in his youth.

[62] Poggio Bracciolini, *Facezie*, trans. by Marcello Ciccuto (Milan: Rizzoli, 1983), p. 110, refers to himself as one 'qui ad levationem animi haec et ad ingenii exercitum scripsit' ('who has written these things to raise the spirit and exercise the intellect').

[63] Lucas Gracián Dantisco, *Galateo español* (1575), ed. by Margarita Morreale (Madrid: CSIC, 1968), p. 155, cited in *Novelas amorosas de diversos ingenios*, ed. by Rodríguez Cuadros, p. 18.

[64] *El día de fiesta por la tarde*, ed. by Cristóbal Cuevas (Madrid: Castalia, 1983), p. 387, cited in *Entre la rueca y la pluma*, ed. by Rodríguez Cuadros and Haro Cortés, p. 35.

[65] Bandello's original Italian title (at least in the earliest printed editions) appears to have been *Novelle*; the French and English translations add 'tragic', to which the Spanish further adds 'exemplary'.

[66] *Novelas amorosas de diversos ingenios*, ed. by Rodríguez Cuadros, pp. 51, 53, 55, 57.

[67] Although exemplarity is not addressed in the *Poetics*, 'Aristotle does indeed set out to argue

exemplary,[68] he pointed up an affinity between the two modes: in both there is an immediate meaning in the text and a further meaning.[69] Satire does not necessarily identify itself as such, and sometimes the reader has to use his acuity to see through a satire, unless it is only thinly veiled.

A small number of Spanish novella collections have theoretical introductions, as in Lugo, Tirso, and Lope de Vega; Piña supplies an epilogue.[70] All of them appear between 1621 and 1635, so there is an initial untheorized period from the *Novelas ejemplares* to 1621, a group of theoretical considerations from 1621 to 1635, and after that interest in theory disappears. Lugo shares with Francesco Bonciani, in his *Lezione sopra il comporre delle novelle* of 1574, an approach to prose fiction that is calqued on Aristotle's discussion of drama.[71] The influence of Bonciani on Lugo has not been examined. Tirso (*Deleitar*, pp. 7–14) is in the Horatian *prodesse–delectare* ('benefit–delight') tradition. There is also some discussion of the novella in miscellanea (such as Suárez de Figueroa), and courtesy books (Gracián Dantisco).[72]

Although the majority of exemplary tales display both promythium and epimythium, it is also common to encounter a mismatch of tale and epimythium. Livy's exempla have been described as 'inordinately pliant'.[73] In the tradition of the Seven Sages of Rome the tale *Mel* is used in the Spanish to teach that one should not act precipitously and in the Persian that one should nip trouble in the bud:[74]

A huntsman finds a hive and takes it to a merchant to sell it. A drop of honey falls on the ground—A bee jumps on the honey—The merchant's cat jumps on the bee—The

in his own way for poetry's intellectual and moral status' (Stephen Halliwell, *Aristotle's 'Poetics'*, rev. edn (Chicago: University of Chicago Press, 1998), p. 2).

[68] Avellaneda, *El ingenioso hidalgo don Quijote de la Mancha*, p. 195.

[69] Ellen Douglass Leyburn, 'Notes on Satire and Allegory', *Journal of Aesthetics and Art Criticism*, 6 (1948), 323–31.

[70] Joseph Gibaldi, 'The Renaissance Theory of the Novella', *Canadian Review of Comparative Literature*, 2 (1975), 201–27; Lugo, *Teatro popular*, pp. 13–27; Rafael Bonilla Cerezo, '"Proemio" e "Introducción a las novelas" del *Teatro popular* de Francisco Lugo y Dávila: estudio y edición', *Edad de Oro*, 30 (2011), 25–68; Tirso, *Deleitar*, pp. 7–14; Lope de Vega, *Novelas a Marcia Leonarda*, ed. by Antonio Carreño (Madrid: Cátedra, 2002), pp. 103–07, 181–84; Juan Izquierdo de Piña, *Novelas ejemplares y prodigiosas historias*, ed. by Encarnación García de Dini (Verona: Università degli Studi di Pisa, Dipartimento di Lingue e Letterature Romanze, 1987), pp. 215–29.

[71] Francesco Bonciani, *Lezione sopra il comporre delle novelle*, in *Trattati di poetica e retorica del Cinquecento*, ed. by Bernard Weinberg, 4 vols (Bari: Laterza, 1970–74), III (1972), 135–65, 493–96. I have not seen María José Vega Ramos, *La teoría de la 'novella' en el siglo XVI: la poética neoaristotélica ante el 'Decameron'* (Salamanca: Cromberger, 1993).

[72] Christóval Suárez de Figueroa, *El pasagero*, ed. by Francisco Rodríguez Marín (Madrid: Renacimiento, 1913), p. 55; Lucas Gracián Dantisco, *Galateo español*, p. 155. See Thomas Frederick Crane, *Italian Social Customs of the Sixteenth Century and their Influence on the Literatures of Europe* (New Haven: Yale University Press, 1920), pp. 565–659, on Spanish novels and courtesy literature.

[73] Jane D. Chaplin, *Livy's Exemplary History* (Oxford: Oxford University Press, 2000), p. 197.

[74] Sofía Kantor, *El Libro de Sindibād: variaciones en torno al eje temático 'engaño–error'* (Madrid: Real Academia Española, 1988), pp. 81–83.

huntsman's dog jumps on the cat—The merchant kills the dog—The huntsman kills the merchant—The merchant's kin kill the huntsman—A vendetta ensues—In the end all are dead.

In the Spanish, the narrator Sendebar concludes: 'Do not act precipitously'. But in the Persian, Sindibad deduces: 'cette histoire montre qu'il ne faut pas tarder à arracher l'épine du désordre, sous peine de malheurs inévitables'.[75] Chaucer's version of Patient Griselda in the Clerk's Tale has an epimythium that goes counter to the majority of versions, which praise Griselda for her submissiveness.

The mismatch of tale and epimythium is paralleled by a potential mismatch of tale and frame. The question of inappropriate reader reaction was addressed as early as Petrus Alfonsi (Petrus was printed in Cervantes's time in the *Ysopete* collection):

[The master tells two stories of the wiles of women.] At this the pupil said: 'What I have just heard is marvellous. But I pray you, instruct me further so that I may be better informed of the deception practised by women, and may therefore be more on my guard to keep myself protected.' The master answered him: 'Good; so I will tell you a third story, but you must be content with my stories that I give you to educate you.' The pupil said: 'Please, I will be content as you wish.'[76]

As we saw, in Juan Ruiz and the *Panchatantra* tradition, tales can be perverted by the internal narrator. In Lugo's *El andrógino* the lover disguises himself as a woman to gain entry to his lady's house; when discovered, he claims to have just changed sex. He employs an 'expert' to 'prove' that such things are possible. This is really a tale of trickery but it pretends to answer the question that was posed in the informal friends' academy: 'Do androgynes exist?'[77]

I have argued that the *Novelas ejemplares* should be viewed in a context of continuity leading from antiquity to after Cervantes's time. Exemplarity has a long tradition. Authors of all types claimed exemplarity, some in earnest and some in jest. And the exemplum could include the *exemplum vitandum* ('example of what to avoid').[78] As Cristóbal Suárez de Figueroa says: 'Las novelas, tomadas con el rigor que se debe, es una composición ingeniosísima, cuyo

---

[75] *Le Livre des sept vizirs*, trans. by Dejan Bogdanović (Paris: Sindbad, 1975), p. 163.

[76] Eberhard Hermes, *The 'Disciplina clericalis' of Petrus Alfonsi*, trans. by P. M. Quarrie (London: Routledge & Kegan Paul, 1977), p. 121.

[77] *Teatro popular*, pp. 191–270.

[78] The locus classicus is Livy, praefatio: 'Hoc illud est praecipue in cognitione rerum salubre ac frugiferum, omnis te exempli documenta in inlustri posita monumento intueri; inde tibi tuaeque rei publicae quod imitere capias, inde foedum inceptu foedum exitu quod vites' ('In acquiring knowledge of things this is what is especially wholesome and fruitful: to observe the lessons of every exemplum, enshrined in some great work, and to derive therefrom, for yourself and your country, on the one hand that which is worthy of imitation, and on the other those things—rotten from start to finish—which you must avoid').

ejemplo obliga a imitación o escarmiento. No ha de ser simple ni desnuda, sino mañosa y vestida de sentencias, documentos y todo lo demás que puede ministrar la prudente filosofía.'[79] Authors expressed exemplarity in different topics over time: in terms of the kind of biblical integument used in the fables of Walter the Englishman, included in the *Ysopete* collection; of Horatian *delectare-prodesse* as in Tirso's *Deleitar aprovechando*; of fruit/flowers (Walter again); or the bee (Tirso's *Deleitar* again).[80] Exempla could mean different things in different contexts, and the relative weight of pleasure and profit in a work varies according to the individual author. At certain points these commonplaces are made real issues, as at times of censorship: the Ban of 1625 and Tirso's acquiescence in censorship. But exemplarity meant as much or as little as the author wanted. The major difference between medieval and Renaissance poetics, I think, is the rediscovery of the Aristotelian concept of verisimilitude.[81] Otherwise, the Renaissance critics write about the novella as medieval ones had written of the exemplum.

How does Cervantes compare with the norm? He has no frame, no epimythium, no end,[82] and a prologue which shows awareness of the issues of exemplarity but refuses to assign the *Novelas ejemplares* a place in the discussion. I see this as part and parcel of Cervantes's artistic personality, characterized by evasion and avoidance of explicitness. As was noted above, the *Novelas ejemplares* succeeded in reviving the short-story collection in Spanish, and at the level of plot exercised an influence on Zayas and Lugo.[83] But exemplarity was not rendered obsolete by Cervantes's work. The novella after him, like history and tragedy, whether in prose fiction or on the stage, continued to look to the end. Others did not follow his lead: perhaps he was too innovative and the old ways (which were certainly very old) were too deeply ingrained.

THE BRITISH LIBRARY   BARRY TAYLOR

[79] Christóval Suárez de Figueroa, *El pasagero*, p. 55, cited in *Novelas amorosas de diversos ingenios*, ed. by Rodríguez Cuadros, p. 19.

[80] Tirso, *Deleitar*, ed. by Palomo and Prieto, p. 9, says the bee mixes a product which is both 'saludable' and 'dulce'.

[81] For Riley verisimilitude, or bringing fiction closer to the rigours of history, was essential to Cervantes's theory of the novel.

[82] Cervantes has one frame in the *Novelas ejemplares*: the *Coloquio de los perros* is enclosed in *El casamiento engañoso*, but there is no sign of a promythium and epimythium (ed. by García López, pp. 536–37, 623). See Jorge García López, 'Finales de novela en las *Ejemplares*', *Anales Cervantinos*, 35 (1999), 185–92; Caterina Ruta, 'Los comienzos y los finales de las *Novelas ejemplares*', in *Memoria de la palabra: actas del VI congreso de la Asociación Internacional Siglo de Oro*, 2 vols (Madrid: Iberoamericana, 2004), I, 111–38.

[83] Agustín G. de Amezúa y Mayo, *Cervantes, creador de la novela corta española* (Madrid: Consejo Superior de Investigaciones Científicas, 1956).

APPENDIX

Early Editions of Novelle, Chiefly in Spanish[84]

T	translations
bold	collections
*	academy setting

T1489   *Ysopete* [+at least 30 editions to 1750]

T1493   *Exemplario contra los engaños del mundo* [9 editions to 1547; with *Ysopete* 1541, 1546, 1550, 1621]

T1496   Boccaccio, **Ciento novelas** [1524, 1539, 1543, 1550]

1567   Timoneda, **El patrañuelo** [1576, 1578, 1580, 1759]

1575   Don Juan Manuel, **El conde Lucanor** [1642]

1575   Gonçalo Fernandes Trancoso, **Contos e histórias de proveito e exemplo** [+10 editions to 1681]

T1580   Straparola, **Primera parte del honesto y agradable entretenimiento de damas y galanes** [2a pte 1581; 1582, 1585, 1598, 1612]

T1589   Bandello, **Historias trágicas ejemplares** [1596, 1603]

T1590   Giraldo Cintio, **Primera parte de las cien novelas**

1613   Cervantes, **Novelas ejemplares** [+19 editions to 1700]

1613   Sebastián Mey, **Fabulario**

1614   Alonso Jerónimo Salas Barbadillo, *La ingeniosa Elena* [1993]

1617   Juan Cortés de Tolosa, **Discursos morales**

1620   Diego Ágreda y Vargas, **Doce novelas morales, útiles por sus documentos** [1620, 1724]. French translation 1621

1620   Antonio Liñán y Verdugo, *Guía y avisos de forasteros* [1980]

1620   Juan Cortés de Tolosa, **Lazarillo de Manzanares y cinco novelas** [1974]

1620   Alonso Jerónimo Salas Barbadillo, **Casa del placer honesto** [1927]*

1621   Lope de Vega, *La Filomena*

1622   Francisco de Lugo y Dávila, **Teatro popular. Novelas morales** [1906]. French translation 1628

1623   Gonzalo Céspedes y Meneses, **Primera parte de las historias peregrinas y ejemplares** [1630, 1647; 1906, 1970]. French translation 1628

1624   Lope de Vega, *La Circe*

1624   Tirso de Molina, **Cigarrales de Toledo** [1630, 1631; 1996]

1624   Juan Pérez de Montalbán, **Sucesos y prodigios de amor en ocho novelas ejemplares** [12 editions 1626–1702; 1949, 1999].[85] Italian translation 1637; French translation 1644

---

[84] These data are based on Begoña Ripoll, *La novela barroca: catálogo bio-bibliográfico (1620–1700)* (Salamanca: Universidad de Salamanca, 1991), and Isabel Colón Calderón, *La novela corta en el siglo XVII* (Madrid: Laberinto, 2001).

[85] *Obra no dramática*, ed. by José Enrique Laplana Gil (Madrid: Fundación José Antonio de Castro, 1999).

1624   José Camerino, *Novelas amorosas y prodigiosas historias* [1736]

1624   Juan Izquierdo de Piña, *Novelas ejemplares y prodigiosas historias* [1987]

1625 EDICT OF THE JUNTA DE REFORMACIÓN

1625   Alonso Castillo Solórzano, *Tardes entretenidas* [1908; 1992]

1626   Alonso Castillo Solórzano, *Jornadas alegres* [1909]

1626   Baltasar Mateo Velázquez, *El filósofo del aldea, y sus conuersaciones familiares, y exemplares, por casos, y sucessos casuales*

1627   Juan Izquierdo de Piña, *Varias fortunas*

1627   Alonso Castillo Solórzano, *Tiempo de regocijo y Carnestolendas de Madrid* [1907]

1627   Gabriel Bocángel, *Rimas y prosas*

1628   Juan Izquierdo de Piña, *Casos prodigiosos y cueva encantada* [1907]

1628   Miguel Moreno, *El cuerdo amante* [1906]

1629   Juan Izquierdo de Piña, *Segunda parte de los casos prodigiosos*

1629   Alonso Castillo Solórzano, *Huerta de Valencia: prosas y versos en las Academias della* [1944]*

1631   Alonso Castillo Solórzano, *Noches de placer* [1906]

1632   Pérez de Montalbán, *Para todos* [10 editions 1633 to 1691; 1999].[86] French translation 1685*

1632   Pedro de Castro y Añaya, *Auroras de Diana* [. . .] *con privilegio y prohibición* [1632, 1634, 1637, 1640, 1654; 1949, 1989]. French translation 1683, 1685

1634   Alonso Castillo Solórzano, *Fiestas del jardín: que contiene tres comedias y cuatro novelas*

1635 END OF THE PROHIBITION ON PRINTING NOVELS AND PLAYS IN CASTILE

1635   Alonso Castillo Solórzano, *Novelas de varios sucesos*

1635   Ginés Carrillo Cerón, *Novelas de varios sucesos*

1635   Tirso de Molina, *Deleitar aprovechando* [1677, 1765; 1981, 1994]

1636   Jacinto Amaral, *El forastero*

1637   María de Zayas y Sotomayor, *Novelas amorosas y ejemplares* [1638, 1648; 2000]

1640   Alonso Castillo Solórzano, *Los alivios de Casandra*. Includes *En el delito, el remedio*, written without A. French translation 1640

1640   Francisco de Navarrete y Ribera, *Flor de sainetes*. Includes *La novela de lostres hermanos, escrita sin el uso de la A* [1871].[87]

1640   Matías de los Reyes, *Para algunos*

1641   Alonso de Alcalá y Herrera, *Varios efectos de amor en cinco novelas ejemplares y nuevo artificio de escribir prosa y verso sin una de las letras vocales excluyendo vocal diferente en cada novela* [1671; and in Robles 1666]

1641   Andrés Sanz del Castillo, *La mojiganga del gusto en seis novelas* [1734; 1908]

1642   Alonso Castillo Solórzano, *La garduña de Sevilla* [1972]

---

[86] In *Obra no dramática*.

[87] In *Biblioteca de autores españoles*, XXXIII.

1647   María de Zayas y Sotomayor, *Parte segunda del sarao y entretenimiento honesto* [*Desengaños amorosos* 1649; 1983]; *Primera y segunda parte de las novelas amorosas y ejemplares* [1659, 1664, 1674; 11 editions 1705–95]. French translation 1658, 1680

1648   Jusepe Alfay and Martín Navarro [publishers], *Novelas amorosas de los mejores ingenios de España*. By Lope de Vega and Castillo Solórzano [1649, 1650]

1649   Alonso Castillo Solórzano, *La Quinta de Laura; que contiene seis novelas, adornadas de diferentes versos* [1732]

1649   Alonso Castillo Solórzano, *Sala de recreación* [1977]

1654   Matías de Aguirre del Pozo y Felices, *Navidad de Zaragoza**

1654   Manuel Lorenzo de Lizarazu y Berbinzana, *Acasos de fortuna y triunfos de amor. En dos novelas. La una escrita sin a.*

1654   Fernando Jacinto Zurita y Haro, *Méritos disponen premios. Discurso lírico*

1655?   [Leonor de Meneses], *El desdeñado más firme* [1999][88]

1662   Francisco la Cueba, *Mojiganga del gusto en seis novelas*

1663   Andrés de Prado, *Meriendas del ingenio y entretenimientos del gusto en seis novelas*

1663   Mariana de Carvajal y Saavedra, *Navidades de Madrid y noches entretenidas* [1728; 1988; 1993]

1662   Cristóbal Lozano, *Soledades de la vida y desengaños del mundo. Novelas y comedias ejemplares* [+15 editions 1672–1761]

1666   Jacinto de Ayala, *Sarao de Aranjuez en varios versos y novelas*

1666   Isidro de Robles [publisher], *Varios efectos de amor en once novelas ejemplares* [1692, 1709, 1709, 1729, 1760]

1679   Ana Francisca Abarca de Bolea, *Vigilia y octavario de San Juan Bautista* [1993]

1681   Antonio Vital Pizarro y Cuña, *Excesos amorosos en cuatro novelas ejemplares*

1683   José Penso de la Vega, *Rumbos peligrosos*

1685   Luis de Guevara, *Intercadencias de la calentura del amor: sucesos tragicos [. . .] ya dichosos*

1698   Miguel de Montreal, *Engaños de mujeres, y desengaños de los hombres* [1709]

---

[88] In *Entre la rueca y la pluma*, ed. by Rodríguez Cuadros and Haro Cortés, pp. 337–93.

MODERNITY AND THE CULTURAL MEMORY CRISIS IN GUSTAVO ADOLFO BÉCQUER'S *LA CRUZ DEL DIABLO* AND *EL MONTE DE LAS ÁNIMAS*

Gustavo Adolfo Bécquer's reputation as a despondent and suffering poet was in reality a carefully designed fiction created by his friends and colleagues to propagate what Rica Brown aptly entitled 'the Bécquer legend'. In her analysis Brown rectified this erroneous and romanticized image of Bécquer to portray instead a more encompassing and realistic vision that showed the eclectic and critical side of the renowned nineteenth-century writer.[1] More inclusive studies on Bécquer have since revealed a perspicacious critical mind and an individual who regarded the changing socio-cultural landscape of Spain with increasing circumspection as it moved ever more rapidly toward a technologized and secular modern world.

Furthermore, analysis of Bécquer's writings, according to Rubén Benítez and Robert Pageard, should not discount the political affiliation with *moderantismo* that reflected the conservative ideology which permeates his critical and literary writings. The historians Bahamonde and Martínez state that the *moderados* may have represented an eclectic conglomerate of individuals who differed in the degree of their adherence to conservative ideals, but as a united party embraced the notion of a codified national system underwritten by national traditions.[2] The *moderado* political temperament valued the benefits of modernization while remaining faithful to the cultural traditions that had carried the nation to this historical juncture. Bécquer professes this ambivalence in his writings by advocating the preservation of those customs that protected against the erosion of communal bonds while simultaneously praising the advances of modernization.

In the fourth letter in *Desde mi celda*, Bécquer verbalizes this inner conflict:

Yo tengo fe en el porvenir. Me complazco en asistir mentalmente a esa inmensa e irresistible invasión de las nuevas ideas que van transformando poco a poco la faz de la Humanidad, que merced a sus extraordinarias invenciones fomentan el comercio de la inteligencia, estrechan el vínculo de los países, fortificando el espíritu de las grandes nacionalidades, y borrando, por decirlo así, las preocupaciones y las distancias, hacen caer una tras otras las barreras que separan a los pueblos. No obstante, sea cuestión de poesía, sea que es inherente a la naturaleza frágil del hombre simpatizar con lo que perece y volver los ojos con cierta triste complacencia hasta lo que ya no existe, ello es que en el fondo de mi alma consagro, con una especie de culto, una veneración profunda por todo lo que pertenece al pasado, y las poéticas tradiciones, las derruidas fortalezas, los antiguos usos de nuestra vieja España, tienen para mí todo ese indefinible

[1] Rica Brown, 'The Bécquer Legend', *Bulletin of Hispanic Studies*, 18 (1941), 4–18.
[2] Ángel Bahamonde and Jesús A. Martínez, *Historia de España: siglo XIX* (Madrid: Cátedra, 1994), pp. 246–48.

Modern Language Review, 110 (2015), 473–90
© Modern Humanities Research Association 2015

encanto, esa vaguedad misteriosa de la puerta del sol en un día espléndido, cuyas horas, llenas de emociones, vuelven a pasar por la memoria vestidas de colores de luz, antes de sepultarse en las tinieblas en que se han de perder para siempre.[3]

This passage captures the duality felt by Bécquer as he negotiated the challenges of a liminal period, as one cultural moment erodes and a new one has yet to assert itself. In other words, Bécquer reveals a historical moment in which the social customs and the overarching infrastructure are not aligned and thus interfere with communal bonds and stability. Within this framework, the present article will elaborate on this transitional cultural period and how it manifests itself in two of Bécquer's *leyendas*, *La cruz del diablo* and *El monte de las ánimas*. These two legends serve as testimonial texts reflecting the shift of knowledge management, particularly with reference to the decline of oral traditions and modernity's ascension of what Michel de Certeau terms the scriptural economy.

De Certeau regards the shift to print culture as one of the prevailing signs of the modern world-view: 'Thus one can read above the portals of modernity such inscriptions as "[h]ere, to work is to write," or "[h]ere only what is written is understood".'[4] In his analysis of the scriptural economy he explains that the modern Western perception of the world has seen that '[t]he "oral" is that which does not contribute to progress; reciprocally, the "scriptural" is that which separates itself from the magical world of voices and tradition. A frontier (and a front) of Western culture is established by that separation.'[5] The transitional process from predominantly oral traditions to written systemization of knowledge introduces new understandings of the world as well as significant changes in individual consciousness. Individuality and solitary reflection become the dominant status of human consciousness rather than one integrated into a communal network of voices.[6] Walter Ong makes this distinction between the underlying dynamics of an oral culture versus a chirographic or written one: 'Oral communication unites people in groups. Writing and reading are solitary activities that throw the psyche back on itself.'[7] He continues: 'More than any other single invention writing has transformed human consciousness.'[8] This is perhaps most evident in the shift from oral memory rituals to the reliance on external sources for storing cultural and historical knowledge.

---

[3] Gustavo Adolfo Bécquer, *Obras completas*, ed. by Joan Estruch Tobella (Madrid: Cátedra, 2012), pp. 407–08. Henceforth cited as *OC*.

[4] Michel de Certeau, *The Practice of Everyday Life*, trans. by Steven F. Rendall (Berkeley: University of California Press, 2011), p. 134.

[5] Ibid.

[6] Ibid.

[7] Walter Ong, *Orality and Literacy: The Technologizing of the Word* (London: Methuen, 1982), p. 69.

[8] Ibid., p. 78.

The scriptural system's conquest of the practice of memory rituals has been interpreted in oppositional ways. On the one hand, writing creates higher, abstract thinking that has contributed to the numerous advances in conceptual and technological fields. Yet it lessens the demands on memory, thus introducing a dependence on external sources for cultural and historical knowledge. These external sources infiltrate the consciousness individually rather than through vetted communal processes. Ong considers that communal and oral processes for knowledge management provide a community with agency in selecting which cultural system it retains and perpetuates. Oral traditions may be handed down by institutionalized sources that originate outside of the community's boundaries, but they change according to the needs of the specific collective body. Furthermore, the importance of oral traditions is not based exclusively on the information they convey but also on the social processes that are generated through these rituals that fortify the collective's sense of cultural unity.

The supersession by writing of oral memory rituals does not occur without causing anxiety over the impact this transformative process has on human behaviour.[9] Richard Terdiman argues that the disjunction between the two forms of managing cultural knowledge was felt with particular acuity in Europe throughout the nineteenth century: 'In this period people experienced the insecurity of their culture's involvement with its past, the perturbation of the link with their own inheritance, as what I want to term a "memory crisis": a sense that their past had somehow evaded memory, that recollection has ceased to integrate with consciousness.'[10] A deep sense of loss and isolation emerged from this dislocation of the past from memory. The consequences of the split between memory and history evoked feelings of ambivalence over the myth of progress that Terdiman notes was caused by 'a deep perception of the memory crisis as a historical disaster'.[11] In an effort to preserve connections with oral manifestations of cultural memory, writers implemented diverse tactics that could mediate the corrosive forces of modernization without halting the progressive march through history; perhaps one of the most recognized resources was found in folkloric expression.

Integrated folkloric expression in the guise of beliefs, practices, stories, and so on had played a fundamental role in earlier literary works throughout

[9] These moments of transformation in predominant modes of communication are not limited to the period covered in this article, but rather comprise the historical flow of human development. In a recent study by Kim von Arx, the author notes that the conquest of CMC (computer-mediated communication) has changed human behaviour and, consequently, perceptions of the world: see Kim von Arx, 'LitOral: A New Form of Defamation Consciousness', *Canadian Journal of Law and Technology*, 1 (2002), 63–76.

[10] Richard Terdiman, *Present/Past: Modernity and the Memory Crisis* (Ithaca, NY: Cornell University Press, 1993), pp. 3–4.

[11] Ibid., p. 24.

Spanish history, but during the first half of the nineteenth century were often at the service of conservative Romantic nationalism. As Montserrat Amores elucidates:

La atracción por lo natural, lo salvaje, lo exótico se integró dentro de un movimiento de primitivismo cultural que menospreciaba lo "artificial", lo "pulido", y que propició la identificación entre lo antiguo, lo distante y lo popular. Por otra parte, esto último pasó a ser pronto fundamento del nacionalismo. La identidad nacional se manifestaba en las creaciones del pueblo, y por ello los estudios y trabajos sobre el folclore adquirieron un evidente significado político.[12]

Under this premiss, Amores identifies Cecilia Böhl de Faber as one of the principal figures to popularize the ethnopoetic sensibilities of Romantic nationalism through the collection and re-elaboration of folkloric works.

While Böhl de Faber popularized literary folklore, in part, to propagate what she envisioned as an authentic Spanish nationalism, Romantic historiography had also sought to recover autochthonous, and Christian, origins in its remote medieval past that had been cast aside by the rationalistic minds of the eighteenth century. Derek Flitter explains that the Romantic historiographers 'exalted the sacred traditions of a God-fearing society underpinned by stable and enduring values, an historical age that had inspired humanity with the sublimity of its magnificent deeds and with the idealism of its chivalric enthusiasm'.[13] Flitter points out that Romantic historiography vindicated popular sources as a vehicle for transmitting cultural knowledge; in its 'mediaeval revivalism', the Romantic historiographers attempted to redress the harm caused predominantly by the eighteenth-century sceptics. In addition, he adds: 'at a period of crisis intensified by the far-reaching breakdown of religious beliefs and established values for which the Enlightenment was increasingly held responsible, the harmonious and unitary belief-system and cultural patterns of the mediaeval period began not just wistfully to be eulogized and imaginatively to be evoked but ideologically to be reasserted'.[14] In this medieval revivalism historiographers restored traditional and popular sources to the status of valid historical knowledge. As non-empirical resources, oral rituals were revered for preserving cultural memories that had been expunged from history by the *philosophes* of the preceding century.[15]

---

[12] Montserrat Amores, *Fernán Caballero y el cuento folclórico* (El Puerto de Santa María: Ayuntamiento de El Puerto de Santa María, 2001), p. 5.

[13] Derek Flitter, *Spanish Romanticism and the Uses of History* (London: Legenda, 2006), p. 11.

[14] Ibid., p. 9.

[15] Hayden White comments: 'The Enlighteners believed the ground of all truth was reason and its capacity to judge the products of sensory experience and to extract from such experience its pure truth content *against* what the imagination wished that experience to be. Thus, as Voltaire maintained in his *Philosophy of History*, it appeared to be a simple matter to distinguish between the true and the false in history. One had only to use common sense and reason to distinguish

Philip Silver posits that Bécquer practised a poetic historicism through his vindication of oral traditions inherited from Romantic historiography:

the critical historian with his documents would not leave out any famous names, but he would certainly discount their more fabled aspects. The poetic historian, on the other hand, would focus on just such traditional sources, inasmuch as they were genuine repositories of Spanish values. The poetic historian would work intuitively with these to reveal the 'ideas' that popular tradition attached to these famous names. Thus, for Bécquer as a national-romantic, oral tradition and ruins of religious monuments were the preferred source of national values and hence more precious than historical 'truth'.[16]

Bécquer embraced both poetic and critical historicism as early as his *Historia de los templos de España* (1857). In the introduction, and spread throughout the *templos* project, he validates the necessary collaboration between archival and poetic sources to acquire authentic historical and cultural knowledge. While the religious origins of national identity pervade this work, the preservation of collective cultural memory also receives attention, yet is often overlooked in studies of *Historia de los templos*. In one instance, as Bécquer completes the detailed historical account of the church of Santa Leocadia, he adds the non-empirical description of its miracles and traditions:

Pareceríanos que faltaba el complemento de la reseña histórica de Santa Leocadia si, aunque en postrer lugar, no diéramos cabida en este artículo a las diversa tradiciones que, acerca de la efigie del Cristo que se ve en su altar mayor, corren con más o menos aceptación entre los toledanos. (*OC*, p. 988)

He then adds that this artefact had been preserved in cultural memory in Zorrilla's legend *A buen juez mejor testigo* (*OC*, p. 989). The emphasis on cultural memory and oral traditions moves from an afterword in these chapters of *Historia de los templos* to a position of much greater prominence in the *leyendas*, which underscores one of the primary characteristics of legends as a folk genre providing source material for the investigation of oral memory rituals and cultural knowledge.

The predominance of published legends throughout the nineteenth century testifies to an intermediary stage between oral and written cultures. They belong to a category of residual ritualization of knowledge that occurs as older forms of practising culture give way to the new print culture. In fact, Jack

---

between the truthful and the fabulous, between the products of sensory experience as governed by reason and such products as they appeared under the sway of the imagination, in the historical record.' He continues: 'This meant that whole bodies of data from the past—everything contained in legend, myth, fable—were excluded as potential evidence for determining the truth about the past' (Hayden White, *Metahistory: The Historical Imagination in Nineteenth-Century Europe* (Baltimore, Johns Hopkins University Press, 1973), p. 52).

[16] Philip W. Silver, *Ruin and Restitution: Reinterpreting Romanticism in Spain* (Nashville: Vanderbilt University Press, 1997), p. 76.

Goody categorizes legends within formal oral recitations typically 'told on ritual occasions'.[17] The ritualization of these oral histories is essential for disseminating knowledge of the past and associating it with the specific temporal markers or events in which ritual activity assists in recalling foundational cultural events. Goody also notes that there are some cultures more prone to retaining orality than others: 'the Roman Catholic countries of southern Europe continue to encourage the telling of saints' stories (or legends, a feature of the oral tradition of written cultures), whereas these stories almost entirely disappeared from the Protestant north when the saints themselves were largely banished'.[18] As Benítez and later Silver have argued, Bécquer's desire to protect oral culture was rooted in his belief that the peasantry had retained the ideals of a more harmonious Christian period in Spain's history and that the truth of history was embedded in these oral productions. In a brief scan of the contemporaneous periodicals, reference to legends as a way of storing cultural, medicinal, hygienic, or patriotic information was frequently encountered.[19]

As it is my intention to show here, legends are specifically adept at portray-

---

[17] Jack Goody, *Literacy in Traditional Societies* (Cambridge : Cambridge University Press, 1968), p. 54.

[18] Ibid., p. 56

[19] There are several cases in periodicals from the mid-nineteenth century that demonstrate resistance to purely critical forms of disseminating knowledge. While legends were most often associated with fantastical stories, they were also cited as providing the kind of valuable information not available in more sceptical written documents. In one such periodical, *La Ilustracion: Periódico Universal*, 339 (27 August 1855), 342, the editors include a legend entitled *El pescador de corral* that relates a supernatural tale in which a proud and selfish character, Romualdo, sells his soul to rid himself of his rival and childhood companion, Jaumy. The legend relates typical events imbued with supernatural incidents, but more importantly for our analysis are the reflections on memory and its necessary function as part of a cultural source of knowledge. The narrator laments the effects of time on memory after Jaumy has disappeared a month before his wedding to his beloved Marta: 'Ellos [months passed] traen el olvido de las penas y la esperanza; ellos calman la aflicción más amarga, y el velo del olvido, más tupido de año en año, oculta en sus pliegues los deleites y los infortunios pasados. Así se había casi borrado de la memoria de sus compañeros el recuerdo de Jaumy, cuando se despertó de nuevo el día de la Asunción, que era el señalado para los desposorios de Marta con el pobre pescador.' It is only through the ritual acts associated with the Assumption and veneration of the patron saint that memory is resuscitated, and with that process Jaumy returns from what is perceived as a supernatural land beyond our earthly existence. The narrator confirms the power of memory as he remarks its fundamental power from the vantage-point of the present. The chapel that had united the community, sparking their memory of Jaumy, serves as a memory site for the fisherman of the present to recall the very real maritime dangers that lurk in treacherous waters: 'Esta leyenda es referida hoy mismo por los viejos pescadores de la costa á los viajeros que recorren aquellos parajes, mostrándoles una capilla ruinosa sobre un promontorio. La yedra crece y se enreda en paz entre sus quebradas paredes; las sabandijas asoman sus cabezas por entre las piedras dislocadas: los insectos se arrastran por la yerba que obstruye la puerta apolillada. Pero esta capilla solitaria, mudo testigo de tantas borrascas, conserva el espíritu grave melancólico de monumentos grandes ó pequeños, trayendo á la memoria hechos de épocas lejanas, y aun la contemplan los pescadores del país como una centinela vigilante y benéfica que los protege contra las olas tempestuosas, del mismo modo que había protegido a las generaciones pasadas.'

ing social conflicts as well as emphasizing the intricacies and implications of an oral cultural tradition. In fact, as Linda Dégh notes, legends 'more than any other folklore genre, can make sense only within the crossfire of controversies. Even if participants occasionally do not seem to be in fierce disagreement with the legend's proposition, the commonly known opposing opinion of society at large always makes its presence felt'.[20] Dégh highlights two key components of legends: the participatory aspect that subtly incorporates the targeted audience, and the controversy at the centre of the story that foregrounds a greater tension afflicting that same audience. Both of these constitutive parts of the genre play an important role in Gustavo Adolfo Bécquer's legendary stories first published between 1858 and 1864, in various journals that reflect this greater trend towards preserving cultural memory through oral and communal storytelling rituals.

The orality in these legends forms part of their structural component, in which an internal narrator tells a story that communicates the origin or incident loosely associated with some aspect of cultural knowledge. As Russell P. Sebold indicates, the role of group dynamics is part of Bécquer's poetic of the fantastic, in which orality is the dominant mode of communication. Sebold identifies several versions of listening groups within the stories that assist in conveying a different type of authority rooted in collective group unity: 'La mera sugestión de auditorio, público, reunión de testigos, coadyuva a la consecución de la aceptabilidad cuando se trata de lo fantástico; pues lo que se oye entre dos o más personas posee, por increíble que de otro modo sea, cierta rudimentaria objetividad que no tiene lo experimentado por una sola persona.'[21] While Sebold characterizes this as part of the process by which the sceptical listener becomes a willing believer in the fantastic, his observation underscores the psychology of group dynamics that unifies highly oral cultures. Furthermore, he has noted that among Bécquer's *leyendas*, *La cruz del diablo* portrays the highest register of orality in which a group is brought into a unifying circle. In fact, the storytelling act functions as a connective thread throughout the tale, and the question of its purpose repays further study. A similar scenario is present in *El monte de las ánimas*, and although Sebold differentiates this legend as containing 'un auditorio implícito', from a cultural perspective it creates the same connective processes as the more explicit forms of group storytelling present in *La cruz del diablo*: 'En fin, he aquí en esta narración un verdadero congreso de cuentistas, narradores y relatores de todas las edades y ambos sexos, cada uno con un sendo público.'[22] Sebold emphasizes the reaction of the listeners as they internalize the supernatural

[20] Linda Dégh, *Legend and Belief: Dialectics of a Folklore Genre* (Bloomington: Indiana University Press, 2001), p. 2.

[21] Russell P. Sebold, *Bécquer en sus narraciones fantásticas* (Madrid: Taurus, 1989), p. 71.

[22] Ibid., p. 73.

elements, moving from disbelief to belief, and the power of this process as it occurs in a group dynamic. While I essentially agree with Sebold that Bécquer is attempting to draw in the sceptical implicit audience, my focus points to an underlying criticism of the isolating and empirical forms of managing cultural knowledge, and consequent erosion of the communal unification inherent in oral traditions.

Bécquer's *leyendas* emphasize the oral dissemination of knowledge that is intrinsically linked to iconic or commemorative objects, and locations are permeated with strong religious connotations that have evolved into sacred spaces, existing apart and distinct from profane, everyday life. The sacralization of these sites assures the continuity of cultural understanding by demanding a ritualized acknowledgement of their significance. In both *La cruz del diablo* and *El monte de las ánimas*, it is not only the specific objects and sites that are imbued with sacred meaning, but also the act of storytelling. In both legends the physical ruins—the cross and the mountain on the specific *Noche de los difuntos*—and the verbal stories become part of a memory ritual. The stories become ritualistic in that they have 'a quality of specialness not the same as other things, standing for something important and possessing an extra meaningfulness and the ability to evoke emotion-filled images and experiences'.[23] These sacralized sites are passed down generationally through ritualized memory in the guise of supernatural and folkloric stories. The ritualization of the stories instils in them a special and sacred form that contributes to asserting 'a certain identity, history, and value system'.[24] The relating of the story becomes part of the ritual-like activity that assists in disseminating the internal and poetic historicism that Bécquer had advocated in his narratives. In this way, the violent experiences undergone by the characters who disregard the memory rituals are understood within the context of a desecration that requires a blood sacrifice in order to restore harmony to the community. In both cases the dismissal of ritualistic storytelling produces violent consequences. Whereas Bécquer's critical essays explicitly confront the crisis of modernity in which the associated transformations had begun to disenfranchise the collective from its cultural awareness and inherited values, his *leyendas* are an exercise in theory in which the separation from living memory changes how communities perceive and process cultural knowledge in their interpretation of the world. In the first legend, however, the cultural move is from disunity to unity, thus avoiding continued violence and death, whereas in the second this shift operates in the opposite direction—from unity to disunity—leading to the death of the two main characters.

As we turn to Bécquer's two legends to examine how the cultural crisis

---

[23] Catherine Bell, *Ritual: Perspectives and Dimensions* (New York: Oxford University Press, 2009), p. 157.

[24] Ibid., p. 159.

manifests itself, it is necessary to point out that this analysis does not pursue the status of belief in the supernatural as the central conflict within the stories, but rather belief as it assists in the transmission of authentic cultural values. Contributing to the ritualized memory that underscores this aspect of conveying poetic historicism, the dialectic of belief and disbelief, as posited by Sebold in relation to Becquer's *leyendas*, plays a fundamental role in the transmission of internal cultural knowledge and communal unity. It is because these ritualized mnemonic acts of storytelling are shrouded in supernatural references that connective semantics are constituted. Sebold indirectly describes how connections are sustained through Bécquer's use of fantasy in what he calls *el casi creer*: 'Uno de los principales componentes del relato fantástico en la mayoría de sus manifestaciones modernas es el asombro u horror de los personajes y lectores escépticos al sentirse llevados a prestar fe a sucesos cuya maravillosa índole está en contradicción con cualquier concepto convencional de la posibilidad física natural.'[25] It is not my purpose here to dismiss the importance of the dialectic between belief and disbelief in the supernatural, as the interplay between the two creates the scenario in which the underlying cultural past is relayed to the implied reader. What is foremost in this analysis, however, is to show how the ability to sustain collective unity as well as awareness of a cultural heritage is a question of intercepting and accepting the internally shared cultural history that is embedded in the retelling, or collective remembering, of supernatural stories.

In the first legend, *La cruz del diablo*, a community is forced to contend with oppressive violence committed by the cruel overlord, el señor del Segre, and, after the villagers murder him, the Devil's continuation of violent attacks. It is not until the community as a whole repents and unites in a ritualistic oration that the Devil is defeated, thus restoring peace and harmony to the village. This legend clearly underscores an overarching Christian discourse as the villagers are able to free themselves from violence by submitting to religious penance; yet underlying the overtly religious tone in this tale is evidence of the memory crisis.[26] By dismissing the stories that are passed down through living memory practices, the community exposes itself to repeated danger, and, as a consequence, the characters are punished for ignoring the organically disseminated knowledge of the past in this legend.

The legend begins with an outer layer in which a riding party heads towards the outskirts of Bellver, where the narrator, as the sceptical outsider, discovers

---

[25] Sebold, *Bécquer en sus narraciones fantásticas*, pp. 21–22.
[26] As Silver notes: 'Although Bécquer never collected ballads and other popular poetry the way Fernán Caballero did, he nevertheless shared her high estimate of their value as "remnants" of a happier, more harmonious Christian society; this view matched his ultimately Herderian belief that the ways of peasants were inherently "poetic", and that such folk were even likely to create poetry themselves' (*Ruin and Restitution*, p. 74).

an old cross by the side of the road. In what appears to be a mechanized response to a distant memory, the narrator kneels before the cross: 'Impulsado de un sentimiento religioso, espontáneo e indefinible, eché maquinalmente pie a tierra, me descubrí y comencé a buscar en el fondo de mi memoria una de aquellas oraciones que me enseñaron cuando niño.' (*OC*, p. 110) For the narrator, the cross appear as a relic connected to a distant past which he tries to recover, with apparent difficulty, through memory. It is here that Bécquer begins to develop the role of memory as part of cultural awareness. The narrator's response to the cross is emblematic of the cosmopolitan spirit that has transformed cultural symbols and objects into impenetrable and petrified vestiges rather than expressions of living traditions.[27] The guide's interaction with the cross, on the contrary, expresses a complex living belief system; it underscores not only a religious piety, but also awareness of a cultural history that has lived in synchronicity with the symbol, thus explaining what appears to be an excessive reaction to the narrator's attempt to kneel before the image:

de improviso sentí que me sacudían con violencia por los hombros. Volví la cara: un hombre estaba al lado mío. Era uno de nuestros guías, natural del país, el cual, con una indescriptible expresión de terror pintada en el rostro, pugnaba por arrastrarme consigo y cubrir mi cabeza con el fieltro que aún tenía en mis manos. (*OC*, p. 110)

The guide explains that this particular cultural symbol 'pertenece a un espíritu maligno, y por eso la llaman *La cruz del diablo*' (*OC*, p. 110). The supernatural aspect introduces a sense of intrigue that helps to induce the incredulous members of the riding party to listen to the tale, albeit at first simply to satisfy their curiosity; however, there is a significant historical lesson embedded in the image of the cross that the guide is able to embed within the story of *La cruz del diablo* and transmit to his audience.

In typical storytelling fashion, the travellers gather round a fire to listen to the story of the cross. In contrast to critical, official historical records, the guide searches for the past and the shared culture in his memory: 'el héroe de la fiesta guardó silencio durante algunos segundos, como para coordinar sus recuerdos' (*OC*, p. 111). The guide verifies his recollection of the story through the testimony of objects: 'Aún testifican la verdad de mi relación algunas informes ruinas que, cubiertas de jaramago y musgo, se alcanzan a ver sobre su cumbre desde el camino que conduce a este pueblo' (*OC*, p. 111). Here the cultural memory lives embedded in these sites and assists

[27] Bécquer's religious conservatism has been amply studied by critics and does not need to be elaborated here, but it is necessary to point out that religion is the overarching cultural expression that lends itself to the cyclical repetition of unofficial and organic customs and traditions. A religious icon will often be intertwined with folkloric representation, thus making it more of an organic product of culture rather than an expression imposed by official and institutionalized forces such as the Church. For further reading see Robert Pageard, *Bécquer: leyenda y realidad* (Madrid: Espasa-Calpe, 1990).

the storyteller in his role as guardian of the organically remembered past.[28] The guide is also able to draw his listeners into the cultural link by incorporating them into the community that forms part of the legend: 'Hace mucho tiempo, mucho tiempo, yo no sé cuanto, pero los moros ocupaban aún la mayor parte de España, se llamaban condes nuestros reyes' (*OC*, p. 111). The subtle yet vitally important 'nuestros' makes this legend belong to the entire group. Furthermore, the reference to the occupation of the Moors conjures up connective bonds between the storyteller and the audience as they identify with a nationally fortifying and shared cultural heritage.

Once the connective semantics have been established, the legend proper takes the foreground. The guide relates the story of the villagers of Bellver, who had suffered under the rule of a cruel feudal lord, el señor del Segre. After a long though indeterminate interval, *el mal caballero* decides to sell his land to the inhabitants and join the Crusades.[29] The villagers, in a collective effort, combine resources to pay for their freedom from *el mal caballero* and, with their liberation from his cruelty, develop a fruitful and peaceful life. The memories of the cruel señor del Segre are relegated to the 'exclusivo dominio de las viejas, que en las eternas veladas del invierno la relataban con voz hueca y temorosa a los asombrados chicos' (*OC*, p. 112). The reference to old women telling tales by the fire, a typical symbol of the traditional folk tales, casts doubt on the veracity of the remembered past in spite of the fact that the existence of el señor del Segre has already been established. The inhabitants' incredulity vis-à-vis their own past exposes them to renewed danger as they are ill-prepared to deal with the return of *el mal caballero*, at first considering the renewed cruelties perpetrated upon the villagers to be merely imagined fantastical stories. However, after a series of violent acts committed against members of the community, the inhabitants acknowledge that *el mal caballero* has indeed returned, which causes them to rise up against el señor del Segre, of whom the narrator says: 'Aquello no era pelear para vivir: era vivir para pelear' (*OC*, p. 113). Finally, in a collective effort, the inhabitants are able to defeat and kill el señor del Segre along with his violent cohorts.

Once again, time passes and the stories of el señor del Segre fall back into

[28] Barbara A. Misztal emphasizes this process as part of the connective nature of memory: 'A group's memory is linked to places, ruins, landscapes, monuments and urban architecture, which—as they are overlain with symbolic associations to past events—play an important role in helping to preserve group memory. Such sites, and also locations where a significant event is regularly celebrated and replayed, remain 'concrete and distinct regardless of whether they are mythological or historical' (*Theories of Social Remembering* (Philadelphia: Open University Press, 2003), p. 116). These places and sites are recovered for the members of the national community that had abandoned organic cultural memory for the critical recollection of history.

[29] The legend vacillates between specifying a fixed period and a vaguer impression of time's passing. As part of organic memory, the relaxation of chronological time—which is fundamental to critical history—places more emphasis on the subjective inner recollection of the events as experienced by members of the community.

the realm of terrifying folk tales believed to be only a projection of over-active imaginations. This dangerous attitude of the inhabitants towards oral forms of memory invites a new threat into the village. The guide explains:

Si de aquí no hubiera pasado la cosa, nada se habría perdido. Pero el diablo, que a lo que parece no se encontraba satisfecho de su obra, sin duda con el permiso de Dios, y a fin de hacer purgar a la comarca algunas culpas, volvió a tomar cartas en el asunto. Desde este momento las fábulas, que hasta aquella época no pasaron de un rumor vago y sin viso alguno de verosimilitud, comenzaron a tomar consistencia y a hacerse de día en día más probables. (*OC*, p. 114)

Indicative of the effects of a memory crisis is the villagers' outright dismissal of the stories on account of their fantastical elements. As a result, they expose themselves to a resurgence of brutality by ignoring the warnings that circulated through these shared *fábulas*. Under the new threat, there is even greater suffering than what they had experienced under el señor del Segre, and in their attempt to protect themselves from continued harm they appeal to a venerable and saintly hermit. He advises the members of the community: 'encargándoles [. . .] que [. . .] no hiciesen uso de otras armas para aprehenderlo que de una maravillosa oración que les hizo aprender de memoria, y con la cual aseguraban las crónicas de San Bartolomé había hecho el diablo su prisionero' (*OC*, p. 117). Here, memory is upheld as the ultimate protection against danger over other sorts of weaponry or defence. And in fact the villagers carry out the instructions successfully, capturing the unknown violator who had occupied the armour of el señor del Segre.

During the offender's trial, the inhabitants demand that he lift his visor to reveal his identity. At that moment, the entire suit collapses to the ground, verifying 'que el diablo, a la muerte del señor del Segre, había heredado los feudos de Bellver' (*OC*, p. 119). The villagers lock the armour away while they request advice from the archbishop and the Conde de Urgel, who both advise hanging it in the plaza. Upon their return, the jailer, who had been left in charge of guarding the possessed armour, comes running to the door begging forgiveness:

¡Perdón, señores, perdón!
¡Perdón! ¿Para quién? —dijeron algunos— ¿Para el diablo que habita dentro de la armadura del señor del Segre?
Para mí —prosiguió con voz trémula el infeliz, en quien todos reconocieron al alcaide de las prisiones,— para mí [. . .] Porque las armas [. . .] han desaparecido. (*OC*, p. 120)

As the prison guard explains what happened, he reveals that his own failure to believe in the story of the armour led to his exposing the entire community to danger:

Yo no acertaré nunca a dar la razón; pero es el caso que la historia de las armas vacías me pareció siempre una fábula tejida en favor de algún noble personaje a quien tal vez altas razones de conveniencia pública no permitían descubrir ni castigar. [. . .] Una noche, por último, aguijoneado por la curiosidad y deseando convencerme por mí mismo de que aquel objeto de terror nada tenía de misterioso, encendí una linterna y bajé a las prisiones, levanté sus dobles aldabas y, no cuidando siquiera (tanto era mi fe en que todo no pasaba de un cuento) de cerrar las puertas tras de mí, penetré en el calabozo. (*OC*, p. 120)

The jailer realizes too late that he had made a grave error in dismissing the circulating stories, and as a result the possessed armour escapes. The violence commences once again until the village, as a united collective, is able to recapture the offender and complete the process by which the armour would be permanently immobilized. Through their unified efforts and 'El constante trabajo, la fe, las oraciones y el agua bendita consiguieron, por último, vencer al espíritu infernal, y la armadura se convirtió en una cruz' (*OC*, p. 122). Through a ritualized connective practice, the community overcomes the violence and persecution. The circulating stories of *el mal caballero* certainly transgress the boundaries of verisimilitude that critical history requires, but underlying the supernatural element is a ritualized connective process which refortifies communal unity, something absent from the new historicism.

This legend very clearly suggests that by dismissing the events related in shared cultural stories a community opens itself to pernicious forces. In the first instance, in a span of just three years the inhabitants had converted the image of el señor del Segre from reference to an actual individual into a fictional menace. While they continued to talk about the violence he had committed, these stories were banished to the realm of the imaginary, in which they were considered puerile and irrelevant, thus leaving the community vulnerable to renewed abuses once *el mal caballero* had returned. This is clearly reflective of the changes ushered in by modernity, whereby acts of oral memory, no longer considered relevant to historical knowledge, were dismissed as unimportant. In fact, once el señor del Segre returns, for several days the members of the community continue to believe that the stories of renewed violence were no more than made-up tales. The same dynamic occurs once the armour has been possessed by the Devil. The inhabitants continue to ignore the warnings embedded in the circulating stories as they regard them simply as childish tales. Furthermore, this time the violence against the community is much worse than what they had suffered under el señor del Segre, making their continued refusal to believe in the stories more puzzling. Eventually, in what appears to be an almost unanimous decision, the community immobilizes the armour. However Bécquer is not quite done with his disbelieving community, and makes them suffer one more time. In the last incident, in which the jailer fails to heed the warnings in the story of the possessed armour, the community is once again exposed to violence. It is only with full co-operation and the unifying belief in the story that the community is able to rid itself of an ever-present danger.

El monte de las ánimas is somewhat more complex in regard to the under-lying historical lessons embedded in the circulating story. In this legend, the danger arises when Beatriz returns after many years of living in Paris, and mockingly dismisses the beliefs embraced by the inhabitants. After the nar-rator's brief introduction, the legend begins mid-scene, with a hunting party led by Beatriz's cousin, Alonso, reconvening in order to leave the mountain before nightfall. A sense of urgency is apparent as Alonso calls out to his rid-ing party: 'Atad los perros, haced la señal con las trompas para que se reúnan los cazadores y demos vuelta a la ciudad. La noche se acerca, es día de Todos los Santos y estamos en el Monte de las Ánimas' (*OC*, p. 129). For the mem-bers of the cultural group, this announcement needs no further elaboration: it is an integrated component of their identity and practised living culture maintained through collective memory rituals. However, Beatriz, culturally distanced from the customs and practices embedded in the group's memories, counters with what may be interpreted as shocking disbelief: '¡Tan pronto!'; to which Alonso responds: 'A ser otro día, no dejara yo de concluir con ese rebaño de lobos que las nieves de Moncayo han arrojado de sus madrigueras; pero hoy es imposible. Dentro de poco sonará la oración de los Templarios, y las ánimas de los difuntos comenzarán a tañer su campana en la capilla del monte' (*OC*, p. 129). The historical event is weaved into the belief practices that have been passed down generationally and maintained by cultural mark-ers that connect the members of the community. As Beatriz responds with scepticism to the hunting party's fears, Alonso relates the originating incident that transformed this particular cultural site into dangerous ground. He be-gins: 'Ese monte que hoy llaman de las Ánimas pertenecía a los templarios, cuyo convento ves allí, a la margen del río' (*OC*, p. 130). Here, this memory site is intended to encourage the sceptical Beatriz to recognize the physical remains of the events, which gives greater credence to the story in spite of its supernatural elements.

As in the previous legend, Alonso also situates the events within a shared past that had constituted the foundational cultural unity and identity of Spain: 'Conquistada Soria a los árabes, el rey los hizo venir de lejanas tierras para defender la ciudad por la parte del Puente, haciendo en ello notable agravio a sus nobles de Castilla, que así hubieran solos sabido defenderla como so-los la conquistaron' (*OC*, p. 130). Alonso establishes the legacy of heroism and nobility of his ancestors, who had ably defended their land. However, the intrusion of outsiders had initiated an imbalance in the world order of the noblemen of Castile as they saw the Knights Templar appropriate the

mountain and indulge themselves with abundant hunting and excessive consumption: 'Entre los caballeros de la nueva y poderosa orden y los hidalgos de
la ciudad fermentó por algunos años, y estalló al fin, un odio profundo. Los
primeros tenían acotado ese monte, donde reservaban caza abundante para
satisfacer sus necesidades y contribuir a sus placeres' (*OC*, p. 130). A great
battle ensues, with all the members of both sides perishing in what has been
passed down as the bloodiest and deadliest encounter in the land's history.
As a result of the deadly conflict, Alonso relates, the King had the mountain
condemned in commemoration of these ill-fated events, the story of which
had been passed down through generations as a reminder of the violent outcome. This historical occurrence might have been lost over time had it not
been transmitted with the cultural warning:

Desde entonces dicen que cuando llega la noche de difuntos se oye doblar sola la
campana de la capilla, y que las ánimas de los muertos, envueltas en jirones de sus
sudarios, corren como en una cacería fantástica por entre breñas y los zarzales. Los
ciervos braman espantados, los lobos aúllan, las culebras dan horrorosos silbidos, y al
otro día se han visto impresas en la nieve las huellas de los descarnados pies de los
esqueletos. Por eso en Soria lo llamamos el Monte de las Ánimas, y por eso he querido
salir de él antes que cierre la noche. (*OC*, p. 130)

The supernatural element connected with *la noche de los difuntos* ensures that
the historical knowledge embedded in the story of *El monte de las ánimas*
continues to be transmitted through organic, living memory rituals.

While sceptical outsiders like Beatriz mock the story because of its supernatural element, Alonso and his hunting party interpret the memory as part
of their intimate cultural identity; not only does the recollection inculcate a
sense of shared culture, it also sustains the foundational memory and victorious acquisition of the land by the noblemen of Soria. The story points
to the dangers of external influences on the socio-cultural balance of the
community. Thus, they remember the past not only to assert their own identity as part of a cultural framework, but also to recall the dangers of not
protecting the boundaries that define their collective culture. This process of
remembering a foundational historical event unites the present inhabitants to
their cultural heritage and instils a sense of belonging to the community. By
continuing to respect the dictates of cultural practices passed down through
generations, the inhabitants propagate the internal history of their region and
fortify inner-group unity.

Alonso wants Beatriz to acknowledge this memory in order to integrate her
into the cultural fold; not only does it substantiate the living practices that
comprise the community, but it also makes her more accessible as a possible
wife. His awareness of the need to make good her lack of cultural knowledge is
clear in the following sentence: 'Tú ignoras cuanto sucede en este país, porque

aún no hace un año que has venido a él desde muy lejos' (*OC*, p. 129). In a later conversation, when the hunting party has safely retired to Alonso's estate, he reiterates her status as outsider in a tone that pardons her disdain while subtly defending his homeland: 'las áridas llanuras de Castilla, sus costumbres toscas y guerreras, sus hábitos sencillos y patriarcales, sé que no te gustan; [. . .] Tal vez por la pompa de la corte francesa, donde hasta aquí has vivido —se apresuró a añadir el joven— De un modo o de otro, presiento que no tardaré en perderte' (*OC*, p. 131). At first glance, the contrast he draws between the simplicity of Castile with the elaborate splendour of France appears to denigrate the local customs; however, Alonso then adds: '¿Te acuerdas cuando fuimos al templo a dar gracias a Dios por haberte devuelto la salud que viniste a buscar a esa tierra?' (*OC*, p. 131). He reminds her that in this apparently less civilized land she was saved from some undisclosed threatening illness. The underlying message is that only by reconstituting a connection with her homeland is she able to recover the bodily health and harmony that the artificiality of the French court was unable to supply, but it is also implied that Beatriz's illness may have originated as a result of her cosmopolitan lifestyle.

As in the other legend analysed above, storytelling has a binding effect on group unity. The hunting party has returned to Alonso's palace, where the members have gathered round the fire to listen to the old women telling folk stories to the younger members of the group: 'Las dueñas referían, a propósito de la noche de difuntos, cuentos temorosos, en que los espectros y los aparecidos representaban el principal papel; y las campanas de las Iglesias de Soria doblaban a lo lejos con un tañido monótono y triste' (*OC*, p. 131). The transmission of stories from the older generation to the younger creates the cultural bond that ties all members to a shared past. Furthermore, Bécquer makes use of the sound of church bells tolling throughout the town to emphasize a connection between the past and the present. The bells in the town echo the solitary bell tolling from the condemned church in the mountain that marks the return of ancestral apparitions. And, with this aural trigger, the group remembers the original founding event that led to the stories surrounding *El monte de las ánimas*.

Alonso and Beatriz, on the other hand, are set apart and outside of the unified group in what appears to be an ideological struggle between belief and disbelief. The fact that he is isolated from the group listening to tales at the fireside makes him more vulnerable to his cousin's exhortation to transgress the cultural norms of the community. After establishing that on any other night he would be willing to enter the mountain without fear, on this night, he explains, he is afraid:

Las campanas doblan, la oración ha sonado en San Juan del Duero, las ánimas del monte comenzarán ahora a levantar sus amarillentos cráneos de entre las malezas que cubren las fosas...¡Las ánimas!, cuya sola vista puede helar de horror la sangre del más valiente, tornar sus cabellos blancos o arrebatarle en el torbellino de su fantástica carrera como una hoja que arrastra el viento sin que se sepa adónde. (*OC*, p. 132)

To which Beatriz responds with disdain: '¡Oh! Eso, de ningún modo. ¡Qué locura! ¡Ir ahora al monte por semejante friolera! ¡Una noche tan oscura, noche de difuntos y cuajado el camino de lobos!' (*OC*, p. 132). Confronted with her mockery and overwhelmed by the desire to impress and win over the affections of his cousin, Alonso ignores the cultural taboo associated with this particular night and leaves for the mountain to recover Beatriz's lost blue scarf.

In the last segment of the legend, Beatriz returns to the isolation of her room after encouraging Alonso to go back to the mountain. She superficially attends to the rituals associated with the Day of the Dead, then falls into a fitful sleep. Her state of mind is infected by the penetrating sounds of the church bells, mingled with what she perceives as her name being pronounced in the distance. In a certain sense, the continued tolling of the bells represents the persistent effort of the cultural ritual to penetrate Beatriz's cosmopolitan attitude. Yet, she asserts her sense of cultural superiority and otherness that has kept her separated from the representative community of Soria in the palace: '¡Bah! —exclamó, volviendo a recostar su hermosa cabeza sobre la almohada de raso azul del lecho— ¿Soy yo tan miedosa como estas pobres gentes cuyo corazón palpita de terror bajo una armadura al oír una conseja de aparecidos?' (*OC*, p. 134). The devastating consequences of her isolation from connective bonds of community lead to her dismissal of cultural belief in *El monte de las ánimas*, and this results in both her and Alonso's death:

Cuando sus servidores llegaron, despavoridos, a noticiarle la muerte del primogénito de Alcudiel, que a la mañana había parecido devorado por los lobos entre las malezas del Monte de las Ánimas, la encontraron inmóvil, crispada, asida con ambas manos a una de las columnas de ébano del lecho, desencajados los ojos, entreabierta la boca, blancos los labios, rígidos los miembros, muerta, muerta de horror. (*OC*, p. 134)

Beatriz puts her cousin in harm's way by instigating his return to the mountain and provoking his violation of a cultural taboo. Furthermore, she is punished for her transgression, so that in death her spirit is condemned to wander the mountain in a desperate and frantic search for Alonso.

While Beatriz is often portrayed as a coquettish female who cruelly induces Alonso to commit an act that defies his cultural convictions, in the present context she may rather be considered emblematic of the increasing isolation characteristic of the scriptural economy. As a result of this process, memory rituals in the form of cultural stories are condemned as insignificant and puerile. Alonso's typical depiction as the victim of Beatriz's manipulation is likewise reconfigured in the analysis offered here: he too is punished for dismissing the implicit lessons embedded in cultural memory. His ancestors had fought to the death to protect their land and customs, and the community remembers, through transmission of the supernatural story, the values that define their cultural identity. Just as the noblemen of the past had warded off the introduction of external customs into Soria by attacking the Knights Templar, so too Alonso is expected to defend his cultural identity from external threats. However, in this situation the threat is ideological in that Beatriz represents the cosmopolitan spirit which denigrates and dismisses the essential cultural identity of Soria, as embodied in Alonso. The moment he acquiesces in Beatriz's desires, he allows the new modern spirit to transform his relation to his culture and collective past, and this leads to the only possible outcome, namely death—the metaphorical depiction reflecting the overarching message portrayed in this legend.

In these two legends Bécquer advocates the protection of poetic historicism in the guise of collectively shared stories. He saw the danger of the exclusivity of critical history in recording the past as well as the isolation characteristic of the new modern and technological social order. Both posed a risk to cultural memory by dissociating the collective body from an internal and organic understanding of its identity. Organic culture passed down through memory rituals sustains the collective living consciousness of the nation. Without this internally practised historical continuity, a nation was at risk from external forces that could easily overwrite the living traditions and impose values which were contradictory or pernicious to the nature of the cultural collective. Bécquer attempts to restore this fractured cultural bond by vindicating the act of storytelling as one of the means of circulating and practising poetic historicism. In a more general sense, these legends demonstrate the tensions that accompany transitions from one source of cultural communication to another, whereby perceptions of the world undergo radical transformations.

Virginia Tech   Sarah Sierra

ZURICH DADA'S FORGOTTEN
MUSIC MASTER: HANS HEUSSER

The eight Zurich Dada soirees, from 1916 to 1919, were the central event in the founding of Dada as a spectacular international phenomenon. They have remained famous ever since in the history of the development of European art. But a key figure in those soirees has been almost completely forgotten: the composer Hans Heusser. He provided the first work to be performed at the first soiree, and the last work programmed at the final soiree; his work was performed at all but two of the soirees, and occupied the entirety of one of them. And yet most specialists of the period hardly recognize his name.

This article has three aims. The first is to resuscitate the figure of Hans Heusser, and to sketch his contribution to the Dada soirees. The second is to relate how he was immediately and efficiently erased from the history of Dada. And the third is to suggest that this process of erasure was not a simple omission. It was (and remains) motivated by the extraordinarily complex and paradoxical relationship between the fundamental principles of Zurich Dada, and the very concept of music.

The few hard facts known about Hans Heusser's life are quickly summarized. He was born in Zurich in 1892. His early published compositions were songs and short piano pieces; and it was indeed works for piano and voice, and short piano pieces, that constituted his main contribution to the Zurich Dada soirees, from 1916 to 1919. However, his subsequent career took him in a different direction. He specialized in a capella choral music for female voices, and wind band music. In 1924 he became director of music for the town of Sankt Gallen in Switzerland. There he remained until his death in 1942. The only music by Heusser that is still performed today, and still readily available, is his wind band music. The music website notendatenbank.ch, for example, lists a dozen pieces by Heusser for wind band, including probably his most famous, the 'Sankt Gallen Marsch' and the 'Russische Rapsodie', for which one can order parts. None of the songs or piano works from his earlier period is thus available. Indeed, the general opinion seems to be that they are largely lost—and if they are not lost, they might as well be.

Almost nothing is known about Heusser's life in Zurich during the Dada years. Raimund Meyer, in *Dada in Zürich*, provides a full and careful assessment of the available biographical facts and gives their sources, which are of only three types: contemporary newspapers; the accounts of other Dadaists; and the brief obituary of Heusser that appeared in the *Sankt Galler Tagblatt* in 1942. He was unable to find out more: 'Nachforschungen bei den Nachlassverwaltern und Bekannten aus dem Kreise um Heusser haben keine weiteren Informationen über das Zürcher Leben von Heusser gebracht' ('Enquiries

Modern Language Review, 110 (2015), 491–509
© Modern Humanities Research Association 2015

directed to Heusser's executors and to those acquainted with his circle have
not yielded any further information concerning Heusser's life in Zurich').[1]
At least Meyer took the trouble to scrutinize those few available sources of
biographical information, and draw what conclusions he could from them.
Heusser's music of the Dada period has, on the other hand, been scrutinized
by nobody.

The academic neglect of Heusser's music is symptomatic of a more general
critical reluctance to acknowledge the place of composed music in Zurich
Dada. In his article 'Duchamp: Dada Composer', Leigh Landy writes:

Inspecting documents which include lists of programmes of Dada soirées, one sees
that relatively little accent was given to composed—as opposed to an occasional
improvised—music. In Zürich Hans Heussen [*sic*] presented 'antitunes', and equally
unknown composers H. Samuel Sulzberger and Suzanne Perrottet are named. Surprisingly a couple of the young Schönberg's works were played there as well. If ever there
was an undadaist personality, it was he![2]

This reflects quite accurately the stereotypical view of Dada music. Factually,
however, it is quite misleading. Why does Landy characterize Heusser's music
as 'antitunes'? This description does not correspond at all, as we shall see,
to what we find in the pieces by Heusser that have come down to us. I find
it difficult not to suspect that, like almost all the other scholars who have
written about Dada music, Landy had not actually looked at Heusser's published scores. Furthermore, the programmes of the Zurich Dada soirees make
it perfectly clear that 'composed—as opposed to an occasional improvised—
music', by contemporary composers, was in fact a regular feature of the
soirees. Satie and Cyril Scott are listed in those programmes, as well as
Schoenberg, Heusser, Sulzberger, Laban, and Perrottet. Schoenberg seems
quite at home in this company if one considers that these are all composers,
born between 1860 and 1880, who were lucidly aware of the ties, as well as
the rifts, between their music and the great nineteenth-century melodic and
tonal traditions.

Certainly, in the history of Dada, there were types of music which completely rejected those melodic and tonal traditions. Richard Huelsenbeck, in
En avant Dada, published in 1920,[3] provides a wonderfully clear account of
the historical conflict within Dada between the composed music with its roots
in the nineteenth-century artistic tradition, and a new type of music, based

---

[1] Raimund Meyer, *Dada in Zürich: Die Akteure, die Schauplätze* (Frankfurt a.M.: Luchterhand,
1990), p. 162. All translations throughout this article are mine.

[2] Leigh Landy, 'Duchamp: Dada Composer and his Vast Influence on Post-World War II Avant-
Garde Music', in *Marcel Duchamp*, ed. by Klaus Beekman and Antje von Graevenitz (Amsterdam:
Rodopi, 1989), pp. 131–44 (p. 131).

[3] Richard Huelsenbeck, *En avant Dada: Eine Geschichte des Dadaismus* (Hanover: Steegemann,
1920).

on noise, which contested not only that tradition, but the very concept of art that subtended it, and with it, the word 'music' itself. He begins from a firm distinction between 'Musik' and 'Bruitismus'. Both, he says, were present in Zurich Dada. They corresponded to two distinct strands of its aesthetic. He makes it clear that for his own brand of politicized post-war Berlin Dada, it was 'Bruitismus' that mattered, not music. But Zurich Dada was very different.

One of the main concerns of Zurich Dada was, Huelsenbeck tells us, the movement towards the identification of true art with abstraction. In that movement, music was of central importance, as it had been throughout the previous half-century. The very concept of abstract art had grown to maturity through the development in the nineteenth century of the notion of absolute music, and through the subsequent application of that notion of absoluteness to the other arts. Music had thus become the keystone in the edifice of abstract art, hence of art in general as the Zurich Dadaists wished it to become. Huelsenbeck, proclaiming a new post-war phase in the history of Dada, wanted to remove that keystone from the edifice, to remove music from Dada by replacing it with 'Bruitismus', and thus to cause the construction of art to collapse. But he never sought to deny that music, together with a profound belief in art, had been present in the earlier phase of Dada, at the Cabaret Voltaire (where Heusser also performed) and during the Zurich soirees. All the evidence from the Zurich Dada period itself confirms that Huelsenbeck was right. When the Zurich Dadaists wrote about, programmed, and performed music, their concept of that art remained firmly rooted in the nineteenth-century concept of music as an art form with an exemplary tendency towards abstraction.

Sébastien Arfouilloux, in his article 'La Musique aux temps de Dada', has very little to say about the Zurich Dada soirees. Like Landy, he does not note the full number of contemporary composers cited in the programmes. Like Landy again, he dismisses Heusser in a single sentence. But unlike Landy, he relates Heusser to classical and nineteenth-century traditions:

Lors de nombreux spectacles entre 1916 et 1919, le jeune musicien suisse Hans Heusser propose des pièces de facture classique pour piano, nommées dans le style des compositions du xixᵉ siècle: *Lune au-dessus de l'eau, Humoresque turque, Cortège de fête à Capri*.[4]

In his book *Que la nuit tombe sur l'orchestre*, he adds that Heusser was an 'ancien élève de la Schola Cantorum'.[5] It is indeed generally maintained that Heusser went to Paris before the war, studied with both Debussy and

---

[4] Sébastien Arfouilloux, 'La Musique aux temps de Dada', in *Dada circuit total*, ed. by Henri Béhar and Catherine Dufour (Lausanne: L'Âge d'Homme, 2005), pp. 522–30 (pp. 524–25).

[5] Sébastien Arfouilloux, *Que la nuit tombe sur l'orchestre: surréalisme et musique* (Paris: Fayard, 2009), p. 84.

d'Indy, and wrote an opera entitled *Kismet* that was performed there. Jean-paul Goergen, whose article on the music of Zurich Dada is doubtless the best-informed and most careful on the subject to date, states: 'In Paris, where he had also studied with Vincent d'Indy, he created a sensation with his opera "Kismet".'[6] However, I have been unable to find any trace of an opera of this title performed in Paris at the time. *Kismet*, for the Parisian public of the pre-war years, was not an opera but a very popular play, written by Jules Lemaître. I suspect that the assertion that Heusser wrote an opera with that title arose from a deliberate confusion between the title of the play and that of a little piece by Heusser called 'Danse orientale pour piano, extraite de la suite *Kismet*', which was indeed published in Paris, in 1914—and that the inspiration for this confusion came from Heusser himself, or from his fellow Dadaists.

The origin of the notion that Heusser wrote an opera called *Kismet* seems to be an article in the *Neue Zürcher Zeitung*, dated 24 May 1917. The article is a trailer for the 'Hans-Heusser-Soirée' which took place the following day. It states: 'Hans Heußer ist ein Schüler Vincent d'Indys und Debussys. In Pariser Musikkreisen erregte er Aufsehen mit seiner Oper "Kismet"' ('Hans Heusser is a pupil of Vincent d'Indy and of Debussy. In Parisian music circles he caused a stir with his opera *Kismet*').[7] But can one necessarily believe what one reads in the papers, especially when the copy has clearly been furnished by a Dadaist? After all, the *Neues Wiener Journal* was fooled into publishing a lengthy review of a Dada soiree that never took place at all. [8] There is, to my knowledge, only one piece of objective evidence that Heusser ever actually went to Paris. It is an inscription, in what must be Heusser's own hand, on the copy of 'Danse orientale' held by the Zentralbibliothek in Zurich.[9] Under-neath the printed dedication, on the front cover, 'à mon ami Otto Uhlmann', Heusser has written, 'Zur Erinnerung an unsere fröhliche Studienzeit in Paris | Hans Heusser | Paris Juni 1914' ('In memory of our happy time as students in Paris | Hans Heusser | Paris June 1914'). Otto Uhlmann was a composer and conductor, born in 1891. I have been unable to find any other verifiable information concerning Heusser's Parisian exploits.[10] Seen from the stand-

---

[6] Jeanpaul Goergen, 'The Big Drum: Boom Boom Boom Boom. The Music of Zurich Dada', in *Crisis and the Arts: The History of Dada*, ed. by Stephen C. Foster, 9 vols (New York and London: G. K. Hall and Prentice Hall International, 1996–2004), II: *Dada Zurich: A Clown's Game from Nothing*, ed. by Brigitte Pichon and Karl Riha (1996), pp. 153–67 (p. 157).

[7] Richard Sheppard, 'Dada Zürich in Zeitungen', in *Dada Zurich*, ed. by Pichon and Riha, pp. 191–259 (p. 216). All my quotations from newspapers are taken from this invaluable and authoritative collection of articles.

[8] Sheppard, 'Dada Zürich in Zeitungen', pp. 251–53.

[9] Hans Heusser, 'Danse orientale pour piano, extraite de la suite *Kismet*' (Paris: Roudanez, 1914).

[10] Further evidence that Heusser had studied with Debussy is generally held to be provided by a letter from Hugo Ball to August Hoffmann dated 2 June 1916, in which he refers to a young

point of academe, the clearest fact about Heusser's career before Dada is its elusiveness.

His work with Dada, on the other hand, is firmly documented by the programmes of the Zurich Dada soirees, which have been preserved, and which are confirmed by contemporary accounts as a fairly accurate record of what was actually performed—or at least, of what the Dadaists intended to be performed. An inspection of those programmes leads to the astonishing conclusion that Hans Heusser was actually one of the two central figures of the Dada soirees in the sense that his music occupied more stage time than the work of anyone else except Tristan Tzara. It was performed (always with Heusser himself at the keyboard, sometimes with others singing, reciting, or perhaps playing stringed instruments) at six of the eight soirees. The first opened, appropriately enough, with his 'Prélude'. One of the soirees, the sixth, entitled the 'Soirée Hans Heusser', was dedicated entirely to his work (the only other soiree devoted to a single person was the Tristan Tzara soiree). What, then, can explain his almost total invisibility in the picture that is generally painted of Zurich Dada?

Two answers to this question are implied by Dada scholarship to date. Heusser's works, it is usually said, are largely lost. Furthermore, the Dadaists who left accounts of the soirees had almost nothing to say about Heusser. Does this not suggest both that he was not central to the Dada aesthetic and that there is little point trying to revive interest in him? I shall be suggesting that, on the contrary, the conspiracy of silence can be explained precisely by his centrality to the Dada aesthetic; that his works are not as lost as is generally believed; and that if we take the trouble to return him to his rightful position in the history of the movement, that history will be decisively inflected.

According to the programmes of the Zurich Dada soirees, Hans Heusser performed only his own works, at the piano or harmonium. (Works by other composers were generally played by Suzanne Perrottet.) Most were short piano pieces. Some were songs or 'gesprochene Gesänge' ('spoken songs'), always for female voice. Only one work called for greater instrumental forces:

Swiss composer playing in the Cabaret Voltaire: 'Ein junger Schweizer hat in Paris bei Debussy studiert und spielt ab und zu eigene Kompositionen' ('a young Swiss who studied with Debussy in Paris plays from time to time his own compositions') (Hugo Ball, *Briefe 1911–1927*, ed. by Annemarie Schütt-Hennings (Einsiedeln: Benziger, 1957), p. 56). Was this Heusser? It may well have been; or it may have been Sulzberger, as Chris Walton points out (see 'The Many Lives of Marcel Sulzberger', *Musical Times* (Winter 2013), 5–18 (p. 13)). But even if Ball was referring to Heusser, it would prove nothing more than that Heusser had told Ball he had studied with Debussy. I have found no confirmation of this from any source that does not lead quite directly back to Heusser himself. There is no reference to Heusser in Debussy's correspondence, or in any of his other published works. Similarly, if he studied with d'Indy at the Schola Cantorum, this cannot be verified (the archives of that institution are not open to the public). I am grateful to Katharine Ellis for her advice on tracking down Heusser's references to his time in Paris.

his piano quartet, which, as we shall see, may never have been performed. So much is clear. But what do we know about the character of these works, and of their reception? We have well-known accounts of the soirees from no less than six of the other participants at those events (Perrottet, Tzara, Ball, Huelsenbeck, Richter, and Glauser). Most have absolutely nothing whatever to say about the character of Heusser's music. Ball's *Flucht aus der Zeit* names Heusser only when listing his contributions to the soirees; there is no description of his music at all. The same is true of Tzara's *Chronique zurichoise*, and in Suzanne Perrottet's reminiscences,[11] as well as in Huelsenbeck's *En avant Dada*. Friedrich Glauser, in his atmospheric essay 'Dada', first published in 1931, gives a description of the 'Abend neuer Kunst' ('Soiree of New Art') in April 1917, which famously includes a cameo of a composer leaning his forearm on all available keys of a harmonium as he simultaneously plays a piano.[12] This has always been taken by critics as a portrait of Heusser at work. Goergen, for example, quoting Glauser's description, simply states: 'the musician involved must have been Heusser'.[13] However, this is, to say the least, a highly problematic inference. Heusser's name is mentioned nowhere in Glauser's essay. The soiree Glauser claims to be describing is in fact one of only two in which none of Heusser's music was performed. He did not participate in it, nor was there a harmonium present. (He did play the harmonium at another soiree, but no contemporary account suggests he did so in the manner described by Glauser. We will come to what the reviewer of that soiree had to say about his harmonium-playing; it certainly does not imply a forearm on the keys.) It is, then, impossible to believe that the scene painted by Glauser is an accurate representation of Heusser's participation in the 'Abend neuer Kunst'. It is far more likely, as are many elements of Glauser's testimony, to be an imaginative reconstruction, based on several conflated half-remembered episodes, and distorted by the twin lenses of hindsight and polemic. This is so obvious that one must ask oneself why critics have always taken it unproblematically as a description of Heusser, even though Glauser never names him and he was absent from the soiree in question. The only possible answer is that it corresponds too readily to the stereotype of the Dada composer, which we have already encountered: a stereotype built on noise, improvisation, and 'antitunes'. Hans Heusser, however, does not correspond to that stereotype.

The American composer Otto Luening, writing in 1980, provides the nearest thing we have, to my knowledge, to a cameo of Heusser in the Dada years.

---

[11] As transcribed by Giorgio Wolfensberger in *Suzanne Perrottet: Ein bewegtes Leben* (Bern: Benteli, [n.d.]). This fascinating volume consists largely of Wolfensberger's edited transcriptions of Perrottet's memories of her life, as recounted to him between 1981 and 1983.

[12] See Friedrich Glauser, *Dada, Ascona und andere Erinnerungen* (Zurich: Arche, 1976), p. 56.

[13] Goergen, 'The Big Drum', p. 158.

Luening was only sixteen years old at the time, and a student at the Conservatoire in Zurich. He does not describe any of the Dada soirees, which he doubtless did not attend. But he does describe an evening at the Cabaret Voltaire, in which both he (accompanying the cellist David Rubinstein) and Heusser performed. Heusser, according to Luening, was not only a performer at the Cabaret; he was also 'the professional music director for the Dada group' (as well as a fellow student at the Conservatoire),[14] and responsible for programming the music at the Cabaret.

Heusser, Rubinstein, and I played at the Meierei one night at 1:30 A.M. The program included one of my compositions for cello and piano, known as the 'Wet Dream Gavotte'! We also played an aria and a one-step. Why Rubinstein and I also played Saint-Saens' 'The Swan', I don't know, but Heusser found it suitable for his interesting programs. These included his own works for voice, piano, and harmonium, which were much hated by the Establishment. African dancers with masks were accompanied by Arabian tunes and tambourines. One-steps, ragtimes, noise music, balalaika concerts, music with magic lantern slides, piano improvisations, folk songs, brothel songs, and bass drum solos rounded out his programs. There was a huge crowd, an unearthly din, and blue smoke clouds, and everybody talked. Nobody listened except Heer, the Swiss poet.[15]

Although it was written over sixty years after the event, this accords very well with what we learn of the music at the Cabaret from other sources. It ranged from noise (including the bass drum), through folk music and exotic or popular African and American music, to tonal music in the great European tradition. And what of Heusser's compositions? Luening tells us that they were for piano, harmonium, and voice, and that they were 'hated by the Establishment' (how did he know this? the Establishment was not present at the Cabaret). But he says absolutely nothing about their character or style.

We have, in fact, only two sources of descriptions explicitly of Heusser's music at Dada events that do purport to reveal its character. One is a couple of reviews in contemporary Swiss newspapers; they are certainly intriguing and revealing, although they were evidently written by journalists without much knowledge of contemporary music. The other is the testimony of Hans Richter, in his *Dada: Kunst und Antikunst*. There is, as we shall see, a most striking contrast between the newspaper reviews and the assertions of Richter; such a contrast, indeed, that we must ask ourselves who is telling the truth about the nature of Heusser's music.

Would it not make sense, then, to begin by looking at Hans Heusser's music itself, to see what it was really like? Goergen writes: 'Unfortunately, most of

---

[14] Otto Luening, *The Odyssey of an American Composer* (New York: Charles Scribner's Sons, 1980), p. 126. I am very grateful to Chris Walton for drawing my attention to this book, and for much other guidance.

[15] Ibid., p. 127.

Heusser's compositions from his Dada time are lost. Among others, his "Orientalischer Tanz" ["Oriental Dance"], composed in 1915 and performed at the Heusser Soirée, and "Sumatra. Ragtime—One Step" have been preserved.'[16] It is true that the majority of the titles given in the Zurich Dada soiree programmes do not correspond to those of any pieces by Heusser that currently appear in the catalogues of public libraries. However, the Zentralbibliothek in Zurich has a collection of piano pieces and songs by Heusser which includes all of those on the programme of the first half of the 'Soirée Hans Heusser'.[17] That programme begins with a piece entitled 'Prélude', which is also the title of the first piece played at both the first and second soirees.[18] So we are entitled to think that with this piece, we have the music that inaugurated the first Dada soiree. Its opening is given as Figure 1.[19] We may note, before going any further, that the first sound heard at the first Dada soiree was not a noise, nor an improvisation, nor an 'antitune', but a C major chord, leading into a composed tonal tune.

The programme for the 'Soirée Hans Heusser' lists the pieces to be performed thus (the dates given in brackets are presumably intended to indicate when they were composed):

(1912) 1. a) Prélude.
           b) Adagio.
           c) Certosa di Pavia.
           d) Novellette.

(1914) 2. a) Die Wanderer (Hans Rœlli).
           b) Tiefgelbe Rosen (Hans Rœlli).
           c) Herbst.
           d) Tanzweise (Huggenberger).
           (Gesungen von Frl. Emmy Kæser, Zürich)

(1915) 3. a) Danse triste.
           b) Danse orientale.

(1917) 4. a) Fragmente aus der Bühnenkomposition: 'Der gelbe Klang',
              (von W. Kandinsky).
           b) Impressions orientales. (Für Harmonium).

(1916) 5. Sheherezade: (Else Lasker Schüler)
           a) Ich tanze in der Moschee.

[16] Goergen, 'The Big Drum', p. 158.
[17] I have been unable to locate in any library any music by Heusser from his Dada period that is not also in the Zurich Zentralbibliothek. The Dada archives at the Kunsthaus in Zurich have nothing by Heusser; nor does the International Dada Archive at the University of Iowa.
[18] Hans Heusser, 'Praeludium' (Zurich: Holzmann, 1917). This 'Praeludium' is clearly the same piece as 'Prélude', since it is listed on the score, exactly as in the 1917 soiree programme, as the first of four pieces in a series, the others being 'Adagio', 'Certosa di Pavia', and 'Novellette'.
[19] The illustration may be viewed in greater detail in the online version of this article, available at www.jstor.org.

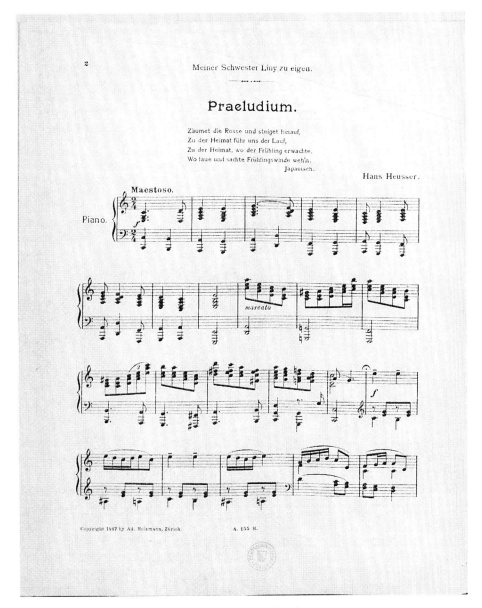

FIG. 1. Hans Heusser, 'Praeludium', opening page

b) Apollides und Tino kommen in eine morsche Stadt.
c) Das Lied meines Lebens.
(Gesprochene Gesänge Käthe Wulff).
d) Heimlich zur Nacht.
e) Der Tempel Jehovah.
f) Der Epilog spricht. (Nietzsche).
(Gesungen von Frl. Meta Gump).

(1916/17) 6. a) Humoresque turque.
b) Mond über Wasser.
c) Zwei arabische Tanzrhythmen.
(Gespielt vom Componisten).

The music in the Zentralbibliothek corresponds to what Heusser presented as his earlier work, composed in and before 1915. It does not, therefore, include the music composed during the Dada period itself, which began in 1916.

Might one speculate that Heusser's later work was somewhat different in character? His titles do not suggest any change in style. They continue to refer either to 'oriental' dances or impressions, or to contemporary literature. The 'gesprochene Gesänge' must certainly have been formally different from the songs and piano pieces that preceded them. However, they too reference both dance and contemporary poetry; and the contemporary newspaper review (cited below) describes them as more old-fashioned, not more modern, than Heusser's other works. After the 'gesprochene Gesänge', Heusser returns to more traditional song, before concluding with a pair of oriental dances. Little further evidence is provided by what we know of his compositional activities in the years around 1919. There is a song in the Zurich collection entitled 'Augen, meine lieben Fensterlein', whose publication date is given as 1925 (whereas the works in the Zurich collection that were performed in 1916 and 1917 were published no later than 1917). It seems to show some later stylistic influences; otherwise, though, it is very similar to his earlier songs. Like them, it is short, clearly tonal, conventional in its notation, and quite conventional in its word-setting. 'Sumatra—Ragtime', which Goergen mentions as a rare Heusser survival, was recorded in 1919 by Marek Weber on Parlophon. However, the composer's name on the record label appears as 'Heuller' rather than 'Heusser'; and in any case, the piece is absolutely conventional in style and harmony, containing none of the eclecticism and harmonic oddities of Heusser's music of the previous few years. Certainly, then, the music we have provides no reason to suppose that Heusser's style altered radically after 1915.

It would thus seem likely that the music Heusser performed at the Dada soirees was not written in a specifically 'Dada' style with those soirees in mind, but rather resulted from his general evolution as an artist in the years leading up to that time. And this would correspond to the way that composed music in general figures in the Zurich Dada soiree programmes. Schoenberg,

Cyril Scott, and Satie did not write works for the 'soirees' with a specifically Dada character; nor, doubtless, did Perrottet and Laban. The Dadaists were interested in their work, as they were interested in Kandinsky, Apollinaire, and Picasso, because, although not created as part of the Dada movement, it embodied certain of the core values of that movement. The same must have applied to Heusser.

What can we make of those pieces that comprise the first half of the 'Soirée Hans Heusser'? The first characteristic that strikes the listener is that they are short, and apparently quite simple. They remind one more of Satie, in this sense, than of Debussy or Schoenberg. They are, however, very unlike Satie's work of the time in their lack of obvious experimental audacity. Heusser plays none of Satie's games with repetition and pointed parody. He sticks to all the conventions of traditional notation, including bar lines and key signatures. There is always a clear tonality. The pieces are generally quite tuneful. They also produce quite rapidly the unmistakable impression that they belong to a very individual creative character. It is difficult to define exactly how; it has something to do with the way that Heusser, apparently without radically disrupting the rules of the genre of the song or piano miniature, manages to slip in, almost in passing, moments that evoke a curious variety of contemporary styles and sonorities, from folk music to Satie, Debussy, or even Mahler (plus, in one piece, the unmistakable sound of the overtones of a carillon), which flit by without disrupting the apparently simple flow of the music. It is also connected, again in a way that might remind one of Satie (but, again, without Satie's assumed radicality), with a deceptive apparent ingenuousness, a lack of ample rhetorical gestures and of complex development, with suggestiveness and juxtaposition taking the place of grand form, and hovering knowingly between irony and naivety. One can see why contemporary audiences should have been charmed, intrigued, and rather baffled by these little works.[20]

The only accounts of Heusser's playing we have that were actually written during the Dada years are newspaper reviews, of which by far the most substantial is of the 'Soirée Hans Heusser'. Given its uniqueness, I shall quote it at length:

Was die Kunst Heußers trotz ihrem lockern Gerüste vor einem formlosen Verschwimmen in Klangfabeleien bewahrt, ist ein stark ausgeprägter Rhythmus, der freilich zuweilen in recht exaltierte Schwingung gerät. Daß Heußer der traditionellen Harmonie konsequent aus dem Wege geht und als Träger seiner musikalischen Ideen schrille Dissonanzen sucht, muß, in Anbetracht der Kunsttheorien, welche die Dadaisten verfechten, wohl als selbstverständlich hingenommen werden. Es fragt sich nur, ob Heußer dank seiner entschiedenen Begabung im musikalischen Ausdruck nicht weiterkäme, wenn er weniger exponierte Bahnen wandeln und seine Kunst etwas vernehmbahrer

---

[20] I am grateful to Peter Nelson for his help in listening to Heusser.

und einheitlicher auch im Sinne des Melodischen gestalten wollte. Nicht ungeschickt verwertet Heußer für seinen Expressionismus (er nennt ihn vielleicht anders) das Harmonium, das gewissen damit verbundenen Klangnüancen eher gerecht wird, als das Klavier. In seinen orientalischen Tänzen versucht er Anlehnung an rhythmische Klangfiguren primitiver Völker und vermag hier tatsächlich *exotische turbulente Stimmungen bis zu einem sehr hohen Grade zu steigern.* Diesen aufreizenden, wilden Tänzen stehen die Begleitungen zu den rezitativischen Gesängen in ihrer Tonalität fast diametral gegenüber, da sich Heußers Diktion hier wiederum mehr der Weise *alter* Kirchentonarten und dem Oratorienstil nähert, während er in seinen lyrischen Klavierstücken *extrem Futuristisches mit archaistischen* Tendenzen zu verbinden trachtet.[21]

Heusser's music lacks a solidly constructed framework, but it is saved from dissolving into mere pretty soundscapes by its strongly marked rhythm, which sometimes, indeed, becomes quite powerfully intoxicating. Heusser consistently avoids the path of conventional harmony, and he seeks strident dissonances to express his musical ideas; this is only to be expected in view of the theories about art which the Dadaists defend. One might, however, wonder if Heusser, given his clear gift for musical expression, would not travel further if he chose a less exposed route, and developed his art more melodiously, in a more uniform and comprehensible way. He makes clever use of the harmonium for his expressionism (perhaps he has another term for it), which inspires certain nuances of sound better suited to that instrument than to the piano. In his oriental dances, he profits from the rhythmic sound figures of primitive peoples, and here he indeed succeeds in creating *exotic and turbulent moods of remarkable intensity.* These wild and exciting dances are almost diametrically opposed in tonality to the accompaniments for his recitativo songs; in these, Heusser's diction moves back towards the styles of oratorio and of the modes of *old* Church music, while in his lyrical piano pieces, he seeks to combine *the most futuristic with archaic* tendencies.

In most ways, this corresponds well to how one might have imagined an intelligent provincial reviewer in 1917, with a conservative sense of harmony and unused to avant-garde formal experiments, reacting to the pieces by Heusser that have come down to us. We can readily agree with him that Heusser has a decided gift for musical expression; that his style is eclectic, and his harmonies unconventional (if one limits 'conventional' to the classically tonal); that in his dances, rhythmic drive carries the listener forward; and that generally, what is missing in Heusser's work, judged by the standards of the classical tonal musical tradition within which the reviewer was plainly operating, is extended melody and tight formal structure. As we shall see, in its perception that Heusser unites the archaic or primitive with the futuristic, the review corresponds precisely to Zurich Dada's own definition of its art in May 1917. What, on the other hand, should we make of the 'schrille Dissonanzen' which the reviewer heard? The pieces we have are rarely very dissonant. Was the reviewer thinking of other, later pieces? Or were his ears more sensitive to dissonance than we expect? Doubtless we should bear in mind that he

---

[21] Sheppard, 'Dada Zürich in Zeitungen', p. 218.

was writing in Zurich, not in Vienna or Paris. But there is another possible explanation.

The text we have is given in 'Dada Zürich in Zeitungen' as an article from 'Der Landbote (Winterthur)'. However, the critic from *Der Landbote* (named only as 'C.R.') clearly did not himself attend the soiree, nor does he claim to have written the review. He presents it in the form of a long quotation, taken, he tells us, from the *Neue Zürcher Zeitung*. The passage I cite above is part of that long quotation. After the quotation, 'C.R.' gives his own, extremely derogatory, opinion of the new music, Dada, and modern art in general. The italicized words in the quoted text of the review have clearly been emphasized to support that opinion. I know of no evidence that the review actually did appear in the *Neue Zürcher Zeitung*, nor of who might have written it. There is, then, a complex and tenuous link between Heusser's performance and the only contemporary critical account of it that has reached us. It is at the very least possible that 'C.R.' has modified the text of the review he quotes, to support his own prejudices, based on complete ignorance of the music he is discussing. As we have seen, he would certainly not be alone in writing about Heusser's music without having heard a note of it.

The last Zurich Dada soiree was the eighth, held on 9 April 1919. We have several contemporary accounts, all of which, with one exception (Richter's, to which we shall come shortly), give reasonably compatible versions of the events. The house was full, with probably over a thousand people attending; but the audience was less favourably disposed than at previous soirees. The programme was in three parts, all of which contained musical items. In the first, Suzanne Perrottet played piano music by Schoenberg, Cyril Scott, and Satie. In the second part, Hans Heusser played some of his own recent compositions, including his *Drei Tanzrhythmen*; then Perrottet played some more Schoenberg. After this, Walter Serner read out his 'Manifest'; and it was at this point that the audience, which previously had been only mildly hostile, became aggressively disruptive, feeling insulted, apparently, by Serner's deliberately provocative assertions concerning the nature of art.[22]

The programme for the third and final part was divided into four sections: a dance, 'Noir Cacadou', led by Käthe Wulff; poems by Serner and Tzara; a 'Proclamation Dada 1919' by Tzara; and finally, two piano pieces by Heusser, followed by his piano quartet in E flat major. The accounts given in newspapers after the event, and by Tzara in his *Chronique zurichoise*, suggest that the quartet was not performed. There was such an uproar while Tzara and Serner read out their work that it must have seemed hopeless to perform a

---

[22] *Letzte Lockerung: Manifest Dada* [*Last Loosening: Dada Manifesto*] is Serner's published version of this text (Hanover: Steegemann, 1920).

tonal piano quartet. According to Tzara, the soiree ended with another dance, perhaps a repetition of 'Noir Cacadou'.[23] He does not mention the quartet. Nor do any of the reviews in the newspapers mention it, though one of them, as we shall see, does suggest that Perrottet might have been getting ready to play when the performance broke up in chaos.

The exception to the consensus concerning the events of the evening is Hans Richter's *Dada: Kunst und Antikunst*. Richter describes the end of the soiree thus: 'Der Abend endete mit eigenen Kompositionen von Hans Heusser, die an Zwölftönerei nichts zu wünschen übrig ließen. Das Publikum war gezähmt ... (Ob überzeugt, das war eine Zeitfrage, die man erst heute nach 40 Jahren beantworten kann)' ('The soiree ended with Hans Heusser playing his own compositions, which were as twelve-tone as anyone could wish. The audience was tamed ... (Whether it was convinced is a question which required time; only today, forty years later, can we answer it)').[24] This is surprising in three ways. One: it contradicts the other accounts in stating that the evening ended with Heusser's work. Two: it describes Heusser's compositions as twelve-tone. And three: it is the only account by any of the Dadaists of audience reaction to Heusser's work. Clearly, Richter wishes to present us with a contrast between the reception of the words of Serner and Tzara, which incensed the audience, and the reception of Heusser's music, which calmed the audience.

Whom should one believe, concerning the question of whether or not the soiree ended with Heusser's music? I am inclined not to believe Richter. He was writing more than forty years after the event, as he indicates; his memories may have become muddled over time, and if he relied on the soiree programme as a document to remind him of what happened, this may have falsified his recollections concerning the order of events during the actual performance. Furthermore, some of his other statements concerning the contents of the soiree are clearly inaccurate. He states that Perrottet danced to the music of Schoenberg and Satie, rather than playing it;[25] but this corresponds neither to the programme, nor to Perrottet's own recollections,[26] nor to any other accounts, either of the soiree itself or of Perrottet's part in the Dada manifestations. It seems to me more than likely, then, that Richter is a less reliable witness than those who wrote nearer the time. My guess is that none of Heusser's music was actually played at the end of the soiree, and it seems to me fairly certain, given that even Richter mentions no string players, that the piano quartet was not performed.

The stereotypical view of Dada soirees is doubtless that they were always

---

[23] See Tristan Tzara, 'Chronique zurichoise', in *Œuvres complètes*, ed. by Henri Béhar, 6 vols (Paris: Flammarion, 1975), I, 561–68 (p. 568).

[24] Hans Richter, *Dada: Kunst und Antikunst* (Cologne: DuMont Schauberg, 1964), p. 82.

[25] Ibid., p. 81.

[26] Wolfensberger, *Suzanne Perrottet*, pp. 137–38.

provocative, always designed to create a hostile reaction in the audience, and often degenerated into tumult. Of the Zurich Dada soirees, however, only one fitted this stereotype: the last. All the others were relatively well received. There is no evidence that at the first seven soirees any items on the programme were not performed because of negative audience reaction. The only victims of public outrage at Dada provocation, the only pieces on any Zurich Dada programme not to be performed, were Hans Heusser's piano quartet and, probably, the two piano pieces scheduled to precede it. No one seems to know what became of the quartet. I have no reason to think it was ever performed, or that the parts survive.

At what point during that extraordinary evening, when an audience of many hundreds was making its displeasure forcibly known to the score of Dadaists on stage, was the decision taken to abandon the last item? There is a rather haunting description in one of the newspaper accounts, which would suggest that at least one of the performers for the quartet was on the stage and ready when they realized they would have to abandon the work because they would not be able to make themselves heard: 'eine unglückliche und schöne Dame mußte am Klavier kraftlose Töne üben. Ihre Hände und Arme bewegten sich edel und still, und sie wendete das Haupt ab' ('a beautiful and unhappy lady could bring forth from the piano only powerless tones. Her hands and arms made calm and noble movements, and she turned her head away').[27] Who was the 'schöne Dame'? The only likely candidate is Suzanne Perrottet, since she was the only woman who played the piano at the soirees (although one might wonder why she, and not Heusser himself, was at the keyboard; had she come on stage to play the violin part?). It coincides strangely with her own recollections of her relationship with Dada, as recounted over sixty years later to Giorgio Wolfensberger:

Es kam eine Zeit, wo ich immer noch mitgemacht habe bei den Dadaisten, aber bemerkt habe, dass einige nicht mehr so von innen aus begeistert waren für die Sache, sondern nur Freude daran hatten, die Bürger zu ärgern. Das hat mir dann missfallen. Und schliesslich habe ich bemerkt, ich bin doch kein disharmonischer Mensch, ich hatte nur ein disharmonisches Stadium, ich suchte mein Wesen zu verbessern und hatte im Moment diese Spontanität nötig.[28]

There came a time when I was still collaborating with the Dadaists, but I saw that some of them were not really so deeply inspired in their hearts by the cause; instead, they were just enjoying provoking the bourgeoisie. That didn't please me. And in the end I realized that I'm not a disharmonious person, I was just going through a disharmonious phase, I was trying to improve my way of being and at the time I needed that spontaneity.

It must have been, precisely, at this eighth and final Zurich Dada soiree that

27 Sheppard, 'Dada Zürich in Zeitungen', p. 242.
28 Wolfensberger, *Suzanne Perrottet*, p. 139.

Perrottet was displeased by the enjoyment certain Dadaists found (Serner above all, but also to a certain extent Tzara) in provoking the bourgeois. It is revealing that for her, the question of what she finds acceptable in Dada is inseparable from the question of harmony. She is not, in the end, a disharmonious person; she must go through disharmony, but in pursuit of a deeper harmony. This theme, of an endless quest for harmony, is evident throughout *Suzanne Perrottet: Ein bewegtes Leben*.

Hans Heusser is not the only key figure in the Zurich Dada soirees whose contribution has for decades been underestimated. As Ruth Hemus has so clearly shown, women, as dancers, singers, writers, designers, and visual artists, were central to those soirees, though many have since been largely forgotten.[29] Suzanne Perrottet was one of them. She had a long and distinguished career as a highly innovative dancer, but above all, perhaps, as a theorist and teacher of dance. To the Dadaists, she was a dancer, a pianist, a composer, and a violinist. Her engagement with Dada, like Heusser's, was limited to the Zurich Dada years, from 1916 to 1919. Dada, for Perrottet just as for Huelsenbeck, contained within it two contradictory approaches to music. Plainly, the approach that triumphed at the end of the final soiree was not the one that had drawn her to the movement. It is, however, the one that is now generally remembered. Everyone knows that Dada provokes its audience to uproar. Who remembers that Zurich Dada included the music of Schoenberg, Scott, and Satie, let alone Heusser? And, more to the point, that whereas audience provocation was dominant only towards the end of the last soiree, such composed music was an important element of almost all the soirees—and had originally been programmed to conclude the last?

But let us return to the other unusual element of Hans Richter's account of the final soiree. Whereas none of the other Dadaists has anything whatever to say concerning the style or content of Heusser's music, Richter implies it is 'twelve-tone'. Nothing in the pieces by Heusser which have survived, or in anything else known about Heusser, suggests he would ever have composed in a style that could reasonably be described thus. The designation of the piano quartet as 'in Es-dur' surely demonstrates that Heusser's Dada music never abandoned tonality. Why, then, would Richter have described it as 'twelve-tone'? The answer is given by his subsequent parenthesis. Writing in the 1960s, Richter is assimilating the fate of Heusser's piano music (totally unknown by 1960) to that of the avant-garde music of its time in general, notably Schoenberg's. To him, it is a kind of art which, in its refusal of tonality and thus of traditional harmony, can only, in the end, fail to convince the general public. But that is not at all how it appeared in 1919. To Perrottet, the music performed at the Dada soirees was not disharmonious in its essence.

[29] Ruth Hemus, *Dada's Women* (New Haven and London: Yale University Press, 2009).

It was entirely compatible with a striving towards inner harmony. Had music not always, after all, been built on a play of harmony and dissonance? Plainly, Perrottet did not see the music of Schoenberg, Scott, Satie, and Heusser as a radical refusal of those fundamental principles. The provocations of Serner and of Tzara, however, obstructed those same principles, and after those provocations had prevented the performance of Heusser's quartet, she turned her head away from Dada.

Going by the available evidence, Heusser also turned his head away from Dada after that fateful evening. There is not the slightest trace of his involvement with any of the subsequent Dada performance series, in Berlin, Paris, or elsewhere. Like Perrottet, I suspect, he could not collaborate with a Dada that prevented music from being heard.

We have, then, several answers to the question of why Heusser's contribution to Zurich Dada has been so completely forgotten by posterity. One is that Dada tends to be remembered, today, as a fundamentally provocative and anti-art movement. Of the two faces of Dada that Huelsenbeck describes, the musical and the 'bruitist', it is the latter that has come to be stereotypically identified with the sound of Dada in general. Heusser's music does not fit that stereotype; therefore, it has been evacuated from the collective memory of Zurich Dada.

A second reason for Heusser's fall into oblivion is the simple fact that none of the Dadaists had anything whatever to say about his music at the time; and the inaccurate later recollections of Glauser and Richter have only muddied the waters. That contemporary silence about music is, to me, relatively easy to understand. After all, none of the Dadaists said anything, either, about the music by Schoenberg, Scott, and Satie performed at the soirees. Nor did the male Dadaists have much to say about the distinctive contribution of the women—Suzanne Perrottet, but also Käthe Wulff and Sophie Täuber—who were associated with the Laban school, and who had a view of art that reserved a vital place for a search for harmony. This need not be taken to indicate straightforward hostility or incomprehension on the part of the male Zurich Dadaists at the time, any more than Perrottet's silence on the subject of Heusser should be taken to indicate hostility towards his music. As my work over the past decade has all aimed to show,[30] during this period as in the late nineteenth century, there was a powerful aesthetic principle at work which prized above all silence around music. About music itself, one should say nothing; there is nothing to say. The more famous and more verbally deft composers of the time, including Satie and Schoenberg, but also Stravin-

---

[30] See e.g. *Music Writing Literature, from Sand via Debussy to Derrida* (Aldershot: Ashgate, 2006), or 'Apollinaire's Music', *Forum for Modern Languages Studies*, 47 (2011), 36–48.

sky and Debussy (whose music was much appreciated by Hugo Ball, and of whom, as we have seen, both Heusser and Sulzberger proclaimed themselves students), found ingenious ways to maintain this principle, while nonetheless providing the verbal accompaniment to their musical activities without which their professional success might not have been achieved. Heusser, however, as far as we know, said nothing. Before giving the description of Heusser's music quoted above, the reviewer of the 'Soirée Hans Heusser', as quoted by 'C.R.', wrote, 'Um mich ganz dem "Genusse" dieser Musik hingeben zu können, dazu fehlten mir die nötigen Kommentare' ('In order to give myself over entirely to the "pleasure" of this music, I would have needed commentaries which were not provided').[31] The absence of any commentary on Hans Heusser's works has remained both exemplary and absolute ever since.

Is a third reason for the silence around Heusser's music to be found in its quality? Is he, quite simply, a poor composer, not worth resuscitating? I think it is fair to say that this is the spontaneous assumption of those who note the contrast between his presence in the Zurich Dada soirees and his absence from Dada historiography. It would seem the best explanation of the lack of attention accorded to his work. However, given that no musicologist, no Dada historiographer, no academic, has ever, as far as I can tell, actually thought about or even looked at Heusser's Dada music, it has clearly been condemned without a fair trial.

There is an instructive comparison to be made with the other pianist-composer who performed his own work at a Dada soiree (the 'Sturm-Soirée', on 14 April 1917): H. S. (or Marcel) Sulzberger. 'Sulzberger', writes Chris Walton, 'is mentioned in none of the current literature on those involved with the Dadaists in Zurich.'[32] Similarly, the Dadaists themselves left nothing on the record concerning their reactions to his music.[33] Does that mean it is of no value? That has doubtless been the general assumption. Landy, for example, as we have seen, dismisses him along with Heusser. However, Walton, the first critic to take Sulzberger seriously and to seek out his music, demonstrates that this assumption is based on shaky principles. Surely being unknown, being the object of no critical commentary, does not prove that a composer is of no value. It could, on the contrary, be held to indicate that the composer in question is behaving in accordance with one of the true spirits of Dada.

Of the strands that Zurich Dada wove together, one lent itself to endless

[31] Sheppard, 'Dada Zürich in Zeitungen', p. 218.

[32] Walton, 'The Many Lives of Marcel Sulzberger', p. 13.

[33] Ball and Tzara did, however, express privately their appreciation of Sulzberger's music in an enthusiastic letter they sent to him two days after his performance at the soiree. It is in the collection of the Zentralbibliothek in Zurich; see <http://www.zb.uzh.ch/ausstellungen/mam/ausstellung_6293/bilder_dokumente_jQ10/mus_nl_30_bc_1_fremde_dichter_0210.jpeg> [accessed 25 September 2014].

verbiage: the one that provoked audiences by challenging their preconceptions about art. Another refused all verbiage: the musical. The former, after 1919, rapidly drowned out the latter. The moral of this tale is simple: it is difficult to remember an art which is not defended in words. And defence of music in words is precisely what the musical Dadaists refused, it seems to me on principle, to provide. There had been three key players in Zurich Dada who had performed composed music on the piano: Ball and Heusser in the Cabaret Voltaire, Heusser and Perrottet at the soirees. All of them had abandoned the movement by the end of 1919, as the words of Tzara, Serner, and others began to create a public perception of Dada that did not leave space for their music. It would simply have been impossible for them to fight against that public perception, in words, in the name of music. They did not try.

Nonetheless, one should not think that the words of the Zurich Dadaists, in Zurich and after, simply stood in opposition to the music played by Ball, Perrottet, Sulzberger, and Heusser. If one looks carefully at the vociferations of the Zurich Dadaists (as I hope to in a future publication), one can find therein the evidence of the true value they placed on music, as something that escapes their words. Zurich Dada's energy was born of its determination not to let the operations of traditional logic, rationality, and language get in the way of the truth where the truth, as it so often seems to do where art is concerned, refuses to be recuperated by those operations. The Dadaists were certainly not alone in thinking that the truth about music is that it is inaccessible to words. But more than any other movement of the time, Dada refused to betray music in that inaccessibility to words; the Dadaists honoured it by saying nothing. Hans Heusser's Dada music had no life outside Dada, and never acquired any body of words around it. Therefore, in our current cultural environment, where the unsaid has no secure place, it has vanished. If, however, we can give it back its place, we will be doing justice, not only to Heusser, but to music itself, as Dada saw it.

UNIVERSITY OF EDINBURGH   PETER DAYAN

REVIEWS

Bon usage et variation sociolinguistique: perspectives diachroniques et traditions nationales. Ed. by WENDY AYRES-BENNETT and MAGALI SEIJIDO. Lyon: ENS Éditions. 2013. 338 pp. €23. ISBN 978-2-84788-389-3.

At first sight—and especially to anyone who thinks of both Vaugelas and Grevisse as legislators rather than commentators—there is a paradox in juxtaposing *bon usage* and *variation sociolinguistique*. Not so, and this collection does a good job of showing how and why. Most *remarqueurs* (in France and elsewhere) do provide evidence of less than *bon usage* in terms of forms, words, expressions which they comment on or suggest are stigmatized, and in this regard they are also sociolinguists *avant la lettre* (and sometimes *malgré eux*). The collection begins with a useful introduction before Part I, 'Les Origines de la tradition française'. Danielle Trudeau writes informatively on Henri Estienne's hardly known treatise *De latinitate*, an early 'stylistique comparée' of Latin and French; Francine Mazière discusses Louis Meigret, Jean Macé, and the Académie's 1694 dictionary in terms of what they have to say about *bon usage*; Chantal Wionet presents the libertine La Mothe Le Vayer, an entertaining enemy of Vaugelas's *Remarques* (for example, emphasizing the role of the people as 'le Maistre des langues' (p. 55)); Marc Bonhomme and André Horak discuss Ménage, who was tolerant of competing expressions, e.g. *a mesme temps, au mesme temps, dans le mesme temps, en mesme temps* (p. 69): all are 'tres-bonnes, & tres-naturelles' (an interesting adjective); Ménage proves to be generally but by no means invariably in favour of Parisian rather than provincial forms, and offers 'un excellent témoignage sur les pratiques sociales du français vers le milieu du XVIIe siècle' (p. 75). Gilles Siouffi shows how Bouhours marks an important phase in the development of *bon usage* because of his use of textual attestations leading to a 'corpus de référence' (p. 86) that would be used by later (eighteenth-century) commentators. Éric Tourette analyses the Abbé de Bellegarde's detailed social and sociolinguistic comments, such that 'les *Réflexions* sont devenues un précieux révélateur de connotations sociales' (p. 96); Christine Cuet, in an essay focusing on phonological variation indicated in Richelet, shows how the dictionary covers diatopic and diastratic variation more generally, using a mixture of sources (oral for phonology, and texts for other aspects). Finally, Philippe Caron points out how the Académie, like others following in the wake of Vaugelas, has a tendency to simplify the latter's position, to remove nuances, and thus to be more prescriptive than him; but the pronouncements of the Académie on language are much more hesitant than might generally be imagined. Part II deals with 'de 1700 à nos jours'. Chantal Rittaud-Hutinet discusses a little-known *Essay d'un dictionnaire comtois-françois* of 1753, designed to 'reform' the speech of the author's compatriots; it is a useful source of information about regionalisms and its information is corroborated by later works; Jacques-Philippe Saint-Gérand presents the nineteenth century and the first third of the twentieth as a period of evolution towards a greater degree of uncertainty; Pi-Ying Chen shows how

Alfons Haase's 1898 *Syntaxe française du XVIIe siècle* misrepresents Vaugelas; Christophe Rey and Isabelle Pierozak explain how the Académie's ninth edition of its dictionary still does not adequately represent regional terminology. Anna Bochnakowa discusses the evidence of linguistic interest in *Le Figaro* from 1996 to 2000; Wim Remysen observes definitional problems in and around acceptable usage (Canadian or French?) among Canadian *chroniqueurs de langage*; Jean René Klein (pp. 195–203) analyses the shift within *Le Bon Usage* (1936–2007) towards more explicit prescriptivism. Part III, 'Traditions nationales', discusses (mainly) languages other than French, often showing how the French tradition led the way (predictably enough, given the dominance of France and French in the seventeenth century). Two essays discuss Germany: Nicola McClelland covers the notion of *bon usage* from 1200 to 2000 and Odile Schneider-Mizony focuses on the twentieth century and, in particular, the development of educated lay guidance, which reveals a continuity in the problems discussed (suggesting stable variation). Gijsbert Rutten and Rik Vosters, writing about the Netherlands (1686–1830), point out important differences between north and south, with the former being concerned about language standards much earlier. Two contributions look at English: Ingrid Tieken-Boon van Ostade deals with the eighteenth century, whose first manual (by Robert Baker) was explicitly prompted by Vaugelas; the English tradition goes on to deploy criticism of 'best authors', rather than necessarily following them. Jacqueline Leon analyses Randolph Quirk's *Survey of English Usage*, based on usage, corpus methodologies, and a non-prescriptive approach, although Quirk has nevertheless argued for 'standard English', not least as a world language. Sylvie Archaimbault, writing about the norms of literary Russian, emphasizes that this was a constant in discussions during the eighteenth century and through to modern times, with a hierarchy (going back ultimately to Quintilian), in which literary language is the highest form. Finally, Anne-Marie Houdebine and Ferenc Fodor compare the development of linguistic norms in French and Hungarian: the latter began to be standardized relatively late (in the sixteenth century), and effectively had two competing forms (eastern and western) in the seventeenth and eighteenth centuries, prior to the emergence of a spontaneous common supra-regional form (a type of koineization). The comparative dimension which this third part adds is very welcome (and the fact that all the chapters are in French is a welcome reminder that it is still an international scientific language). A particular strength of the volume is that all the contributors have stuck to the subject, and thus that the different essays provide broadly comparable information about the two areas of the collection's title. There is an extensive bibliography and a very useful index. This is a good and enlightening collection of essays which usefully brings together a great deal of important information on a significant topic about which there is clearly still a good deal to be learnt.

ABERYSTWYTH UNIVERSITY   DAVID TROTTER

Pain and Compassion in Early Modern Literature and Culture. By JAN FRANS VAN
   DIJKHUIZEN. Cambridge: Brewer. 2012. xii+272 pp. £60. ISBN 978-1-
   84384-330-6.

We might be forgiven for thinking that pain is a 'universal' phenomenon: an un-
pleasant but (with luck) temporary physical sensation that we have to endure as
human beings with flawed and fragile bodies. And yet, as Jan Frans van Dijkhuizen
demonstrates in this timely and illuminating book, pain has a cultural history, in
which its earlier religious meanings have been increasingly lost as developments in
medicine have encouraged us to regard pain as avoidable and isolated from other
realms of experience. Van Dijkhuizen traces such cultural shifts back to the Renaissance, which he suggests was a 'crucial chapter in the history of pain' (p. 5). At this
time, Protestant thinkers attempted to redefine the spiritual meaning of pain, and
rejected the emphasis on Christ's bodily suffering built into late medieval and early
modern Catholic pain discourses. The book focuses on the relationship between
physical suffering, compassion, and religious experience, and how such ideas are
explored and debated in literary texts—in particular devotional poetry—of the
period 1560–1660.

   After a wide-ranging introductory chapter, Chapter 2 offers a detailed survey of
early modern religious discourses of pain, and discusses works by Catholic writers
such as Teresa of Avila, Ignatius of Loyola, and Luis of Granada, all of whom invoke
the notion of *imitatio Christi*—an intense identification with Christ's suffering. We
then see how Protestantism attempted to downplay the physical aspects of Christ's
pain and to focus instead on his mental anguish. At the same time, however, van
Dijkhuizen demonstrates that some Protestants were divided and ambivalent: in
the Passion sermons of Lancelot Andrewes and Joseph Hall there remains a fascination with the bodily aspects of pain, and a strong degree of identification with
the suffering of Christ. This substantial chapter provides the cultural and religious
background for the three chapters that follow. Through a series of careful close
readings, van Dijkhuizen demonstrates how such religious debates are played out
in the poetry of Alabaster, Donne, Herbert, Crashaw, and Lanyer, and how the
meaning of pain is 'linked to issues of poetic form and expression' (p. 89). Both
Donne and Herbert ask whether co-suffering with Christ is possible, and whether
the Passion is beyond poetic representation. But while Donne's explorations of
physical suffering convey a sense of 'spiritual and poetic deadlock' (p. 113), van
Dijkhuizen suggests that Herbert is more optimistic, that his poems can offer
a 'possible site of participation in the passion' (p. 116). Chapter 5 extends this
argument, and concludes that Herbert, Crashaw, and Lanyer elevate poetry to a
'sacramental status' (p. 171) as a way of compensating for the increasing lack of
embodied or material religious experiences in the period.

   Two additional chapters take the book's chronology and scope in a slightly
different direction. Spenser and Milton are brought together somewhat awkwardly
in Chapter 6. The chapter does, however, offer some suggestive comments on
the aesthetics of pity in *The Faerie Queene*, and how storytelling is figured as a

'conduit of compassion' (p. 199). The final chapter offers an attractive discussion of Montaigne's *Essais*, and yet the focus here is the 'almost complete lack of a religious dimension' in Montaigne's obsession with suffering (p. 216). This chapter concludes with a brief but tantalizing analysis of *The Tempest*, which takes the focus of the book still further from the devotional poetry of its central chapters. Arguably, then, van Dijkhuizen attempts to provide two things at once: a narrowly focused account of pain in early modern religious poetry and a wider consideration of suffering and compassion in the period. The result is that the book sits between these two stools, and some readers may wish that van Dijkhuizen had considered a wider range of genres, frameworks, and cultural contexts throughout. There is also a tendency to interpret poetic and metaphorical descriptions of the pain of early modern readers too literally at times. Overall, however, this is an intelligent and thought-provoking book that opens up many avenues for further research. It not only reminds us of the reality that physical suffering had for early moderns—and the meanings they ascribed to it—but also points to the cultural constructedness of our own assumptions about pain and the suffering of others.

University of Hull   Richard Meek

Boccaccio's Fabliaux: Medieval Short Stories and the Function of Reversal. By Katherine A. Brown. Gainesville: University Press of Florida. 2014. viii+227 pp. $74.95. ISBN 978–0–8130–4917–5.

Katherine A. Brown's study argues that manuscript collections of Old French fabliaux are key to our understanding of Boccaccio's literary practices in the *Decameron*, that the internal organization of these manuscripts affects our understanding of the tales within them, and that the manuscripts were privileged as sources for the narrative framework of the *Decameron*.

The Introduction gives a brief history of short stories, from the oral tradition to anthologized collections of tales, before explaining the importance of the fabliaux manuscript tradition and clarifying terms used in later discussion, including reversal, the bringing together of linguistic and thematic opposites, and dialectic, the exploring of opposite sides of an argument in search of truth. Examples show how Boccaccio uses inverted fabliaux—for example, by reversing the traditional gender or social roles within a specific novella—and also structures his *Decameron* in such a way as to consciously set individual tales against each other to create humour and avoid didacticism.

Brown's first chapter studies how both fables (which have an explicit moral appended to them) and fabliaux (which are used primarily to entertain rather than instruct) use chiasmus as a type of reversal in plot structure and language. In Chapter 2 Brown focuses on a late thirteenth-century Venetian manuscript, BNF fr. 2173, chosen because of its French and Italian origins, having been produced by a French copyist and a Venetian artist. She examines two key themes within the fabliaux: ambiguity, as seen in the use of puns, homophones, the misunderstanding of idioms, and the reversal of traditional roles; and how the organization of manuscripts helped to avoid didacticism and promote the need to interpret tales. She argues that, within this specific manuscript, fables and fabliaux often deal with similar subject-matter in very different ways, yet 'it is the role of the fabliaux [. . .] to challenge singular interpretations and reveal alternatives' (p. 82).

It is not until the third chapter, 'Medieval Story Collections and Framing Devices', that Brown applies these arguments to individual tales from Boccaccio's *Decameron*. She states that Boccaccio's *cornice* offers a structure similar to that of earlier fabliaux manuscripts, also briefly mentioning oriental collections as another possible source for the frame narrative. Brown argues that our interpretations of individual novelle of the *Decameron* are shaped by the text's frame narrative, just as fabliaux could be read in the context of other tales in collections: the theme set by the Day's ruler (where there is one) indicates how we should read the tales of that Day.

In her final chapter Brown looks at a few individual *novelle* of the *Decameron* to illustrate her arguments, focusing especially on *Dec.* IX. 2, the story of Isabetta and the abbess Usimbalda, as a way of exploring how Boccaccio came into contact with his source text, the fabliau *La Nonete*. Although she concedes that Boccaccio would probably have been dependent upon adaptations of many of the fabliaux, she suggests that he may have come into direct contact with Jean de Condé's manuscript of *La Nonete* in Naples. She further posits that many of Boccaccio's tales were intended to be read in pairs (for example, III. 1 and III. 10, IX. 2 and I. 4), and this enables readers to see more clearly the latent inversions and reversals within the text. Brown's study thus indicates possible new sources both for some of Boccaccio's stories and for his frame narrative. A helpful appendix lists the fabliaux manuscripts consulted and the analogues they contain for the novelle of the *Decameron*.

UNIVERSITY OF LEEDS   SARAH TODD

India and Europe in the Global Eighteenth Century. Ed. by SIMON DAVIES, DANIEL SANJIV ROBERTS, and GABRIEL SÁNCHEZ ESPINOSA. (Oxford University Studies in the Enlightenment, 2014:01) Oxford: Voltaire Foundation. 2014. xii+ 341 pp.; 13 ills. £65. ISBN 978-0-7294-1080-9.

The essays included in this volume were compiled largely from a symposium held at Queen's University Belfast in 2011. The stated aim was to move away from the standard orientalist understanding of eighteenth-century history to create a more nuanced, modern conception of the relationship between Europe and India during that period.

A number of essays deal with French, Spanish, and Dutch attempts to understand 'India' in a manner widely divergent from the British orientalist creation. Anthony Strugnell delves into the multiple influences which drove Raynal's widely read *Histoire des deux Indes*, and notes that among the Enlightenment *philosophes* and British political and merchant travellers to India who contributed to it, the emerging political rivalry between France and Britain over the 'Indian empire' certainly played an important role in how sympathetically India and Indians were portrayed. Felicia Gottmann's essay on Voltaire's *Fragments sur l'Inde* also accords primacy to a French text in the creation of an enlightened idea of the Orient as a 'fallen paradise', capable of regaining its glory, rather than the more common British colonial projection of India as a place devoid of civilizing impulses, and therefore needing British civilization. Florence D'Souza's essay on Surat, the international focus of commerce in eighteenth-century India, demonstrates the fluid understanding of trade and ethnic communities in the different contexts provided by European observers such as the French savant Anquetil-Duperron as opposed to the English doctor John Fryer and the Anglican missionary John Ovington. In exploring the commercial lure that India held for Europe during the eighteenth century, Gabriel Sánchez Espinosa on the Spanish attempt to 'understand' India through Bernardin Saint-Pierre's *La Chaumière indienne* and Mogens Nissen's focus on the Dutch Asiatic Company provide an important corrective to the dominant British Empire model of Indian history.

A second theme consists of examinations of British writers not solely influenced by colonialism or by orientalism. The presence of several major orientalist works underscores the need to re-evaluate them as simple pieces of orientalist literature as Said once imagined. Javed Majeed notes the important influence of eighteenth-century Gothic understanding, as well as Richardson's marginal position as a Scotsman in the British Empire, in creating and analysing John Richardson's *A Dictionary of Persian, Arabic, and English*. Sonja Lawrenson's essay on *The Orientalist*, similarly analyses the liminal position of the female author as Irish in post-Union Ireland. The author offers this work as a marginalized Irish female critiquing the hyper-masculine environment of nationalism and colonialism in eighteenth-century England. The status of 'outsider' also forms the core of Daniel Sanjiv Roberts's argument that the appropriation of Bernier's *Histoire* by ideological opposites, Robert Southey and Sydney Owenson, can be better understood through their respective English and Irish lineages than by addressing their proselytizing missions. Deirdre Coleman emphasizes the influence of anti-colonial sentiment and philosophical conceptions of India in the poetic works of Keats. Similarly James Watt examines three novels written as critiques of the colonial mission and Britain's role as civilizer.

The last essays deal with the position of the 'native'. Long considered passive objects of description, native linguistic collaborators are brought to the fore by Claire Gallien, who highlights the ongoing dialogue between native voices and European translators of early Persian literature into English. Lakshmi Subramanian emphasizes the need to rethink the description of native pirates, who were primarily understood within prescribed British standards of piracy. Thus, a global, fluid understanding of trade and commercial relations between India and Europe in the eighteenth century is necessary to break out of the confines of the limiting orientalist paradigm and the Eurocentric focus imposed by it. Seema Alavi provides examples of trade and commercial practices in Mughal India which can be understood better in the context of a developing global trading economy rather than the binary orientalist opposition. Finally John McAleer's study of the material collections of the East India Company in Britain's India Museum proves that these can be revisited, and the understanding of the culture of colonization and of the notion of colony rethought using the same sources but different lenses of comprehension.

This volume is an ambitious project: Simon Davies, Daniel Sanjiv Roberts, and Gabriel Sánchez Espinosa have spread a wide net and acquired several worthy additions to the study of eighteenth-century globalization, the Romantic oriental movement, and the geopolitical movement of Britain towards empire in South Asia together with its concomitant effects on intra-European political relations. While some essays seem only loosely linked to the larger theme, this is due to the paucity of works viewing colonial relations from a broader vantage-point than the simple binary of colonizer versus colonized proposed by Said. The essays are admirable not just in their depth of research, but in the further questions provoked with regard to the global, colonial history of the eighteenth century. The clear message is that context matters; and in the case of colonial or imperial works, it is not sufficient to attribute one dominant influence to any individual writer. The essays demonstrate that pan-European political relations mattered, as did individual ideological influences and social standing within the national and colonial world.

MORGAN STATE UNIVERSITY   JYOTI MOHAN

The Realist Author and Sympathetic Imagination. By SOTIRIOS PARASCHAS. London: Legenda. 2013. xi+223 pp. £45. ISBN 978-1-907975-70-7.

Nineteenth-century realist fiction is richly populated with characters who are able to read the thoughts and feelings of others. In this cogently argued study, Sotirios Paraschas explores the concept of sympathetic imagination across a wide spectrum of French and British texts, focusing in particular on the works of Honoré de Balzac and George Eliot. The first part of the volume examines the ways in which both novelists sought to elicit, and sometimes undermine, the sympathy of their readers. In *Le Père Goriot* Balzac assures us that the events depicted in this 'effroyable tragédie parisienne' are true, and suggests that they might even cause the reader to shed tears over the plight of the eponymous father. Equally, at the level of plot, Balzac and Eliot portray characters who are either endowed with unusual powers of intuition—a skill memorably deployed by Vautrin in *Le Père Goriot*—or who, like the fictional poet Latimer in Eliot's 'The Lifted Veil', demand sympathy but offer little understanding in return. As Paraschas explains, those characters who are capable of identifying with others enjoy privileged status in nineteenth-century realist fiction, where they often appear as 'doubles' of their creators. Thus, when the antiquary intuits the thoughts of Raphaël de Valentin in *La Peau de chagrin*, he echoes Balzac's conceptualization of the author as a Protean figure blessed with heightened observational powers and the ability to penetrate the hearts and minds of others. In the second half of the volume Paraschas proceeds to consider the ways in which Balzac and Eliot employed these authorial doubles to assert their rights of ownership over their creative work. In his portrayal of Vautrin, most notably, Balzac represents the double as a paternal figure who jealously guards his 'offspring', Lucien and Rastignac, whose careers the master criminal attempts to control. Similarly, in *Daniel Deronda* metaphors of property and possession can be seen to reflect Eliot's fear that her artistic property would ultimately be taken away from her. During a period in which the courts offered little protection against the theft of intellectual property, the authorial double functioned as a key instrument through which Balzac and Eliot articulated their grievances against the inadequacy of their respective legal systems. As more rigorous copyright legislation began to take effect in the late nineteenth and early twentieth centuries, so too, then, did the intuitive characters beloved of earlier writers begin to fade from the literary landscape, where they were replaced—albeit not entirely—by copyists and slavish imitators such as Flaubert's Bouvard and Pécuchet.

Despite occasionally exposing its origins as a doctoral thesis, this is an impressive volume that has been researched with meticulous care. In arguing for a more nuanced understanding of the realist mode, Paraschas has written an important contribution to nineteenth-century French studies, and a book that will serve as an invaluable reference for students and scholars alike.

UNIVERSITY OF BIRMINGHAM   ANDREW WATTS

Prepositions in English Grammars until 1801, with a Survey of the Western European Background. By TOM LUNDSKÆR-NIELSEN. (RASK Supplement, 19) Odense: University Press of Southern Denmark; London: Modern Humanities Research Association. 2011. 307 pp. DKK 275. ISBN 978–87–7674–565–3.

In contrast to his earlier *Prepositions in Old and Middle English* (Odense: Odense University Press, 1993), a contribution to historical linguistics centring on the syntax and semantics of English *at*, *in*, and *on* up to 1400, Tom Lundskær-Nielsen here changes his perspective to prepositions as a word class—that is, to the history of linguistics. While the title seems to advertise a book on English prepositions, its primary aim is rather 'to provide a survey of the main trends in the linguistic description of prepositions and of parts of speech in general' (p. 97). The focus is thus on word classes in the English grammatical tradition, a tradition which is much influenced by Latin and the Latin grammatical system(s) throughout the timespan investigated (see Chapters 1–3 on the Greek and Latin traditions and their tenacious impact on grammar writing in the Middle Ages and the Renaissance). Word classes in the grammatical tradition, however, have already been investigated thoroughly—for example, in excellent studies by Ian Michael (*English Grammatical Categories and the Tradition to 1800* (Cambridge: Cambridge University Press, 1970)) or Vivian Law (*The History of Linguistics in Europe* (Cambridge: Cambridge University Press, 2003)). While these works are taken as cornerstones or are at least cited, more recent research, such as that of Ingrid Tieken-Boon van Ostade and her team (see the bibliographies at <http://codifiers.weblog.leidenuniv.nl/>), has not been considered at all. Thus, with regard to word classes in the grammatical tradition, the book is partly outdated and provides very few new insights.

In his aim of examining the treatment of prepositions as a part of speech within the English grammatical tradition from the late sixteenth until the end of the eighteenth century, Lundskær-Nielsen chooses to provide a 'survey of the main trends' (p. 97) taken from a selection of fifty English grammars, from William Bullokar's *Bref Grammar for English* (1586) up to John Dalton's *Elements of English Grammar* (1801). This survey fills about two-thirds of the book (pp. 97–266) and is subdivided into the 'The Sixteenth Century', 'The Seventeenth Century', 'The Eighteenth Century', and 'One Nineteenth-Century Grammar'. These dreary headings are characteristic of the fashion in which the—often very fascinating—material is presented in this book. Unfortunately, Lundskær-Nielsen has chosen to 'present the texts in strict chronological order, according to their year of publication' (p. 102), which means that a grammar focusing on Latin might be adjacent to another focusing on English, or those modelled on Donatus or (later) Lily might be juxtaposed with others of independent construction. Furthermore, practical and pedagogical grammars both precede and follow philosophical and universal ones. Lundskær-Nielsen argues that 'this zigzag course [. . .] will help to demonstrate that the grammatical texts used here do not constitute a step-by-step linear advance in grammatical description' (p. 100), confuting an argument no one interested in the subject would ever be likely to advance. Lundskær-Nielsen himself is aware that 'such a procedure runs the risk of overwhelming the reader with a somewhat confusing and impenetrable mass of data and no clear overview' (p. 102). Unfortunately, this is indeed what has happened.

Lundskær-Nielsen is unremitting in describing each and every one of his fifty grammars in the same fashion: after a short passage giving biographical information, he painstakingly retells what he found, 'noting in each case what they have to say about the parts of speech in general and about prepositions and prepositional constructions in particular' (p. 102). Readers are generally left alone with this wealth of often very repetitive material: while the 'Summary' (pp. 267–78) outlines at least some of the main trends (in particular the dependence of the respective grammars on Latin, following Michael's 1970 study), the reader is not granted any assistance by, for example, cross-referencing or a comprehensive word index. Such an index would be crucial for linguists interested in, for instance, what the early grammarians have to say about particular prepositions or specific morphological or syntactic phenomena. This is an opportunity missed, since many of the aspects discussed in these early grammars are discussed in similar fashion today. Among them are preposition stranding or the conceptualization of (certain) prefixes as prepositions in Latin-based grammars (as in Lily's definition, in turn copied from Priscian, which was to be repeated with slight modifications by many English grammarians: 'A preposition is a parte of speeche most commonly sette before other partes, eyther in apposition: as, *Ad patrem* [to the father], orels in composition: as, *Indoctus* [untaught]' (p. 92)). The most relevant issue, however, is the concept of a word class 'particles' by the younger grammars, comprising prepositions, adverbs, and conjunctions (and in some grammars also interjections) and thus similar to the recent—and much-discussed—categorization of the *Cam-*

bridge Grammar of the English Language (ed. by Rodney Huddlestone and Geoffrey K. Pullum (Cambridge: Cambridge University Press, 2002), p. 19).

Despite its structural shortcomings, the book still provides a valuable overview of the treatment of prepositions against the backdrop of word classes. For more overarching questions, prepositions may at first glance seem an odd choice, since, following the Greek/Latin tradition, they have long been considered a minor part of speech—hence Priscian's 'Ergo natura quidem posterior est, constructione vero principalis' ('Hence it [the preposition] is subsequent by nature but the first in the construction' (p. 56)). Through Lundskær-Nielsen's meticulous reports, however, we are also made aware that ideas recently developed in discourse analysis and cognitive linguistics have been considered at least since Locke. This is reflected in descriptions which consider 'particles' the most essential elements, as in the grammar of George Dalgarno (*c.* 1616–1687): 'particles, which are to speech what the soul is to man, what the nerves and ligaments are to the body, or what cement is to the building. For, if particles are taken away from speech, what remains? What else but a dead body [. . .]?' (p. 132).

In other philosophical grammars we find conceptualizations which are (including their illustrations) startlingly reminiscent of present-day cognitive research (pp. 137–39 on John Wilkins). It would have been highly welcome if Lundskær-Nielsen, with his outstanding expertise and his wide reading of metalinguistic texts, had presented these approaches in a more comprehensive and reflective way. In its present form, however, those interested have to undertake the wearisome job of reading the book from cover to cover. In sum, this volume may be best described in Lundskær-Nielsen's own words, borrowed from his evaluation of Collyer's grammar: 'there are glimpses of insights in his book, but the shackles of tradition are often too strong' (p. 185).

LUDWIG-MAXIMILIANS-UNIVERSITÄT, MÜNCHEN   URSULA LENKER

The English Martyr from Reformation to Revolution. By ALICE DAILEY. (Reformations: Medieval and Early Modern) Notre Dame: University of Notre Dame Press. 2012. xv+352 pp. £32.50. ISBN 978-0-268-02612-7.

This book, based on Alice Dailey's Ph.D. dissertation (UCLA, 2003), examines the development of English martyrological writing from the medieval to the early modern period, and includes a 'Postscript' on perceptions of martyrdom in the aftermath of the events of 11 September 2001. Its central premiss is that 'martyrdom is not a death but a story that gets written about death' (p. 2), and so it sets out to examine 'the relationship between the paradigmatic martyr story and the unruly exigencies of history' (p. 2). Through an examination of the literary construction of a number of texts, including *The Golden Legend*, medieval Corpus Christi plays, John Foxe's *Acts and Monuments*, the writings of Cardinal William Allen, John Mush, and John Gennings, as well as Charles I's *Eikōn basilikē* and John Milton's *Eikonoklastēs*, Dailey explores the paradigmatic structure of martyrological writing, laying heavy emphasis on the 'victim's anticipation of being narrativized' (p. 5) and how this concern structured their response to their situation.

Dailey's eloquent prose takes the reader through a detailed assessment of both the 'dominant performative and narrative topoi' (p. 6), during which she identifies key texts whose very form and content determined and reinforced the essential character traits and actions expected of a martyr. Her assessment of the martyr/ heretic paradigm leads to a close analysis of the impact the charge of 'treason' (rather than 'heresy') had on Elizabethan Catholics (p. 99 onwards). Dailey posits that this shift in prosecution tactics disrupted the martyological paradigm, and so led to new forms of discourse, which are then further explored.

In this altered discourse, Catholics such as Clitherow and Gennings become 'caught in the representational crux between martyr and traitor or martyr and sui-cide' (p. 162). 'Miraculous intervention' becomes central to proving their 'sanctity' (p.162) in such circumstances. Charles I's role as 'martyr' depends on subverting the paradigm, for he 'would naturally occupy the role of persecutor in the paradigms of Christian martyrology' (p. 209); his role as 'victim' is made possible only by his altered position from powerful to powerless. Milton subsequently challenged Charles's rhetoric, seeing not confessional truth in his words but mere literary artifice. For Milton, Charles merely 'acted over us so stately and so tragically' (cited on page 239); his words and actions are those of a player, not a martyr.

The close textual analysis is commendable, although at times more detailed refer-encing would have been helpful. There is a tendency, in places, to lay little emphasis on scholars who have examined the primary sources previously. For example, the narrative of events in the lead-up to the death of Edmund Campion makes little reference to work done by others in the field, and it is surprising to see Gerard Kilroy's work on Campion reduced to a single footnote. Similarly, the account of Margaret Clitherow gives minimal acknowledgement to the work of Peter Lake and Michael Questier. Often Dailey is at pains to state where she sees modern scholarship to be in error. Yet this frequently happens without actually identifying just who these scholars are. In the discussion of 'recent criticism' of John Foxe's narrative, for example, those with whom Dailey disagrees remain elusive (p. 54).

Dailey's analysis of martyrological writing takes the reader on a grand tour through a wealth of material on saints, miracles, biblical and medieval narratives, as well as key early modern texts in this most fascinating of genres. The breadth of texts and timesepan covered is commendable in its ambition and in its engaging narrative style.

Harvard University   Elizabeth Evenden

Miserere Mei: The Penitential Psalms in Late Medieval and Early Modern England.
    By Clare Costley King'oo. Notre Dame: University of Notre Dame Press.
    2012. xix+283 pp. £34.95. ISBN 978–0–268–03324–8.

Over the last decade, historians and literary scholars have begun to revisit the issue of late medieval and early modern penitential theory and practice before, during, and after the Reformation. Long understood to serve as a definitive point of theological rupture, the transformation of Catholic penance into Protestant repen-tance is currently being re-evaluated as a moment of genuine cultural change that nevertheless contains surprising narratives of continuity. Clare Costley King'oo's *Miserere Mei* joins this still new conversation by focusing on one of the most crucial groupings of penitential texts, the seven penitential psalms, and investigating their curiously prominent status in both pre- and post-Reformation penitential practice. Given the emphasis in the medieval Church on their spiritual efficacy, why would Lutheran and Reformed Churches, for which penance was at best theologically gratuitous, maintain such prominent interest in these psalms? Drawing on an impressive array of resources and methodologies, King'oo shows that the value of these psalms is rooted in multiple aspects of culture—the market for manuscripts and printed books; the popularity of devotional songs; the utility of literature as a medium for political commentary—that both shaped and were shaped by the theological upheavals of the Reformation. The book offers itself both as a valuable cultural history of the penitential psalms and as a model for rethinking outdated yet still dominant modes of historical periodization.

This value is acutely perceptible in contexts that have been underworked. King'oo's first chapter, on illustrated versions of the penitential psalms, demonstrates that a late medieval shift in visual depictions of David (from penitent in agony to voyeur) indicates a corresponding narrowing of focus to the examination of specifically sexual transgressions. In doing so, King'oo also argues for a more nuanced view of the landscape of late medieval penitential practice, still a rarity among early modernists. Her discussions of early modern literature call attention to the importance of the multitude of literary forms used by early modern writers to consider the penitential psalms as elements of penitential practice. King'oo's fifth chapter, which addresses the surprising status of parody in sixteenth-century translations and adaptations, shows that Protestant authors such as Gascoigne and Harington were remarkably aware of the interpretative tradition that identified the penitential psalms as soteriologically efficacious, and their own adapted psalms and psalm sequences develop a lyric speaker capable of lampooning this tradition humorously (Gascoigne) or sardonically (Harington). In Protestant discourse, the penitential psalms were the site of reflection and critique, carrying with them an awareness of past practices while providing the opportunity to refine developing understandings of the practical role of repentance within a vastly different theological framework.

King'oo's subject-matter is, to be sure, somewhat diffuse, and it might be objected that this diffusiveness inhibits the development of a more comprehensive, cohesive argument that would challenge current critical narratives of the pre- to post-Reformation development of penitential practice as such. This objection, however, would be shortsighted. *Miserere Mei* is meticulously aware of the nature of its critical project, which is to trace the penitential psalms across the confessional (and implicitly temporal) divide of the Reformation and examine their striking appearances in a variety of cultural forms, as well as to point to ways in which its analysis might enrich other areas of study. One can readily see how King'oo's lines of enquiry might profitably be extended further into the seventeenth century; to Fulke Greville's reworking of the sonnet sequence in *Caelica*, for instance, and even to Milton's psalm translations. As such, the book is important and useful both for the arguments it offers and for the conversations that it begins.

ITHACA COLLEGE   DAN BREEN

'*The Breviary of Britain*' (1573), with Selections from '*The History of Cambria*' (1584). By HUMPHREY LLWYD. Ed. by PHILIP SCHWYZER. (MHRA Tudor and Stuart Translations, 5) London: Modern Humanities Research Association. 2011. ix+208 pp. £24.99 (pbk £12.50). ISBN 978-1-78188-081-4 (pbk 978-0-947623-93-7).

One set of publications influenced by the current 'translation turn' in early modern studies is the MHRA Tudor and Stuart Translations series. While indebted to the aspirations of its predecessor, Tudor Translations (W. E. Henley 1892-1909; David Nutt Press 1924-27), the new collection seeks 'to restore to view a major part of English Renaissance literature which has become relatively inaccessible and to present these texts as literary works in their own right' (http://www.tudor.mhra. org.uk). This twenty-first-century outlook is clearly exemplified in its inaugural output. By contrast with those sixteenth-century imperatives which sought to re-claim classical literature or works from the early modern European traditions, Philip Schwyzer's smartly informed edition of Humphrey Llwyd's *The Breviary of Britain* and selections from *The History of Cambria* examines texts brought forth from Tudor England's archipelagic concerns. Indeed, as you might expect from the author of *Literature, Nationalism and Memory in Early Modern England and Wales* (Cambridge: Cambridge University Press, 2004) and the co-editor (with Simon Mealor) of *Archipelagic Identities: Literature and Identity in the Atlantic Archipelago, 1550-1800* (Farnham: Ashgate, 2004), Schwyzer's introductory essay keenly establishes the cultural politics of translation, simultaneously scrutinizing Llwyd's critical neglect, Anglo-Welsh relations, and the texts' wider contribution to our understanding of sixteenth-century English literature and culture.

Working out from a compelling account of Llwyd's deathbed epistle to the Flemish map-maker Abraham Ortelius, Schwyzer inducts his reader into the car-tographic and textual networks of *Commentarioli Britannicae descriptionis frag-mentum*, which was printed in Cologne in 1572 and swiftly translated a year later by Thomas Twyne as *The Breviary of Britain*. As Schwyzer recounts the ways in which the self-proclaimed 'Cambro-Britain' (p. 4) gained posthumous recognition 'as the leading authority on the antiquity and geography of Britain' (p. 3) until the publication in 1586 of Camden's *Britannia*, we learn, for example, how Llwyd's Macbeth (awkwardly rendered into the English vernacular) recasts Fleance's son Walter as 'a Welsh prince who fled to Scotland to escape a murderous Welsh tyrant. Hence the ruling Scottish dynasty is entirely Welsh in origin' (p. 7). While responding to contemporaneous antiquarian impulses, Llwyd offers a striking view of 'England, Scotland and Wales (treated in that order)' (p. 5) mediated via a Welsh 'panoptic' lens (p. 7). When it comes to Twyne's version—made with the help of the Welsh-speaking lawyer Thomas Yale—the translator's curial address to Edward de Vere, which announces that 'it were a foul shame to be inquisitive of the state of foreign lands and to be ignorant of our own' (ll. 40–42), foregrounds humanist agendas. At the same time, as Twyne subsumes Llwyd's Cambrian outlook into a homogeneous shared experience, Elizabethan England's colonialist gestures are tacitly exposed.

Gifted by Hugh Broughton to Gabriel Harvey, *The Breviary of Britain* is framed by six liminal poems (one by the Welsh courtier Lodowick Lloyd). The book also engendered a lively trans-European discussion between Hubert Languet and Philip Sidney. Alongside his examination of these foregoing meta- and paratextual concerns, Schwyzer shows how *The Breviary of Britain* is woven into the fabric of English canonical writings such as John Dee's *General and Rare Materials* (1577) and Edmund Spenser's and Michael Drayton's verses. The five carefully chosen extracts from David Powel's 1584 translation of Llwyd's *Cronica Walliae* (*The History of Cambria*), the Welsh author's version of the medieval Welsh chronicle *Brut y Tywysogion* (*The Brut of the Princes*), bespeak a similar intertextual reach and ideological tenor: the second edition of Raphael Holinshed's *Chronicles* (1587), Thomas Churchyard's *The Worthines of Wales* (1587), Book III of Spenser's *Faerie Queene* (1590), Drayton's *Poly-Olbion* (1612), and John Milton's *A Mask Presented at Ludlow Castle* (1634) bear traces of Llwyd's work. If Twyne arguably takes a discreet approach to the appropriation of *Commentarioli Britannicae descriptionis fragmentum* into the cultural and social milieu of 1570s England, Powel's addition of 'twenty-five pages devoted to "The Princes of Wales of the Blood Royal of England", from Edward II to Elizabeth' (p. 24) betrays the subsequent decade's ardent sensibilities. In a work dedicated to Philip Sidney, it is not altogether surprising that Powel effaced Llwyd's view of 'an ignorant English audience' (p. 18) in favour of supporting Henry Sidney's local concerns as the Lord President of the Council in the Marches of Wales. While invested in the material conditions of textual production, Schwyzer has fashioned an engaging, scholarly edition which is as much concerned with its critical apparatus as it is with the ways in which Llwyd's texts have impacted on 'the ideological origins of *Britannicum imperium*' (p. 30). *The Breviary of Britain* and the stimulating episodes from *The History of Cambria* are accompanied by detailed notes, glossaries, indexes, a list of authors, and a bibliography, thus inviting further studies of Llywd's writing and its afterlives at the level of the signifier and beyond.

LANCASTER UNIVERSITY   LIZ OAKLEY-BROWN

Spenser's Ruins and the Art of Recollection. By REBECA HELFER. Toronto: University of Toronto Press. 2012. xiii+391 pp. £57.95. ISBN 978-0-8020-9067-6.

Rebeca Helfer's monograph makes an invaluable contribution not only to Spenser scholarship but, more generally, to memory studies of the early modern period. Helfer's particular enquiry focuses on the intricate textual relationships between history, memory, and poetry in the cultural formulation of authorial and, indeed, collective identities in the sixteenth century: 'the art of memory would be better understood as a story about history, a means of participating in a broad conversation about how the ruins of the past survive in the memory of later minds' (p. xi). In a carefully researched study that acknowledges the rich critical heritage of memory studies executed by classicists and medievalists which early modernists have inherited, one of Helfer's most innovative and dynamic contributions is its refusal to allow its discussion to become locked into a familiar, linear reading experience in which Plato, Augustine, and Cicero, for example, are shed early on in favour of an emphasis upon contemporaneous interventions in the early modern memory debate. Helfer insists that Plato, Augustine, Cicero, and, indeed, Dante and Petrarch are integrated again and again into differing appreciations of Spenser's poetic undertakings, and this stimulates a wide-ranging account of cultural exchange and intellectual debate in late Elizabethan England: 'In Alma's Castle, Spenser not only remembers Augustine, Cicero, Plato, and Aristotle, but he also remembers Augustine remembering these earlier writers' (p. 215).

The decision to link Spenserian formulations of memory with the topos of the ruin (or rather the 'renewal', the regeneration, of the ruin) places Helfer's discussion in lively conversation with a number of other critical debates reflecting upon how the archaeology of the early modern landscape communicated multiple memorial prompts to a post-Reformation culture—a landscape in which sacral (or formerly sacral) places might be invested with strategic memorial status, compelling the inhabitants to attend to the convergence of edifice and edification in a manner which shadowed rhetorical practices promoted in antiquity. The account of these converging lines of devotional and secular memory gives rise to a wider consideration of how early modern investments in remembering transform and endure as the sixteenth century progresses and of how Spenser, in particular, attends repeatedly to the collaborative nature of the labours of memory. In the analysis of *The Shepheardes Calender*, for example, Helfer enquires tellingly, 'At the heart of this debate lies the question of exactly who builds literary immortality: the author or the audience?' (p. 95). Another clear commitment of this ambitious study is made explicit at the outset by Helfer as she indicates her intention to attend to the breadth of Spenser's poetic career and not simply allow *The Faerie Queene* to be the centre of gravity for subsequent discussions. This decision not only allows *The Ruines of Time* to enjoy an enhanced status in the chapters which follow, but helpfully returns attention in a persuasive manner to the importance of Jan Van der Noot's *Theatre for Voluptuous Worldlings* ('the *Theatre* likely showed Spenser the possibility, even the pleasure, of ruin' (p. 21)), the *Mutabilitie Cantos*, and, indeed, *A Vewe of the Present State of Ireland* (where Spenser may be found to play 'the part of historiographer in order to expose the fictions that make up history' (p. 245)).

There is very much to admire in this stimulating and substantial study of Spenser's fascination with 'the desire and duty to remember the past' (p. 133) across an authorial career devoted to 'endles souenaunce' ('November', in *The Shepheardes Calender*, l. 5). The contribution which *Spenser's Ruins and the Art of Recollection* offers to the ongoing scholarly account of the early modern debate of memory is significant and strategically opens up a number of possible fruitful avenues for further enquiry.

BANGOR UNIVERSITY   ANDREW HISCOCK

Early Modern Drama and the Bible: Contexts and Readings, 1570–1625. Ed. by ADRIAN STREETE. (Early Modern Literature in History) Basingstoke: Palgrave Macmillan. 2012. xi+267 pp. £60. ISBN 978–0–230–30109–2.

The notion of a discernible divisibility of early modern literary culture into secular and sacred has been common currency in academic circles for generations. Its most conspicuous, and hitherto least contested, applicability is to the Elizabethan and Jacobean stage, from which, it has routinely been asserted, religion was largely evacuated, as the Church-inspired morality play gave place to more heterogeneous, commercially driven fare. In this critical orthodoxy, the Bible and biblical allusion swiftly exit stage left, if they have been able to inveigle their way into a script in the first place. Displaying quiet authority, this book demurs. For Adrian Streete and his contributors, the Bible is a pervasive, if often refracted, presence in early modern theatre.

The comparative material absence of the Book from the early modern stage is, it should be acknowledged, readily conceded throughout the volume. Why its non-appearance is so manifest, when mass printing in the vernacular had demystified it, is, according to the opening essay by Michael Davies, bound up with theatrical censorship and Protestant iconoclasm (the latter permits a rare on-stage appearance, but of a Vulgate edition, discarded unceremoniously by Marlowe's Faustus). More significantly, we must also look to the Bible's revered place in the public and private sphere ('its status as a holy object remained undiminished' (p. 28)), and its potency as a symbol and agent of magisterial power, instanced in title-pages regularly bearing the royal portrait.

Its physical elusiveness does not, however, preclude Davies from positing the 'possible presence of a Bible at key moments' in early modern drama (p. 43), notably in the unidentified reading matter of eponymous Shakespearian characters. When holding this presence to underscore debates on princely legitimacy, as in *Henry VI, Part III, Henry VIII*, and *Richard II*, one suspects the author is on slightly firmer ground than when suggesting that Hamlet's potential Bible-reading ('Enter Hamlet, reading on a book') signals 'a particularly Protestant kind of "inwardness"' (p. 44). Nevertheless, Davies puts down a marker for profitable discussion in the remainder of the volume on the dramatic effects to which veiled uses of Scripture are put.

One of these uses concerns the understudied overlap between preaching and playing, carefully analysed in an essay by Emma Rhatigan. This chapter's twin focus is on Thomas Adams's sermon *The White Devil* (1613) and John Webster's play of the same name, first performed a year earlier in London. Here, Rhatigan argues, pulpit and stage combine to indicate divergent but complementary treatment of biblical tropes on hypocrisy; dual minatory warnings, saturated in apocalyptic imagery, on women's capriciousness and Catholic clerical rapacity. To her credit, and to the betterment of the discussion, the author seeks not only to elucidate the 'hints of some form of if not collaboration then at least creative reciprocity' between these writings (p. 186), but also to gauge the respective audience reception. Ultimately, despite the inclusion of Shakespeare, Marlowe, and, to a lesser extent, Heywood, the full range of texts under discussion seems insufficiently canonical for the sacred/secular divide to be dismissed as anachronistic (p. 223). However, one finishes the book newly apprehending that, like most binaries, this one is rather less illuminating than it claims to be. As Streete argues in his Introduction, and as the remainder of the book amply demonstrates, in sixteenth- and seventeenth-century drama 'the divine may no longer be represented mimetically but biblical language, imagery, and tropes were very much part of a dramatist's arsenal' (p. 8). At a time when it is fashionable to write—and read—religion out of, or at least minimize its impact on, the culture of earlier epochs, this study stands as a useful corrective, reminding us of the Bible's elevated position in early modern literature and drama, and its capacity to navigate between the two.

BIRKBECK, UNIVERSITY OF LONDON   PHILIP MAJOR

Railing, Reviling and Invective in English Literary Culture, 1588–1617: The Anti-Poetics of Theater and Print. By MARIA TERESA MICAELA PRENDERGAST. (Material Readings of Early Modern Culture) Farnham: Ashgate. 2012. xii+ 246 pp. £55. ISBN 978-1-4094-3809-0.

'Railing', 'reviling', and 'invective' are words not often associated with coherency. Their textures suggest a lack of control in the delivery of verbose and unstructured vituperation. However, in her wide-ranging and meticulously researched book, Maria Teresa Micaela Prendergast demonstrates that late Elizabethan and early Jacobean railing formed a clear narrative that responded to varying political, religious, and sociological events. Since engaging in such discourses was unlikely to escape the notice of the censors, Prendergast argues that the railers circumvent censorship through focusing upon perversion. Perversion, in the early modern sense of the word, not only connotes depraved acts, but also brings into focus an inversion or discarding of the 'correct' meaning of words. This insight into the meaning of railing allows Prendergast to contend that the 'rhetorical perversions of railing dominated the English literary landscape from 1588 to 1620, inspiring writers to rant about a variety of topics that they deemed to be immoral' (p. 1). Despite the writers of railing pamphlets' assertion of their dominance of the moral high ground, the appropriation of the rhetoric of perversion to voice discontents undermines this moral positioning. Bodily corruption, scatology, general putridity, and degraded sexuality are thus used to sensational effect by these writers.

While connections between the body politic and the body natural in early modern culture are well established, Prendergast uses this relationship to elucidate the complex and multivalent modes that are adopted by railers. For Prendergast, early modern attitudes to gender and sexuality—perhaps especially with regard to how gender is performed on stage and ambiguities as to whether or not a male writer adopted a female persona in print—render conceptions of gender unfixed, and this fluidity of gender makes for fruitful queer readings. These queer articulations, coupled with early modern medicine, allow the body and bodily perversion (and the sense of disgust that it implies) to become sites of discontent. The rhetoric of femininity or effeminacy in particular is used by way of invective. Beginning with the Marprelate controversy, Prendergast suggests that because 'this controversy led to the deaths of two men involved in printing the Marprelate pamphlets, the four other major waves of railing in theatre and print moved away from politically sensitive material and towards controversies around gender and aesthetics' (p. 3). From the Marprelate controversy, Prendergast moves roughly chronologically and thematically to examine the Nashe–Harvey pamphlets, connect *Troilus and Cressida* to the *Poetomachia*, and examine railing as a way to articulate disillusionment with the aristocracy in *Coriolanus* and *Timon of Athens*, before finally discussing gender instability in female railing.

Rather than showing the relationship between railing texts through the ways in which they make topical allusions, Prendergast focuses upon the aesthetic connections between the Marprelate controversy, the Nashe–Harvey pamphlets, and the war of the theatres. It is this recognition of the aesthetics (or anti-aesthetics) of railing that allows Prendergast to explore a poetics of perversion and enhance our understanding of the symbiotic relationship between railing, printed text, and playhouse. However, it also gives her scope to explore what happens when railing moves beyond a narrow focus on the topical to represent an ailing aristocratic identity. Marginality takes on many guises, whether in the shape of religious grievances, in an emerging literary popular culture, in the decline of social elites, or in the relationship between men and women. Prendergast identifies many unforced connections between railing rhetoric and contemporary queer theory and uses them productively. This book offers a fresh and invigorating perspective on railing, its relationship to the subject, and the paradoxical way in which railers both relish and revile the rhetoric that they employ.

Bangor University   RACHEL WILLIE

John Milton: An Annotated Bibliography, 1989–1999. By CALVIN HUCKABAY and DAVID V. URBAN. Ed. by DAVID V. URBAN and PAUL J. KLEMP. Pittsburgh: University of Duquesne Press. 2011. xvi+488 pp. $100. ISBN 978-0-8207-0443-2.

This is the third and final part of the late Calvin Huckabay's bibliography of twentieth-century Milton scholarship, completed and edited by David V. Urban and Paul J. Klemp. Tellingly, the final volume covers only the last decade of the century, and annotates 2411 items. There could hardly be a clearer indication of how Milton scholarship mushroomed in the latter half of the twentieth century, as doctoral and academic research became increasingly professionalized. This expansion is sometimes disparagingly termed the 'Milton industry', but it should rather be seen as a tribute to how Milton's reputation as a writer has been not only sustained but recognized more fully, particularly in relation to the prose writings and to categories of thought central to Western liberalism: toleration, political liberty, nationhood. The items annotated here range from ground-breaking monographs to brief notes, and the volume helpfully includes (some) doctoral dissertations and translations, many of which would otherwise remain obscure. Anyone looking for Chinese versions of *Samson Agonistes* should start here. In a departure from the previous volumes, the notes even include references to reviews. The annotation is brief and informative but not evaluative, which is probably the right approach, despite the daunting amount of material; it is difficult to pick up on even the slightest hint of editorial disapproval in the annotations. It is hard also to quarrel with the way the editors have divided the material: 'Bibliography and Reference Works'; 'Biography'; 'Editions'; 'Translations'; 'General Criticism and Miscellaneous Items' (perhaps a little capacious); 'Criticism of Individual Works'; 'Style and Versification'; 'Editions, Translations, and Illustrations: Criticism' (an unexpected category); and 'Fame and Influence'. *Paradise Lost* of course gets the largest section, both in 'Individual Works' and in the volume as a whole, and that is how it should be; but it is a sign of shifting critical approaches that the section on 'Prose Works' is almost as long as that on 'Shorter Poems'. That shift is likely to be sustained if there is a subsequent volume on the first decade of the twenty-first century.

UNIVERSITY OF EXETER   NICHOLAS McDOWELL

Gulliver's Travels. By JONATHAN SWIFT. Ed. by DAVID WOMERSLEY. (The Cambridge Edition of the Works of Jonathan Swift) Cambridge: Cambridge University Press. 2012. civ+806 pp. £80. ISBN 978–0–521–84164–1.

The Cambridge Edition of the Works of Jonathan Swift continues apace, and David Womersley's impressive contribution will form the centrepiece of this important academic endeavour. Appropriately, Womersley's introduction to the volume provides probably the fullest understanding of the *Travels*' place within Swift's œuvre. The introduction is remarkable in its breadth of knowledge in this respect, but refers sparingly to the wider cultural context and to previous criticism: perhaps wisely, given the innumerable books and essays devoted to this most famous of satires.

Diligent attention to the author is also evident in the choice of copy text: George Faulkner's 1735 Dublin edition has been selected, with the convincing rationale that it represents Swift's final intentions, including his attempts to restore original meaning to inflammatory passages suppressed by Benjamin Motte and Andrew Tooke for the 1726 editions. The *Travels*' full textual history, an intriguing tale of secret printing and publisher 'mangling', is examined meticulously in a dedicated section.

Unlike *A Tale of a Tub*'s fifth edition (1710), the *Travels* did not come burdened with Swift's own footnotes, and this allows the majority of Womersley's annotations to sit conveniently at the bottom of each page. The notes range from the brief gloss of phrases such as 'Kentish pippin' (p. 211), to the detailed exposition of 'Austrian lip' (p. 45), with generous quotation of parallel passages. Rather than always adhering to our knowledge of Swift's own reading, many of the identified analogues instead point towards a broader sense of the cultural resonance of particular usages, furnishing us with an idea of possible contemporary reception as well as motivations behind composition. Some annotations also serve purposes more interpretative than descriptive, and while purists might baulk at this, such glosses will aid undergraduates and non-Swiftian scholars immensely.

In addition to the footnotes are the 'Long Notes', each of them at least a page in length, situated at the end of the volume. This binary system of annotation inevitably raises the issue of why certain topics have been deemed worthy of extended commentary. The 'Long Note' on 'standing armies' (pp. 487–96) is a case in point: having already received significant annotation in Marcus Walsh's recent edition of '*A Tale of a Tub' and Other Works* (Cambridge: Cambridge University Press, 2010), it might have been considered prudent for this later volume to gloss the theme more moderately and so conserve space for other, more exclusively Gulliverian aspects.

The edition usefully includes all of Swift's known correspondence related to the composition, publication, and reception of the *Travels*, together with the commendatory verses (many probably by Pope) that soon greeted the Dean's most popular and enduring work. Given that these verses receive extensive annotation, it is somewhat curious that the more substantive variants included in the 'MS readings from particular copies' are not annotated in their own right. For instance, the profoundly allegorical 'Lindalino' passage (pp. 742–43), found in the interleaved Forster copy originally owned by Charles Ford, is crucial in understanding the importance of the Wood's halfpence affair to the 'Voyage to Laputa', but receives only bibliographical explication in this edition (pp. 722–23).

Nevertheless, this weighty tome fulfils with aplomb the considerable demands required of a new standard edition of Swift's masterpiece, and will be essential reading for scholars of the eighteenth century.

UNIVERSITY OF LIVERPOOL   GREG LYNALL

Anna Letitia Barbauld and Eighteenth-Century Visionary Poetics. By DANIEL P.
 WATKINS. Baltimore: Johns Hopkins University Press. 2012. xvi+245 pp.
 $60; £31. ISBN 978-1-421-40458-5.

Anna Letitia Barbauld (née Aikin) burst onto the literary scene in 1773. Two hundred and forty years later, we are recapturing something of the excitement which greeted her first volume. Thanks to the tireless biographical and editorial endeavours of William McCarthy and other scholars, her work has now begun to receive serious critical attention; this, however, is the first book-length study of her ground-breaking debut volume. As Daniel P. Watkins brilliantly shows, *Poems* (1773, reprinted 1792) is a fascinating volume, not least because of its changeable, at times conflicted, nature. The poems move between different modes, shifting in genre, voice, and form, through which Watkins confidently guides us. A key example is his analysis of the shift between the first two poems, 'Corsica' and 'The Invitation'. Reading these together helps us fully to appreciate the 'complicated relationship between pastoral and prophecy' in Barbauld's work (p. 56). She is at once attracted to and made anxious by the prophetic mode which 'Corsica' at first seems to embrace, and the changes within and between the poems further demonstrate her awareness of human experience as 'vexed and multilayered' (p. 71) and her self-consciousness about her own idealism. Analysing the 'self-reflective and self-correcting character' (p. 49) of Barbauld's poetics, Watkins shows how she constantly interrogates her own standpoint.

The study, then, is attentive not only to the specifics of individual poems, but to the ways in which they answer, echo, and correct one another, an endeavour which lies at the heart of this monograph. As the preface explains, the book began life as a three-volume study comparing Barbauld's *Poems*, Ann Yearsley's *Rural Lyre* (1796), and Joanna Baillie's *Metrical Legends* (1821). These books share interests in ideals of love and benevolence, 'human betterment', and the ways in which this might be achieved, inflected by the authors' backgrounds in Protestant Dissent. But, with engaging and persuasive frankness, Watkins makes the case that each volume should have the tribute of a close, detailed analysis. They are, he maintains, 'among the most important poetic statements of the late eighteenth and early nineteenth centuries and should be placed alongside works by Blake and Wordsworth for their visionary sophistication and revolutionary thought' (p. xi).

'Visionary' is a key word here, since a central concept for Watkins is that of 'visionary poetics', inherited from Joseph A. Wittreich (see, for example, *Visionary Poetics: Milton's Tradition and his Legacy* (San Marino, CA: Huntington Library, 1979)). The study diverges from Wittreich, however, in showing the importance of women writers, and the ways in which they intervene in, and challenge, male traditions of visionary thought and poetics. In the eighteenth century, argues Watkins, such traditions 'took an odd but important detour into the imaginations of many women writers' (p. 202), and, while it focuses on Barbauld, this reading of female visionary poetics also reflects on a range of poets including Mary Leapor, Elizabeth Hands, and Anne Bannerman to demonstrate the wider application of his theories. Thoughtfully engaging with major trends in critical perspectives on female poetics, Watkins's goal, explored in his introduction, is to enlarge our discussions of women's writing in the period partly through his awareness of this larger span of visionary thought, and partly through close attention to form and style, the 'particulars of poetic expression' (p. 8).

This, indeed, is the great strength of his discussion of Barbauld as visionary and as poet: he seeks to bring out the allusive richness of each poem while remaining alert to the larger aims of the volume as a whole. *Poems*, he argues, is marked by a 'visionary tension between the world as [Barbauld] wants it to be and the world as it is' (p. 47): this important study helps us to respond to Barbauld's vision, and to recognize its depth and complexity.

UNIVERSITY OF LEICESTER   FELICITY JAMES

Bodies and Things in Nineteenth-Century Literature and Culture. Ed. by KATHA-
    RINA BOEHM. (Palgrave Studies in Nineteenth-Century Writing and Culture)
    Basingstoke: Palgrave Macmillan. 2012. xi+254 pp. £50. ISBN 978-0-230-
    36938-2.

Moon-faced automata, locks of hair, pieces of china, pregnant women, bath towels, manuscript albums, and Egyptian mummies represent a sampling of the bodies and things to which this volume turns its attention. These items bring with them narratives that transform the relationship between subject and object from binary division into shifting network. The essays in this collection turn to human bodies when they are disaggregated and objectified and to objects when they are endowed with subjective agency. This allows *Bodies and Things* to offer thoughtful new readings of canonical authors such as Oscar Wilde, Charles Dickens, and Jane Austen, but also to probe some of the stranger materials of which Victorian literature and culture are made.

The collection is introduced eloquently by Katharina Boehm, who situates it among previous work on material culture in the Victorian period, and particularly in relation to the developments of the last decade since Bill Brown first set out 'thing theory' in 2001 ('Things', *Critical Enquiry*, 28 (2001), 1–16). Brown himself provides an epilogue which lends kudos to the work and helps to make it a sure addition to the reading lists of those interested in the theorization of materiality. Isobel Armstrong contributes a brilliantly wide-ranging first chapter which forges fascinating connections between (among other things) Jane Eyre's favourite plate, Karl Marx's commoditized table, and several grotesque vases from the Great Exhibition. These pieces set up a number of theoretical questions regarding the relationships between bodies and things: how far can one go in reading the presence of an object and its 'associative connections' in a text (p. 20), following the example of Elaine Freedgood (*The Ideas in Things: Fugitive Meaning in the Victorian Novel* (Chicago: University of Chicago Press, 2006))? How might we contemplate a 'poetics of things that is not always met by their material histories alone' (p. 20)? How are oppositional relationships between bodies and artefacts governed (or circumvented)? And how might readers continue to think beyond the framework of consumption and commodity culture in exploring the social and cultural agency of objects? *Bodies and Things* is worth picking up for Armstrong's essay alone, but the rest of the collection does not disappoint in taking up the questions she sets out.

The rest of the book is divided into three sections: 'Spaces', 'Practices', and 'Performances'. In the first of these, the spaces of Fanny's dressing room in Austen's *Mansfield Park* and the Turkish bath in Trollope's story of the same name are examined by Kirstyn Leuner and Catherine Spooner respectively, before Muireann O'Cinneide goes on to discuss the writings of Victorian women in conflict zones.

O'Cinneide demonstrates these women's 'capacity to refigure their own relationships with objects as a mode of narrative response' to their traumatic experiences
(p. 85). She argues convincingly that travel writing warrants particular attention
from scholars of material culture as it insists upon the presence of the writing body
in the narrative in contrast to its frequent effacement in the Victorian realist novel.
The practices and pleasures of collecting books, pieces of handwriting, locks of hair,
and other artefacts are discussed as bodily substitutions in stimulating essays in the
middle section of the volume. The final two essays, by Anne Anderson and Stefania
Forlini, make a neat pairing in their turn to the end of the century to examine
the aesthetic woman's body in relation to her objects and to read Arthur Symons's
decadent poetry through the lens of Thomas Henry Huxley's conscious automaton
theory. These works by historians, art historians, and scholars of literature and
culture are well marshalled into a collection that makes a significant intervention
into the study of the object in the nineteenth century.

UNIVERSITY OF SURREY   BETH PALMER

Pioneer Performances: Staging the Frontier. By MATTHEW REBHORN. New York:
   Oxford University Press. 2012. x+207 pp. £41.99. ISBN 978-0-19-975130-3.

This book on nineteenth-century theatre explores performance of American pioneers and native Americans, or as the author puts it, 'performing the frontier'
(p. 6). In his introduction Matthew Rebhorn examines the well-known concept of
'manifest destiny' as demonstrated or undermined by two late nineteenth-century
performers, the famous Buffalo Bill Cody and his Wild West Show, and the now
obscure Gowongo Mohawk, a native American cross-dressing actress who offered
an alternative image of the untamed West. The dynamic contrasts in these performances stand for the contradictory images of the frontier and manifest destiny
that follow in chapters dealing with native American, African American, and white
frontiersmen, and women. Cody's manufacture of the western drama and Mohawk's invention of violent but entertaining trickery with transparent role-playing
underscore the melodramatic nature of all of the plays and performances that the
author analyses. The juxtaposition of Cody's culturally safe presentation of decor-
ous Annie Oakley with Mohawk's portrayal of a wildly dangerous warrior involved
a contrast that demonstrates the dichotomy of the thesis.

   The author begins his case studies with performances by Edwin Forrest of
Metamora (1829), by John Augustus Stone. Rebhorn has drawn on many sources
of evidence, but it is surprising that he has ignored Richard Moody, who wrote
the first important and detailed examination of Forrest's career and style (*Edwin
Forrest: First Star of the American Stage* (New York: Alfred Knopf, 1960)). He does,
however, note with some merit that most accounts of Forrest's performance of
the native American character rely more on the text of the play than on evidence
of his performance choices. He discusses 'the grammar of the passions' (p. 28),
Forrest's extensive Indian research, and connects the actor's performed passion to
'bolstering American nationalism' (p. 36). He calls Forrest the '"king" of a new

acting style' (p. 39). Utlimately he finds Forrest presenting sympathy for the Indian while simultaneously supporting Jacksonian Democracy, which advocated Indian removal.

With the 1831 melodrama *Lion of the West* by James Paulding, Rebhorn explores the wonders of the unsophisticated but sympathetic stage frontiersman, one Nathan Wildfire, who 'mobilizes the fantasy of the frontier' (p. 50). But Wildfire is also seen here as a 'disruptive agent' for the ideology he supposedly upholds. More intriguing, however, is the author's examination of the 'blackface pioneer' (p. 71) in Chapter 3. Blackface parodies of frontiersmen in minstrelsy pit Jim Crow against Davy Crockett, or even portray Jim Crow *as* Davy Crockett. He finds some minstrelsy unsettling to the dominant ideology of the perceived frontier spirit. In Chapter 4 the author takes on Dion Boucicault and his infamous play *The Octoroon* (1859). This play is seen here as coalescing frontiersmen, native Americans, blacks, and mulattas while seeking 'pleasure in black-and-white identity politics' (p. 99). A melodrama of amalgamation, *The Octoroon* explores character and racial suffering with both spectacle and 'bad taste' (p. 106). He also links the play to the aesthetics and sensationalism of P. T. Barnum, who presented the play after its first run.

Rebhorn sees the Civil War as a great divide, bringing about a remarkable shift in perceptions of the frontier as plays lost their present-tense presentation of the frontier and resorted to transmissions of 'the memory of the frontier' (p. 148). The afterword is a bit heavy-handed, with an abrupt shift to George W. Bush and the film *Brokeback Mountain*, topics which contribute little to the value of the book. On the whole, however, I find that Rebhorn provides important additions to the study of theatre's involvement in the creation of the idea of manifest destiny for the white population in a westward expansion of the United States.

INDIANA UNIVERSITY   RONALD WAINSCOTT

Women Writing Crime Fiction, 1860–1880: Fourteen American, British and Australian Authors. By KATE WATSON. Jefferson, NC: McFarland. 2012. viii+ 252 pp. £34.95. ISBN 978-0-7864-6782-2.

Women's crime writing, once neglected in crime-genre criticism, has received a surge in attention since the 1990s. While the majority of this consideration has been devoted to women crime writers of the 'Golden Age', as well as to feminist revisions of the 1980s–1990s, the contributions of women to the early development of the genre have been comparatively overlooked, though a few nineteenth-century women writers, such as Anna Katharine Green and Mary Elizabeth Braddon, have been recognized by critics, including Stephen Knight in *Crime Fiction 1800–2000: Detection, Death, Diversity* (Basingstoke: Palgrave Macmillan, 2003), Catherine Ross Nickerson in *The Web of Iniquity: Early Detective Fiction by American Women* (Durham, NC: Duke University Press, 1998), and, more recently, Lucy Sussex in *Women Writers and Detectives in Nineteenth-Century Crime Fiction: The Mothers of the Mystery Genre* (Basingstoke: Palgrave Macmillan, 2010). In *Women Writing Crime Fiction, 1860–1880*, Kate Watson 'seeks [. . .] to resolve what was perceived as an absence of women's crime narratives' (p. 1) in the early stages of the genre's formation, providing the first study of early women crime writers that includes Australia as well as Britain and the United States.

Beginning with Britain and then travelling to the United States and Australia, the three chapters that make up this monograph each commence with a social and historical analysis of early crime fiction and the publishing industry in the nation under consideration. The chapters are then divided into short sections, each outlining a woman crime writer's life and contextualizing her work in the early development of the genre. The first chapter, on British crime fiction, includes Catherine Crowe, Caroline Clive, Elizabeth Cleghorn Gaskell, Mary Elizabeth Braddon, and Mrs Henry (Ellen) Wood. The second chapter, on the United States, considers the work of Harriet Prescott Spofford, Louisa May Alcott, Metta Victoria Fuller Victor, and Anna Katharine Green. Chapter 3, on Australia, examines Céleste de Chabrillan, Caroline Woolmer Leakey (Oliné Keese), Eliza Whitstanley, Ellen Davitt, and Mary Helena Fortune. Watson chooses to profile both nineteenth-century women who are known specifically for crime writing, such as Anna Katharine Green and Mary Helena Fortune, and those, such as Elizabeth Gaskell and Louisa May Alcott, usually recognized for their middle-class, domestic fiction. Her study thereby emphasizes the indistinct borders of the developing crime genre.

Watson's focus on previously critically neglected writers and on little-known works of more famous nineteenth-century women writers is justification enough for this study. But this work goes further, arguing that 'these women can and do enact [. . .] subversion through and within gendered publishing and social orthodoxies' (p. 9). Watson supports this argument through her competent close readings of moments of gender instability in the texts. She often makes the valid point that though gendered hegemonies are sometimes challenged in the work of women writers, subversiveness is just as often 'safely' contained in the narratives' conclusions: for example, when active female characters succumb to either death or domesticity. These perceptive readings could be further enhanced by at least some employment of contemporary gender theory, though Watson acknowledges in the introduction that her methodology 'concentrate[s] on the [. . .] interaction of multi-voiced and multi-national criminographic and gendered conversation/s in the period, instead of reading [. . .] through the lens of a particular literary theory' (p. 11). Though the sociohistorical basis for Watson's analyses is an efficient approach for this type of work, there are sometimes unconvincing moments when she interprets texts based on assumptions about the writer's intentions or feelings; for example, at one point Watson suggests that a character's 'decided and independent voice' might reflect the 'ideas and emotions' of Australian writer Ellen Davitt (p. 167). Such occasions, though few, take away from otherwise persuasive arguments. Nevertheless, Watson's work is well organized and compellingly argued, and her recognition of the significance of Australian women writers in the development of the crime genre makes *Women Writing Crime Fiction, 1860–1880* an important contribution to the field.

University of St Andrews　　　　　　　　　　　　　　　Megan Hoffman

British Women's Travel to Greece, 1840–1914: Travels in the Palimpsest. By Churnjeet Mahn. (The Nineteenth Century) Farnham: Ashgate. 2012. ix+167 pp. £55. ISBN 978–1–4094–3299–919–9.

In this book Churnjeet Mahn sets out to address the critical neglect of Victorian women's travel writing about Greece and the academic blind spots contributing to this. Mahn takes a loose definition of 'travel literature', going beyond the 'travelogue' form, so as to include Jane Harrison's and Agnes Lewis's translations of Greek-authored travel texts, Harrison's articles and academic books (Chapter 2), and Felicia Skene's travel poetry (pp. 80–88). This definition of travel literature illuminates hitherto under-appreciated Victorian women travellers to Greece and revises the traditional critical emphasis on female 'armchair' travellers, which has characterized such travel writing as 'derivative', Byronic imitation (p. 1). Mahn's book goes further than creating interest in individual non-canonical writers, however. Her real strength is in showing these writers to be participating diversely in a wider cultural nexus of representation.

Mahn's discussion of Victorian guidebooks in Chapter 1 not only provides an insight into the cultural lens through which British women travellers viewed Greece, but also maps a narrative layer of Greece to be contested and overwritten in a bid for representational authority by these same travellers. Furthermore, Mahn uses the guides to emphasize topography as 'process', detailing the shift from 'the selection and compilation of Greece from an exotic oriental space in 1840 to a vast open-air museum by 1909' and the colonial agenda underpinning this topographical instability (p. 11). The result is a much more complex mapping of Greece than that traditionally afforded it by Travel Studies, which has historically portrayed Greece as the gateway to the Orient, a threshold rather than a territory (p. 4).

Shaping the remaining chapters using the disciplinary frameworks of archaeology, anthropology, and tourism, Mahn's aim is to demonstrate 'how women use their travel in Greece as a vehicle for exploring women's relationship to knowledge and their role in society outwith the home' (p. 7). Nevertheless, her analysis highlights not only the strengths but also the limitations of each writer's approach. Harrison, for instance, while aiming through her books at granting women wider access to a classical education, nevertheless estranges herself from her audience by performing professionalism through the role of 'eccentric scholar' (p. 52). Similarly, Chapter 3 celebrates the authority that first-hand ethnography could grant British women formally denied access to the study of anthropology (p. 74), while also exposing its negative side, whether through the imperialism underpinning Skene's sentimental anecdotes of reformed Greek prostitutes (pp. 82–86) or the implicit threat to Greek 'integrity' by vampiric 'Balkanization' in G. Muir MacKenzie and A. P. Irby's narratives (pp. 93–94).

By emphasizing the complexity of these women's travels, Mahn succeeds in critiquing the overarching narrative of women's travel literature as concerning itself with 'the minutiae of domestic life' still persisting in Travel Studies (p. 1). Although focusing on the seemingly traditional ground of the fashion-oriented lady traveller for her final chapter, Mahn's originality here is her tour de force as she makes the insightful parallel between the fictional 'New Woman' and her precursor, the 'Lady Traveller' (pp. 112–13). Locating the discourse of danger surrounding Victorian women's travel 'in the bodies of the [travelling] women themselves' (p. 111), Mahn reads Isabel Armstrong, Catherine Janeway, and Emily Pfeiffer as self-aware, 'image-conscious' travellers 'fashion[ing] a new type of travelling subjectivity, one which by travelling, was making a defiant move in claiming the right to public space' (p. 111). While Mahn's complex, revisionist mapping of Greek history and historiography makes this book essential reading for travel studies on Greece, her fresh and subtle approach to Victorian women's travel literature and its relationship with early feminism recommends the book to a wider travel-literary audience and to scholars of gender studies alike.

BANGOR UNIVERSITY   REBECCA BUTLER

The Song of the Lark. By WILLA CATHER. Ed. by ANN MOSELEY and KARI A. RONNING. (Willa Cather Scholarly Edition) Lincoln: University of Nebraska Press. 2012. xi+925 pp. £50. ISBN 978-0-8032-1402-6.

This scholarly edition of the American writer Willa Cather's novel *The Song of the Lark* is a beautifully presented and carefully assembled volume. Offering the 1915 edition of *The Song of the Lark*, the book also contains a wealth of biographical information and contextual material of interest to students and scholars of Cather's life and work. The Willa Cather Scholarly Edition series has been overseen by Guy J. Reynolds and the late Susan J. Rosowski, who, in their foreword to the volume, emphasize the importance of adhering to Cather's stated preferences in relation to the presentation of the text.

The Song of the Lark tells the story of a female artist, tracing the evolving artistic sensibility and development of its protagonist, Thea Kronborg, from country girl to renowned singer. The essays and commentaries included provide historical, cultural, and literary background to Cather's work. The novel itself is followed by two main sections, the first entitled 'Historical Apparatus', the second 'Textual Apparatus'. This structural division of material provides a helpful overview of the contents, which makes the information easily accessible and user-friendly for readers and scholars engaging in research activity.

Ann Moseley's meticulous 'Historical Essay' traces the myriad influences from Cather's world and surroundings on *The Song of the Lark*, and discusses the novel's publication and reception. Moseley also examines the influence of Henri Bergson in relation to Cather's representation of self and the artist's perception. The 'Illustrations' section presents a visual dimension to the volume, in the form of an illustrative series of photographs of people, places, and images, for instance of a promotional leaflet for *The Song of the Lark*. These illustrations offer stimulating visual representations and provide an added dimension to Cather's work, thereby allowing scholars a unique insight into the writer's preoccupations and her contemporary culture. The 'Explanatory Notes' to the novel, which form part of the 'Historical Apparatus' section, present a variety of detailed and carefully assembled contextual information for the reader to peruse.

In the 'Textual Apparatus' section, Kari A. Ronning's 'Textual Essay' is of particular interest to scholars conducting research into the historical and creative dimensions of Cather's publishing. Ronning explains the reasoning behind using the 1915 first edition as the source for the present University of Nebraska Press edition. The essay throws light on the novel's editing and printing history, and the extent of Cather's own involvement in decision-making processes. The 'Emendations' and 'Notes on Emendations' included in the 'Textual Apparatus' section will also be of interest to readers and scholars wishing to explore the editorial processes behind Cather's fiction.

Cather's own preface to the 1932 edition of *The Song of the Lark* offers the writer's reflective assessment of the issues faced by her female artist figure, and the consequences of pursuing her art. In this novel Cather presents a compelling narrative of female artistic accomplishment. As evidenced by the absorbing material in this edition, Cather's portrayal of the female artist in *The Song of the Lark* is as pertinent today as it has ever been. The edition will have a broad appeal for undergraduate and postgraduate students, but also contains material which will be useful to advanced researchers. This volume and the Scholarly Edition series overall reflect a sustained interest in Cather's life and writing, and the enduring fascination that they hold.

University of Gloucestershire   Charlotte Beyer

Analogie et récit de voyage: voir, mesurer, interpréter le monde. By Alain Guyot.
   (Études romantiques et dix-neuviémistes, 29) Paris: Classiques Garnier. 2012.
   369 pp. €29. ISBN 978–2–8124–0629–4.

What is there left to say about travelogues? The elusive nature of travel writing continuously calls for further consideration but, as early as 1994, Adrian Pasquali's *Le Tour des horizons: critique et récit de voyage* (Paris: Klincksieck) indicated that many approaches to travel literature showed signs of saturation.

Alain Guyot, professor in Nancy but previously at the Travel Studies stronghold of Grenoble, suggests new routes, placing the notion of 'analogy' at the heart of his study of travel in the crucial period towards the end of the Enlightenment and early Romanticism. Analogy is an excellent choice as a core notion: travel presents unfamiliar elements through familiar expressions and images. While aspects of the 'pensée analogique' have been studied by such authorities as Paul Ricœur, Michel Foucault, and François Hartog, this approach cannot be deemed saturated.

The resulting research questions are not always new, but the variety of approaches in this work validates them. Nothing new in his comment that figures of analogy are not innocent; less usual is the subsequent call to read them also as the author's attempt to orient his readers, to de/valorize the unknown item (as well as the 'domestic' point of comparison). Similarly, while the claim that metaphors were less numerous in travelogues when these books were mostly informative is a truism, it is enriched by the use of near-statistical methods.

The book opens on a brief *mise au point poétique*, defining the starting-points of the analysis. A second, historical chapter tackles the use of analogy since antiquity. A lengthy chapter on analogies in Bernardin de Saint-Pierre and Chateaubriand is accompanied in the index by an unusual table of analogical figures. The last chapter represents a total—and very salutary—change of perspective: the study of the presentation of the valley of Chamonix in travelogues is based on the reading of over a hundred texts, representing an almost 'serial' approach, unfortunately rare in literary analysis of travels.

The variety of approaches is remarkable, but not without dangers. The brief historical chapter rushes through questions which have received considerable attention already, such as scientific travels or instructions to travellers (where the almost total lack of English secondary literature is evident), or deals too quickly with authors such as Béat de Muralt.

The case of Muralt reveals another point where further considerations are needed. Was he really wholeheartedly favourable to England, or was this only the perception of his work? Thus, can figures of analogy and comparison be considered only from the side of the emitter, the author? An important tradition of travel scholarship, mostly neglected here, suggests that it is only through the study of reception that we can hope for a full picture. The success (or failure) of analogies is part of the *pacte de lecture* that links authors and readers of travel.

This relative neglect of reception is visible in the choice of source texts too. With the exception of the last chapter, only the better-known texts are studied, seldom stepping away from the rather narrow canon of travelogues used by most works, a choice sometimes based more on later literary merits than the importance of a given text in its time. Thus, Bernardin de Saint-Pierre's travelogue was far from being a success—he himself admitted finding travel writing problematic. On the contrary, Volney's *Voyage en Égypte et en Syrie* was considered at that time a perfect travelogue, and even the royal censor applauded its 'ton de vérité'. It is thus puzzling to see it—and Volney generally—mostly neglected.

Nevertheless, Alain Guyot's work does achieve the goal it set itself. The study of the shifting use of analogies in travels and the conceptualization of their reading make it an important reference for future studies, and the stepping-stone for the necessary continuation of this work: considering the perception and reception of analogies in travelogues.

University of Aberystwyth   Gabor Gelléri

Manual of Anglo-Norman, 2nd edn. By IAN SHORT. (Occasional Publications Series, 8) Oxford: Anglo-Norman Text Society. 2013. 178 pp. £39. ISBN 978-0-905474-57-1.

Keith Busby wrote of the 2007 paperback edition, 'Despite the protestations of modesty in his foreword, Ian Short has produced a small book that will henceforth become a vade mecum for all those working, or thinking of working, in Anglo-Norman studies' (*Speculum*, 84 (2009), 774–75). These pages are the product of a lifetime of study by the doyen of Anglo-Norman studies. They merit careful reading and pencilling.

The voice of Anglo-Norman at the Museum of London, the author is better known as the past honorary secretary of the Anglo-Norman Text Society (ANTS), a position he held for nearly four decades. In the selective bibliography, I count twenty-two editions of Anglo-Norman literary texts that passed through his hands during the Birkbeck years, but the number of published volumes vetted by him for ANTS exceeds fifty.

In this second, hardback edition Short sets out to 'correct some of the errors and omissions in the original (2007) version' (p. 15). The second edition improves on the first in its use of IPA symbols throughout to approximate the pronunciation of words. The volume organizes in concise and convenient format the knowledge acquired about Anglo-Norman over the past eighty years. The pagination has changed but not the reference numbers of the notes on Anglo-Norman language. A prominent theme is the author's desire to encourage further research in the field.

Though selective in its examples and references, the second edition puts readers on a firm footing in Anglo-Norman. The introduction surveys the development of Anglo-Norman over more than four centuries (1066–*c.* 1500), including again a discussion of the language of the Conqueror's court and commentary on the process by which the French-speakers of England (*Franci*) came to self-identify as English.

Short augments the second edition by some thirty pages, owing principally to a new excursus on the language of the Oxford *Chanson de Roland*. He updates the bibliography with the addition of recently published critical editions. He again includes many useful comparisons of Anglo-Norman usage with both medieval and modern French and English.

For newcomers to this fair field, Short's work might be further improved by the simple expansion of arcane abbreviations such as *ZrPh* (pp. 9, 15), ZfSL (p. 53), and Pphil. and RPhil. (p. 55), and others, to aid scholars' research efforts. A few typos have carried over from the first edition, notably p. 41, line 33, p. 62, line 29, and p. 99, line 12.

MEREDITH COLLEGE   BRENT A. PITTS

*Exchanges in Exoticism: Cross-Cultural Marriage and the Making of the Mediter-
ranean in Old French Romance.* By MEGAN MOORE. Toronto: University of
Toronto Press. 2014. xii+184 pp. $65. ISBN 978-1-4426-4469-4.

Megan Moore's *Exchanges in Exoticism* provides a timely focus on the role of
women in cross-cultural exchanges, and highlights the importance of the Mediterranean in romance as a space of contact between East and West. In particular, this
study underscores the power of women actively to shape relations between men
in a manner that has often been underestimated. Taking the relationship between
Byzantium and the West as the central arena for her analysis and uniting Old
French and Medieval Greek romances, Moore argues for fluid regional networks of
trade and interaction that revolve around marriage and familial practices.

The study is divided into four chapters that focus on gaps 'through which alterity
constitutes culture' (p. 18). Chapter 1 explores anxieties about gender structures
and fecundity within cross-cultural marriage in *Cligès* and *Digenis Akritas*, and
argues that women negotiate exchanges of culture across frontiers beyond their re-
productive roles. Moore's subsequent treatment of *Floire et Blancheflor* in Chapter 2
is important for its reassessment of pagan identity in this text. She looks beyond
the Christian–Muslim labels that are generally attributed to the protagonists and
reframes the tale within an economy of exoticism that is deeply rooted in Byzantium and which reveals a 'multiplicity of easts' (p. 51). The Mediterranean acts
as a 'founding centre' (p. 79) for the building of lineage where, in contrast to the
orientalism of Edward Said, masculinity may be figured rather than challenged
through exoticism. Chapter 3 of the study signals the changes in attitudes towards
the East following the fall of Constantinople in 1204 and explores the relationship
between love and empire. Situating the *Roman de la Manekine* and *La Belle Hélène
de Constantinople* in a historical framework, Moore notes the importance of distinguishing self from other in these texts and sets the victories of women against the
deviancy of Eastern male rulers. The role of women in economies between men,
she suggests, thus demonstrates a politicized and moralized movement towards the
West that refuses a narrative of Eastern patriarchy. In the final chapter, this move
to Western self-reflexivity is epitomized in the staging of King Arthur within a
Mediterranean context as found in *Floriant et Florete*. *Translatio* is examined in
this section as a way to expose 'the cultural stakes of the moment of (re)writing'
(p. 107), where the reinscription of Arthur resists the genealogization of Eastern
glories and reveals a decline in the value of 'Mediterranean connectivity' (p. 118).

The strength of Moore's study lies in her reframing of cross-cultural exchange
as the norm rather than the exception in medieval social interactions and in her
prioritization of female agency. At times the analysis tends to assume a certain coherence to Mediterranean noble identity that could be further explored. However,
the focus on marriage in this study is especially enlightening as it brings together
the ideal, the literary, and the lived, reminding us that intermarriage is not simply
a literary imagining but a real practice. Marriage practices also allow Moore to
demonstrate the ability of women to shape the building of empires and bring their

ideological forces to bear on the political backdrop around them; similarly, her attention to gender addresses assumptions made about the construction of masculinity by highlighting exchanges of love rather than conquest and crusade scenarios. While the interpretation of 'exotic' and 'exoticism' could have been further clarified and notions of gender perhaps nuanced with reference to her theoretical readings, Moore maintains a highly accessible style. Her use of engaging examples make this study a pleasure to read, one which combines questions of hybridity, exchange, and gender in fruitful ways.

UNIVERSITY OF ST ANDREWS   VICTORIA TURNER

Violence and the Writing of History in the Medieval Francophone World. Ed. by
   NOAH D. GUYNN and ZRINKA STAHULJAK. (Gallica, 29) Cambridge: Brewer.
   2013. x+210 pp. £50. ISBN 978–1–84384–337–5.

This volume of twelve essays explores a diverse selection of texts from the eleventh to the fourteenth centuries. 'Francophone' is defined at the outset, in the editors' excellent introduction, as representing not only the pluralities of French in this period, but also the fluid, multilingual world in which the authors operated. Leah Shopkow's study of Lambert of Ardres's Latin chronicle, for example, highlights how Lambert's Latin wordplays worked just as well in French, while Jeff Rider's longitudinal survey of Flemish historiography skilfully demonstrates how Romance inflections entered Latin-language texts *before* they were translated into the vernacular. Simon Gaunt, meanwhile, draws on Agamben and Nancy to tease out the difference between the earlier, Franco-Italian vision of a 'coming community' in Marco Polo's *Divisement*, and its disappearance as that text became more standardized and Eurocentric (and hence more intolerant of difference) in its French version.

'History', too, is interrogated as a term: many of the essays utilize works that were not written *as* histories, but display a self-consciously historical sensibility. A major aim of the book is to read such texts on their own terms, rather than sifting them for elusive, 'factual' information. Deborah McGrady traces the poetic exchanges between the imprisoned Charles d'Orléans and his cousin Philippe, duke of Burgundy. As McGrady points out, Charles's subsequent editing of his writings, identifying Philippe as his correspondent, politicized the exchange and brought it into the historical realm as he and the duke established more concrete ties by marriage and political collaboration. Noah Guynn challenges the historical 'reliability' of Geoffrey de Villehardouin's *Conquête de Constantinople* by teasing out the writer's underlying scheme of doubt and faith, and use of rhetorical devices inspired by *chansons de geste*. The deliberate blurring of history and fiction is neatly summarized by David Rollo's reading of Benoît de Sainte-Maure's *Chronique des ducs de Normandie* against the same author's earlier *Roman de Troie*—Benoît's ostensibily flattering portrayal of William the Conqueror in the *Chronique* turns out, on closer reading, to be anything but.

The main theme, violence, is approached from a number of angles. The editors suggest that medieval society was no more violent than present times, but that violence held great cultural and ideological weight. Examining this issue in greater depth, the essays demonstrate that accounts of violence are not unproblematic reflections of acts themselves. Rather, rehearsing violence in texts enabled the formation of ideas and definitions of 'good' and 'bad' violence, definitions that might, as Karen Sullivan demonstrates in her study of the *Canso de la Crozada*, conflict even within the same work. The tedious (to modern eyes) reiterations of single combat, Ros Brown-Grant reminds us, were to a medieval audience a way to reinforce the image of the hero, in this case the knight Jacques de Lalaing. A similar shaping of ideals of behaviour within acceptable parameters is also visible in the Old French epics of revolt, as Andrew Cowell argues. And the accounts of horrible bodily mutilations visible in the study of Edward I's wars by Matthew Fisher, and of treasonous sexual intercourse by Zrinka Stahuljak, utilize acts upon a single body to symbolize much broader concepts of threat to the kingdom. Indeed, the language used in the texts is remarkably similar, and it might have benefited the volume as a whole to bring out such parallels and links in a brief conclusion. A rich and challenging collection, of interest to linguists and historians alike.

University of Winchester   Patricia Skinner

The Medieval Shepherd: Jean de Brie's 'Le Bon Berger' (1379). Ed. and trans. by Carleton W. Carroll and Lois Hawley Wilson. (Medieval and Renaissance Texts and Studies, 424) Tempe: Arizona Center for Medieval and Renaissance Studies. 2012. x+226 pp. £38. ISBN 978–0–86698–472–0.

Dedicated to Charles V of France in 1379, *Le Bon Berger* is a practical guide to sheep husbandry by Jean de Brie. Wool was of high economic importance in the late Middle Ages—the growing demand for wool being the primary factor in the transition from arable agriculture to animal husbandry (p. 7)—and sheep-raising had long been honoured in France, but this 'shepherd's manual' is the first of its kind. After a biography of Jean de Brie and an introduction to the usefulness of the treatise, the hands-on manual provides the reader with general shepherding rules, advice on meteorological conditions, tasks to do month by month, and an overview of specific diseases and their cures.

Unfortunately, no original manuscript of *Le Bon Berger* has survived. The Middle French text is preserved in four sixteenth-century editions, each existing in a single copy, respectively the Vostre (V), Trepperel (T), Jonot (J), and Bogart (B) editions. Carleton W. Carroll and Lois Hawley Wilson's critical edition is mainly based upon V, as it is the oldest edition and 'relatively free of gross errors' (p. 29), but B and T have also been examined in their entirety. The result is an easily accessible edition of the Middle French text accompanied by a facing-page English translation. Variants are taken into account as footnotes to the edited text, whereas the footnotes added to the translation clarify technical vocabulary (e.g. identification of plants, birds, or illnesses). More detailed background information is provided in sections following the actual edition containing textual notes and supplementary comments, each structured by chapter. The index, on the other hand, does not distinguish between the edited text and the translation, as it contains Middle French and English forms of proper names and includes names of plants, animals (except the various names for sheep), and diseases.

This first critical edition of *Le Bon Berger* (the so-called 1879 edition is in truth a reprint of the Jonot text: *Le Bon Berger, ou Le vray régime et gouvernement des bergers et bergères, composé par le rustique Jehan de Brie, le bon berger* (Paris: [n. pub], 1541; repr. Paris: Lyseux. 1879)) touches upon an impressive range of aspects of daily life in the late Middle Ages. For instance, the treatise expands on the usefulness of dried sheep bowels as cords for a range of musical instruments such as 'almaduries' or 'cytholes' (p. 60), describes the art of telling the weather by reference to different birds, and demonstrates specialized knowledge of local fauna (pp. 76–81). This specialized knowledge in various fields is reflected in the language by the presence of various lexical fields (for medical–botanical lexis see Tony Hunt, 'L'Art d'élever les moutons: le lexique médico-botanique du *Bon Berger* de Jean de Brie', in *'Qui tant savoir d'engin et d'art': mélanges de philologie médiévale offerts à Gabriel Bianciotto*, ed. by Claudio Galderisi and Jean Maurice (Poitiers: Université de Poitiers, Centre d'études supérieures de civilisation médiévale, 2006), pp. 301–10). Striking a balance between necessary annotation and keeping the text readable thus becomes a complicated feat, which the editors manage by means of a select critical apparatus in the text, and more extensive background research in supplementary comments after the edition. With notes and comments being supported by a wide range of reference works as well as by on-the-ground experience in managing a farm flock, this edition provides fascinating insights into sheep husbandry around 1379.

University of Sheffield   Catharina Peersman

La Fauconnerie à la Renaissance: Le 'Hieracosophion' (1582–1584) de Jacques Auguste de Thou. Ed. by Ingrid A. R. De Smet. (Travaux d'Humanisme et Renaissance, 520) Geneva: Droz. 2013. x+691 pp. SwF 85. ISBN 978-2-600-01703-9.

Jacques Auguste de Thou was still only a fledgling poet when he composed his didactic Latin epic on the art of falconry. Yet the *Hieracosophion* would appeal largely to a royal court under the influence of the pronounced Valois passion for hunting, and the poem soon won respect for its literary merits and its mastery of the technicalities of falconry. In this impressive and scholarly volume, Ingrid de Smet—an established authority on de Thou—has produced a new critical edition of his magisterial poem complete with a detailed commentary, the first modern translation of the poem into French, and a comprehensive historical survey of falconry in sixteenth-century France.

De Thou's poem is divided into three books: the first lists the qualities of different types of falcon; the second describes how to train your falcon; and the third explains how to treat it for various common diseases. De Thou's handling of his hybrid combination of didactic, scientific, and epic poetry is deft: the detailed technical information, tempered by short mythological and aetiological digressions, is conveyed with clear conciseness and lightness of touch, and the same deftness is felt in the accuracy and fluency of De Smet's highly readable translation. The commentary expands on the poem's literary and linguistic features, and contextualizes its technical descriptions of falconry through comparison with the Renaissance ornithological works on which de Thou drew.

The extended introduction explores the literary, cultural, and social status of falconry in Renaissance France. Both the men and the women of the Valois house are shown to have participated in this most aristocratic and magnificent of pastimes, as did various Renaissance cardinals and popes—despite the sixth-century decree that banned the clergy from hunting (perhaps in anticipation of the Huguenot disapproval of hunting as a symbol of debauchery). A combination of strict hunting laws and prohibitive expense (de Thou recommends feeding ailing falcons on such costly ingredients as saffron and fine cuts of beef) preserved falconry as an exquisitely noble pursuit, but its wider sociological repercussions were felt through the growing trade in birds and bird products as well as through the multiple associated crafts required to support the industry of falconry. Royal enthusiasm for hunting is, however, shown not to have placed it above criticism: the luxurious opulence of an activity whose utility as military training decreased as the use of gunpowder grew exposed it to moral scrutiny, as did its place during the religious wars, when instead of being seen as a means of distracting men from fighting, hunting simply demonstrated the violent tendencies that it failed to purge. Early conscientious objectors to the cruelty of killing animals included Michel de l'Hôpital and Montaigne—whose ethical stance against hunting may have been quite independent of his professed incompetence as a hunter.

One of the great pleasures of this wide-ranging volume is its wealth of unexpected *faits divers*, reflecting a fondness for incidental detail that de Thou and De Smet seem to share. Where de Thou cites the Renaissance belief ('Experti credunt', p. 238) that a sheepskin drum will be silenced by the sound of its wolfskin equivalent, demonstrating the abiding posthumous fear in animal products of their natural predators, De Smet includes the anecdote of the hanged man's corpse that Gaspard de Saulx-Tavannes thought fit to place in the comtesse de Crussol's bed ('Délits de chasse', p. 77), demonstrating Renaissance hunters' energetic, if ghoulish, taste in practical jokes. Overall, this accessible, informative, and richly detailed volume makes an excellent case for directing Renaissance scholars' attentions back to both the *Hieracosophion* itself and the art it so carefully describes.

University of St Andrews   Emma Herdman

Marivaux et la science du caractère. By Sarah Benharrech. (SVEC, 2013:06) Oxford: Voltaire Foundation. 2013. xii+319 pp. £60. ISBN 978–0–7294–1067–0.

The starting-point for Sarah Benharrech's study of Marivaux and *caractère* is the fact that the eighteenth century was a time when the relationship between the sciences and the arts was still close enough for practitioners often to be able to move back and forth between the two. Nevertheless, Marivaux felt that there was a prejudice in favour of science which he fought against: the writer was just as much an observer of human nature as the scientist was of nature itself. One significant feature of science at the time was the desire to classify, and Benharrech compares this scientific classification of species, minerals, etc. with the concept of the classification of fixed personality types, *caractères*, associated most closely in French literature with La Bruyère, but dating back to the work of Theophrastus. Much of the argument centres on the way this notion of *caractère* as a fixed and definable type moves in the works of Marivaux towards a more modern notion of *caractère* as the unique personality of an individual, although Marivaux also uses the word in the sense of 'moral fibre'. Benharrech shows that, despite some vestiges of the Theophrastian idea of *caractère*, particularly with regard to minor characters, Marivaux is moving towards a more modern sense of not only individuality, but also changeability, of which the most extreme example is what she describes as the *sans caractère*, typified, she says, in Marivaux's work by the Trivelin of *La Fausse Suivante*, but more famously to be found in Diderot's Neveu de Rameau and the Figaro of *Le Mariage*.

This is a wide-ranging study, and consequently the title, although not technically inaccurate, is still perhaps misleading: there is too much concentration on Marivaux for this to be regarded merely as a general study of *caractère* in the later seventeenth and the eighteenth centuries, but he also disappears from view for such long stretches that it is difficult to feel that it is a book about Marivaux—indeed, the last two of the nine chapters are concerned with Crébillon *fils* and Diderot. Marivaux is also cast into the background for much of the discussion of different methods of depicting *caractère* and characters, an impressively detailed discussion, but which sometimes left this reviewer with the impression of not being able to see the wood for the trees. When more detailed examination of Marivaux does arrive, there is interesting work on *Le Paysan parvenu* and *La Vie de Marianne*, but the studies of individual plays, despite having points to make, felt too short to be fully effective. When other authors were discussed at length, it was not always clear whether we were to understand that they had been influenced by Marivaux (or, in the case of Crébillon, were reacting against him), or whether we were simply dealing with similarities—more clarification and detailed evidence for any direct influence would be useful.

This is an impressively broad study, with a wide frame of reference, which will certainly be of interest not only to those with an interest in the development of the depiction of character in eighteenth-century French literature but also to those interested in Marivaux or the other authors who are foregrounded. However, anyone looking for a full 300-page monograph on Marivaux may well be disappointed by the low profile he keeps for much of the time.

SWANSEA UNIVERSITY					DEREK CONNON

Correspondance littéraire. By FRIEDRICH MELCHIOR GRIMM. Ed. by ULLA KÖL-
VING. Vol. VIII: *1761.* Ed. by ULLA KÖLVING, ELSE MARIE BUKDAHL, and
MÉLINDA CARON. Fernay-Voltaire: Centre International d'Étude du XVIIIe
Siècle. 2013. lxx+523 pp. €150. ISBN 978-2-84559-097-7.

The year 1761 began with a grave event for Grimm: intercepted letters led to his
being accused of spying for Prussia, and, as a result, being forced to resign his role
of representative of the city of Frankfurt to the French court. Now spending all of
his time in France, he is more obviously taking full control of the *Correspondance*
than in the years immediately preceding.

Perhaps the most significant literary event of the year is the publication of the
literary phenomenon that is *La Nouvelle Héloïse.* Grimm's review begins with a
comment to the effect that it is difficult to make a reliable judgement so soon after
its publication on a work that has been so eagerly awaited; thereafter, his judgement
is damning, and even admirers of the novel will find it difficult to disagree with all
his criticisms. One might expect a more positive review of the Parisian premiere
of his friend Diderot's *Père de famille*, but, having already reviewed the work itself
very positively on its publication in 1758, here Grimm comments mainly on the
performance, generally taking the high quality of the play for granted, but criticizing most of the actors and the cuts they made to the text. The play, he suggests,
succeeds despite them, although he does permit himself some minor criticisms at
the end of a second review.

Following Diderot's review of the biennial salon in 1759, Grimm continued to
entrust this task to him, and his report for this year is both more comprehensive
and more detailed than its predecessor. Taking up a major proportion of four issues,
this is the most significant complete text to be included during the course of the
year, but another interesting inclusion is a series of four dialogues that have often
been attributed to Diderot, but are here unambiguously presented by Grimm as the
work of Mme d'Épinay. One feels that if anyone should know who wrote them—his
best friend or the woman he was living with—he should. Useful appendices look
at both this question of attribution and changes and additions Grimm made to
Diderot's original text of his article on the salon. Other important inclusions are
Boufflers's *Reine de Golconde* and a large number of short pieces by Voltaire, the
continuing legacy of the friendship Grimm forged with him in 1759.

As usual, it is the arts which dominate, but, towards the end of the year, texts
related to the campaign of the Parlement against the Jesuits emerge, and the subject
of inoculation is raised in the first issue for December in a lengthy review of
d'Alembert's *Mémoire sur l'inoculation.* As always with this series, the introduction
and critical apparatus provide copious background and contextual information.
The edition is establishing itself as an essential tool for anyone interested in the
French eighteenth century.

SWANSEA UNIVERSITY   DEREK CONNON

Narrative Responses to the Trauma of the French Revolution. By KATHERINE AST-
 BURY. London: Legenda. 2012. x+186 pp. £45. ISBN 978–1–907975–42–4.

A generation of French scholars has found the fiction of the 1790s wanting: most
authors of the period are judged to be timid and old-fashioned because they refused to engage explicitly with the epoch-making events of the French Revolution.
Worse yet, they continued the generic conventions of the old regime: sentimental
novels and pastorals thrived. In *Narrative Responses to the Trauma of the French
Revolution*, Katherine Astbury challenges this conclusion. She contends that many
novels of this era did indeed respond, both explicitly and implicitly, to the Revolution. Inspired by British studies of English novels of the 1790s, Astbury proposes
that sentimental fiction can pack a political punch. In other words, novels that
appear to be about families, love, and marriage may in fact be political. This idea is
hardly new: Fredric Jameson's concept of the 'political unconscious' introduced the
literary world to this type of analysis in the 1980s. What is new is Astbury's willingness to analyse in depth neglected and often maligned novels of this all-important
decade.

The project begins with a study of the pastoral and its persistence throughout
the 1790s. Astbury seizes on this ancient generic form to make three important
points: she underscores how the Revolutionary pastoral breaks with its Ancien
Régime cousin; she demonstrates that the apparently non-political does engage
with politics; lastly, she shows how writers of different political parties deployed
the form to their own ends. To make her argument, Astbury offers sustained
reading of six little-known pastorals by authors such as Fournier de Tony, Baron
de Bilderbeck, and Moutonnet de Clairfons. In the next chapter she turns her
attention to better-known literary figures, J.-P. Claris de Florian and Jean-François
Marmontel, to trace their evolution from Enlightenment to Revolutionary authors.
Again, Astbury analyses how each author, while deploying traditional generic
forms—the chivalric and moral tale—sought explicitly to contribute to the moral
regeneration of the French nation: a project near and dear to the heart of most
early Revolutionaries. Astbury bolsters her claims about the literary significance of
these works through a chapter-length examination of the periodical press.

The second half of the book interprets novels written during and after the Terror
through the lens of trauma theory. Borrowing from Holocaust studies, Astbury
demonstrates how sentimental novels such as Mme de Genlis's *Les Chevaliers du
Cygne* (1795) register an experience of trauma (even if the novel is apparently about
the court of Charlemagne) and bequeath a kind of eyewitness account of Revolutionary events to posterity. She performs a similar analysis of Ducray-Duminil's
Victor, ou l'enfant de la forêt (1797), exposing the psychological trauma caused by
the Revolution that is inscribed within the narrative. According to trauma theory, there is an inevitable belatedness in understanding or coming to terms with
traumatic events. In final chapters of the book, Astbury reads émigré fiction and
Chateaubriand's writings during the Revolution as examples of this belated capacity

to write more explicitly about the painful experience of exile and emigration and thus to reconnect productively with the past.

Whether or not one finds Astbury's use of trauma theory compelling, she succeeds in changing the terms of a debate that had relegated a decade of literature to virtual oblivion. Astbury is absolutely right to insist on the historical and literary significance of the fiction of the 1790s. Given the historical impact of these years, it seems extraordinary that later generations of scholars have expressed such little interest in these works.

INDIANA UNIVERSITY SOUTH BEND   LESLEY H. WALKER

The Economy of Glory: From Ancien Régime France to the Fall of Napoleon. By
    ROBERT MORRISSEY. Trans. by TERESA LAVENDER FAGAN. Chicago: University
    of Chicago Press. 2014. xii+258 pp. $45. ISBN 978–0–226–92458–8.

Robert Morrissey is known to many as the director of the Project for American and French Research on the Treasury of the French Language (ARTFL). In this work, which originally appeared in French as *Napoléon et l'héritage de la gloire* (Paris: Presses Universitaires de France, 2010), he follows themes developed in his *L'Empereur à la barbe fleurie: Charlemagne dans la mythologie et l'histoire de France* (Paris: Gallimard, 1997) and in *Héroïsme et Lumières* (Paris: Champion, 2010). His goal was to 'explore the conditions of Napoleonic glory in the light of the collective *longue durée*' (p. 193). He traces the transformation of the idea of glory through time, beginning with a twenty-six-page tour of the pagans and the early Christians, including Augustine, Ambrose, and Aquinas. The next chapter (only twenty-five pages) proceeds from the medieval, including the *chansons de geste*, through Louis XIV. The chapter on the Enlightenment discusses glory as either 'a political instrument or a societal principle' (p. 73) and focuses on the well-known Montesquieu and Marat, and the less-known Antoine-Léonard Thomas and Jean-Baptiste Salaville, among others. In the pages on the Revolution Morrissey uses the transfer of Turenne's remains to the Temple of Mars to underscore that 'the notion of glory had always been at the heart of French identity' (p. 91). During the Empire glory became 'a principle of self-legitimation and a mechanism for governing' (p. 193). An exculpatory note sounds when Morrissey argues that Napoleon was 'the prisoner of a vision with a long history or, at least, that he had little room for manœuvre, given the complex period in which he was living' (p. 143) or when he claims that 'the waves of glory would have laundered the Revolution' (p. 159). One of the strongest chapters, although bedevilled by literary jargon, is an *explication de texte* of the *Mémorial de Sainte-Hélène*. This approach means that the reader sees Saint Helena only through the admittedly skewed perspective of Napoleon. The last chapter traces Napoleon's effects on literature, with a focus on nineteenth-century France.

Specialists will appreciate this illumination of the Napoleonic moment and will debate the role of glory in fusing pre- and post-Revolutionary France. Still, this is not a book for the uninitiated; the author neither sets some of the themes within a larger context nor identifies in any significant way many of the authors. The historical literature is virtually omitted, as are the victims of this quest for glory. Some sentences are constructed in a language that makes them obscure. For example, 'This is true of the Ignatian type of meditation, which unlike Salesian contemplation, is made up of discursive and reflective acts, freely admits love, and thus often has recourse to "the whole interest-based vocabulary of hope and fear"' (p. 50); or, 'The transcendence in immanence that characterizes glory has the same universality as the instinct for survival, but also the same psychological and cultural relativity' (p. 60). Many large block quotations both in the French and in a graceful English version are printed in the text. The reader can thus consult the French without in most cases turning to the endnotes. The illustrations appear only in black and white, but are well chosen and interpreted. A more extended analysis of both the artistic contribution and the classical legacy would have been welcome. There is no bibliography but there are two indexes, a general one and one of authors cited.

UNIVERSITY OF MONTANA   LINDA FREY
KANSAS STATE UNIVERSITY   MARSHA FREY

Zola Autodidacte: genèse des œuvres et apprentissages de l'écrivain en régime naturaliste. By OLIVIER LUMBROSO. (Histoire des idées et critique littéraire, 469) Geneva: Droz. 2013. 423 pp. €61.99. ISBN 978–2–600–01718–3.

With the final novel of his *Rougon-Macquart* cycle, *Le Docteur Pascal* (1893), Zola wished to produce a sense of circularity, 'quelque chose [. . .] du serpent qui se mord la queue', as he put it to Edmond de Goncourt. If tying the ends of his series together proved to be a difficult task, it was, it seemed, a measure of the transformations that a novelist, and a fictional project, could undergo in the *longue durée*—for Zola, over two decades. Between the first (*La Fortune des Rougon*, 1870) and the last novel of the cycle, writes Olivier Lumbroso, 'Zola n'est plus le même homme, plus le même écrivain, plus le même artiste' (p. 21). Lumbroso's highly engaging study presents Zola's dynamic self-transformation as an ongoing *autodidaxie*, which spans his entire career, developing far beyond the period usually associated with his initial apprenticeship as a writer (1858–67). Lumbroso addresses the play of influence, rejection, and imitation that characterizes these early years (Chapter 1), but the bulk of the book is dedicated to tracing the less readily discernible development of his aesthetic and professional writing practice from 1869 onwards, that is, over the course of the planning and composition of the *Rougon-Macquart*. With its focus set on the preparatory texts (Chapters 2 and 3), Lumbroso's study appears as part of a wider development of interest over the past two decades in the 'metatextual' Zola. (The Équipe Zola—CNRS-ITEM—has been instrumental in fostering genetic studies of Zola's works. Colette Becker's monumental, and ongoing, project of editing the *dossiers préparatoires* of the *Rougon-Macquart* aims to make accessible the material on which such research depends.) These new investigations into the Zolian 'avant-texte' are bound to reframe our understanding of Zola's authorial self-actualization; and Lumbroso's wide-ranging study already masterfully sets out the new insights and questions such close lexical and semantic analysis can produce. The point of this approach is not to schematize, and Lumbroso insists throughout on the instability and mutability of Zola's *dossiers*, which are held to participate in a perpetual process of creative reinvention ('un devenir d'artiste', p. 123). Such an account involves treating with some caution Zola's own single-minded declarations about the unity of his project and his fidelity to its original intentions. Instead, what emerges with Lumbroso's analysis is a sense of Zola's ongoing adaptation and, above all, reflexivity: how could he maintain an aesthetic coherence without being systematic? How could he manage, and also renew, the expectations of readers and critics for whom his aesthetic might be acquiring a certain predictability? What compromises were to be made between fostering a sense of unity in the cycle and the diversity necessary to avoid self-imitation? Far from programmatic, then, the *dossiers* appear at once as the tangled locus of the writer's intimate reflections and internal dialogue, of his negotiation with his own critical reception, and of the cultivation of his self-image for posterity. Lumbroso teases out Zola's developing creative consciousness, and self-consciousness, in the *dossiers*, as well as the terms of his metadiscourse, which, underpinned by a dual impulsion to creation and destruction, he relates in turn to the fantasies and anxieties about the creating subject that are played out in *Les Rougon-Macquart* (Chapter 4). Such self-reflexivity in Zola's fiction might not lead us towards a modernist aesthetic in quite the same way as Flaubert's, but Lumbroso's attention to Zola's self-development as a writer successfully reveals the more dynamic, provisional character of literary naturalism. This valuable study raises far-reaching questions, not least about the periodization of Zola's career, and the relationship between naturalist doctrine and practice, which will surely prove influential.

PETERHOUSE, UNIVERSITY OF CAMBRIDGE   CLAIRE WHITE

Photobiography: Photographic Self-Writing in Proust, Guibert, Ernaux, Macé. By AKANE KAWAKAMI. London: Legenda. 2013. x+193 pp. £45. ISBN 978–1–907975–86–8.

This book studies how photography influenced self-writing in four writers of the twentieth century. If the ur-example of 'photobiography' is *Roland Barthes par Roland Barthes* (Paris: Seuil, 1977), the special relationship of photography with the referent goes back to another 'photomane', Proust. Akane Kawakami begins by setting up three types of photographic content in a text: literal, metaphorical, and analogical. While the first category is clear, as in photo-texts, there appears to be some blurring in the latter two.

The chapter on Proust homes in on the analogical photograph that Marcel sees of his grandmother upon his return from Doncières, when he sees her outside of the love that he has for her, and therefore for the first time located in the unmerciful onset of time. Kawakami demonstrates that the moving passage is the first step in the creative process of *A la recherche du temps perdu*. One could have wished for a comparison with the actual photograph of the grandmother taken by Saint-Loup at Balbec.

The chapter on Hervé Guibert discusses photography as an act of love for this self-writer and photographer. Kawakami goes back to an early work to study how fact and fiction as well as text and photographs mix in Guibert's praxis of writing the body. Writing in the shadow of photography was a staple of his prose, only accentuated by his AIDS writing in the final novels. The critic analyses Guibert as *spectrum* whether in his selfies or in the works of his friend and fellow photographer Hans Georg Berer. Kawakami concludes that 'autofiction and photographs come together in Guibert to create a strangely death-defying genre' (p. 78), which might sound banal but not to anyone who has actually read his words and seen his photographs, some of the most moving of which are included in *Photobiography*.

For Annie Ernaux the desire 'to make writing into a referent' (p. 106) leads her to the important work *Les Années* (Paris: Gallimard, 2008), a third-person narrative that includes descriptions of photographs in an enterprise that is at once Proustian and anti-Proustian. Ekphrasis and *mémoire collective* (ethnotext) go hand in hand in Ernaux's book. This chapter contains references to Kawakami's correspondence with Ernaux, and a written interview appears in an appendix.

The final writer to be studied is Gérard Macé, the least known of the authors included in the corpus despite an œuvre of more than twenty books. His 'self is never explicitly present in his works' (p. 132), but his reflections on mirror and other reflecting images, including dreams, site him as someone who is used to 'seeing photographically' (p. 144). The actual readings of the photographs by Macé, several of which are reproduced, are among the best in Kawakami's book.

Among the strengths of *Photobiography*, I would point to her use of the first person in her own prose, her very complete use of relevant criticism, and her mastery of works of differing if overlapping genres. It was a wise decision not to belabour the initial tripartite distinction. Nothing is really done with the gay gaze or gay (self-)consciousness. Macé does not quite fit in with the authors discussed, and Claude Simon, of an earlier generation, would have been an excellent choice because of his self-writing and his own photography as well as his use of postcards. Complete with extensive notes and bibliography, this is an excellent contribution to a field that has numerous pedagogical implications, given students' penchant for all things visual.

The University of British Columbia (Vancouver)   Ralph Sarkonak

'Fièvres d'Afrique', suivi de trois récits inédits: 'La Recluse', 'La Duchesse' et 'Minne Water: Lac d'Amour' (extraits). By Louis Charbonneau. Ed. by Roger Little and Claude Achard. Paris: L'Harmattan. 2014. xxviii+211 pp. €24. ISBN 978–2–343–02555–1.

Mambu et son amour. By Louis Charbonneau. Ed. by Roger Little. Paris: L'Harmattan. 2014. xl+163 pp. €21. ISBN 978–2–343–02463–9.

Louis Charbonneau (1865–1951) was a French colonial merchant with the sensibility of an artist. From the late 1880s until 1922 he undertook a variety of commercial and mining enterprises in Africa, shuttling between the French and

Belgian Congos and Portuguese Angola. Although a more or less unremarkable colonial businessman, Charbonneau produced a body of writing that reveals in fascinating detail the complexities of everyday life in colonial West and Central Africa around the turn of the century. A portion of Charbonneau's œuvre has sadly been lost, but Roger Little's editions of *Fièvres d'Afrique* and *Mambu et son amour* bring his reflections on colonial Africa and rich personal narratives to new, twenty-first-century audiences.

Both of these books offer fictionalized autobiographical accounts of Charbonneau's travels throughout the region as well as his dealings with local administrators, missionaries, and indigenous colonial subjects. He never questions the inherent benevolence of European interests and governance in Africa, but neither does he uncritically accept the idea of African inferiority on which the colonial question hinges. *Fièvres d'Afrique* deals with this ambivalence most directly: in 'Une aube nouvelle', a section of a lengthy dreamscape set off by a feverish delirium, he optimistically and perhaps stubbornly asserts that 'les nations blanches ont enfin compris qu'il n'était pas de prospérité possible pour le continent africain sans le concours de la race noire' (p. 57). The affirmation of a certain idea of indigenous dignity goes hand in hand for Charbonneau with successful colonial rule, and the tension between these two ideas persists throughout the two books, informing his reflections on the colonial situation at its broadest level.

What drives the narratives in both of these texts, however, is Charbonneau's abiding love for an African woman named Mambu, with whom he lived informally for several years during the 1900s. The relationship began awkwardly as Mambu's brother, Charbonneau's local business associate, offered her to the Frenchman as a sort of transactional token. But it went on to become a full-fledged *mariage colonial*, as such liaisons between (often already married) European men and indigenous African women were frequently termed in French. There is little doubt for the reader that Charbonneau remained passionately attached to Mambu for the rest of his life, long after her untimely death in 1906 and his loving pilgrimage to her resting place the following year. Constructed as a series of journal entries and thinly fictionalized (as Little points out in his introduction), *Mambu et son amour* tells their love story and suggests that their intimate contact was responsible for Charbonneau's optimistic openness regarding the future of Africa. Indeed, his friend Raymond Escholier points out in the preface that this is the story of 'la petite négresse qui *civilisa* un Blanc' (p. 4, emphasis original). Mambu's memory haunts *Fièvres d'Afrique*, which takes place fifteen years after her death and sees Charbonneau (fictionally rendered as 'Libono' or 'Lici') return to the region where he started his African career, come down with a tropical illness, and reflect deliriously on the geological and social history of Africa with his deceased companion serving as spiritual guide.

This romantic relationship, which at times takes the form of a tragic obsession, comes to inflect Charbonneau's sense of literary style as well. The organization of the narratives as journal entries lends no small amount of intimacy to the reader's engagement with the text, and the reading experience is often tinged with a sort of colonial voyeurism. At the same time, though, Charbonneau's realism infantilizes Mambu: in their dialogues she speaks only in *français petit nègre*, and this feature brings the colonial relationship into the textual renderings of their most intimate interactions: 'Libono, je suis contente! Serre petit peu contre toi... moi aussi... je suis petit poussin pour toi!' (*Mambu*, p. 39). Fascinatingly, Charbonneau's characteristic ambivalence towards race and the colonial situation becomes part of his aesthetics, such that every dialogue or journal entry is both intensely personal and expressive of broader political and racial considerations.

These are rich and illuminating colonial documents, and Little has done well to bring them out in new editions. Aside from 'La Duchesse', a lengthy short story appended to *Fièvres d'Afrique*, the other previously unpublished texts in this collection do not add as much to our understanding of Charbonneau's work as one might hope. Nonetheless, they do testify to Mambu's lifelong hold on his literary psyche. Little's critical introductions to both texts offer helpful overviews of Charbonneau's writerly output as well as the challenges involved in piecing together his biography and literary works. Although he might have drawn out for non-specialists Charbonneau's connections to other colonial writers of his time, Little's editorial work is careful and conscientious in its attention to a colonial writer who reveals himself to be complexly and painfully human on every page.

BROWN UNIVERSITY   JUSTIN IZZO

Südlich der Sahara: Afrikanische Literatur in französischer Sprache. By JÁNOS RIESZ. Tübingen: Stauffenberg. 2013. 465 pp. €49.90. ISBN 978–3–86057–299–3.

János Riesz is regarded as one of the leading experts in the field of African literatures in French. Educated as a traditional scholar of Romance languages and literatures whose publications span the *Novellino*, Calderón, and Mallarmé, as well as European classics, he has devoted a great part of his career since the 1980s to the exploration of African literatures in French. *Südlich der Sahara* represents the essence of more than thirty years' work on African literatures.

The book regards itself as a handbook of literary history. It can also be used as an encyclopedia, but additionally—and that is the merit of Riesz's book—it can be read as a captivating narrative of the development of a literature against the backdrop of African and European histories.

Riesz subdivides his work into three main parts: 'Corpus', 'Sprache' (Language), and 'Kultur' (Culture). This subdivision ensures that the book does not give the impression of being a mere sequence of important texts as in a lexicon, but instead, that the pieces of information are contextualized through larger narratives. The part entitled 'Corpus' sheds light on the history of francophone African literatures, from their beginnings in the 1920s to *négritude*, the anticolonial novel of the 1950s and 1960s, to the more recent movements of the 'children of the postcolony' (Abdourahman Waberi, 'Les Enfants de la postcolonie: esquisse d'une nouvelle génération d'écrivains francophones d'Afrique noire', *Notre Librairie*, 135 (1998), 8–15). This part embeds the literatures in their historical context and thus renders them more understandable. The second part is dedicated to the conflictual implementation of the French language in francophone Africa and explores how the historical problem of language (language of the colonizers and 'indigenous' languages) is mirrored in literature. This part can be read as the leitmotif of Riesz's accomplishments, since he previously produced an important work, tellingly entitled *Französisch in Afrika: Herrschaft durch Sprache* (Frankfurt a.M.: IKO, 1988). In the third part, Riesz illuminates how African authors enter into a literary dialogue with European stereotypes about Africa, and how a distinct literary identity develops out of this dialogue.

Riesz's historical approach is obvious, particularly in the first part. By means of facts, numbers, and cartographic material, Riesz tells the history of colonization in order subsequently to link key texts by African authors to this context. The connection of literary production with the context of its genesis is one of the specific characteristics of Riesz's analysis. The analyses refer to well-known classics of African literatures 'south of the Sahara', and even when Riesz presents one or more of the less well-known key texts of African literatures (for example, *La Violation d'un pays* by Lamine Senghor, which today can only be obtained with difficulty), the interpretation and analysis of the text remain understandable throughout because they are embedded in larger historical contexts.

The selection of authors under discussion ranges from writers such as Bakary Diallo from the beginnings of francophone African literatures to Kossi Efoui, writing today. Riesz is also to be given much credit for incorporating popular culture, which is so important in African cultures, into his historical considerations. Thus, important passages on contemporary singers such as Alpha Blondy or Tiken Jah Fakoly can be found in *Südlich der Sahara*. For those without a knowledge of contemporary popular culture, today's francophone African literatures are impenetrable.

Riesz's book thus covers a century of literature, never forgetting that literature is always a product of its respective sociohistoric situation. His great strength lies in narrating one century of the history of francophone African literatures and, along with it, one hundred years of the history of francophone Africa. Without reverting to obscure academic jargon, he intelligently and comprehensibly creates interrelations which turn the book itself into a narrative. The only regret is that at present only speakers of German are able to enjoy this work.

JOHANNES GUTENBERG-UNIVERSITÄT MAINZ   THORSTEN SCHÜLLER

Le Blanc qui s'était fait nègre. By RENÉ GUILLOT. Ed. by MARIA CHIARA GNOCCHI. Paris: L'Harmattan. 2013. xxxviii+143 pp. €19. ISBN 978-2-343-00799-1.

With this volume, Guillot joins an extensive list of authors (including René Maran and Maurice Delafosse) whose texts have been resurrected within the Autrement Mêmes series so well established by Roger Little. Originally published in 1932, *Le Blanc qui s'était fait nègre* tells the story of Barail, a French soldier who leaves Bordeaux for Africa with the colonial forces. He is accompanied by Giraud and Sidoine, and the relationship between the three progresses with as much tension and violence as their colonial strategies. At the end of the novel, Barail has established a village at Dougouni and dies there beside the narrator to whom he has recounted the tale.

In her introduction, Maria Chiara Gnocchi argues that the text is one of the first French rewritings of Joseph Conrad's *Heart of Darkness* (p. xiii). Her intertextual analysis helpfully draws attention to the colonial encounter, similar characters, and parallel story progression. It is a shame that the bibliography makes little mention of the vast corpus of anglophone criticism on Conrad, and this reveals the barrier which exists more widely between anglophone and francophone critics. Nonetheless, such a comparison effectively draws out the theme of Otherness which is so important in this series.

Two key elements are highlighted by Gnocchi: the journey metaphor and the question of madness. Describing the text as a 'voyage au bout de l'altérité' (p. xxiv), she adeptly introduces the characters' encounters with places, people, and aspects of themselves which are strikingly 'autre' (p. 100). These continue where Guillot's text diverges from Conrad's, with Barail's return to France and seamless insertion into the late Sidoine's family. If we prolong Gnocchi's attention to intertextual play by reading *Le Blanc qui s'était fait nègre* alongside more recent francophone literature, we will find further rewritings of journey, migration, and encounter which speak into discussions of belonging and subjectivity in French as well as African contexts.

The crux of the drama stems from Barail's madness as he moves from calm pragmatism to fits of rage. Gnocchi's use of Sigmund Freud to explore the protagonist's unconscious as an 'Afrique intérieure' is insightful (p. xxx)—exploring how he is 'driven' by the opposite (and potentially invented) characters of Sidoine and Giraud—and is more convincing than the references to Flaubert (p. xvii). The narrator's conclusion that having internalized the two, 'il n'est pas fou, il est double' (p. 110), illustrates Guillot's exploration of a complex, conflicted subject. The title misleadingly suggests a centralization of race which is absent from the text, obscuring the focus on subjectivity which continues to merit our attention.

UNIVERSITY OF WARWICK   HANNAH GRAYSON

Into Disaster: Chronicles of Intellectual Life, 1941. By MAURICE BLANCHOT. Trans. by MICHAEL HOLLAND. New York: Fordham University Press. 2013. vi+ 151 pp. £16.99. ISBN 978–0–8232–5097–4.

Desperate Clarity: Chronicles of Intellectual Life, 1942. By MAURICE BLANCHOT. Trans. by MICHAEL HOLLAND. New York: Fordham University Press. 2013. vi+228 pp. £16.99. ISBN 978–0–8232–5100–1.

We tend to think of the young Maurice Blanchot (1907–2003) primarily as the author of dark, unsettling novels: *Thomas l'obscur* appeared in 1941, quickly followed by *Aminadab* (1942). Yet this is only a part of the picture.

In his early years Blanchot wrote a great deal of journalism, both political and literary. We still await a collection, even in French, of the youthful right-wing pieces in *Le Rempart, Combat*, and elsewhere, which need to be set against his later left-wing writing, now mostly gathered in French and translated into English, in order to understand his political itinerary; it was nothing if not radical. At least we have most of his early literary reviews, edited by Christophe Bident, and published by Gallimard under the title *Chroniques littéraires du 'Journal des débats'* (2007). Those reviews appeared weekly from April 1941 to August 1944: a total of 173 pieces. Along with three articles published in *L'Insurgé* and one in *Revue française des idées et des œuvres*, a number of the contributions to *Journal des débats* were slightly recast and included in *Faux pas* (1943). The book was completed with an unpublished essay, 'De l'angoisse au langage'. The two volumes under review represent the pieces in *Journal des débats* published in 1941 and 1942; two further volumes are to come, covering the years 1943 and 1944. None of the articles included in *Faux pas* is reproduced either in the French or in the English collections, but that is understandable. Needed far more urgently than a full set of the *Chroniques littéraires* is a volume of Blanchot's early fugitive literary criticism as it appeared in *Aux écoutes*, *L'Insurgé*, and other little magazines of the day.

Now we are in a better position than ever before to get a sense of Blanchot's early engagement with literature and of his evolving style of literary criticism. Perhaps the first thing to say about these reviews is that they could never be published in a weekly paper today: beautifully written though they are, their density would alarm a subeditor of even a high-toned literary supplement, and their range of cultural reference would be too highbrow for most readers of book reviews. These are essays of serious intellectual reflection, centred on literature, and referring widely to philosophy, religion, politics, and history. So we find Blanchot thinking deeply about Dante and Montesquieu, Descartes and Mallarmé, Mauriac and Valéry. If we look to the pieces chosen for *Faux pas*, we find rewarding discussions of Balzac, Baudelaire, Claudel, Gide, Lautréamont, Melville, Rimbaud, Woolf, and other canonical writers.

Not that Blanchot had the luck to review only enduring works; there is also a range of now forgotten books considered, though even here he has memorable things to say. Few people today read Franz Hellens's *Nouvelles réalités fantastiques* (1941), yet Blanchot's remarks on fantasy, aided by E. M. Forster's advice on how to distinguish plots from stories, remain fresh and sharp. Inevitably, Blanchot's preoccupations of the time come through in review after review: his interest in surrealism, his commitment to contestation, his fascination with obscurity, his distaste for anecdote, and his view of silence as a counterweight to the noise of words. We begin to see the outline of the obsessive author of *L'Espace littéraire* (1955) and the other collections that have made him a towering figure in modern French literature.

One of the most remarkable things that appeared in the *Chroniques littéraires* is a three-part article on Jean Paulhan's *Les Fleurs de Tarbes* (1941). The whole thing was published as *Comment la littérature est-elle possible?* in 1942, and then the second and third parts were recast as a chapter in *Faux pas*. 'Terror in Literature', the first instalment of the sequence, appears in *Into Disaster*. There we find the author wondering if *Les Fleurs de Tarbes* hides 'a sort of time bomb, that, though invisible today, will one day explode, and so devastate literature that it will become unfit for use' (p. 102). In his reflections on Paulhan, turning on the ambiguities of rhetoric and terror (the elimination of cliché), Blanchot uncovers that bomb. It is in the spirit of Kant's Copernican Revolution: literature does not revolve around thought but around language. One can read the pieces that compose *Comment la littérature est-elle possible?* as foreshadowing what Jacques Derrida was to call deconstruction some twenty-five years later. True, Blanchot knew some Heidegger, but his reading of Paulhan is original and fecund. That it appeared in a weekly paper, not an academic journal, is an index of his clarity, to be sure, but also an index of what is now no longer possible in literary journalism.

Michael Holland has exquisitely translated both volumes. His introductions, though not long, are rich and remarkably sensitive to the cultural and political nuances of wartime France. They make essential reading for anyone interested in Blanchot.

University of Virginia   Kevin Hart

Contesting Views: The Visual Economy of France and Algeria. By Edward Welch and Joseph McGonagle. (Contemporary French and Francophone Cultures, 27) Liverpool: Liverpool University Press. 2013. viii+236 pp. £70. ISBN 978-1-84631-884-9.

Over fifty years now after the end of the Algerian War (1954–62), which led to Algerian independence from French colonial rule, the Franco-Algerian relationship continues to generate a great deal of interest, in both the public and academic spheres. This rich study of visual culture and the 'visual economy' of France and Algeria succeeds in providing a fresh, engaging, and insightful outlook on this particular relationship. Not only do Edward Welch and Joseph McGonagle examine visual culture in various forms, they also focus on the ways in which images 'circulate within and between the two countries, and what sort of images tend to dominate those flows' (p. 7); what they term, following Deborah Poole, the 'visual economy'.

The book is divided into two parts, each comprising three chapters. Part I looks towards the past and analyses how visual images during and since the colonial period and the war have shaped historical understanding of these periods; Part II focuses on the ways in which the legacy of the Algerian War and ongoing manifestations of the Franco-Algerian relationship are played out in contemporary visual culture.

Chapter 1 is made up primarily of a discussion of nostalgic visions of French Algeria as represented in *pied-noir* photo-books, but an interesting counterpoint to these visions is provided by the examination of photographs taken by Pierre Bourdieu and Marc Riboud. While the majority of the photographs analysed in this chapter allows 'a return to lost worlds which remain in pristine condition' (p. 37), those taken by Bourdieu and Riboud destabilize this vision of unchanged history and present history as in progress.

In Chapter 2 the authors challenge the prevalent notion of photography being viewed simply as a historical resource, and assert the potential of the photograph to shape historical understanding. This provides the basis for the ensuing analysis, which includes discussion of pro-French Algeria visual representations during and at the end of the Algerian War. These perspectives are offset by images taken by conscript soldiers, which problematize the role of the conscript as an agent of history or as an innocent bystander caught in the unfolding of history.

The possibility of photography shaping historical understanding is pursued in Chapter 3, which examines the iconography of 17 October 1961, including images televised and printed at the time of the events, as well as contemporary representations. The chapter ends with a discussion of victimhood as portrayed in these contemporary images, and outlines the problems associated with such representations, which deny the agency of the subjects they depict.

Part II begins its analysis of the legacy of the Algerian War with a discussion in Chapter 4 of three films: Mehdi Charef's *Cartouches Gauloises* (2007); Thomas Gilou's *Michou d'Auber* (2007); and Michael Haneke's *Caché* (2005). Though Haneke's film has received wide critical attention, the analysis of it in this chapter remains compelling, somewhat overshadowing the discussion of the other two films. Chapter 5 takes as its focus visual representations of the Mediterranean Sea, including in photography, documentaries, and art installations from both sides of that particular space, which is presented as binding France and Algeria together, rather than as a dividing line. Finally, Chapter 6 returns to film to explore the paradoxical nature of the Franco-Algerian relationship, one which is, on the one hand, indicative of a French/Algerian transnational space, a space of potential consensus and reconciliation, but remains, on the other hand, a relationship that continues to be defined by borders and exclusion. This concluding notion, which is reinforced through discussion of the photography of Yann Arthus-Bertrand at the end of the chapter, reinforces the overall aim of the book to present the Franco-Algerian relationship, and the transnational space which it has engendered, as a site of contestation.

University of Liverpool   Jonathan Lewis

Language and Literary Form in French Caribbean Writing. By Celia Britton. Liverpool: Liverpool University Press. 2014. x+220 pp. £70. ISBN 978–1–78138–036–9.

In this compelling book Celia Britton further develops a methodology central to her work: the study of what is theoretically and politically at stake in the formal and linguistic analysis of postcolonial literary discourses. The topics, authors, and genres analysed are wide-ranging and heterogeneous, and include works by Glissant, Césaire, Ménil, Chamoiseau, Confiant, Depestre, Condé, Schwartz-Barth, Pineau, and Maximin. In her introduction Britton stresses the often problematic relationship between postcolonial studies and formal textual analysis, despite the strong influence of the (post)structuralist linguistic turn and postcolonial critics'

initial concern to develop a literary counter-discourse. However, in the last decade language and literary form in postcolonial writing have become increasingly
important areas of research, charged with potentialities for future analysis. From
Britton's perspective, greater attention to formal aspects could help to renegotiate
the relationship between postcolonial literary texts and the political, producing
a more nuanced and less schematic understanding of it. A formal and linguistic
analysis, avoiding self-referentiality, should help to overcome an 'easy automatic
correlation between the formal features of a text and its possible political significance' (p. 4). This leads to a consideration of how realism and the realist novel
in francophone postcolonial literature may be redefined in a way that is different
from both naturalism and the Western experimental novel, such as the *nouveau
roman*, and may re-evaluate realism itself. For instance, in the interview concluding
this volume, Maryse Condé considers how realism may combat ideological stereotypes and exoticism, including through the use of irony. Condé's novel *Traversée
de la mangrove*, analysed in Chapter 5, breaks the conventional codes of literary
discourse, but her irreverent transgression and dismantling of cultural stereotypes
entails an even deeper engagement with the real.

The first three chapters of the book consider issues of difference and exoticism from different perspectives, starting with the seminal work of the review
Tropiques, before moving to the *créolité* movement and the role played by the
'postcolonial exotic' in current marketing of Caribbean literature for a Western
audience. This raises a key question in postcolonial studies: how to enhance a
cultural aesthetic that sustains autonomy and difference, while avoiding the risk
of becoming trapped in forms of auto-exoticism, including folkloric and nostalgic
visions of cultural identity, ambiguously aimed at consumption by a metropolitan
readership. In Chapter 1 Britton explores this issue from different angles, such as
the Negritude's ambivalent attitude towards primitivism, ethnography, and surrealism. In Chapter 2 this 'abnormal type of exoticism applied to their own society'
(p. 27) is analysed in the *créolité* movement, specifically in Patrick Chamoiseau's
Solibo magnifique and Raphaël Confiant's *Le Nègre et l'admiral*. In these novels the
authors risk repeating cultural stereotypes about the Antillean other, producing a
more attractive and 'authentic' version of them for the Western literary market.
This line of analysis is further developed in the third chapter, where Britton considers the tropes of taste and consumption in relation to the marketing of Caribbean
literature and identifies one of the main 'ideological apparatuses' of neo-colonial
domination in the age of global capitalism: 'to consume the Other as a commodity
which is valued precisely for its difference' (p. 59).

Britton's extensive investigations are sustained by an original and effective use of
analytic tools drawn from literary theorists and philosophers, including Bakhtin,
Barthes, Benveniste, Lacan, Althusser, and Deleuze. The second part of the book
collects a series of illuminating essays on Édouard Glissant, who has always been
a point of reference for this scholar, taking into account his novels and essays
from *Le Quatrième Siècle* to *Une nouvelle région du monde*. In particular, the last
chapter takes an innovative and fruitful approach to his œuvre, considering from a

philosophical viewpoint the complex entanglement between a work of art and the real. This book gives further confirmation that Britton is currently one of the most important and prolific scholars in the field of French Caribbean literature.

UNIVERSITY OF BIRMINGHAM   ALESSANDRO CORIO

Writing, Reading, Grieving: Essays in Memory of Suzanne Dow. Ed. by RUTH
     CRUICKSHANK and ADAM WATT. (Nottingham French Studies, 53.1) Edin-
     burgh: Edinburgh University Press. 2014. ix+114 pp. £45.50 (download:
     http://www.euppublishing.com/toc/nfs/53/1). ISSN 0029-4586.

This elegant and imaginatively conceived tribute to the late Suzanne Dow is both a celebration and an engaged taking forward of its subject's adventurous intellectual work. The eight essays form an important contribution to our understanding of modern, avant-garde, and postmodern writing in French: punning and pastiche, the multiform challenge to reader reception, poetics of equivocation and the strategic disruption of assumptions, and the interrelation of psychoanalysis and literature provide key vectors of the volume. The editors have created a dialogic space where the contributors engage directly or implicitly with Dow's scholarship.

The opening essay, by Dow, is a lively and previously unpublished reading of Beckett in and for Lacan. Dow muses playfully on the near-total occlusion of Beckett in Lacan's work. Working from Joyce's letter/litter equivocation, she challenges Žižek by arguing for Beckett as a crucial 'silent partner' (p. 1) of Lacan who offers a 'discourse without speech' and a site of ethico-political values in minimalist anticipation of Lacan's primary engagement with Joyce. Katherine Shingler assesses the serious game of punning in avant-garde poetics in a substantial, illustrated reading of Apollinaire. Exploring the visual and semantic dimensions of punning, Shingler makes fruitful links with the simultanist aesthetic and with the poet's foray into psychiatric medicine and the punning capacity of the pre-rational mind. Lucy O'Meara focuses on crime fiction and its affinity with Oulipian constraint via a comparative reading of Perec and Garréta that examines the variable disruption of normative expectations among truth-fetishizing readers. Reading Nina Yargekov's debut novel *Tuer Catherine* (2009), Katie Jones approaches the text through the prism of Dow's work on female authorial anxiety and evolving constructions of madness-as-play, offering intriguing insights into the intradiegetic pastiches of the canonical nineteenth-century novel. Helen Vassallo probes the conjunction of cultural and political values of 'freedom' in the Lebanese writer Darina Al-Joundi's *Le Jour où Nina Simone a cessé de chanter* (2008), mobilizing Said's affirmative vision of exile. Complementing Dow's work on Beauvoir, Ruth Cruickshank re-reads tropes of eating and not eating in *Les Belles Images*, alert to cultural, social, colonial, and, especially, global contexts. Cruickshank is primarily concerned with the global reach of Beauvoir's critique and its implications for twenty-first-century market-bound experience. Two contributions on Proust develop a further avenue of Dow's research. Thomas Baldwin, on Barthes's engagement with Charlus's discourse, considers the significance of *Comment vivre ensemble* in bringing both confirmation and a corrective to Barthes's structuralist approach to (Balzacian) discourse in *S/Z*, and thus challenges the critical construction of a disjunction between Barthes's structuralism and poststructuralism. In a powerful and poignant closing essay, Adam Watt assesses afresh the deep, affecting influence of Proust on Barthes, taking *Journal de deuil* as a narrative of the intimate afterlife of mourning shared by the two writers.

In their prospective engagement with facets of Suzanne Dow's frontier research—from explorations of punning and playfulness, via psychoanalysis and postcoloniality, to reappraisals of madness, mourning, and modernist aesthetics—the contributors develop innovative readings in key areas of modern and contemporary writing and critical thought in this finely crafted collection of essays.

University of Bristol   Susan Harrow

Conversations with Kenelm: Essays on the Theology of the 'Commedia'. By John Took. London: UCL Arts and Humanities Publications and Ubiquity Press. 2013. 201 pp. £13 (download: doi.org//10.5334/baa). ISBN 978–1909–18800–6.

This volume is made up of eight essays, bracketed by a foreword and afterword, and taken together the contributions act, as the title indicates, as a sustained set of 'conversations' with the work of the distinguished Cambridge *dantista* and Thomist scholar, Kenelm Foster. As John Took notes, this is a 'conversation going on between those standing within the theological circle but inclined to deconstruct and reconstruct the argument according to the properties of formation and temperament' (p. ii). Chapter 1 ('Between Philology and Friendship: Dante and Aquinas Revisited') examines afresh questions regarding Dante's reading of Thomist texts, stressing the complexity and radically qualitative and personal nature of such reading in Dante. The chapter provides a helpful and lucid overview of many of the earlier positions regarding Dante's so-called 'Thomism', as well as an interesting survey of some of the ways Dante reads against the grain of Aquinas's *Summa contra Gentiles*. It also offers reflections on the relationship between theology and the crisis of existence in Dante. Chapter 2 ('The Twin Peaks of Dante's Theology in the *Paradiso*') considers the poet's treatment of the theologies of atonement and salvation (in Canto vii, on the one hand, and Cantos xix and xx, on the other). There is a useful account here of Anslem's *Cur Deus homo*, which is counterpoised with a close reading of *Paradiso* vii in ways that draw out some of the similarities but also the differences given what Took calls the 'agapeic' rather than the apologetic dimension of Dante's thinking through of the Christ event (p. 65). The chapter moves on to consider election theology on the basis of Thomist texts, and again stresses the particularities and peculiarities of Dante's treatment of what Took terms 'love-magnanimity' and 'love-responsiveness' (p. 79). The third essay ('Dante and the Modalities of Grace') takes as its starting-point Antonio Mastrobuono's contribution to the relationship of nature and grace in Dante, and develops concerns with how the individual is encouraged and emancipated by grace and with grace as a principle of ecstasy. Another important moment in English-language

Dante scholarship is the cue for the fourth essay ('Events and their Inner Life: An Essay in Actual Eschatology')—Alan Charity's book on events and their afterlife in Dante (A. C. Charity, *Events and their Afterlife: The Dialectics of Christian Typology in the Bible and Dante* (Cambridge: Cambridge University Press, 1966)). In this chapter, Took offers considerations in relation to the way eschatology 'turns upon the historical instant and the contentfulness thereof as the whereabouts of ultimate self-interpretation' (p. 119). He does so by paying close attention to the *Inferno*, in particular the episodes involving Francesca, Pier della Vigna, and Guido da Montefeltro, in each of which he assesses the 'ascendancy of the vertical over the horizontal as a plane of the eschatological awareness in the *Commedia*' (p. 112). The fifth essay ('Two Dantes or One? An Essay in Transcendence and Theatricality') handles, as its title states, the best-known Foster essay of all, namely, that concerning the tensions in Dante between the pagan and the Christian, and the essay does so with close attention to elements of consistency and resolution brought about in the poem. The sixth essay ('Complementarity and Coalescence: Dante and the Sociology of Authentic Being') explores Dante's treatment of the ways in which the individual stands alone and how this is qualified by 'a sense of the presence of the self of the next man as a parameter of ontological awareness' (p. v). The essay begins again with Foster and his sense of the social aspect of the *Inferno* but moves on to explore social issues in relation to Pauline models of social configuration and Trinitarianism. The final two essays in the volume ('Dante and the Protestant Principle' and 'The Courage of the *Commedia*') enter into dialogue with the German American theologian Paul Tillich and are concerned with how Dante rethinks elements of soteriology and election theology, and with how the self gains the ability to self-govern.

As a whole, the collection is of value to the specialist and advanced student and is of interest to all those concerned with the status of, and questions related to, theology (and not only in the late Middle Ages), as well as its forms in Dante and the potential value of dialogue between its Dantean manifestations and contemporary concerns. Though the book is not always easy reading, it is elegantly written, and the notes offer rich documentation of the critical bibliography and some interesting and important suggestions of models and parallels in Dante's likely interlocutors. Dante scholars will probably take most from the chapters or parts of chapters that directly address the relationship with Foster, but the book will also be of interest to theologians and historians of religion.

University of Warwick   Simon Gilson

Francis of Assisi and his 'Canticle of Brother Sun' Reassessed. By Brian Moloney. New York: Palgrave Macmillan. 2013. xxvi+169 pp. £55. ISBN 978-1-137-30696-8

An introduction to the first poem of the Italian literary canon, this volume does exactly what it proposes to do in its title and carries out a 'reassessment' of the 'Canticle' as connected to the life, works, and spirituality of Francis of Assisi. Since the text is a declared expression of its author's strong spiritual perspective, an analysis of its contents and its various aesthetic elements grants the opportunity to revisit and remeditate crucial aspects of Francis's mysticism, his renewed approach to religious life, and the creation of a new mendicant order.

After an overview of the book's contents and an introduction to the subject-matter in Chapter 1, Chapter 2 draws a historical and cultural picture of Francis's world, before offering an account of the composition of the canticle in Chapter 3. Chapter 4 is about the language of the poem and the long-lasting critical question related to the polysemous preposition 'per'. Chapter 5 deals with the sources, while Chapter 6 analyses the impact of Francis's mysticism on the writing of the canticle. Chapter 7 delves into the more specific issue of calling death 'sister,' which seems to contradict the use of attributes of brotherhood and sisterhood solely for God's creatures—and death is not one of them, for human beings brought it upon themselves through disobedience. Chapters 8 and 9 are historical. Chapter 8 places the text in the cultural context of thirteenth-century Italy and addresses the issue of Catharism, which Francis indirectly refuses when he emphasizes the beauty and goodness of nature, in opposition to the Manichaean doctrine of the Cathar Heresy. Chapter 9 deals with the impact of chivalric culture on Francis. Chapter 10 is a close, line-by-line reading of the poem, and Chapter 11 summarizes and concludes the arguments made throughout the study. The volume also contains the original Italian text of the canticle as well as two translations by the critic, one of which makes the original choice of rendering the 'per' referred to the various creatures with 'from', instead of the more common 'for', 'by', or 'through/by means of '.

While offering a thorough and comprehensive overview of some of the most important interpretations (Luigi Foscolo Benedetto, Leo Spitzer, Giovanni Miccoli), the volume adds some interpretative points of its own. When considering the philological sources of the canticle in Chapter 5, the author adds the twelfth-century Cistercian monk Idung of Pruefungen as possible inspiration for Francis's idea of inanimate creatures being able to praise God (p. 58). The long discussion on chivalric culture as possibly affecting Francis's attitude and the subsequent Franciscan movement is convincing, but it does not have much bearing on the interpretation of the poem. The author himself states that there is 'no explicit reference in the canticle to the code or ethos of chivalry' (p. 120), although a small hint may be detected in 'the optative subjunctive' of the refrain, which 'may appear to be more courtly than the imperative' (p. 121). The argument about the composition of the canticle is directly related to the significance of a religious poet's inspired condition. If the poem was indeed written in three separate sessions (as transmitted by hagiographies), then it would be difficult to view it as inspired by the poet's mysticism (Moloney argues), which supposedly would have to come in one single urge of creativity. The critic eventually reconciles these two (only apparently) contradictory positions by stating that Francis may have been equally inspired by mysticism when he wrote part two and part three as well as when he wrote the first section of the poem. Some missing references to criticism in the bibliography are noticeable, such as the work of Lawrence Cunningham, Vito

Cutro, Joan Mowat Erikson, John Fleming, Giovanni Getto, and Adolfo Oxilia. Considering the long and articulate section of the volume dedicated to the preposition 'per', the omission of Antonino Pagliaro's illuminating article on the subject is remarkable. Chiara Frugoni is quoted in the text (p. 117), but then she appears as Carlo Frugoni in the bibliography (p. 154).

This book is comprehensive, well informed, and clearly presented. It certainly serves the purpose of introducing first-time readers to the canticle by offering all the essential ingredients to interpret and analyse it from a literary, theological, and spiritual point of view.

RUTGERS UNIVERSITY   ALESSANDRO VETTORI

Pinocchio, Puppets and Modernity: The Mechanical Body. Ed. by KATIA PIZZI. London: Routledge. 2012. xvii+228 pp. £90.03. ISBN 978-0-415-89096-0.

This interesting collection of papers stems from a symposium held in London in February 2006, and deals with several topics related to the Italian author Collodi, alias Carlo Lorenzini (1826–1890), and to the marvellous and ever-inspiring character he created: Pinocchio, the puppet which desires to become a real boy of flesh and blood.

The editor, Katia Pizzi, and other leading scholars contributing to this volume have chosen a bifocal approach. On the one hand this involves investigation of the cultural context around Collodi, viz. nineteenth-century French and Italian literature with special regard to George Sand and Giuseppe Mazzini, but also to Hoffmann's tales and Hans Christian Andersen's fairy tales. This implies stories in which automata or dynamic, strange beings move their rhythmical and mechanical bodies. On the other hand, the approach looks at the future and the numerous metamorphoses of Pinocchio as a puppet/donkey/boy: from Monsieur Ubu or marionettes and mannequins in the theatre of Dario Fo, to the rewritings of Pinocchio's adventures by Luciano Folgore in radio and television programmes for children, or Pinocchio's transitions from Collodi's page to screen or to the digital world. The book gives a vivid sense of the great influence of this human/not human puppet/boy who/which is able to raise fundamental questions about the condition and fate of contemporary man.

In Chapter 1 Jean Perrot, author of an interesting monograph on Sand and Collodi (*Le Secret de Pinocchio: George Sand et Carlo Collodi* (Paris: In Press, 2003)), considers *Pinocchio* as an original transformation of Sand's (children's) book *Histoire du véritable Gribouille* (1850). Although Collodi was familiar with French literature and a connection is therefore possible, the hypothesis seems to have a limited scope in relation to an extremely stratified text such as *Pinocchio*. In Chapter 2 Ann Lawson Lucas compares Pinocchio's story with the most famous tales or novels whose protagonists are puppets, automata, or mechanical beings: among them, *Der Sandmann* by E. T. A. Hoffmann (1816) and *Frankenstein* by Mary Shelley (1818). In her view, Pinocchio represents an innovation because it/he is a puppet which/who stands up against adults' power and wants to be independent: for this reason Pinocchio can be seen as a universal symbol of freedom.

The differences between Pinocchio and Frankenstein are also noted and analysed, among other things, by Charles Klopp in Chapter 3 . According to him, Pinocchio's vitality and its/his experiential curve is an ascending and triumphant one that is starkly different from the descent into degradation of Shelley's Creature.

In Chapter 4 Jill Fell carefully deals with Alfred Jarry's creation: the drawing/caricature/silhouette/puppet Monsieur Ubu. Special attention is paid to the 'theme' of the nose, considered as both a caricatural element and a symbol of death. In Chapter 5 Christopher Cairns provides a very stimulating discussion of Fo's innovative use of mannequins, as inspired by De Chirico and Carrà, but probably by the Bragaglia brothers and Totò too.

'Unpainting Collodi's Fireplace', by Stephen Wilson, is the title of Chapter 6, which is accompanied by an interview conducted by Susan Lawson in which Wilson describes his artistic work as inspired by the puppet's adventures. In Chapter 7 Katia Pizzi brilliantly explores Luciano Folgore's papers dedicated to Pinocchio and to his 'pinocchiate', that is, his comic rewritings and free reinventions of the puppet's adventures. The entertaining mixture of fairy-tale characters suggests the presence of the great model of Sergio Tofano's *Il romanzo delle mie delusioni* (1917). Chapters 8 and 9 are both written by Salvatore Consolo, who first describes the mythological and heroic dimension of Pinocchio, and then analyses the transition from Collodi's page to the silver screen, paying special attention to Roberto Benigni's film and its mixed critical reception. In the final chapter, devoted to the 'Digital Pinocchio', Massimo Riva remarks that Pinocchio embodies a fundamental ambivalence of modernity: its myth of endless renewal and growth. As a combination of virtual and physical, Pinocchio maintains its appeal because 'it is focused on that evanescent threshold, on that crucial transition from childhood to young adulthood' (p. 203). Once again, *The Adventures of Pinocchio*—or simply *Pinocchio*—confirms its status as a universal and timeless literary masterpiece, written for both children and adults.

COLLODI-PESCIA   DANIELA MARCHESCHI

Un paese senza eroi: l'Italia da Jacopo Ortis a Montalbano. By STEFANO JOSSA. Rome and Bari: Laterza. 2013. xii+283 pp. £23.09. ISBN 978–88–581–0666–2.

A few years after *L'Italia letteraria* (Bologna: Il Mulino, 2006), Stefano Jossa brings to our attention another significant literary study on Italian national identity, but this time more focused on national iconography, and with an original and sharp-sighted line of argument: Italy is a country with no (literary) heroes.

In compelling chapters, where literary criticism stands aloof from dry erudition in order to embrace a historical, philosophical, sociological, anthropological, and political dialogue, the reader is convincingly led to recognize that if Italian literature has not produced a celebrated national hero equivalent to Robin Hood, d'Artagnan, or William Tell, this is actually a positive thing. In fact—Jossa argues—while the national hero can have a detrimental effect on society, 'l'eroe funziona come un mito salvifico per chi lo desidera e mito narcisistico per chi s'identifica'

(p. 27), the anti-hero, on the contrary, acts according to his/her ethical values, and not for opportunistic reasons. The clear allusion to some Italian historical leaders who, sometimes for better but most often for worse, have become legendary (Garibaldi, Mussolini, Berlusconi) is not difficult to perceive.

The ethical conduct of the anti-heroes who have become heroes at a personal rather than historical level can be recognized from the first Italian novels, among which Foscolo's *Jacopo Ortis* and Nievo's *Confessioni d'un Italiano* are masterfully explored. If critical insights into the reasons why D'Annunzio's *superuomo* failed to be appreciated as the potential national hero are very much pertinent to Jossa's line of enquiry, where his book utterly mesmerizes is when he examines the 'little' heroes of our Italian pedagogic literature: *Pinocchio*, *Enrico*, and *Gian Burrasca*. All three literary characters, as Jossa discusses, could have been considered ideal candidates for the role of national hero inculcating the educational values of the new Italian nation, and indeed *Pinocchio*'s iconic character was reshaped and exploited by Fascist propaganda. Fortunately, however, Collodi, De Amicis, and Bertelli endowed these three little characters with such a complex nature, which is so caught up in the emotional universe of childhood upbringing, that they have managed to escape the cold symbolic destiny of heroic characters.

Another captivating analysis occurs in Chapter 8, where Pirandello's and Svevo's *inetti esistenziali* are examined. They are considered to be neither heroes intent on dominating their time, nor anti-heroes proudly standing against the compromises of their experience, but modern *personaggi* aware of the multiplicity of viewpoints. Yet the antagonistic nature of Mattia and Zeno, as well as the ideological divergence of the two novels, is clearly identified.

The most gripping part of the book, however, is perhaps Chapter 9. The ever-present risk of writing 'glorious' literature is here expressed through Calvino's own reflections on the difficulties, in post-war Italy, of creating a national literary role model. Pin and Kim, therefore, but also Fenoglio's *Johnny*, are not heroes of the Italian Resistance, but 'true' literary figures who provide an ethical model to all the readers who experienced the Resistance as partisans and as children. Consequently, it is not by chance that this chapter, which reflects also on heroism as interpretation of historical class experience, ends with Pratolini's *Metello*, who, though far from being a righteous hero, can nonetheless be recognized as a true man of the working class.

The last romantic anti-hero of Italian literature, Don Fabrizio di Salina, opens the sharp discussion in Jossa's last chapter, which is, however, mainly focused on Camilleri's mass hero Montalbano. If in Tomasi di Lampedusa's *Gattopardo* we are reminded of the dialectics between the historical hero (Tancredi) and the individualistic, disenchanted anti-hero (Don Fabrizio), the analysis of Montalbano's rise to exemplary model of the Italian nation gives our author the chance to confirm his line of argument: the need on the part of the mass to create myths to feed public opinion. In his concluding remarks, therefore, Jossa emphatically invites the reader to distinguish a (national) hero, who most often is a superficial figure of adoration, from a (true) hero, who in ethical terms has maintained a solid resistance to ideological instrumentalization.

This is an insightful analysis, and a fascinating read throughout. Although one might argue that the absence of female heroines/anti-heroines is a regrettable oversight, it is unquestionable that Jossa's rich and intellectually coherent discourse on the *dignitas hominis* of Italian literary anti-heroes is a precious addition to scholarship in Italian Studies. It is not surprising, therefore, that this volume was shortlisted for the Viareggio Rèpaci Book Award in 2014.

UNIVERSITY OF SUSSEX   AMBRA MORONCINI

Amor che move: linguaggio del corpo e forma del desiderio in Dante, Pasolini e Morante. By MANUELE GRAGNOLATI. Milan: Il Saggiatore. 2013. 236 pp. €19. ISBN 978–88–428–1865–6.

In this stimulating and well-executed study, Manuele Gragnolati uses what is called a diffractive approach, a methodology taken from the theoretical work of Donna Haraway, whereby texts that may not appear to have any apparent or obvious connection are put into contact with one another in order to produce new and resonant interconnections of a non-hierarchical nature, as they bounce off one another, analogously to the way in which diffracted light spreads out. He succeeds admirably in doing just that: Dante, Pasolini, and Morante all benefit from his flexible and yet quite rigorous interpretation and application of this methodology, which, as I understand it, is essentially a critical mode that proposes to avoid traditional comparative paradigms and straightforward source studies. The authors included in Gragnolati's volume do have well-known and already studied connections, of course, but this diffractive approach allows for the discovery of additional ways in which their works create cross-dialogues and cross-references that are not easily discerned or explicitly expressed by more standard approaches.

The emphasis of Gragnolati's book is on the topics of desire, the body, and language as they are expressed in Dante's *Vita nuova* and *Commedia*, in Pasolini's *La divina mimesis* and *Petrolio*, and in Morante's final novel, *Aracoeli*. What is most remarkable to my mind is how the structure of his book perfectly reflects the content and critical approach, for we move in a genuinely diffractive manner from Dante to the other authors and then back to Dante and again to the modern authors in a fluid, wave-like, and ultimately cumulative manner, as resonances collect and meanings gradually deepen. This is also a book that openly embraces a 'queer' approach, which does not mean simply concentrating on the gay or non-heterosexually normative elements of the texts, but rather veering from traditional or standard readings in order to search for the oblique aspects that a less 'queer' approach would most likely miss.

Gragnolati's claims begin with the idea that Dante's *Vita nuova* creates, perhaps for the first time, the performative and therefore modern author, while Pasolini's *Divina mimesis* destroys this figure. In the *libello* there is the exemplary *auctor* but there is also the character who is individualized and whose experiences are personal, not only universal. Thus the modernity of this author-character is born and shaped into a cohesive totality, and is, of course, continued in the *Commedia*. Pasolini, instead, embraces fragmentation and lack of unity and completeness in *La divina mimesis*, which reveal the mechanisms of performativity that Dante's text synthesizes into a unity of poetry and prose, past and present. Pasolini thus highlights the failure of the figure of the modern author that Dante brought to life. Continuing his study of Pasolini, in the next chapter Gragnolati analyses the extremely fragmented and unfinished (perhaps interminable) novel *Petrolio*, in which he discerns not only the performativity of *La divina mimesis*, but also a quite specific form of desire and sexuality, which is 'queer' as the term is defined by Leo Edelman: that is, a position which refuses temporality seen as progress and future-oriented reproductivity in favour of non-teleological repetitivity and negativity, both of which are tied to a form of subversive, non-reproductive sexuality. Both *La divina mimesis* and *Petrolio* are, in Gragnolati's view, provocatory gestures that refuse the normative, capitalist order of progress, as well as textual linearity and psychological wholeness.

There is a return to Dante in the next two chapters, in both of which the concept of 'eschatological anthropology' is proposed, by which Gragnolati seeks to explore the meaning of desire and corporeality in the *Commedia*. Of particular interest is the fact of the physicality of the spirits in the afterworld, imagined by Dante to have aerial bodies that are in essence an effect of their souls' status. The body remains a site of desire in Dante's poetic vision, as is perhaps most forcefully seen in the impossible embraces that signal a persistence of the corporeal even in the *Paradiso*. Gragnolati posits that this persistence of the bodily is a way of highlighting the singularity of each spirit, as well as the affective dimension of his/her past lived life. The affective realm is also strongly linked to the maternal, both thematically and linguistically, and the following chapter on Morante's final novel *Aracoeli* investigates the centrality of relationality and intersubjectivity by means of the search for the resurrected mother. The tormented protagonist of the novel, Manuele (who is based on Morante's dear friend Pasolini), is torn between the affective and corporeal realm of the maternal, as represented by the (literally) maternal language, or language of his mother, which is Spanish, and the hierarchical and disciplinary realm of the paternal language, Italian, which is strongly tied to Fascism. The last pages of the book sum up the points of connection among the texts studied, and convincingly argue for a Dante whose great poem is much more open to 'queer' readings than centuries of commentary have understood or acknowledged.

UNIVERSITY OF CHICAGO   REBECCA WEST

Italian Crime Fiction. Ed. by GIULIANA PIERI. (European Crime Fiction) Cardiff: University of Wales Press. 2011. xi+159 pp. £24.99. ISBN 978-0-7083-2432-5.

The Importance of Place in Contemporary Italian Crime Fiction: A Bloody Journey. By BARBARA PEZZOTTI. Madison, NJ: Fairleigh Dickinson University Press. 2012. viii+213 pp. £42.97. ISBN 978-1-61147-552-4.

Methods of Murder: Beccarian Introspection and Lombrosian Vivisection in Italian Crime Fiction. By ELENA PAST. Toronto: University of Toronto Press. 2012. x+353 pp. $59.34. ISBN 978-1-4426-4388-8.

The Black Album: il noir tra cronaca e romanzo. By MARCO AMICI and MASSIMO CARLOTTO. Rome: Carocci. 2012. 138 pp. €13. ISBN 978-88-430-6568-4.

Since the mid-1990s, the sales of crime fiction in Italy have soared. With the Sicilian patriarch Andrea Camilleri and his *commissario* Montalbano leading the way, a plethora of Italian crime-fiction authors have dominated the top list of best-selling books, undermining the top-ranking positions traditionally held by translated foreign (particularly American) novels. Massimo Carlotto, Gianrico Carofiglio, Giancarlo De Cataldo, Marcello Fois, and Carlo Lucarelli are some of the other best-known contemporary crime writers; their works are widely translated abroad and have often inspired successful cinema and TV adaptations; in some cases (Lucarelli and De Cataldo) authors have turned themselves into TV stars.

This phenomenon, initially unexpected but by now well established, has interested journalists as well as critics. Many scholars have overcome the established academic distrust of all forms of 'para-literature'—a definition for popular genres, challenged already in the late 1970s and 1980s by the pioneering work of scholars such as Giuseppe Petronio and his collaborators in Trieste (mainly in the field of sociology of literature) and Umberto Eco (on mass communication and on the pleasure of reading). In 1989 crime fiction found its place in the canonical *Letteratura italiana* directed by Alberto Asor Rosa, with a chapter on 'Il poliziesco' by Benedetta Bini; since then, monographs and articles have appeared on specific authors and on crime fiction as a genre, often presented in historical perspective. Nowadays it is not uncommon to find panels on crime fiction at all major conferences of Italian Studies, promoted by respected scholars in the field—mostly working in English-speaking countries and in continental Europe (e.g. Claudio Milanesi, director of the Atelier sur le Roman Policier at Aix-en-Provence), with fewer but essential names from Italian universities (Vittorio Spinazzola and his research group centred on the journal *Tirature* in Milan; Elisabetta Mondello in Rome; and Gisella Padovani in Catania).

In this respect, the repeated claim by scholars working on crime fiction that they are challenging the traditional highbrow canon seems rather anachronistic. It is true, though, that many critical works are in Italian and/or have appeared in journals and series focused on the Italian context, while knowledge of Italian crime fiction in the international literary scene is relatively scant. Three recent books contribute to broadening the interest in the genre beyond Italian national borders, by presenting to English readers the Italian manifestation of crime fiction, its history, and some insight into its protagonists, with a strong focus on the contemporary scene (post-1990s).

Italian Crime Fiction, a collective volume edited by Giuliana Pieri and co-authored by some of the best-known scholars in the field based in the UK, Ireland, and Canada, represents a suitable introduction to the Italian case. After an overview of the genre in its early stages in the 1920s and 1930s (Jane Dunnett), the following chapters focus on Giorgio Scerbanenco, the front runner of popular *gialli* in the 1960s (Jennifer Burns), and on the masters of the highbrow rewriting of the detective novel in the second half of the twentieth century, such as Carlo Emilio Gadda, Leonardo Sciascia, Umberto Eco, and Antonio Tabucchi (Joseph Farrell). The second half of the book has both a geographical focus, with chapters devoted to the representation either of the urban realities of Milan (Pieri) and Bologna (Luca Somigli), or of the South (Mark Chu, who analyses the Sicilian novels by Camilleri, the Sardinian *noirs* of Fois, and the Apulian stories of Carofiglio), and a gender focus, by concentrating on women writers of crime fiction (Pieri and Lucia Rinaldi). The annotated bibliography (Rinaldi) is a useful tool for those who are starting to navigate the critical production in this area. If some sections appear more derivative than original, it is worth highlighting that the aim of the collection is precisely to provide the English reader with an overview both of Italian crime fiction and of its milestones. The book enriches the European Crime Fiction series of the University of Wales Press, which includes volumes on French, Iberian, and Scandinavian noir, and on crime in capital cities, in order to foster the dialogue between anglophone and European crime writing.

An informative value can also be traced in Barbara Pezzotti's *The Importance of Place in Contemporary Italian Crime Fiction: A Bloody Journey,* which explores the distinctive geographical rootedness of Italian *giallisti* and *noiristi*—a trait explained by the combination of the realist drive typical of crime fiction (internationally and historically) with the mosaic-like nature of Italian national identity. Her map includes novels set in Milan (by the duo Piero Colaprico and Pietro Valpreda, Andrea G. Pinketts, and Sandrone Dazieri), Turin (Bruno Ventavoli and Piero Soria), Naples (Massimo Siviero), Palermo (Santo Piazzese), Bologna (Lucarelli), the North-East (Carlotto), Sicily (Camilleri), and Sardinia (Fois).

In view of the abundance of crime-fiction texts and authors, Pezzotti selects only novels organized in series and first published between 1992 and 2001, but sometimes she finds herself prisoner of her own selection criteria: her map is heavily weighted in favour of the North, Rome is absent (the exclusion of *Romanzo criminale* by De Cataldo, although not fulfilling the 'crime series' criterion, is problematic), and even Carofiglio's Bari is not there. In addition, the passage from city-based to island-based analysis (Chapters 1–6 vs. 7–8) could be clearer, and the final sections on Sicily and Sardinia tend to present stereotypically homogeneous island identities (the discussion would be different if, for Sicily, Piazzese's Palermo were analysed in the same chapter with Camilleri's Vigàta; for Sardinia, the crime series by Giorgio Todde, set in Cagliari, would provide elements for a meaningful comparison and contrast to Fois's Nuoro). An imbalance can also be found among the writers selected, who are unequal in terms of literary ambition and achievements, as well as their fame among readers. Nevertheless, by following the urban wanderings of fictional detectives as if they were the heirs of Walter Benjamin's *flâneur*, Pezzotti offers an interesting overview of literary representations of Italy at the end of the twentieth century, caught in the traumatic and fragmented passage from local pre-modernity to *glocal* postpostmodernity, with the sense of nostalgia that this process entails; the Veneto and Emilian urban sprawls identified in Carlotto's and Lucarelli's crime series are the most convincing examples of this troubled metamorphosis of the Italian space. The book is now available in Italian translation (goWare 2014, epub format only), and is followed by another introductory text useful for didactic purposes, *Politics and Society in Italian Crime Fiction: An Historical Overview* (Jefferson, NC: McFarland, 2014).

More original is the theoretical framework underpinning Elena Past's *Methods of Murder: Beccarian Introspection and Lombrosian Vivisection in Italian Crime Fiction*. The author argues that, although it is true that Italy arrived late in the production of crime fiction, the discourses of modern criminology have a long-term tradition in the country, which was the birthplace of founding texts such as Cesare Beccaria's *Dei delitti e delle pene* (1764) in the Enlightenment and Cesare Lombroso's *L'uomo delinquente* (1876) in the Positivist era. Their influence has expanded beyond the juridical and medical sectors, informing the broader social and cultural field (literature included), with long-term effects. First, the author revisits Beccaria and Lombroso with the support of contemporary philosophers, from Michel Foucault to Giorgio Agamben, and cultural historians such as Carlo Ginzburg. Subsequently she extrapolates two paradigms of epistemology of crime from their writing: the Beccarian perspective, introspective and philosophical, looks at the 'disembodied criminal' in the context of the judicial system, while the Lombrosian perspective is biological and fascinated with criminals and victims as bodies to vivisect, loci of crime and of investigation. Past does not aim to define genealogies, but to explore how, 'underlying the recent outpouring of crime fiction, [. . .] are discernible attitudes towards the problem of crime that in many ways determine the unfolding of the narrative, its style, and its substance' (p. 9). In her analysis, 'Italian fiction is embedded in a centuries-old Italian discussion, and not simply an Anglo-Saxon literary tradition' (p. 16). Persuasively, the Beccarian interpretative framework is applied to Sciascia, Camilleri, and Carofiglio, in whose works the ethical question of the application of justice and its limits features heavily, and the failure of Enlightenment as the 'educating century' is exposed. Crime novels by Gadda and Lucarelli, together with the early cinema of Dario Argento (the animal trilogy, 1970–71: *L'uccello dalle piume di cristallo*, *Il gatto a nove code*, and *Quattro mosche di velluto grigio*), are examined as Lombrosian-style narratives, in which the emphasis on the opening of the victims' bodies at the moment of death raises awareness of the permeability of the 'border of human existence that separates the living from the dead, the inside from the outside' (p. 273).

The Black Album: il noir tra cronaca e romanzo is a conversation in Italian on the history and the articulation of crime fiction between one of its protagonists, Massimo Carlotto, and the scholar Marco Amici. This is a good example of the rare interaction between academics and writers, who in most cases work in hermetically sealed compartments. Since the late 2000s, some Italian writers have been theorizing their writing practices, and especially the issue of the return to the real. The seminal *New Italian Epic: Memorandum 1993–2008. Narrativa, sguardo obliquo, ritorno al futuro* by Wu Ming 1 (discussed at conferences and in online blogs before being published by Einaudi in 2009) highlights the role of mid-1990s detective and crime fiction in starting the process of renewal of Italian literature. De Cataldo links crime fiction and the social novel under the category of 'neo-neorealism' ('Raccontare l'Italia senza avere paura di sporcarsi le mani', *Repubblica* <http://ricerca.repubblica.it/repubblica/archivio/repubblica/2008/06/08/> [accessed 4 October 2014]), while Carlotto looks both at the phase of the 'Mediterranean noir' and to its overcoming ('Legalità d'evasione', *Il Manifesto* <http://www.edizionieo.it/news_visualizza.php?Id=206> [accessed 4 October 2014]). It is time for academic scholars to recognize the existence of this rich, broad literary and cultural discourse, developed at the margins or outside university borders, and often on the Web: acknowledging it, and interacting with its interlocutors, seems nowadays a necessity for all those working on contemporary literature.

UNIVERSITY OF LEEDS   GIGLIOLA SULIS

Adamastor e dintorni: in ricordo di Antonio Tabucchi. Con un frammento inedito. Ed. by VALERIA TOCCO. Pisa: Edizioni ETS. 2013. 185 pp. £13.07. ISBN 978–88–467–3724–3.

In the year following Antonio Tabucchi's death in March 2012, a series of one-day events in his honour were held in Italian universities. This volume contains the presentations made at the Pisa event on 24 September 2012 and in Genoa on 22 March 2013, preceded by a short, previously unpublished excerpt of dialogue and an introduction by Valeria Tocco. The first section is entitled 'Pisa e la filologia', and a number of the essays here emphasize the significance of Pisa in Tabucchi's formation and the influence that his work in Portuguese Studies had on his life and career. The contributors include several former colleagues from the University of Pisa; the essays, which include many personal memories, provide an insight into the early stages of Tabucchi's academic career, as well as his interaction and collaboration with mentors, colleagues, students, and other writers (including Norman Manea and Orhan Pamuk, as outlined in Bruno Mazzoni's essay) over many decades. Valeria Bertolucci Pizzorusso summarizes Tabucchi's achievements, notes the importance of travel for Tabucchi, and, like Francesco Guazzelli, recalls a generous and hospitable friend and colleague.

Salvatore Settis eschews personal memories of Tabucchi to concentrate on 'un tema che gli fu caro, l'impegno degli intellettuali nella vita civile del nostro Paese' (p. 25). He presents Tabucchi as a shining example of a socially committed intellectual, arguing that he stood out in an Italy where this is no longer the norm.

He makes particular reference to Tabucchi's *Gli zingari e il rinascimento* (Milan: Feltrinelli, 1999), a text also highlighted in historian Giuseppe Marcocci's essay, 'Gli zingari e gli inquisitori'.

Alessandro Martinengo presents a rereading of Tabucchi's 1973 essay 'Da Adamastor a Polifemo: l'antinomia acqua/pietra in Camões e Góngora' (*Annali della Scuola Normale Superiore di Pisa, Classe di Lettere e Filosofia*, 3rd ser., 3 (1973), 581–91). Adamastor is the name of the mythical giant created by Luís de Camões; its inclusion in the title of this collection alludes to Tabucchi the Portuguese scholar, but also to Lisbon, Adamastor being an alternative name for the Miradouro de Santa Catarina in the Portuguese capital.

Remo Ceserani's essay is the first to concentrate on Tabucchi's literary output. His wide-ranging chapter concludes with a list of what he considers to be the principal themes in Tabucchi's entire corpus. Blanca Periñán's essay on Tabucchi's 'ludismo linguistico' contains detailed textual references across a very broad range of Tabucchi's texts, from the earliest to the most recent.

Thea Rimini has written an interesting article focusing on Tabucchi's work as a reviewer of Portuguese literary works for the newspapers *Il Corriere della Sera* and *La Repubblica*. Rimini considers Tabucchi's parallel roles as 'lusitanista accademico' and 'lusitanista quotidiano' (p. 85), and analyses how he brought his scholarly eye, philological training, and academic rigour to bear in his newspaper reviews, arguing that his narrative and his journalistic writings are 'strettamente legate l'una all'altra' (p. 94).

The second section of the book is entitled 'Genova per lui'. In contrast to the articles from the day in Pisa, the six essays in this section are less personal and focus on different aspects of Tabucchi's writing. Giorgio Bertone draws up a list of five essential elements which for him characterize Tabucchi's work, paying particular attention to the political dimension in Tabucchi's writing and also to the question of identity. Luigi Surdich, on the other hand, suggests that Tabucchi's texts are linked by 'inquietudine'. Francesco De Nicola's article looks at the links between *Il filo dell'orizzonte* (Milan: Feltrinelli, 1988) and *La testa perduta di Damasceno Monteiro* (Milan: Feltrinelli, 1997), and examines the portrayal of journalists in these two *gialli*, while Silvia Zangrandi explores the fantastic in Tabucchi's texts. Surprisingly, given the title of this collection and the fact that it is published in the Oficina Lusitana series, Roberto Francavilla's contribution is one of very few essays which really foreground the importance of Portugal and all things Portuguese in Tabucchi's texts. Francavilla describes Pessoa as a 'crocevia' (p. 161) through which one must pass on any journey to decipher Tabucchi. In the final essay, Eugenio Buonaccorsi examines the importance of theatre for Tabucchi, claiming that this has seldom been given due recognition.

The retrospective nature of the essays in this collection has allowed contributors to survey the entire corpus of Tabucchi's writing, leading to useful comparisons between earlier and later works and allowing them to trace the development of themes over a long period. In her introduction to this volume Tocco states that the aim of the project was to organize 'una serie di iniziative che non si limitasse a un omaggio circostanziale, ma che toccasse le molte corde dell'universo intellettuale tabucchiano' (p. 15). In this I think that the volume is successful. The diverse contributions underline the breadth of Antonio Tabucchi's interests and the comprehensive nature of his appeal to, and engagement with, those working in many disciplines.

UNIVERSITY COLLEGE CORK   LOUISE SHEEHAN

Gothic Terrors: Incarceration, Duplication and Bloodlust in Spanish Narrative. By
    ABIGAIL LEE SIX. Lewisburg: Bucknell University Press. 2010. 184 pp. £35.
    ISBN 978–0–8387–5747–5.

Gothic Terrors is a short book that does not attempt to trace a comprehensive history of the influence of Gothic fiction on Spanish writers. Instead, Abigail Lee Six proposes to illuminate Gothic studies through an analysis of a selection of Spanish novels covering the nineteenth century up to the contemporary period. The authors covered include Galdós, Pardo Bazán, Unamuno, Cela, García Morales, Espido Freire, and García Sánchez. The approach taken across each chapter is thematic rather than chronological, which limits a discussion of the broader social, historical, and cultural anxieties latent within the Gothic genre. The three chapters cover the themes of incarceration, duplication, and bloodlust, which Lee Six views as key features of Gothic fiction from its inception.

The methodological intention of this study is to open up Spanish fiction to the Gothic mode in order to trace features of this genre across a variety of texts. Lee Six's intention in writing the book is 'to contribute to a fuller appreciation of the Gothic presence lurking in the shadows of Spanish realism, naturalism, *noventayochismo*, *tremendismo*, fantasy, and historical fiction' (p. 19). However, as Lee Six herself attests, the Gothic is such a fluid genre that it proves hard to define it within a series of clear reference-points. One may even go so far as to ask whether the Gothic novel in fact represents a subgenre of the psychological novel, given its propensity to explore, quoting Punter, 'the dark imagination' (p. 17), which is nothing other than the deeper recesses of the individual and collective unconscious. Across each of the chapters, it is often this dark imagination that Lee Six notes in her analysis, rather than clear evidence of the Gothic. Gothic traces are therefore sometimes confused with the deeper themes that run through the work of the Spanish novels and plays under discussion. For example, Rosario's confinement and apparent madness in *Doña Perfecta* does, as Lee Six observes, represent Galdós's empathic understanding of 'the psychological problems created for women by prevailing gender stereotypes' (p. 34), but it is still not clear how the Gothic mode illuminates this theme. Similarly, Gothic thematics are discussed in relation to Unamuno's *Nada menos que todo un hombre*; yet Unamuno's concerns with fears surrounding what constitutes an individual's sense of self are not unique to the Gothic genre. Whether or not the Gothic mode facilitates a greater understanding of the deeper ontological themes in Unamuno's fiction remains moot. The reader is therefore left questioning, on occasion, what it is specifically about

Gothic fiction that illuminates the central themes in the texts under discussion. One wonders whether the bloodlust found in Cela's *La familia de Pascual Duarte* can be usefully expanded upon through a Gothic lens or whether Pascual's act of matricide points to a deeper fear of the maternal figure that exists across a variety of Spanish novels from this period.

Thus, what might have been foregrounded more forcefully is a discussion of the relationship between the Gothic and wider cultural anxieties over identity, gender, and historical change that afflicted Spain from the nineteenth century onwards. When the discussion moves in such a direction, this is where Lee Six's analysis affords a deep insight into the psychological dimension of Gothic fiction and its capacity to reveal a deeper societal unease with historical changes. *Gothic Terrors* therefore leaves the reader searching for further insights into the Gothic genre in Spain. This may indeed be fertile ground, especially when it comes to exploring the relationship between the Spanish novel and its capacity to reflect the recesses of the human psyche—Punter's 'dark imagination' again—as well as the realms of gender and ontological freedom.

University of Bristol										Caragh Wells

Isabel Allende's 'House of the Spirits' Trilogy: Narrative Geographies. By Karen
	Wooley Martin. (Colección Támesis, Serie A: Monografías, 285) Wood-
	bridge: Tamesis. 2010. 194 pp. £50. ISBN 978–1–85566–200–1.

This volume offers a 'geographically-rooted reading' of the trilogy formed by *La casa de los espíritus* (1982), *Hija de la fortuna* (1999), and *Retrato en sepia* (2000), a focus justified by the lack of critical attention to date to the coherence of the trilogy from a strictly geographical perspective. The first chapter, 'Roots and Routes to Utopia: Imagined Geographies in Isabel Allende's Fictional Universe', seeks to defend Allende against her detractors (including Jean Franco) and identifies the novels' common themes, techniques, and characters. Chapter 2, 'Literary Geographies, Borderlands and the Boundaries of Identity', is theoretical, drawing on the works of both cultural geographers and literary critics, with the emphasis on the political implications of space: 'geographics' recognizes that identity is 'dynamic and multi-axial, rather than fixed and easily defined' (p. 34). Particular attention is given to characters' movements through various points of cultural collision, while Foucault's notion of heterotopia is used to signify a 'place of otherness' (p. 36), richly represented in the trilogy by the brothel, the colony, and the boat. Lefebvre's self-declared position as 'the outsider who purposefully chooses to remain out-side' (p. 41) parallels Allende's, while the trilogy's geographic trajectory reflects the author's 'personal spatial displacements and re-anchorings' (p. 43). Chapter 3, 'Mapping Ethnicity: Race, Class and Mobility in the Trilogy's New Narratives', focuses on the contestation of socio-ethnic, socio-political, and socio-sexual boundaries. The domestic space is shaped by architectural styles that demarcate the class divisions between family members and servants. Some characters, notably Eliza Sommers (*Hija de la fortuna*), defy clear categorization in terms of class and race, being located between cultures and leading 'unhomely' lives. Allende inverts racism, presenting it from the perspective of an ethnic minority which fears white brutality (p. 61). Characters such as Eliza and Tao Chi'en become cultural chameleons, adept at mimicking the appropriate codes in line with the cultural context of the moment. Chapter 4 focuses on *La casa de los espíritus*, which 'recentres Chilean history from female and/or minority vantage points' (p. 81) and considers domestic space under Clara's influence. The jubilation attending Allende's victory is tarnished by the continuing invisibility of the indigenous Spanish American, the conclusion noting that writing seems to be the only protected space for the marginalized. Chapter 5 considers gendered spaces and border crossings, emphasizing the importance that Allende attaches to female sexual autonomy in the light of the patriarchal Esteban Trueba's predatory sexual instincts that convert rural space into a site of danger for women. His own power is compromised by the appropriation of his house by his granddaughter Alba and her boyfriend Miguel. Marginalized figures such as homosexuals and prostitutes play a central role in an 'alternative space' (p. 140). Chapter 6 considers 'Transcendent Spaces', i.e. writing and photography. Here, writing as resistance in *La casa* is analysed both as an act of self-preservation for Alba and also as testimony to the horrors perpetrated by the military regime. The novel offers a 'woman-centred version of twentieth-century Chilean history' (p. 150). Portraits, photographs, and daguerreotypes are the trilogy's primary means of protecting the genealogical continuity of the families it represents. The conclusion attempts to defend Allende against charges of naivety and disingenuousness but is not sufficiently incisive or convincing: 'despite the negativity of the world [. . .] the author insists on imparting a hopeful and optimistic message throughout her writings' (p. 173).

The relatively narrow scope of the argument gives rise to repetitiveness, sometimes perhaps understandable, but the partial duplication of critical quotations (for example p. 148, p. 171) is less so, as is the almost routine derivativeness of many other critical references: for example, the quotation from Foucault (p. 129) is referenced as 'qtd. in Grosz 146'. Negative criticism of Allende is mentioned in general terms but usually without identifying individual critics and without engaging meaningfully with their perspectives. Deleuzian concepts are suggested, e.g. in relation to the urban space (p. 143), but the associated theories (such as that relating to smooth and striated space) are not incorporated into the argument. There is a tendency towards generalized assertion—'Allende's tremendous voice and power as cultural critic' (p. 23)—that goes hand in hand with a failure to acknowledge widely perceived weaknesses, such as the portrayal of the coup d'état in *La casa*, that is claimed—without further elaboration—to have 'artistic merit' (p. 82). There are some notable omissions in the bibliography, such as Susan Frenk ('The Wandering Text: Situating the Narratives of Isabel Allende', in *Latin American Women's Writing: Feminist Readings in Theory and Crisis*, ed. by Anny Brooksbank Jones and Catherine Davies (Oxford: Clarendon Press, 1996), pp. 66–84). On the positive side, the work maintains a clear focus throughout and succeeds in filling a gap in Allende criticism by approaching the trilogy from a geographical perspective.

SWANSEA UNIVERSITY   LLOYD HUGHES DAVIES

The Cambridge Companion to Gabriel García Márquez. Ed. by PHILIP SWAN-
   SON. Cambridge: Cambridge University Press. 2010. xii+206 pp. £19.99.
   ISBN 978-0-521-68710-2.

This volume comprises twelve chapters that cover not only the author's creative writing but also his journalism and the cinematic productions based on his work. Following Philip Swanson's lively introduction, the first chapter, 'Gabriel García Márquez: Life and Times', by Gene H. Bell-Villada, discusses the composition of *One Hundred Years of Solitude*, the writer's move to Spain, and the publication of *The Autumn of the Patriarch*, arguably *the* novel of the Latin American dictator-ship. Donald Shaw, 'The Critical Reception of García Márquez', charts the major landmarks, among them Josefina Ludmer's *Cien años de soledad: una interpretación* (1972), still 'the most illuminating book of its kind on García Márquez' (p. 32), while Robin Fiddian considers the early novels *Leaf Storm, No One Writes to the Colonel*, and *In Evil Hour*.

   In Chapter 4, on *One Hundred Years of Solitude*, Swanson discusses the signi-ficance of the calling into question—in the text's final chapter—of the historical status of the banana strike, which 'casts the entire narrative in a state of existential uncertainty' (p. 60). The pervasive incest themes are rich in conflicting associations, both negative and positive: the reader is obliged to adopt an active role in the face of the 'tantalising mix of possible readings' (p. 62). In Chapter 5, Raymond L. Williams offers an eco-critical reading of *One Hundred Years*. Among Colombian precursors, he notes the contrasting works of Jorge Isaacs's *María* (1867) and José Eustasio Rivera's *La vorágine* (1924), and emphasizes, like Swanson, García Már-quez's elusiveness and complexity. Steven Boldy, on *The Autumn of the Patriarch*, shows that the Patriarch is based on dictators mainly from Central America and the Caribbean from the late nineteenth century to about 1960. Boldy highlights links with other texts and draws attention to the repetitive style. He refers to Fuentes, who sees language as being at the root of both literature and power: 'what serves to free us also serves to subjugate us' (p. 90).

   Describing *The General in his Labyrinth* (Chapter 7) as the culmination of García Márquez's career as a writer, Gerald Martin identifies its main themes as solitude, power, and death. He highlights the affinity that García Marquez felt for Bolívar: although his aim was to demystify him, some critics claim that he actually re-mythologized him. In Chapter 8 Mark I. Millington looks at García Márquez's novels of love, highlighting marriage as usually loveless and often associated with suffering. Millington does not avoid engaging with the problematic aspects of Florentino's relationships, notably that with the adolescent América Vicuña: moral issues, says Millington, are covered over with 'deft phrases and witty invention' (p. 120). In his chapter on the short stories, Stephen Hart identifies five features that are all present in those works that represent García Márquez at the height of his imaginative powers: magical realism; fragmented time; punchy dialogue; humour; and allegory. 'The Incredible and Sad Tale of Innocent Eréndira and her Heartless Grandmother' brings together all five traits: the wider implications of indebtedness and prostitution as well as of Eréndira's escape are traced persuasively.

In Chapter 10, Robert L. Sims focuses on García Márquez's non-fiction works, considering the *refrito* or follow-up story that 'provides information discovered or events happening after the publication of the original story' (p. 144). He notes that García Márquez consistently confronts the 'official' version of events. His subversiveness 'aims directly at *how an event occurred* and never at *what happened* [. . .]. The *refrito* affords him the opportunity to liberate the human context' (p. 147). Sims identifies *Living to Tell the Tale* (2003) as a hybrid text that belongs to the realm of *felt history*, refusing to be confined within chronological, official history. In Chapter 11, Claire Taylor discusses García Márquez and film, noting that the writer himself pointed to the limitations of cinema when confronted with the 'magic of the words' (p. 165). In the final chapter, 'García Marquez, Magical Realism and World Literature', Michael Bell characterizes García Márquez as essentially a self-conscious writer of historical reality. He distinguishes between *lo real maravilloso* that refers to a *reality* and 'magical realism' that refers to a literary *mode* (p. 183): the post-*One Hundred Years of Solitude* novels 'are not magical but they are highly, and consciously, literary' (p. 186).

These essays provide an engagingly diverse and lively overview of García Márquez's œuvre, not only offering many new insights into the major texts but also examining the less studied non-fictional works and cinematic adaptations. A theme that might have merited further treatment is the writer's legacy and his reception in and impact upon Europe. In relation to García Márquez, Moretti claims that 'for the first time in modern history, the centre of gravity of formal creation leaves Europe' (Franco Moretti, *Modern Epic: The World System from Goethe to García Márquez* (London and New York: Verso), p. 233). Some reflections on this subject would have contributed yet another dimension to a rich and multifaceted collection of essays.

SWANSEA UNIVERSITY   LLOYD HUGHES DAVIES

Contrastive Register Variation: A Quantitative Approach to the Comparison of English and German. By STELLA NEUMANN. (Trends in Linguistics, 251) Berlin and New York: de Gruyter. 2013. xx+361 pp. €99.95; $140. ISBN 978–3–11–023859–4.

In this monograph Stella Neumann embarks on an ambitious corpus-driven study of eight registers (domains of language use, which in this study include fiction, political essays, instructional manuals, popular science articles, letters by CEOs to their shareholders, promotional tourism texts, and websites) in English and German. She examines three dimensions of variation: between registers, between English and German, and between original texts and their translations into either

English or German. The theoretical framework of Hallidayan Systemic Functional Linguistics is combined with Corpus Linguistics and a battery of statistical tests to examine the extent of linguistic variation within and between the eight English and German registers, and between translations and source texts.

After an overview in Chapter 1, Neumann discusses the theory and methodology underlying her study in Chapters 2–4. In Chapter 5 the CroCo corpus—the corpus of English and German texts and translations from which Neumann draws her data (http://fr46.uni-saarland.de/croco/index_en.html)—is described in detail. The actual analysis of texts begins in Chapter 6, in which Neumann examines English-only texts for linguistic features of register variation. The same is done for German in Chapter 7, and the two languages are compared in Chapter 8. The differences between translations and their source texts are discussed in Chapter 9. Neumann synthesizes her findings in Chapter 10 and provides some concluding remarks in Chapter 11.

Neumann's book provides an excellent overview of salient linguistic features of different registers in English and German, and what the actual social or interpersonal function of these features may be. For example, she finds that the presence or absence of epistemic modal lexis—modal verbs (*must/müssen*) and adverbs (*possibly/vielleicht*) indicating high and low degrees of speaker or writer certainty concerning their assertions—goes hand in hand with how much writer authority is to be conveyed. Tourism texts and instructional manuals, owing to their informative nature, display high degrees of writer authority, and therefore contain significantly fewer markers of epistemic modality than registers where authors wish to hedge their assertions, such as in popular scientific writing. She also finds that translations are often 'bleached' (p. 282) from the source texts, meaning that the prevalence of certain linguistic features in the original is not always as strong in the translations because of a number of linguistic and socio-cultural factors involved in the translation process.

Much of the detailed analysis provided in Chapters 8–11 focuses on only two registers, fictional texts and CEO letters. This is partly because the extensive CroCo corpus requires Neumann to concentrate on only a few registers for a meaningful discussion. Hence the reader is left with a fraction of the possible analyses available for the eight registers in the corpus. On the plus side, this provides many opportunities for future research agendas. In spite of this limitation, Neumann's work is at the cutting edge because it combines advances in Corpus Linguistics and quantitative statistical methods with the qualitative analytic framework provided by Systemic Functional Linguistics to examine not only register variation, but translation techniques as well. So it is worth a read for those interested in contrastive English–German linguistics, register variation, and Translation Studies.

University of Nottingham   Richard J. Whitt

Pragmatischer Standard. Ed. by Jörg Hagemann, Wolf Peter Klein, and Sven
    Staffeldt. (Stauffenburg Linguistik, 73) Tübingen: Stauffenburg. 2013.
    343 pp. €49.80. ISBN 978-3-86057-118-7.

While the general concept of a German standard language, promoted by grammarians since at least the seventeenth century, is a well-researched aspect of the
recent history of German, the field of the pragmatics of the German language has
largely been disregarded in this context. The book reviewed here addresses this
gap, arguing that the term 'pragmatic standard' is itself a useful one and can be
understood in different ways, either as a standard of spoken (as opposed to written)
language use, or as a standard that calls for description on the level of linguistic
action and behaviour (p. 3). These interpretations are not necessarily mutually
exclusive, and both are studied here. The volume concentrates on two main topics:
constructions—typical for, as well as widespread and accepted in, spoken language;
and linguistic behaviours—typical for, as well as widespread and accepted in, certain communicative situations, such as those that can be characterized by the use
of a standard language (see pp. 3–4).

    The book derives from papers presented at a conference held in Würzburg in
2012 and consists of twenty-one chapters, grouped into three main areas. Following an introduction, Chapters 2 to 10 look into general difficulties encountered
in finding and defining pragmatic standards. While it is argued by some that a
clear concept of the standard language is necessary as a point of comparison,
especially for teaching German, a clear codex listing the variants that belong to this
standard language is seen as problematic since it might lead to the stigmatization
of certain variants and discrimination against their users. Spoken standard German can therefore be reconstructed only from a 'Gebrauchsstandard', i.e. actual
spoken language usage, rather than any codified norms found in grammars and
dictionaries. That spoken language contains inconsistency and incompleteness is
shown in various contributions, and these two factors result in the acceptance of
constructions in spoken language that are considered 'wrong' in written language.
Indeed, it is argued that every construction different from other standards can potentially be a pragmatic standard and that everything not noticed as deviant from
the standard, or, if noticed, not judged negatively, can become a standard variant,
also in the written language. That the use of standard versus non-standard German
can influence the production of a particular linguistic action (such as apologies) is
demonstrated in particular by Sven Staffeldt's experimental study.

    While all the chapters in the first section contribute to the understanding of
the theory and methodology behind the term 'pragmatic standard', the subsequent
chapters treat individual case studies, including the use of particular constructions,
such as the 'x-and-x construction', the stigmatized construction '*sein*$_{\text{PRÄT}}$+*gewesen*',
'*dass*-constructions', the '*ja nein* construction', and the combination of *an*-particle
verbs with a *gegen*-prepositional phrase, and it is concluded that these constructions would all form part of a pragmatic standard: some of them even express
ideas that would not be conveyed by their written-standard equivalents. Other

contributions analyse spontaneous, informal language, particular text types (such as newspaper dating advertisements), and the acquisition of complex constructions by children. The analysis of these constructions and forms of language reveals a more complex, varied, and dynamic picture of the German language than standard grammars would suggest (p. 227). Furthermore, it demonstrates that 'spoken language' is a heterogeneous category: that is, a single 'spoken language' cannot exist and is an abstract concept (p. 194). Any confinement of linguistic reality to a single standard variety, therefore, runs the risk of ignoring these variations, and the language would thus lose its dynamic character (p. 237).

Whereas the contributions of the second sections focus on particular case studies, the last three chapters investigate the educational potential and reality of a pragmatic standard more generally. These essays demonstrate that 'German German' (as opposed to 'Austrian and Swiss German') dominates in German textbooks used in the Czech Republic, and that not only textbooks but also language teachers themselves play a crucial role in the process of forming a particular language norm. It is argued that students should be made aware not only of the pluricentric nature of German (p. 314) but also of the characteristics of spoken and written language in order to reduce 'mistakes' in written texts, usages that would not be perceived as 'mistakes' in spoken language. For students, a defined spoken standard would act as a point of orientation between the spoken dialect/sociolect and the demanded standard language in written texts (p. 336).

Pragmatischer Standard undoubtedly generates sufficient conceptual interest in addition to detailed case studies of a pragmatic standard to close a major research gap and to spark further discussions of the subject (a concluding or summary chapter by the editors would have been very useful in articulating precisely what the volume's major gains have been). It would be interesting to test to what extent the theoretical concepts of a pragmatic standard developed in this book can readily be applied to other standardized languages. The volume offers a significant contribution to our understanding of the *actual* norms of standard languages and can be thoroughly recommended to anyone interested in the establishment of any spoken standard language, in particular constructions, and/or in the use of pragmatic standards in (foreign) language-teaching.

UNIVERSITY OF BRISTOL   ANNA HAVINGA

'Das Nibelungenlied' und 'Die Klage', nach der Handschrift 857 der Stiftsbibliothek St. Gallen. Ed. with modern German translation and commentary by JOACHIM HEINZLE. (Bibliothek des Mittelalters, 12) Berlin: Deutscher Klassiker Verlag. 2013. 1750 pp. €148 (leather €248). ISBN 978–3–618–66120–7 (leather 978–3–618–66125–2).

The *Nibelungenlied* is perhaps the archetypal medieval German text in the popular imagination. What has not been at all obvious to the non-specialist, however, is the textual context of which it was a part in its own time; in academic teaching and research, too, it is all too often presented in isolation. This new edition should go a long way to changing that: for the first time in its modern editorial history, the *Nibelungenlied* can now be read in a single volume together with the *Klage*, alongside which it is transmitted in all but one of its complete manuscripts.

The *Klage* is in the first instance a continuation of events in the *Nibelungenlied*. The apparent finality of the latter's monumental tale of love, betrayal, and revenge appears in a very different light when one is aware that the cataclysm at its end actually provided the beginning for a 'new' story. The *Klage* relates the 'clean-up operation' on the battlefield in Etzelburg, describes how news of events reached the outside world, and presents a glimmer of hope for the future when the son of Brünhild and Gunther is crowned king, bringing the court in Worms 'ein teil in vreude' (l. 4099: 'a little joy'). As well as the narrative span that takes shape through the juxtaposition of the two works, aspects of their wider literary-historical setting become clearer than would otherwise be the case. In a classroom setting in particular, the crucial links with oral and written literary culture can be illustrated with reference to the contrast between the archaic strophic form of the *Nibelungenlied* and the courtly rhyming couplets of the *Klage*, or to the account in the epilogue of the *Klage* about how events in Etzelburg found their way into the written medium.

Joachim Heinzle's edition of the *Nibelungenlied* and *Klage* is based on MS B. The text, parallel translation, and commentary bring together an outstanding set of resources in a single volume. Thus, for instance, the passage from the *Klage* quoted above is translated as 'große Freude', but the commentary notes the alternative given here, so the litotes reading is not forced upon the reader. Only in the introductory remarks on pp. 989–1035 might more detail have been desirable. The decision as to which version of the *Nibelungenlied* to present, for example, is set out as a matter of choosing between *B and *C: 'Für die vorliegende Ausgabe, die ein breiteres Publikum erreichen möchte, mußte ich mich für eine dieser beiden Versionen entscheiden. Andere Textformen sind nach dem Stand der Dinge nur für die Spezialforschung von Interesse. (Das gilt auch für die Fassung *A [. . .].)' (p. 1026). It might have been helpful for such a 'wider audience' if more had been said about the distinguishing features of all three main versions of the *Nibelungenlied* before summarily dismissing one of them. Likewise, the introductory material tends to be largely 'traditional' in nature. This is not meant in a pejorative sense—such topics as the circumstances of composition, historical foundations, and Scandinavian analogues are all important. Nonetheless, the non-specialist reader might have welcomed a brief guide to further themes and issues that are raised by these works, such as the literary presentation of space, the configuration of gender roles, or the role of visuality and the body in the social worlds they depict. This could also have provided a conceptual framework for seeing the *Nibelungenlied* and *Klage* together in thematic as well as textual terms—the dominance of the former in the introductory discussion seems at times almost to perpetuate the very exclusivity that the printing of the two works together so rightly calls into question.

At the same time, it is easy to criticize a book on the basis of what it does not do. It should therefore be said very clearly that this new edition is significant, timely, and unrivalled in its exposition of textual detail. It will also provide an invaluable new impetus to research on the *Klage* in particular. One criticism that is less easy to qualify, though, is the cost of the book in its current format. The aim of reaching 'a wider audience' stands at odds with a price tag that will in most cases be prohibitive to the general public, to students, and to those academics who do not have access to a substantial spending allowance. A number of volumes in this prestigious series have gone on to be published in an affordable paperback format, and it is very much to be hoped that this one follows them.

OXFORD   ALASTAIR MATTHEWS

Nibelungenlied und Nibelungensage: Kommentierte Bibliographie 1945–2010. Ed. by FLORIAN KRAGL with ELISABETH MARTSCHINI, KATHARINA BÜSEL, and ALEXANDER HÖDLMOSER. Berlin: Akademie Verlag. 2012. xiv+830 pp. €198. ISBN 978–3–05–005842–9.

This annotated bibliography is an extremely useful reference work, both for students of the *Nibelungenlied* and for scholars working in the field. The bibliography, which aims at comprehensive coverage, provides a (very short) summary of every publication in the designated period. These abstracts seek to convey the essence of the argument and are not in any way evaluative. There is also relatively little difference in the length of abstracts, regardless of whether the publication in question is a short article or a major monograph such as Jan-Dirk Müller's *Spielregeln für den Untergang* (Tübingen: Niemeyer, 1998). While there are some advantages to this scrupulous objectivity, it also means that this bibliography does not provide very much guidance as to the quality and impact of a particular publication—although the provision of references to book reviews (in the case of monographs) does something to redress this.

   The real value of this work lies in the indexes, which enable the reader to search by modern author, medieval author, literary character, keyword, individual strophe or *aventiure*, and manuscript. The range of keywords is particularly well chosen, including many terms relating to literary theory as well as to more concrete items. Under 'T', for example, one will find entries for 'Textimmanenz' and 'Textstringenz', as well as for the more predictable 'Tarnkappe', 'Textilien', and 'Teufel'. Overall, this is a very welcome resource for medieval German studies.

ORIEL COLLEGE, OXFORD   ANNETTE VOLFING

A Ruler's Consort in Early Modern Germany: Aemilia Juliana of Schwarzburg-Rudolstadt. By JUDITH P. AIKIN. Farnham: Ashgate. 2014. xvi+238 pp.; 30 ills. £60. ISBN 978–1–4724–2384–9.

This is a remarkable book about a remarkable seventeenth-century woman. As the author of two hymns still to be found in the Lutheran hymnal, one of which formed the basis for several of Bach's cantatas after her death, Aemilia Juliana, Countess of Schwarzburg-Rudolstadt (1637–1706), has never quite faded from view. This book demonstrates the breadth of her achievements.

Through the accident of her brother's death, Aemilia Juliana, born Countess of Barby, became an heiress and so was able to make a good marriage in 1665 to her cousin, Albert Anton of Schwarzburg-Rudolstadt. She became pregnant just twice, one of these children being a male heir who lived to succeed his father. Having done her dynastic duty, she was then able to educate her young son, run a household of 152 persons, work in the still room, make preserves and jellies, manage the home farms, vegetable gardens, and orchards, entertain guests, and refurbish the 153-room palace of Heidecksburg. She also ran the estate of Cumbach, which Albert Anton had given her on their tenth wedding anniversary, and added to her holdings of land over the years.

All the while she was writing devotional songs and prayers and composing thousands of letters to a wide range of correspondents. She is the author of some 700 devotional song texts, many of which appeared during her lifetime in one or other of her fourteen published collections. Around a hundred of them were in constant use for several centuries after her death. Judith P. Aikin has unearthed another 58 unpublished songs, several manuscript books of pharmaceutical and culinary recipes, and 430 letters. Then there was her active patronage of building and decorating projects, of writers, dramatists, artists, and musicians. She commissioned artists to decorate the palace and to provide engraved frontispieces for her own books, she worked with the dramatist Caspar Stieler (1632–1707) to create theatrical entertainments for various celebrations at court, and with the court Kapellmeister Philip Erlebach (1657–1714) to arrange musical performances, both sacred and secular.

Aikin shows how, while Albert Anton was busy with military matters, with dispensing justice, with hunting and horse-breeding, Aemilia Juliana was not only consoling their subjects with her hymns and prayers, she was also giving them practical help—feeding the hungry, dispensing medicine to the sick, improving the schools, and boosting local industries such as forestry, mining, milling, and potting. She functioned as her husband's partner in all these activities. Aikin also demonstrates Aemilia Juliana's sympathy for, advocacy on behalf of, and practical help to other women, particularly widows. She was the author of a book of devotional songs and prayers to be used by pregnant and birthing women, by midwives and wet nurses: *Geistliches Weiber-Aqua-Vit* (Rudolstadt: Fleischer, 1683). We can safely say that she never drew a breath or completed an action that was not accompanied by prayer and by devotional song. It is therefore no surprise that she 'thoroughly planned her deathbed behaviour and words, as well as her funeral, her sarcophagus, and her epitaph' (p. 188). She died an exemplary Lutheran death, just as she had lived an exemplary Lutheran life.

It is rare to get such a complete and rounded picture of the life of an early modern consort, still less one of someone for whom written communication was so important and who has left so much source material. Aikin has done her subject proud. Every page bears witness to her thorough and painstaking research, to her wide contextual reading, and to the clarity of her style. In addition, the book is helpfully illustrated with portraits, frontispieces of Aemilia Juliana's publications, photographs of relevant places, reproductions of the decorations for her funeral, a dynastic table, and a map. In short, this monograph is a worthy monument to its subject.

University of Oxford   Helen Watanabe-O'Kelly

Ferdinand Raimund: Sämtliche Werke — Historisch-kritische Ausgabe, vol. 1: *Der Barometermacher auf der Zauberinsel; Der Diamant des Geisterkönigs*. Ed. by Jürgen Hein and Walter Obermaier. Vienna: Deuticke. 2013. 624 pp. €39.90. ISBN 978–3–552–06176–7.

This edition of Ferdinand Raimund's first two plays is the first of five volumes that will make up the first critical edition to appear since the work of Fritz Brukner and Eduard Castle in the 1920s and 1930s. Four volumes will each contain two of the eight plays and a fifth will present Raimund's poems, letters, and other texts.

The edition offers an impressive array of critical apparatus, with extensive details on manuscripts, sources, corrections, and variant readings, and on the plays' reception. Dialect and local references are explained; there is a brief survey of modern criticism and an extensive bibliography; and the chapters on music by Dagmar Zumbusch-Beisteiner provide all textual aspects of the score for the plays, although full reproduction of the music was rejected for reasons of cost. The account of the genesis of the plays is based on statements by Raimund and his acquaintances and fellow dramatists, and also includes the full text of the stories that formed key sources for the plays. In the case of *Der Diamant des Geisterkönigs* the editors argue (pp. 385–91) that Raimund drew more fully on his sources than was acknowledged by Brukner and Castle, who were concerned to emphasize Raimund's originality. The sections on the plays' reception are particularly useful in the range and completeness of the material provided. Compared with the Brukner–Castle edition, the ordering of contemporary reviews is predominantly chronological, there are more reviews of later performances, and in particular the reviews are reproduced in full; in the earlier edition it was not always possible to see how the extracts related to the review as a whole, as omissions were indicated only in the middle but not at the beginning and end. Although the sections omitted in Brukner–Castle were often plot summaries, there were also substantive comments on themes or on an actor's performance, and some reviews were given in an extremely truncated form. Among the new material provided, Karl von Holtei's discussion of Raimund's guest performance in Berlin in 1832 is valuable, and also the diary entries of Matthias Franz Perth, a government accountant and keen theatregoer, whose comments provide a useful contrast to those of Raimund's friend Costenoble.

Whereas Brukner and Castle drew on the revised text of the first performance of the plays, this new edition reproduces the first manuscript in Raimund's own hand; only with the first scene and five later scenes in Act I of *Der Barometer auf der Zauberinsel* is a later theatre script used to fill gaps. The text of *Barometer* is longer or more repetitive than later versions, especially noticeable in Quecksilber's opening monologue (I. 2) or Zoraide's first attempts to steal the talismans (I. 12), but also somewhat more crude, as in Zoraide's verbal attack on Linda (I. 13) or Quecksilber's language throughout the play. In the original manuscript of *Der Diamant des Geisterkönigs* the land visited by Eduard and Florian is 'das Land der Sittsamkeit' (or 'Sittlichkeit'), not the land of truth, and its ruler and his daughter are Modestius and Sidi. The changes undoubtedly anticipate likely problems with the censor (p. 512), as does the drastic pruning both of the ruler's demands that his subjects mimic his emotions and of Amine's long list of her supposed crimes (II. 15–16). Overall the original text is longer than the later scripts but lacks Florian's aria in praise of Mariandl (II. 5) and his later quodlibet (II. 14).

The overriding aim of remaining faithful to the earliest manuscript (pp. 147, 151), in line with the recent edition of the works of Nestroy, is particularly evident in matters of spelling and punctuation, where the precise text of the original manuscript is retained, both for orthography—'vieleicht', 'Busta' (='Puszta'), 'verequentirt', 'tuschiren', 'gewieß', 'deutent', 'öfnet' (pp. 22, 24, 26, 37, 43, 61, 99)—and for the frequent confusion of accusative and dative: 'auf keinen Hahn wird nimmer ausgritten, lieber auf einen gebakenen Hendel', 'ich hab Ihnen fragen wollen, wieviel Uhr als es ist', 'wenn ich nur ihm unterzubringen wußt, auf einen Comptoir bei einen Sauerkräutler oder wo' (pp. 51, 52, 92). The proliferation of errors might well be a consequence of Raimund's relative lack of formal education (he left school at the age of fourteen), and was arguably exacerbated by the speed at which the texts were written (particularly that of *Barometermacher*, which was completed within three weeks after Meisl had been unable to provide a play for Raimund's benefit night). Certainly one has the impression that many of the original errors are mere 'Flüchtigkeitsfehler': 'Wer hat Ihnens gschafft daß Sie kommen sollen wären Sie weg geblieben', 'von verschiedne Farben', 'so giengs den Volk besser als uns', 'umöglich' (pp. 36, 62, 75, 92), or instances where the same word is repeated; indeed a number of corrections are already found in the early theatre scripts, listed under 'Lesarten'.

The editors would no doubt argue that it is not their role to adjudicate on such matters, although a different policy has been adopted with the spelling of characters' names, pronominal modes of address, 'daß' and 'das', and also with some missing or indecipherable punctuation. It is perhaps to be regretted that the list of the changes made in the theatre scripts does not indicate orthographical alterations, except when they occur within a more substantive rewriting, and ideally all variant readings and spellings might have been collated rather than being given in separate sections relating to the original manuscript and to the theatre scripts; in that way it might have been possible to establish the point at which the more standard grammar and orthography found in the first critical editions emerged.

One consequence of the editorial policy is that the new edition, with its idiosyncratic orthography, its many brackets and different typefaces, is not always the most pleasing on the eye—'[U]nd weil in das Kabinet was unser[n] alte[n] Herr[n] sein Zauberlabratorium war[,] selten wer kommt' (p. 92)—and scholars who are not concerned with the minutiae of Raimund's spelling may still choose other editions for purposes of quotation. Such reservations do not, however, detract from the significant contribution that this edition makes to research on Raimund, and the editors are to be congratulated on their dedication and attention to detail despite a few minor inconsistencies in the densely packed notes. As subsequent volumes appear, it will be interesting to see how the insistence on presenting the raw material of Raimund's work might change our perception of his later plays, with their increasing use of more weighty or serious themes.

University of Reading   Ian F. Roe

The Very Late Goethe: Self-Consciousness and the Art of Ageing. By Charlotte
  Lee. London: Legenda. 2014. x+152 pp. £45. ISBN 978-1-909662-12-4.

In a posthumously published collection of essays, *On Late Style* (London: Bloomsbury, 2006), Edward Said distinguishes between two qualities that tend to characterize the final phase of an author's output. These are clarity and serenity, on the one hand, beside disharmony and unresolvable contradictoriness on the other. It may seem inappropriate to charge Goethe with the latter type of 'catastrophic' lateness, yet nineteenth-century responses by the likes of Wolfgang Menzel and Friedrich Theodor Vischer demonstrate that the luminaries of the time were frequently unable to discern Olympian qualities in key texts such as *Wilhelm Meisters Wanderjahre* and *Faust II*.

Charlotte Lee's study has two objectives. The first is to reject the view that Goethe's *Spätwerk*, his final creative phase, began around the time of the death of Schiller. This is done by partitioning out a corpus dating from the early 1820s onwards and demarcating it from the rest of his work. Lee argues passionately for a separation of Goethe's mature writings into a 'late' and a 'very late' period. The second, more ambitious task involves putting forward a specific poetics that will bring out qualities unique to the last decade of Goethe's life. In doing so, Lee is obliged to address the conflict between order and chaos as a fundamental of his late style. The two terms that she uses most frequently, 'very-lateness' and 'self-consciousness', are neither elegant nor free of ambiguity, yet they are the key constituents of her discourse and are generally put to intelligent use within it. The term *Alterslyrik* is commonly felt to be appropriate not just because the poet reached a riper old age than most of his contemporaries, but also because it implies the summation of a continuously unfolding talent. Thus, as long as one accepts, as Lee does, that the template underlying Goethe's development takes the form of a spiral or helix reliant on the forces of 'Polarität' and 'Steigerung', it can be difficult to present his 'very late style' as a radically new type of writing.

Not one to insist on the separation of empirical and poetic reality, Lee begins with the relatively uncontroversial observation that at no other point in the poet's career was his work so evidently saturated with allusions to past experiences. This in contrast to those traditionalists who follow Erich Trunz in seeing the ageing poet concealing his true self behind symbols derived from images of Nature. Thereafter, the focus is on strategies of self-referencing, with the aim of showing that they assume supreme importance at the end of Goethe's career. In comparing the poem 'Dem aufgehenden Vollmonde' with the much earlier 'An den Mond', Lee observes not only 'greater control' but also a sense that, by virtue of being able to move in memory between the past and the present, his life still 'has meaning in the world' (pp. 30–31). Much of this must remain axiomatic, just as it appears futile to ask whether the poem 'Harzrcise im Winter' or 'Dornburg, September 1828' is more immediately autobiographical.

Within its relatively restricted scope, this study both succeeds and disappoints. Far from showing us a new Goethe, the author argues that what we see in his final phase is 'on a far grander scale' (p. 11) and 'developed much more fully' (p. 74) than what preceded it. In the 'Marienbad Elegy', we are told, the self-questioning becomes 'more severe than at almost any other point in Goethe's œuvre' (p. 25): more often than not, the difference is one of degree rather than quality. Adumbration and obfuscation do not suddenly enter the poet's toolbox in the final decade of his life; they had become well-refined techniques by the time of *Die Wahlverwandtschaften*. Ottilie's diary, the Architect's reflections, the dramatic account of the 'Nachbarskinder' could be evaluated in similar terms to Makarie's aphorisms and the seemingly distracting subplots and interpolations embedded in the later novel. And yet, the presence of manipulative strategies in earlier works does not of itself demolish the argument that the last years of Goethe's life, from around the time of his Marienbad experience onwards, should be accepted as a distinct unit. The 'fragility of what we think we know' (p. 78) does indeed become more fragile as the poet consciously approaches the term of his life. At the same time, affirmative elements continue to proliferate, defining themselves with the help of memory, as a comparison between the 'Anmutige Gegend' and 'Bergschluchten' scenes in *Faust II* reveals (p. 125); here, the author is able to strengthen her case and the textual evidence she cites throughout is useful and illuminating. The major achievement of this study is to show how simplistic it is to distinguish between clarity and chaos as two distinct types of late style. Neither will serve as an adequate descriptor of Goethe's late-late writing, which is simultaneously highly patterned and controlled, yet ultimately also inchoate and at times bafflingly lacking in transparency.

University of Kent   Osman Durrani

The German Gothic Novel in Anglo-German Perspective. By Patrick Bridgwater. (Internationale Forschungen zur Allgemeinen und Vergleichenden Literaturwissenschaft, 165) Amsterdam and New York: Rodopi. 2013. 607 pp. €130; $182. ISBN 978–90–420–3741–0.

German Gothic novels have led a strange existence on the margins of mainstream literary studies since Jane Austen's list of 'horrid' novels in *Northanger Abbey* secured their infamy among English audiences in 1817. While the anglophone discipline of Gothic Studies has generally followed Austen's lead in misrepresenting the horrific nature of works by writers such as Benedikte Naubert and Carl Grosse, Germanists have seemed loath to acknowledge the idea that Friedrich Schiller's *Der Geisterseher* was only the barely acceptable tip of an iceberg of popular literature being read while Weimar Classicism flourished. Thanks to Patrick Bridgwater's *German Gothic Novel in Anglo-German Perspective*, which brings together the diverse findings of over twenty years of his research, anglophone readers in particular now have a rich bio-bibliographical panorama of key Gothic authors that will help set this record straight in the years to come.

Bridgwater somewhat misleadingly notes in his preface that this book is the 'first full-length study of the outstanding German contributions to the Gothic canon', and its main aims are to review common misconceptions of German Gothic, and provide 'many new insights and pieces of analysis, and some changes of perspective' (p. 8). Bridgwater works on the premiss that uncovering the Gothic alter egos of canonical writers while introducing less-known writers is a way of both casting light on the literary margins of the Gothic and correcting anglophone misconceptions of German Gothic novels. In this latter aim the book is certainly successful, although specialist readers may feel as though they have heard many of these stories before. This is because the author's claim in the cover blurb to have taken account of 'all the relevant secondary material' in order to 'facilitate future research' does not quite stand up to scrutiny. Future researchers will look in vain for many of the central critical works in the field, such as those by Jörg Schönert, Christian Begemann, Hans von Trotha, Stefan Andriopoulos, and the present reviewer, and especially Dirk Sangmeister's excellent '10 Thesen zu Produktion, Rezeption und Erforschung des Schauerromans um 1800' in the *Lichtenberg Jahrbuch* (2010), which challenges some of the genealogical assumptions of Bridgwater's study (in particular relating to Goethe's role as the supposed progenitor of German Gothic). This caveat aside, the author shows himself to be so well read that even experts will find some surprising new insights here.

Part i, the weightier of the two sections of the monograph, presents a panorama of key Gothic novelists from the final third of the eighteenth century, through Romanticism, finishing with a coda on Wilhelm Meinhold, a little-known writer whose *Sidonia von Bork die Klosterhexe* (1847) enjoyed a curiously successful afterlife in Victorian Britain. Bridgwater thereby works through the evolution of the Gothic from the drama of the *Sturm und Drang*, late Enlightenment prose (Naubert, Schiller, Grosse), via the *Kunstmärchen* and night-pieces of Romanticism (Wilhelm Tieck, Bonaventura, E. T. A. Hoffmann), to late Romanticism. This also introduces the key works, contexts, and concepts of the German Gothic novel in its various forms, including historical Gothic (novels of chivalry and *Ritterdramen*), secret society novels, *Geisterseher*-type novels, and brigand novels. Readers will find the broad survey of the forms, movements, and writers of German Gothic illuminating, not least for the panorama of multiple generic codes, or 'subsets' (p. 31), such as the *Ritter-*, *Räuber-*, and *Schauerromane* that emerge here.

Part ii is more diffuse in its focus. After two chapters with a thematic or motif-related focus on secret tribunals and banditry respectively, survey chapters on Anglo-German interactions and Gothic art are followed by a section on the relationship between Gothic novels and fairy tales. Notwithstanding the difficulties of mapping the networks of translation, plagiarism, and forgery of authorship around

1800, the central interest in tracing the acts of cultural transfer between Germany and Britain must be the core component of any future study, and Bridgwater's book is a useful introduction to this complex field, although it is wrong to suggest that there is no current discourse on Anglo-German relations within the Gothic, as scholars such as Dan Hall, Silke Arnold-de Simine, Hilary Brown, and Andrew Cusack have all done sterling work in this field already and can be highly recommended.

The justification for the lengthy digressions in Part II on the so-called *Vehmgericht*, the Sicilian brigand Fra Diavolo, and on art history is not immediately apparent, interesting as they are. Neither these nor the concluding chapter on the interrelationship between Gothic and fairy tale will enable 'agreement among German critics as to what, if anything, constitutes the German Gothic novel' (p. 7), not least because the final section in particular seems unconcerned with developing a systematic answer to this question. That there are interesting links between both modes is unsurprising, given that the fairy tale is a 'Fundgrube' of intertextual traces and connections (p. 589). One longs, however, for a more rigorous, systematic consideration of how the motifs are deployed, transformed, etc. as they change genres, especially because contemporary literary criticism since Todorov distinguishes between the outright marvellous of the fairy tale and the literary fantastic (to which Gothic broadly belongs). Here, as elsewhere in the study, the lack of measured theoretical and conceptual consideration as to what constitutes the Gothic will raise questions for specialist and non-specialist readers alike.

Compared with the interpretative clarity, critical and cultural reflexivity, and theoretical ingenuity with which scholars such as David Punter, Vic Sage, and Fred Botting have established and invigorated Gothic scholarship within English Studies, the present book is likely to disappoint. Readers searching for a more systematic account of the German Gothic can look to some of the newer studies mentioned in this review, while those unfamiliar with German Gothic writing and on the lookout for a veritable goldmine of reading recommendations to correct their lack of familiarity will find this study a useful starting-point. Bridgwater's book thus plays a rather similar role to that of the spirited pioneers of English Gothic Studies such as Montague Summers and Devendra P. Varma, whose passion for the subject and breadth of reading are certainly matched by the knowledge of German texts from the so-called threshold period visible here.

St John's College, Oxford   Barry Murnane

Heinrich von Kleist: Artistic and Political Legacies. Ed. by Jeffrey L. High and Sophia Clark. Amsterdam and New York: Rodopi. 2013. 289 pp. €62. ISBN 978–90–420–3781–6.

The 2011 bicentenary of Kleist's death witnessed no shortage of cultural events, conferences, and publications accentuating Kleist's presence as a major figure in the German and European literary canon. Such commemorations, however, often leave unanswered questions about the lasting fascination with a writer's work and personality in a wider cultural framework and among a broader audience. It is precisely this that Jeffrey L. High and Sophia Clark invite contributors to address in *Heinrich von Kleist: Artistic and Political Legacies*. Based on papers delivered over the course of a succession of panels organized at the annual conference of the German Studies Association between 2007 and 2011, the essays in the volume attempt, according to High, to assay the significance of Kleist's legacy 'beyond the academic' (p. 18); they promise a 'coherent response to one of the more complicated questions that can be asked about a canonical artwork or an artist: What are the characteristics that explain the enduring relevance of the work or the author?' (p. 17).

Whether the essays do constitute a coherent whole is open to question. The editors do not aspire to full or even coverage of works or themes—of the fourteen contributions that follow High's introduction and a foreword by Seán Allan, no fewer than five, for instance, focus principally upon 'Michael Kohlhaas' and/or the theme of terrorism. This is perhaps not surprising, given both the lasting appeal of Kleist's best-known novella and the contemporary salience of the terror question. Methodologically there is also no unifying principle beyond the general umbrella concept of reception (p. 21). Instead the editors appear to have afforded individual contributors considerable latitude to pursue a wide range of approaches. These include literary influence (High and Curtis Maughan on Thomas Mann, and Tim Mehigan on Kafka); intertextuality (Friederike von Schwerin-High on Judith Hermann, Mary Helen Dupree on Ian McEwan, Markus Wilczek on Heiner Müller, and Hans Wedler on David Foster Wallace); transformations and reworkings (Jeffrey Champlin on Eichendorff, Bernd Fischer on E. L. Doctorow and Christoph Hein, Jennifer M. Hoyer on Nelly Sachs, Amy Emm on Othmar Schoeck, Hugo Wolf, Ingeborg Bachmann, and Hans Werner Henze, and Marie Isabel Schlinzig on adaptations of Kleist's suicide by Henning Boëtius, Reto Finger, and Monika Radl); and questions of identification and self-identification (Daniel Cuonz on Robert Walser and Christa Wolf, Carrie Collenberg-Gonzalez on Kleist in the reception of the Red Army Faction).

Such diversity is by no means a weakness: on the contrary, the breadth of approach allows for the emergence of an array of insights which not only extend current perspectives on aspects of Kleist's legacy in popular culture but may also provide useful orientation for subsequent work within the broad field of *Kleistrezeption*. A further striking feature, particularly in the context of the recent flood of Kleist literature, is the inclusion of contributions not only from established Kleist scholars (Allan, Fischer, and Mehigan) but also substantially from those whose expertise lies principally in other areas. The outcome is somewhat ambivalent: some analyses of Kleist's life and works lack historical and contextual precision; but, less burdened by the weight of Kleist scholarship, most readings are able to canvass the specific issue of the author's legacy more freely. To this reviewer's mind the balance tips favourably, and the contributions succeed in bringing a fresh outlook and opening a range of stimulating and distinctive perspectives. For this, the volume warrants recognition as a profitable contribution to Kleist scholarship and deserves a wide readership.

UNIVERSITY OF LUCERNE   STEVEN HOWE

'Der Schimmelreiter': Novelle von Theodor Storm. Historisch-kritische Edition. Ed. by GERD EVERSBERG with ANNE PETERSEN. (Husumer Beiträge zur Storm-Forschung, 9) Berlin: Erich Schmidt Verlag. 2014. 590 pp. €79. ISBN 978-3-503-15506-4.

The stated aim of this edition of Storm's best-known work is to provide a reliable text of the *Novelle* in accordance with current principles of genetic editing. The large amount of manuscript material that is available is deployed so as to render visible the process of the production of the text, in the narrow sense, and thereby to shed light on Storm's way of working—among other things his practice of making detailed changes at a very late stage. Largely eschewing interpretative comment, the editors modestly insist on the auxiliary character of their work, suggesting only that it might contribute to a more comprehensive understanding of the *Novelle*.

The greater part of the volume consists of three texts of similar length. In the first place there is the book publication of 1888, which—proof-read by the author—has the quality of an 'Ausgabe letzter Hand'. This is presented together with all variants and is accompanied by detailed editorial commentary; the reader can thus see the changes made to the text previously published—like the *Novellen* of Heyse and Meyer—in Rodenberg's *Deutsche Rundschau*. There follow the two principal manuscripts, the earlier and more provisional *Concept* and the *Reinschrift*, printed in parallel on opposite pages. These texts are likewise accompanied with variants and, to avoid repetition, less detailed editorial comment. The editors are at pains to treat the unpublished texts as more than stages on the way to a definitive version, and indeed are inclined almost to present them as works in their own right.

This strictly editorial matter is supplemented by a detailed account of the *Entstehungsgeschichte* in the broader sense. This provides clarification of the sources, including the correction of some widely propagated but false assumptions regarding the existence of a *Schimmelreiter* saga, as well as details of the historical and technical research undertaken by Storm and the relation of the work to his own experiences. There follows an extensive and meticulous account of the geographical, cultural, and historical setting of the *Novelle*. This reaches back to the twelfth and thirteenth centuries and brings together accounts of local customs, as well as detailed descriptions of the techniques of dyke construction and their evolution over time, and contributes to the identification of the real-life individuals who may have served as models for the fictional characters. This section—evidently a labour of love for the editors—takes us beyond what would have been available to the author, acquiring a certain independence from the primary task at hand. The impression is created that this material is directed at a readership whose interest is in other matters than state-of-the art editorial scholarship.

This is particularly so where the fictional history and topography of the *Novelle* are 'corrected' by comparison with the authentic landscape and historical fact.

Here might have been the place for more decisive interpretative intervention, for the editors are well aware that the realist Storm is concerned with the 'effect' of reality, that the landscape of the *Novelle* is a 'fictionalized landscape', and that the significance of any factual basis recedes or changes in proportion to the increase in narrative layers. No doubt Storm's departures from ascertainable fact remain consistent with the 'inner logic' of the narrative, but one would have welcomed a more explicit analysis of this inner logic. The editors nevertheless succeed in the somewhat unlikely task of allowing this additional material to acquire a distinct fascination, thus adding to the interest of a valuable and scholarly work.

UNIVERSITY OF WARWICK   JOHN OSBORNE

Hermann Bahr: Österreichischer Kritiker europäischer Avantgarden. Ed. by MAR-
    TIN ANTON MÜLLER, CLAUS PIAS, and GOTTFRIED SCHNÖDL. (Jahrbuch für
    Internationale Germanistik, 118) Bern: Peter Lang. 2014. 214 pp. €57.
    ISBN 978-3-0343-1531-9.

As the editors of this gem of a collection note in their introduction, the sesqui-
centenary of Bahr's birth in July 2013 went virtually unnoticed even among the
international community of scholars working on *fin-de-siècle* Austria. And yet there
has been very significant critical activity of late, centred on the Hermann Bahr Project at the University of Vienna. The team there is led by Claus Pias, with Martin
Anton Müller responsible for a detailed treasure-trove of a website (www.univie.
ac.at/bahr) and Gottfried Schnödl for the edition of *Kritische Schriften* projected in
twenty-three volumes—all downloadable in manageable sections as PDFs from the
Bahr site, which will also include facsimiles of the 4000 or more articles and essays
published by Bahr during a career of more than fifty years.

For this volume of ten essays on aspects of Bahr's life and non-literary writing—
including autobiography, history of art, literary history, philosophy, theatre, and
economics—the three editors have written an unapologetic introduction. They
acknowledge both Bahr's reputation throughout most of the twentieth century
(dominated by clichés such as 'Mann von Übermorgen', 'Verwandlungskünstler',
indiscriminate 'Überwinder', and 'Proteus der Moderne', p. 9), but also—since a
paradigm-shifting conference in Linz in 1998—the critical presence of 'der böse
Bahr', the reactionary, anti-Semite, and political windbag (pp. 8–9). The volume
sees Bahr not as an amorphous harbinger of new trends, but as the complex construct of the pressures and tensions of a vibrant age of cultural and technological
change, and the centre-versus-periphery tension in the subtitle, *Österreichischer
Kritiker europäischer Avantgarden*, nicely reflects the shift that the volume engenders from a focus on Vienna and the provinces to a more comprehensive
perspective. Müller's fascinating essay on *Selbstbildnis* (1923), arguably at the core
of the volume, makes the persuasive new arguments underlying this approach.
He shows how Bahr's controversial autobiography draws together material from
his own and others' works teleologically, in a narrative to justify his conversion,
concluding, 'nicht er wäre Zeitzeuge, sondern die Zeit dazu da, seine Existenz zu

bezeugen' (p. 182). On this reading, Bahr's own particular 'Ich' is far from being 'unrettbar'.

There are some fascinating discoveries presented in these essays, many facilitated by the lapse of copyright in 2005, and the last contribution, by Kurt Ifkovits, provides an informative overview of the history of the Bahr *Nachlass* as it made its way from his widow Anna Bahr-Mildenburg into the Theatre Collection of the Austrian National Library. At the other end of the volume, archival research by Gerd-Hermann Susen establishes that, despite the claims of generations of books on the turn of the century, Bahr was not one of the founders of Samuel Fischer's Freie Bühne in 1890, not even a salaried employee, but a regular freelancer. Alfred Pfabigan explores the canonically hostile relationship between Bahr and Karl Kraus, including the legal action that Bahr launched in 1901, using *Nachlass* material to come to a much more nuanced view of its genesis and of the nature of Kraus's defeat in the courts. Intriguingly, Pfabigan's scrupulous redressing of the balance between 'die Kraus ergebenen Biographen und Biographinnen' (p. 85) and an account from Bahr's perspective yields in the final paragraph to a more partisan view: 'doch [. . .] die Niederlage gegen einen inferioren Gegner [ist] der erste Schritt zum Heldentum' (p. 96).

The archives also disgorge seven letters and postcards from Hans Vaihinger to Bahr, which touch interestingly on the issue of 'das unrettbare Ich', since Bahr saw in Vaihinger's *Philosophie des Als Ob* (1911) the possibility of a condition in which 'das Ich' might be rescued; in addition, '[sie erlauben] die wichtige Rolle Vaihingers für Bahrs Weg zum Glauben nachzuvollziehen' (p. 153). Elsbeth Dangel-Pelloquin writes eloquently on the reception of Eleonore Duse and Isadora Duncan by Bahr and Hofmannsthal and on what this tells us about divergences in their conceptions of modernism; the key essay 'Dialog vom Tragischen' is treated to a subtle reading by Alfred Dunshirn encompassing classical philology, Nietzsche, and the psychology of Freud, Breuer, and Bernays to demonstrate how it incarnates a visionary theory of drama for the modern age. Space does not permit mention of every contribution, and omission here should not be taken as implicit criticism: there are no obvious weak points in this well-conceived, well-presented, and usefully indexed volume. Together with the collection that emerged from the 1998 conference, *Hermann Bahr — Mittler der europäischen Moderne: Hermann Bahr-Symposion Linz 1998* (=*Jahrbuch des Adalbert Stifter Institutes*, 5 (published in 2001)), the current volume will contribute significantly towards refocusing Bahr studies for a new generation of students and scholars.

UNIVERSITY OF BRISTOL   ROBERT VILAIN

Alfred Döblin: Eine Biographie. By WILFRIED F. SCHOELLER. Munich: Hanser. 2011. 911 pp. €34.90. ISBN 978–3–446–23769–8.

Wilfried F. Schoeller's detailed study of Döblin is a timely enterprise. The absence of a full-length biography, as well as the patchy editorial state of his works, has for a long time complicated research on him and made the acquisition of contextual understanding a protracted process. The catalogue of the centenary exhibition in Marbach (1978) and Louis Huguet's *Chronologie Albert Döblin* (in the inaccessible *Annales de l'Université d'Abidjan* for 1978) have remained important guides to his life, but are dated; Gabriele Sander's volume, *Alfred Döblin* (Stuttgart: Reclam, 2000), is invaluable, but inevitably only as comprehensive as its small format allows. With the republication of Döblin's complete works as Fischer Klassik e-books and paperbacks begun in 2013, this biography comes at an opportune moment to boost Döblin's readership outside the academy, as Schoeller sets out to do (p. 15).

Döblin stands out, even in his generation, for the diversity of his interests and concerns. Schoeller's achievement is to have placed his wide-ranging activities side by side, encouraging his readers to connect events that are easily separated in thematic studies or in the collected works. He amasses a wealth of background knowledge and of published and archival material, some (notably the memoirs of Yolla Niclas) used here for the first time. This approach works best for the periods when Döblin's writing was at its most intense and diverse: the 1920s (Chapters 3 and 4), where literary production and *Kulturpolitik* are compellingly interwoven, and his exile in France (1933-40, Chapter 5). Understanding Döblin's education and medical training is greatly facilitated by its clear narration in Chapter 1, and Chapter 2 makes a protracted and successful bid to outline Döblin's political and aesthetic attitudes around the First World War. His persistently awkward relations with his publishers are lucidly traced throughout. On the other hand, where the story is mainly one of frustration—notably, Döblin's Californian exile and the disappointments after his swift return—the danger is a lapse into chronology: subtitles such as 'Zweites Halbjahr 1947' and 'Weiter 1950' suggest that the narrative has lost its shape.

Schoeller's introduction makes much of the paradox that Döblin's works and *Nachlass* are rich in biographical information, but also confound the biographer's task: 'Von seinem Leben inszenierte [Döblin] vor allem die Verweigerung, Auskünfte darüber zu geben' (p. 13). Döblin insisted that the author keep an arm's length from the work, but repeatedly—and enticingly—reflected on his texts in print: the task of judging the connection between the works and the life is thus especially delicate here. Schoeller makes irritating factual errors (many of which were pointed out by Christina Althen and Döblin's son Stephan on literaturkritik.de in 2012). His main problem, however, is in bridging an interest in the author and the excitement of reading him. Seamless quotation, chronological stringency, and proleptic observations construct a compelling story on the one hand, but on the other they tend to fragment the discussion of the many works whose genesis was untidy, and they can obscure context as much as they clarify it (for example, the observation 'ich "las" die Bücher [. . .] wie die Flamme das Holz "liest"', p. 54, refers to *Wallenstein* and was made in 1921, not in Döblin's schooldays, and the description of 'diese sogenannten *Kleinen Schriften*', p. 93, muddies those volumes' real nature and composition). This volume is very rich in the connections it estab-

lishes and makes accessible, and it will engage anyone with an interest in Döblin; it
tends, all the same, to bring the man to life rather than his works.

UNIVERSITY OF BRISTOL   STEFFAN DAVIES

Bertolt Brecht: A Literary Life. By STEPHEN PARKER. London: Bloomsbury. 2014.
    x+689 pp. £30. ISBN 978-1-4081-5562-2.

Since Bloomsbury took over the Methuen Drama series, it has set to work in
some style. Its excellent range of publications on Bertolt Brecht in English now
includes a major new biography by Stephen Parker—the first in English since
John Fuegi's polemical, and much-criticized, 1994 publication (*The Life and Lies
of Bertolt Brecht* (London: HarperCollins)). The volume of material in the public
realm has changed substantially in the intervening years: most importantly, the
Große Berliner und Frankfurter Ausgabe—planned in the 1980s and completed in
2000—has made Brecht's correspondence, notes, dramatic fragments, and the multiple versions of his texts readily available. This vast resource has been augmented
by edited collections of archival documents, such as Brecht's notebooks from the
Weimar Republic and correspondence with his collaborators and lovers. Parker's
biography demonstrates an expert understanding both of Brecht's works and of
the most recent scholarship, and he marshals a vast wealth of detail in a lucid and
compelling narrative.

More than earlier biographers, Parker focuses on the significance of Brecht's medical history, identifying the lifelong complications that arose from his childhood
illnesses and that were not fully understood by his doctors. Untreated bacterial
pharyngitis or 'strep throat' led to the motor neural condition Sydenham's chorea
and inflammation of the heart, which escalated into chronic heart failure, complicated by renal problems. Parker traces Brecht's symptoms through accounts
by his friends and collaborators, and he shows how the young Brecht oscillated
between anxiety and exhilaration, equally conscious of his own mortality and of
his—as yet—unrecognized genius. Parker connects Brecht's medical condition to
the importance of the body in his early works and to the start of his experiments
with epic theatre, arguing that they coincided with Brecht's growing desire to gain
mastery over his body and emotions. This emphasis on emotional self-discipline
did not necessarily lead to a calm rehearsal room—on more than one occasion
rehearsals escalated into threatened or actual violence, directed against Brecht. Nor
did it lead to any restraint in Brecht's treatment of his string of lovers, which was
at times breathtakingly manipulative. Parker argues that Brecht was compulsively
contradictory, and he returns repeatedly to the image in which Caspar Neher,
Brecht's classmate and collaborator, depicted him as Hydratopyranthropos: a man
composed of water and fire, the most antithetical of elements.

Brecht's own voice comes through strongly in this biography, which places his
writing in the spotlight—from his diary entries, notes, essays, and letters through
to his plays and, particularly, his poetry. This approach enables Parker to explore
and indeed celebrate the richness of Brecht's œuvre, and to trace both his public

interventions and his more private reflections. He alerts his readers to the biographical influences in Brecht's works, from the biblical stories told by his mother and grandmother to the folk ballads and storyboards of the Augsburg fairground. Parker demonstrates how Brecht responded to the trauma of exile, and he traces the emergence of a humanist dimension in the plays of the later 1930s, while showing that Brecht would never again achieve such productivity as a writer. Brecht clearly found it harder to write in US exile and, as he had done in the early 1920s, wrote film scenarios that were repeatedly rejected by the industry, with the notable exception of *Hangmen Also Die*. When he returned to Berlin, the scene of his earlier theatrical triumphs, at the newly founded Berliner Ensemble he soon found himself having to resist attempts mounted by long-standing adversaries from the KPD and his years in exile to marginalize his productions. Parker argues that only political circumstances saved Brecht from making a Galileo-style recantation of his aesthetics, when pressure on the GDR leader Walter Ulbricht increased in June 1953.

This biography is an excellent and substantial work of scholarship, which deserves to be translated into German. Parker's achievement lies perhaps not so much in the discovery of new archival material—although there are exceptions here, such as in the section on Brecht's final illness—as in the skill with which he identifies and marshals an extraordinary wealth of detail spread across a wide range of published primary and secondary sources, from Brecht's works, his collaborators' memoirs and collections of archival documents, through to academic studies. Parker makes much of this material available to an English-language readership for the first time, and he illuminates it through his thorough knowledge and understanding of the multiple political and cultural contexts in which Brecht lived and worked, contexts as different as the Wilhelmine empire and Scandinavian exile, as Stalin's USSR and Hollywood. Readers of Brecht in English have had a long time to wait for a balanced biographical reassessment, but Parker's biography has been well worth it.

UNIVERSITY OF EDINBURGH   LAURA BRADLEY

A Companion to the Works of Max Frisch. Ed. by OLAF BERWALD. (Studies in German Literature, Linguistics, and Culture) Rochester, NY: Camden House. 2013. 256 pp. $79.80; £60. ISBN 978–1–57113–418–9.

The newest addition to the Camden House Companion series 'Studies in German Literature, Linguistics, and Culture' is one of an ever-growing number of publications within it to be devoted to Austrian and, albeit to a lesser extent, Swiss writers. Perhaps it is time to consider amending the series title to 'German-Language Literature …' to reflect this. Given the canonical status enjoyed by Max Frisch and his compatriot, friend, and fellow writer Friedrich Dürrenmatt (on whom a Companion must surely already be envisaged), this volume has been a long time coming. It enhances in particular the relatively scant English-speaking secondary literature on Frisch.

As Olaf Berwald notes in his concise and illuminating introduction, Frisch had a special relationship with, and was a frequent visitor to, the United States, so it is fitting that the fourteen essays are by established scholars from the US as well as from Europe. In addition to sketching the essays to follow, the introduction outlines Frisch's relevance for today's reader, reflects on his style, and includes a valuable short biography. Berwald's achievement is significant: working as sole editor for any volume is a major task by any standards, and in addition to the introduction and his own essay (on *Mein Name sei Gantenbein*), Berwald has translated six of the essays into English.

The volume as a whole offers the reader a well-rounded picture of Frisch's works, their literary context and influences, and thematic affinities with the works of other writers. The first five essays discuss Frisch's works for the theatre, while the remaining nine deal with his prose works. As with any multi-authored volume, this presents a variety of approaches and methodologies, combining familiar material, accessible introductions, and new interpretations. With a writer as multifaceted as Frisch, however, it is inevitable that there are certain omissions. No mention is made, for example, of present-day performance practice.

Of the essays looking at Frisch's dramatic works, the two by Walter Schmitz and Klaus van den Berg on four early and two middle-period plays (*Graf Öderland* and *Don Juan*) are the most ambitious, while useful syntheses aimed at the student reader are offered by Amanda Charitina Boyd (on *Biedermann und die Brand-stifter* and *Die große Wut des Philipp Hotz*) and Caroline Schaumann and Frank Schaumann (on *Andorra*). John D. Pizer's 'Eternal Recurrence in Life and Death in Max Frisch's Late Plays' is a fascinating account of the thematic, philosophical, and structural links between *Biografie* and *Triptychon*: he draws on and critiques existing readings, adeptly weaving in Nietzsche's theory of eternal recurrence and Heidegger's positive view on mortality.

Seven of the essays devoted to the diverse prose works focus on Frisch's fiction, one looks at his diaries, and one is on his essays and speeches. Céline Letawe's absorbing 'From Life to Literature: Max Frisch's *Tagebücher*' reflects on the genre and how in these sketchbooks Frisch deliberately conflates reality and fiction, objectivity and subjectivity. The very different *Blätter aus dem Brotsack* and Uwe Johnson's noteworthy editorship of the later diaries are adroitly integrated into the study. Ruth Vogel-Klein's 'Max Frisch's *Montauk. Eine Erzählung*' is an impres-sively exhaustive analysis of Frisch's complex semi-autobiographical narrative. Paul A. Youngman's 'Cybernetic Flow, Analogy, and Probability in Max Frisch's *Homo Faber*' succeeds in making a technical topic accessible and stimulating, and in the process sheds new light on Frisch's understanding and application of cybernetics. Margit Unser's engaging essay on the early fiction justifies an increasing critical tendency to turn back to Frisch's earlier work. His more established narratives are discussed first by Berwald himself in a lucid and tightly argued essay on the experimental novel *Mein Name sei Gantenbein* (drawing on unpublished corres-pondence), by Beatrice Sandberg (on *Stiller*), by Walter Obschlager (whose analysis of *Der Mensch erscheint im Holozän* references Freud), and by Daniel de Vin in brief personal reflections on Frisch's final narrative, *Blaubart*. The closing essay by Régine Battiston on Frisch's own essays and speeches is equally brief, yet it gives an overview of the extensive number of texts and shows how Frisch navigated a path between aesthetics and political engagement.

With some particularly discerning contributions, the volume is an important and informative contribution to Frisch studies in English. It would have profited from more careful copy-editing to eliminate Germanic turns of phrases and ensure consistency in referencing, and the select bibliography is perhaps rather too select, excluding some important older secondary literature in English (such as Michael Butler, *The Novels of Max Frisch* (London: Wolff, 1976), and Malcolm Pender, *Max Frisch: His Work and its Swiss Background* (Stuttgart: Heinz, 1979)) as well as other titles in German that have appeared over the last twenty years, and which are referenced in the notes of several essays. Notwithstanding these desiderata, either in hardback or as an e-book, it is a handsome Companion and an essential library acquisition.

UNIVERSITY COLLEGE DUBLIN   SIOBHÁN DONOVAN

Imagining Germany Imagining Asia: Essays in Asian–German Studies. Ed. by VERO-
    NIKA FUECHTNER and MARY RHIEL. Rochester, NY: Camden House. 2013.
    xii+279 pp. £60. ISBN 978-1-57113-548-3.

The investigation of Germany's many and ambivalent relationships with the so-called 'Orient' has been underway for several decades now. Sizeable works have examined literary orientalism in German and Germany's relationship with the Middle East, there has been a raft of studies devoted to Germany's special relationship with Indian history, language, and culture, and, most recently, the scintillating history of German academic orientalism has been given full treatment. The area continues to provide rich pickings for scholars offering methodological innovation, unearthing new archival material, and publishing in new interdisciplinary configurations. In this context the collection *Imagining Germany Imagining Asia* appears, exploring the various cultural 'spaces' Germany has shared with Asia from the Enlightenment to the present. Opening the collection with a sound discussion of the aforementioned scholarship and the development of German Asian studies, the editors' introduction evokes implicitly Benedict Anderson's notion of the 'imaginary' nature of human communities—'Germany' and 'Asia' are to be flexible and permeable concepts throughout.

The contributions fall into three parts, the first of which examines the diasporic presence of Asians within Germany. Randall Halle's opening essay critiques contemporary theorists of European identity (Derrida and Habermas), positing instead a decentred 'European Intrazone' of cultural linkages illustrated through reference to transnational currents in (German) films and processes of film production. In the context of a globalized world, Qinna Shen's essay analyses the continuities and breakages in the vision of China presented in two German films—shifts which began to dismantle stereotypical political and economic fears of China as the 'yellow peril'. Perta Fachinger's essay focuses on the social and political predicament of Vietnamese immigrants in contemporary Germany: moving beyond the simple binary of the Vietnamese Germans either as the descendants of 'boat people' refugees to West Germany or as guest workers in the former GDR, she examines how these communities are shaped by multiple global forces, and offers a focus on the abiding inequality of Vietnamese women. Quinn Slobodian offers a real-life case study of Xing-Hu Kuo, a Chinese Indonesian immigrant to the GDR, whose position both as a kind of cultural insider and as an outsider offers a productively transcultural intervention in historical work on the Stasi along the thematic axis of memory culture.

The collection's second part, conversely, engages with travel writing by Germans in Asian territories. Kamakshi Murti offers a critical rethinking of her own earlier work, asking how relevant the concept of orientalism still is now that postcolonial scholarship has dispensed with simple East–West binaries. Rereading Günter Grass's *Zunge zeigen*, she sees in its representation of India not an appeal to older orientalist mysticizing traditions, but an instance of how localities and communities are rendered 'translocal' when national boundaries dissolve in a globalized world. Veronika Fuechtner examines the German Jewish sexologist Magnus Hirschfeld's lecture tour through 1930s India, finding his work ambivalent in its attempt to look beyond racial hierarchies: in attempting to present Jews as 'white' it simultaneously restates stereotypes of darker-skinned Orientals and appeals to the exoticism of the *Kamasutra*, rather than contemporary Indian sexology. Medical history, like all intellectual traditions, cannot be seen in isolation from its cross-cultural heritage, according to Fuechtner. Hoi-eun Kim's essay examines the work of anthropologist Erwin Bälz in Korea and Japan around 1900. His racial anthropology underwrote the theory that physically similar peoples should assimilate culturally and politically, which was key not only for the development of racial science in Germany, but also in imperial Japan. Mary Rhiel examines the shifting depictions of the Chinese other in germanophone travelogues from the same period, which demonstrate the attempt to (re)assert a colonializing vision of China, but also more nuanced insights that anticipate colonialism's end. And Perry Myers's subtle essay sees Waldemar Bonsels's travel writing as a 'German' quest for an alternative to modern industrialization and spiritual renewal within India's spiritual heritage, which ultimately led the writer to return to Germany 'empty-handed' and at least in part disabused of his naive ideals.

Finally, the third section challenges the exclusively 'national' nature of the German philosophical canon by teasing out its inherent connection to readings of Asian traditions (p. 8). Sai Bhatawadekar's essay charts not only the foundational role played by Vedānta philosophy in Schopenhauer's ethics, but also how such nineteenth-century European readings of Hinduism fed back into Hinduism's twentieth-century traditions of self-reinvention. Chunje Zhang contrasts popular and highbrow Indophilia in German writing by reading August von Kotzebue's dramas and Friedrich Schlegel's essayistic, but showing how both contribute to the discourses of national identity construction of German around 1800 through a form of 'transcultural symbiosis'. David Kim closes by asking if reading translations of classical Japanese *Genji* through the lens of German Asian studies can free us from essentializing, Western visions of Japan.

Most of the essays deal with the relationship between individual Asian cultures and Germany, so it is perhaps a little odd that the collection did not engage explicitly with the concept of 'Asia' itself, which, Greek in origin, is itself a Western, if ancient, collective imaginary, which compresses into one term a huge range of cultures and languages that do not necessarily mutually relate, and which would bear some unpicking. Quibbles aside, this is a well-edited volume and a welcome addition to scholarship. The tripartite structure aids the conceptual cohesion of its widely varying essays. Most pleasing was perhaps the insight that it is not only material produced during our own self-proclaimed age of globalization, but also texts from the eighteenth and nineteenth centuries, that appear to challenge those simplistic occidental–oriental dualisms we would all do well to dispense with.

WARWICK UNIVERSITY   JAMES HODKINSON

Reframing Antifascism: Memory, Genre and the Life Writings of Greta Kuckhoff. By JOANNE SAYNER. Basingstoke: Palgrave Macmillan. 2013. 304 pp. £63. ISBN 978–0–230–36875–0.

Of the various studies on the debate surrounding anti-Fascism and resistance in the GDR, Joanne Sayner's research into the life writings of Greta Kuckhoff provides a wealth of new material relating to this less well-known figure of Nazi resistance and the GDR public sphere. Most importantly, her book provides insights from the life of a woman in high positions fighting for an appropriate public remembrance of the anti-Fascist resisters she alone outlived. Exploring Kuckhoff's life writings rather than writing a biography, Sayner aims to deliver a much broader insight into Kuckhoff's everyday life, as well as presenting different patterns of memory and experience and contributing to the existing body of research into the few women who held powerful positions in the GDR. Kuckhoff, therefore, stands as a perfect example since she held a variety of important positions—most notably acting as president of the Deutsche Notenbank from 1950 to 1958—but also argued throughout her life for a more appropriate commemoration of the resistance group centred on Arvid Harnack and Harro Schulze-Boysen, better known as 'Die Rote Kapelle', the name given to them by the Gestapo.

Operating in the dichotomy between personal memory and official GDR narratives of anti-Fascism, Sayner convincingly questions memory as a dynamic, socially constructed process within a cultural context, and consequently aims to make these processes visible and to situate them within the power regulations of the time—that is, to investigate their historicity. She therefore explores the various media used by Kuckhoff to challenge the public image of the 'Red Orchestra' with particular focus on her public speeches, radio broadcasts, letters, exhibitions, TV programmes, films, and autobiography. Depicting Kuckhoff's anti-Fascist engagement with the three dominant and interlinked themes of the economic situation of the GDR, denazification, and the situation of women in Germany, the study vividly outlines how the fight of surviving resistance fighters of the Nazi era continued their work in the post-war period, born of the need to convince the public of the moral necessity of their actions, facing resentment and the distribution of imprecise information. These aims are exemplified by the actions of the resistance and prominent figures among the GDR public such as Kuckhoff, who enjoyed a position of privilege and were therefore able to complain about the depiction or omission of the Red Orchestra to Ulbricht, Honecker, or Mielke directly, as evidenced by the various letters she wrote them.

In her most persuasive chapter, Sayner describes the history and influence of the journal to which Kuckhoff contributed, *Die Weltbühne*. She provides evidence for the fact that reports on the Holocaust in the GDR did indeed exist, which has widely been thought not to be the case. Furthermore, this study bears witness to an important chapter of an authentic and mostly intellectual anti-Fascism within the GDR that, despite challenging dominant GDR narratives, was nevertheless present in publications of the time. Kuckhoff's articles thus work as a synthesis of autobiographical memory and political commentary, whereas the latter served to question monolithic perceptions about anti-Fascist discourse in general.

It is likely that Kuckhoff has not become a prominent figure in any collective memory as a result of her reluctance to provide a heroic account of events, preferring instead to deliver a complex picture of the group, which was eventually successful thanks to her autobiography. By showing that both East and West German narratives depicting the 'Red Orchestra' relied solely on Gestapo reports, Sayner's book forms a well-written and convincingly argued contribution to studies of twentieth-century German memory, providing various innovative approaches, especially concerning the perception of the GDR—although it is marred by numerous spelling errors and grammatical mistakes in the German quotations. Sayner's conclusion makes a number of reasonable assertions as to the validity of scholarly interest in memory studies in anti-Fascism, arguing that they may well serve to oppose the simplifications and glorifications of the past encountered in rising Fascist-inspired political movements all over Europe today. Exploring the writings of Greta Kuckhoff thus forms a valuable point of departure.

UNIVERSITY OF BRISTOL   STEPHAN EHRIG

'Aber eines lügt er nicht: Echtheit': Perspektiven auf Hubert Fichte. By ROBERT GILLETT. Hamburg: Textem. 2014. 277 pp. €18. ISBN 978–386485–051–6.

Within the small community of Hubert Fichte scholars, Robert Gillett is a doyen, his books setting a standard within both English- and German-speaking scholarly communities. His bibliography of Fichte's œuvre, for example (*Hubert Fichte: Eine kritische Auswahlbibliographie* (Lampeter: Mellen, 2007)), has put an end to a long-lasting feud and is a hugely useful research tool. In this new book, Gillett contributes significantly to research on Fichte's work and simultaneously updates the theoretical debate within this field. The quotation in his title is from *Versuch über die Pubertät* (Hamburg: Hoffmann und Campe, 1974): 'Wäre er kein Schauspieler müßte man sagen: | Übertrieben! Verlogen! Falscher Ernst! Süßliche Verzweif- | lung! Viel zu lustige Heiterkeit! | Aber eines lügt er nicht: Echtheit' (p. 142), a passage in which the narrator gives a description of a friend, the actor Alex W. Kretschmar. Gillett calls the quotation 'vertrackt' (p. 8), but sees it as programmatic for Fichte's work. It is intricate not just because of the abundance of oxymorons that Fichte uses to describe this character, a stylistic device with which Fichte demonstrates his admiration for the Baroque—it is 'vertrackt' because it invites many diverging interpretations, and like much of Fichte's œuvre, it seems to seduce the reader into pursuing autobiographical allusions. Gillett is very well aware of these multiple layers of interpretation and the pitfalls of autobiographical reference. Even though Fichte's stance towards the writing profession was characterized by irony and by the fact that so much of his writing is inseparable from rites of perfor- mance, Gillett maintains that Fichte insisted on preserving the notion of 'Echtheit', and for Gillett this entails not engaging in biographical readings of individual texts. His goal is to trace and map this poetic programme (p. 8), which contains the key to those aspects of Fichte's work that are still considered 'rätselhaft und irritierend' (ibid.), an element that he sees operating as a form of built-in resistance to simplistic, authoritarian interpretation and thus as the essence of Fichte's camp or queer poetics (p. 9).

The second part of the introduction, in which Gillett sets out to review the latest research on Hubert Fichte and to chart the territory for his own book, is especially fine. Lucid and compelling, Gillett's judgements are fierce without ever becoming polemical. He dismisses the critical paradigm that has labelled Fichte an outsider on multiple levels as factually dubious and heuristically worthless, carrying overtones of benevolent homophobia (p. 10). The diffuse term 'Ethnopoesie' has, in Gillett's view, obstructed a more productive reading of the postcolonial mul- timodality of Fichte's radio features and travelogues, and the trend towards both overemphasizing and idealizing his sexuality has actually underpinned the same patterns of social repression that Fichte aimed to combat throughout his writing career. With this paradoxical poetic programme, Fichte is striving for 'Echtheit' by employing gossip, exaggeration, referentiality, parody, and moral sincerity. By the same token, Fichte's 'Echtheit' defies any attempt to claim an absolute truth, or authenticity, especially in historiography or cultural anthropology (p. 11).

The first of four main chapters deals with Fichte's involvement with Gruppe 47. Reiterating how Fichte has often been viewed as a singular phenomenon, portrayed only occasionally and often unfavourably in autobiographical musings by fellow writers, Gillett sets out to reconstruct the important role Fichte played within that group in the 1960s. Gillett demonstrates that Fichte was heavily involved on dif- ferent levels. He read from his works at several annual meetings of the group, took part in the aesthetic debate at and between those meetings, and documented the convention in Sigtuna in 1964 in an almanac. Far from being merely a footnote to Fichte's intellectual biography and the history of the group, this showcases Gillett's thesis very well: Fichte's ambivalent social performance, his conflicting aesthetic propositions, and his ostentatious non-compliance with group politics are part and parcel of his engagement with the group, and his artistic contribution to its legacy is a genuine one.

Chapter 2, on Fichte and life-writing, is the centrepiece of the book, with far-reaching implications for the interpretation of Fichte's autobiographical texts and for understanding the broader turn to autobiographical writing in West German literature in the 1960s and 1970s. Gillett demonstrates clearly how Fichte's concept of life-writing proved influential for his peers as well as for subsequent generations of young writers. This term, 'life-writing', is an ideal umbrella concept for the different genres appropriated by Fichte, especially in the nineteen volumes of his unfinished *Geschichte der Empfindlichkeit*.

The third chapter focuses on Fichte's texts on Haiti. Although this theme has been discussed extensively—Susan Buck-Morss's book *Hegel, Haiti, and Universal History* (Pittsburgh: University of Pittsburgh Press, 2009) is a compelling case study of the unique role played by the island in the Western imagination—Gillett sheds new light on the works by addressing the multimodality of Fichte's writing, and the sometimes complementary, even contradictory, notions of Haiti Fichte evokes in texts for different media (radio features, newspaper interviews, novels, and photo-book essays). He shows not only how Fichte's anthropological and autobiographical writings mirror each other but also that his life story in fact becomes, in the process, 'Demonstrationsobjekt und Prüfstein für echte Unverlogenheit' (p. 12).

The fourth chapter looks at Fichte's treatment of sexuality and addresses another long-lived 'sacred cow' in research on the author. Fichte is still widely considered an icon of gay literature, and some dismiss his relationship with Leonore Mau (which spanned more than thirty years) as mere social camouflage. Again, it is less biographical accuracy that motivates Gillett here than a concern for the implicit poetic programme in Fichte's works. Gillett argues that Fichte deliberately defies social expectations and labels from all sides and enables his protagonist, Jäcki, to engage in a plurality of modes of loving and living together. The role model for this sexual plurality is, again, the actor Alex W. Kretschmar. Gillett adopts Fichte's own terminology for a poetic 'Programmatik der Bisexualität' (p. 251), based on an ethics of inclusion and employing techniques of montage and collage to incorporate even its own inevitable aporiae (p. 253). The fact that Alex eventually takes his own life demonstrates, as Gillett argues, a twofold defence against social expectations: Alex's suicide is blamed in part on a society that enforces life-threatening phoniness and also denies it the right to judge such matters of life and death. The argument here is perhaps not as strong as in the other chapters: one could argue that Alex's problem is indeed his bisexuality; unlike Jäcki, he cannot forge a coherent life story that aligns his sexual desires with different social roles, and is eventually stuck with the promise of bisexuality, which turns out to be yet another empty label.

Gillett's book will have a lasting effect on Fichte scholarship as a whole. It will be an indispensable point of departure for anyone wishing to contribute to research on Fichte's work, as well as for those working within the field of modern autobiographical writing in German.

UNIVERSITY OF ALBERTA, EDMONTON   ANDREAS STUHLMANN

Born under Auschwitz: Melancholy Traditions in Postwar German Literature. By
 MARY COSGROVE. Rochester, NY: Camden House. 2014. x+234 pp. £50.
 ISBN 978-1-57113-556-8.

In this detailed and cogent study, Mary Cosgrove sets out to explore melancholy as a 'performative discourse' which post-war German-language writers have used in the service of 'a varied and self-reflexive literary language of remembrance' in response to the Holocaust (p. 4). The four chapters provide separate but related case studies of four authors (Günter Grass, Wolfgang Hildesheimer, Peter Weiss, and W. G. Sebald) and examine their respective approaches to European traditions of melancholy as part of an attempt at *Vergangenheitsbewältigung*. This is done through what Cosgrove presents as 'melancholy self-fashioning' (p. 1)—that is, the way in which writers perform melancholy in their quest for a mode of remembrance of the Holocaust. The epilogue (pp. 185–201) treats Iris Hanika's *Das Eigentliche* as a counterpoint to the previous authors, one which marks a departure from the tradition of the 'ethical melancholy man' (p. 199) who is cast as 'the melancholy genius of *Vergangenheitsbewältigung*' (p. 191).

The study is rich in references to discursive frameworks of melancholy, drawing on areas such as medicine, psychology, religion, art, literature, and food. Rather than outlining the extensive and diverse history of melancholy and its traditions, Cosgrove prudently uses the introduction to elucidate selected discourses which appear in the post-war texts, and which recur throughout the different authors' works in the guise of tropes and icons, such as Albrecht Dürer's *Melencolia I*. This approach results in a sustained and dynamic analysis of the authors' works—not least because they have recourse to a wide range of discursive models—while allowing for comparisons to be drawn across the different, often wildly contrasting, texts. Cosgrove considers the tradition of a division between 'good' and 'bad' melancholy, that is to say, the view that melancholy is on the one hand a debilitating affliction, and on the other a mark of creative potential. Cosgrove's discussion of Freud's influence on conceptualizations of melancholy leads to a consideration of melancholy versus mourning, and in turn to post-war theorizing which holds a 'negative assessment of melancholy as a post-Holocaust affective disposition that produces a problematic memory culture' (p. 20).

The case studies that follow are grounded in close reading of the narratives, and an examination of the melancholy traditions and discourses they employ and/or subvert. Cosgrove revisits well-known texts and explores more marginal ones, challenging earlier readings of their melancholy aspects. Grass's *Aus dem Tagebuch einer Schnecke* is an obvious place to start, and is usefully read in the light of *Beim Häuten der Zwiebel*. The analysis weaves together a number of discursive strands, including the notion of *acedia* ('spiritual inertia', p. 51), food melancholy, and Walter Benjamin's 'figure of the melancholy allegorist' (p. 62). Although Grass attempts to 'put in a good word for melancholy' (p. 198), it ultimately serves his self-presentation as a model intellectual (p. 37) by virtue of his distinction between 'good' and 'bad' melancholy. In contrast to Grass, Hildesheimer focuses on the victims' perspective in his novels *Tynset* and *Masante*, primarily through the modes of genial and religious melancholy (p. 83). Cosgrove addresses earlier misreadings of Hildesheimer's melancholy that failed to acknowledge or fully comprehend his intent (p. 82). Here, the performance of melancholy serves to expose the enduring trauma and guilt of victimhood and results ultimately in a far more nihilistic view than in Grass's work.

In his *Ästhetik des Widerstands* Weiss casts a woman in the role of 'troubled melancholy 'genius'' (p. 111), and, in a departure from approaches taken by Grass and Hildesheimer, adopts a more radical stance towards the gendered tradition of female melancholic as 'depressed' rather than 'genial' (pp. 122–23). This approach provides a mode in which to address how language and art can be used to engage with the events of the Holocaust and 'the danger of cultural amnesia' (p. 198). In the final chapter, Cosgrove makes a strong case for the fact that although melancholy in Sebald's works has received significant critical attention, there has been insufficient acknowledgement of its 'fundamental ambivalence' and complexity (p. 145). With reference to his essays and selected prose works, Cosgrove explores Sebald's use of melancholy traditions which are an integral part of his intricate, multiperspectival response to history, the environment, and the contemporary world. Hanika's 2010 *Das Eigentliche*, rooted in the altered memory politics of the Berlin Republic, offers a parody of previous modes (p. 199). While Hanika makes use of discourses found in earlier works, she deploys them to draw attention to a decline in ethical Holocaust commemoration after the *Wende*.

The issue of gender is highlighted at the outset of the study (pp. 10–11), and a solid defence is provided for the inclusion of only one female writer. The book's aim is, after all, 'to trace the rise and decline of a *masculine* type' (p. 10). However, gender is explored throughout: for example, while Grass's depiction of the depressed Lisbeth Stomma reinforces the notion that women cannot aspire to become genial melancholics, Weiss subverts what Cosgrove convincingly sets out as 'traditional conceptions of the depressed woman in the cultural and medical literature on melancholy' (p. 122).

Throughout the study, textual analysis is enhanced by careful attention to the literary, political, and cultural context, and by details drawn from archival material about the writers' knowledge and discussion of melancholy traditions. Cosgrove's strident engagement with earlier critical reception is particularly noteworthy, not least as her study responds to a lack of scholarly interest in post-war Holocaust memory and melancholy, an association that she shows to be worthy of further attention. The chapters on Grass and Sebald in particular weave deftly with existing related studies, such as those on Grass and authorship and some of the many recent publications on Sebald.

The monograph is an original and serious work which provides a highly detailed

perspective on post-war writing about the poetics of remembrance after the Holocaust. As such, it makes an important contribution to the extensive body of recent
criticism on post-war German memory culture. While *Born under Auschwitz* will
certainly appeal to scholars and students from a range of disciplines, the complexity
of the arguments and richness of references and associations may at times challenge
undergraduate readers, despite the publisher's claim that the book is aimed at such
an audience. Nevertheless, Cosgrove's engaging style and rigorous analysis will
certainly make it a challenge well worth taking on.

ST EDMUND HALL, OXFORD   ALEXANDRA LLOYD

Art outside the Lines: New Perspectives on GDR Art Culture. Ed. by ELAINE KELLY
    and AMY WLODARSKI. (German Monitor, 74) Amsterdam: Rodopi. 2011.
    278 pp. £52. ISBN 978–90–420–3341–2.

A decade after the Berlin Wall came down, an exhibition in Weimar, 'Aufstieg
und Fall der Moderne', scandalized critics in both East and West Germany by
its treatment of GDR art. The first of the show's three sections, staged in the
Stadtschloß, was given over to the avant-garde that flourished in Germany in the
1920s. The second and third parts, dedicated to National Socialist and to GDR art
respectively, were set in a decrepit hall to the side of the unfinished NS Gauforum.
Jonathan Osmond summarizes: 'the effect was of an amateur show or flea market'
(p. 223). The denigration of the artistic production of the failed East German state
and its complicated relationship with the broader history of post-war art in both
Germanies is the central theme of this volume. As the editors declare in their introductory essay, '[the] unwillingness to incorporate GDR art works into longer-term
narratives of German cultural history forms the focus of this collection' (p. 1).

    The temptation to compare NS images of contented, Aryan farmers with very
similar GDR paintings of harvest time on the collective farm is, of course, strong.
It also endorses the narrative of an art practice entirely subservient to the goals
of the state. Like the consolidation of an autonomous heavy-industry sector, the
collectivization of agriculture was to be accomplished in the GDR, according to
the party dictates, by the spring of 1960. The function of art, accordingly, was the
pictorial benediction of collectivized and industrialized agriculture. Yet the party
line was neither omnipresent nor omniscient. Even though the GDR insisted on a
'socialist national culture', the reality was so clearly different that even the official
histories recognized regional differences, and distinguished, for example, between
the Dresden, Leipzig, Berlin, and Halle schools of painting, recognizing the distinct
historical traditions on which they drew.

    Virtually every essay in this collection attests to this diversity. In the first chapter,
April Eisman gives a closely detailed account of the controversy surrounding the
murals painted in 1964 for the Hotel Deutschland in Leipzig. She concludes that
'cultural policy in the GDR was far from monolithic' and that 'the discussion
was not limited to the private sphere, but was introduced to the public for a
discussion about art that ultimately lasted many months' (p. 34). Laura Silverberg's

well-researched essay on the Verband Deutscher Komponisten und Musikwissenschaftler confirms that a similar openness to discussion prevailed in the world of music. In the period of de-Stalinization in the mid-1950s a major spat arose between *Sonntag*, the weekly journal of the Kulturbund, and the much more conformist journal of the VDK, *Musik und Gesellschaft*. The composer Paul Dessau condemned those conservatives who 'were happier to orient themselves to Handel than to the great musicians of our century, such as Schönberg, Anton Webern, Alban Berg, Bartók, Shostakovich and Prokofiev' (p. 200), but rather than damning Dessau as a formalist or worse, the official response in *Musik und Gesellschaft* was an offer to discuss the conflicting positions 'in all openness and with total respect for the character of the discussants' (p. 203). As Silverberg notes, 'challenges to SED aesthetic dogma were voiced openly and surfaced at times in party-run newspapers and journals' (p. 194). Yet there were limits: in his persuasive essay on music and discourse, Matthias Tischer retells a possibly apocryphal tale of Dessau pulling the score of a Bartók quartet out of his bag in a session at the Akademie der Künste, only to be told by Hanns Eisler: 'Put it away, Paul!' (p. 162).

Similarly, international contacts were less rare than might be supposed, as is confirmed in the second section of the book, 'Internationalism and GDR Art'. In the context of the Dresden school of painting, Sigfrid Hofer details the reception of Western European and US art, which saw painters such as Hermann Glöckner and Hans Christoph visiting documenta 1 in 1955, and Hans Jüchser 'electrified' by the Jackson Pollock exhibition held in West Berlin in 1958. Although abstract expressionism and Art Informel were known and appreciated in the GDR, they could not be celebrated: Jüchser's own abstract paintings were known only to a small circle of friends and collectors. In the world of literature, by contrast, certain select American impulses were welcome: this is the theme of Sara Lennox's contribution on the reception of African American writers in the GDR. Unsurprisingly in the context of the Cold War, the black liberation struggle was viewed in the GDR from a Marxist-Leninist perspective.

Of all the arts in the GDR, opera was the jewel in the crown, with two outstanding companies in Bertolt Brecht's Berliner Ensemble and Walter Felsenstein's Komische Oper. These were the houses that defined and nurtured *Regieoper*, which released the opera director from conventional settings and stagings. As Joy H. Callico explains, 'the rupture between what one sees and what one hears can produce estrangement. This is the essence of *Regieoper*' (p. 133). While the leading GDR painters, such as Bernhard Heisig, Willi Sitte, or Werner Tübke, were hardly known outside the national boundaries during the Cold War, the top echelon of GDR opera directors—Felsenstein, Harry Kupfer, Ruth Berghaus, Franz Konwitschny—enjoyed international renown.

Although approached in Kristine Nielsen's excellent essay on the massive, fifty-ton monument to Ernst Thälmann in Berlin's Prenzlauer Berg (which apparently has a heated nose to keep the snow off), architecture is the conspicuous omission from this collection. The long and acrimonious debates that preceded the 2008 demolition of the Palast der Republik in Berlin surely deserve mention in any account of the exclusion of GDR culture from the narratives of German history. A further concern is the inconsistent editorial policy on translation, with some German sources translated and others left in the original. One modest volume cannot offer a close reading of GDR cultural policy and production across all the arts, and those seeking detailed accounts of official party policies as they evolved in such discussions as the Bitterfeld conferences in 1958 and 1964 will have to turn to more specialized literature. As a broad and appealing introduction to a complicated subject, however, *Art outside the Lines* is to be warmly welcomed.

UNIVERSITY OF EDINBURGH IAIN BOYD WHYTE

Herta Müller. Ed. by BRIGID HAINES and LYN MARVEN. Oxford: Oxford University Press. 2013. xiv+272 pp. £50. ISBN 978-0-19-965464-2.

When Herta Müller was awarded the Nobel Prize for Literature in 2009, the British media were initially uncertain where to turn for information about her—curiously so, because the German Department at Swansea University had established itself at least a decade earlier as the indubitable centre for Herta Müller studies in the UK, having entertained her as a writer in residence in 1997–98. In this volume, Brigid Haines (Swansea) and Lyn Marven (Liverpool) have provided the broadcasters with precisely the resource they needed: a comprehensive overview in English of Müller's writings and the key issues associated with them.

Müller's writing is well known for its inbuilt resistance to reduction. As the editors put it in their introduction, her prose is typically 'syntactically simple yet interpretatively complex' (p. 15), or as Norbert Otto Eke puts it in his chapter, it aims at the 'deautomatization of perception' (p. 102). It is fitting, therefore, that some of the contributions discuss Müller's poetics and the culture from which she emerged in the German-speaking enclave in Romania, while others focus on particular works or groups of works, or on specific themes.

Katrin Kohl provides a robust initial guide to Müller's sense of poetic mission, bringing out the special character of a kind of life-writing that exploits the tensions between the imperative of precise observation on the one hand and the need to become inventive in order to resist the gravitational pull of conventionality—deceit even—to which linguistic evocation is inevitably subject. In a later chapter, Marven also provides a detailed analysis of the disruptive juxtapositions that characterize Müller's collage compositions, presenting them as 'a textual metaphor for trauma' (p. 135). The historical background to the blending of German and Romanian language cultures that Müller's writing exhibits is explained by Alex Drace-Francis; and Valentina Glajar gives a vivid account of the police state in which Müller grew to adulthood and the importance of that biographical background for the general cast of her writings.

Moray McGowan explores the dense textures with which Müller evokes the world of divided Berlin in her novel *Reisende auf einem Bein*. Beverley Driver Eddy examines the imagery of *Der Fuchs war damals schon der Jäger* and relates it to the literary heritage of Romanian surrealism. Eke brings out the importance of the aesthetics of the 'alien gaze' for the representation of arbitrary power in the two novels that are set in Romania: *Herztier* and *Heute wär ich mir lieber nicht begegnet*. And Haines achieves a suitably cautious and sensitive perspective in her reading of *Atemschaukel*, highlighting its controversial status as a 'fictionalized testimony' of the experience of Romanian Germans in a post-war Soviet labour camp—as Wiebke Sievers brings out in her chapter, there are quite specific echoes of historical experience that Eastern European readers recognize more readily than Westerners in Müller's narratives.

Karin Bauer analyses the complexities in Müller's representation of female sexuality and male homosexuality in the context of oppressive political systems and the power relations that develop within them. Jean Boase-Beier examines the problems that Müller's texts pose for English translators; Sievers provides a remarkably rich account of the international reception of Müller's work, which intensified considerably after the award of the Nobel Prize in 2009; and Rebecca Braun discusses the 'celebrification' process that has ensued (p. 228).

The introduction provides a concise but vivid summary of the issues, and the bibliography is admirably thorough. It is a particularly welcome feature of the volume that quotations appear in the main text in Müller's German, with English translations supplied in footnotes. Swansea is to be congratulated on this excellent contribution to the study of an important contemporary author.

St John's College, Cambridge   David Midgley

Remembering Africa: The Rediscovery of Colonialism in Contemporary German Literature. By Dirk Göttsche. (Studies in German Literature, Linguistics, and Culture) Rochester, NY: Camden House. 2013. viii+485 pp. £60. ISBN 978-1-57113-546-9.

The popularity of African settings in contemporary German fiction is indeed a striking phenomenon. It coincides with a similar wave of African subjects on German television and in the cinema. In this magisterial study, Dirk Göttsche concentrates on historical fiction, that is, on narratives that are entirely or partly set in the past. In his comprehensive bibliography of primary sources, almost 120 of the titles listed appeared in the last twenty-five years, while a few dozen or so from the 1950s to the 1980s illustrate that the current wave had its precursors. Some of these are all but forgotten, such as adventure novels from the GDR, which, in contrast to more recent engagements with colonialism, were able to side unequivocally with the oppressed colonial subjects and to frame their plight within the parameters of class struggle. While Göttsche's chapters normally concentrate on one paradigmatic example each, often complemented by discussions of some similar, though less prominent, works, his aim is to map in a comprehensive way the impressive breadth of subject-matter, literary techniques, and the degrees of reflection of postcolonial and intercultural awareness displayed in this diverse yet distinct field of writing. His scope does not only include stories that are set in Africa, but also literary treatments of historical experiences of the African diaspora in German-speaking central Europe—in both cases including publications intended for the mass market.

Of the many aspects of the topic covered in this study, only a few of the most prominent can be identified here. The historical conditions encountered in different parts of Africa generate quite different literary approaches: as far as the German colonial experience is concerned, the traumatic event of the atrocities committed against the Herero and Nama in German South-West Africa provides the greatest incentive for engagement to German authors, while the Maji Maji wars in German East Africa hardly feature at all—and yet East Africa is one of the preferred settings for more romantic and exoticizing stories. Colonial experiences outside formal protectorates, such as those of the Swiss and Austrians, are often traced through cross-cultural biographies or family histories. The adventure and myth of exploration, aspects of decolonization, missionary activity, the potential and lure of the exotic as a canvas for the imagination of alternative lifestyles, and many other avenues of engagement with Africa are explored. The fictional embellishment of real biographies or events, multigenerational family histories (which allow the linking of the discussion of colonial pasts with that of Fascism and of postcolonial memory discourses on complicity and individual as well as collective responsibility), parallel narration and juxtaposition of past and present, European and African or German and, for example, British experience, self-reflexive, ironic, and occasionally grotesque metafiction—these are just a few of the strategies and formal devices Göttsche identifies as characteristic of those among the writers on Africa who display a keen awareness of the problematics of their subject-matter. Ever since Uwe Timm's seminal novel *Morenga* (1974), authors have been consistently challenged by the difficulty (and ethics) of representing the voices of the subalterns. Some of the most successful writers of African fiction—Blaeulich, Buch, Capus, Hamann, Kracht, Stangl, Trojanow, Wackwitz, to name just a few—thus avoid the insolence of claiming to be able to speak on the colonial subjects' behalf, and rather reflect that inability and their own inevitable prejudice through a variety of devices. These devices of modesty and self-relativization distinguish the more ambitious and more intriguing engagements with the complex interplay between self and other, and facilitate the most nuanced and meaningful encounter of readers with the controversial subject-matter.

Göttsche tackles his vast corpus of material with a refined and elaborate instrumentarium that differentiates clearly between inter-, trans-, and cross-culturality, for example. Importantly, he draws attention to the fact that, in spite of the dominance of postcolonial theory of French and Anglo-Saxon provenance in German academia and worldwide, uniquely German approaches to analysing engagement with the culturally diverse have been developed since the 1970s in the form of 'Interkulturelle Germanistik'. While mostly dealing with very current material, Göttsche furthermore manages to locate the ongoing trend on a historical trajectory from post-war engagement with totalitarianism, the 'Third World Movement' and ideological critique of the 1960s, the anti-imperialist consensus of the GDR, as well as the memory debates and reflections on German history since unification

right down to more recent tendencies to 'normalize' German memory discourses—
a phenomenon that opened the door for a renewed romanticization of the exotic
of a kind that postcolonial critique and literary practice have attempted to purge
from public discourse.

Göttsche's solid framework provides clear criteria for the evaluation of the works
analysed. In summary, 'critical memory of colonial history [. . .] has become the
established norm. [. . .] nostalgia for the colonial world [. . .] is very much the
exception' (p. 415). However, popular fiction in particular—often foregrounding
female characters in search of alternatives to their stale Western existence—cannot
be exonerated from frequently peddling exoticist clichés, generally while pursuing
a naive intercultural agenda.

The study consolidates existing research in the most comprehensive way (plen-
tiful contributions exist on the more intriguing works by the likes of Timm,
Trojanow, Capus, Stangl, and others; almost none exist on the majority of the
material). It thereby provides the touchstone for any future engagement with the
subject-matter. Many of the novels discussed are also eminently teachable. The
usability of the volume would have been increased if the chapter headings had not
only indicated a prevalent thematic or stylistic phenomenon (often using dense
formulations such as 'Transgenerational Postmemory as Literary Meta-Critique of
Postcolonial Memory') but had identified by title the works that form the object of
analysis. But this small impediment will not deter colleagues from recommending
individual chapters and the sturdy introduction to their students.

NATIONAL UNIVERSITY OF IRELAND MAYNOOTH   FLORIAN KROBB

Transitions: Emerging Women Writers in German-Language Literature. Ed. by
    VALERIE HEFFERNAN and GILLIAN PYE. (German Monitor, 76) Amsterdam
    and New York: Rodopi. 2013. 235 pp. €45. ISBN 978–90–420–3689–5.

Valerie Heffernan and Gillian Pye rightly claim that women have never played a
stronger role in German literature than since the turn of the twenty-first century but
that they are still marginalized in academic criticism of recent German-language
writers. This book, comprising ten essays on contemporary women's writing, goes
a long way towards filling that gap. The essays do more than merely introduce
us to emerging authors, however; they also offer new and theoretically informed
interpretations of important works.

In the helpful introduction the editors expound on the overarching theme of
transition. They read contemporary culture as transitional and the theme as central
to art of the present day. They also stress that the experience of evolving identities
and shifting boundaries is rooted in gender, succinctly reminding us of important
ideas of the body as threshold and gender as transitional process in the work of Rosi
Braidotti, Donna Haraway, and Judith Butler. They also make links to more recent
voices, e.g. Karen Barad on post-humanist performativity. Although the editors
contend that the essays are not feminist readings but rather offer 'gender-sensitive
insights into wider concerns and themes', many essays could be interpreted as

feminist as they challenge the perception that there is one fixed experience, narrative, body, or history. Furthermore, German and global culture is subjected to intelligent gendered critique in innovative and fascinating ways.

Several of the essays integrate insights from philosophy and critical theory into the reading of contemporary literature. Linda Shortt, in her reading of the Kazakhstan German author Eleonora Hummel, and Heffernan on Julia Franck's *Lagerfeuer* (2003), draw on Giorgio Agamben. Heffernan's subtle incorporation of Agamben's *Homo Sacer* allows complex readings of nation state, surveillance, borders, and transgression, and feeds into her excellent analysis of Franck's text, focusing on the author's ambivalent representations of Jewishness. Emily Jeremiah's essay on Larissa Boehning's *Lichte Stoffe* (2007) is similarly rich in nuanced readings which interpret the novel's 'black German' protagonist in terms of nomadism, hybridity, and material feminisms. Pye's beautifully crafted and engaging essay on the function of objects in Jenny Erpenbeck's texts argues that everyday items are 'partners in human experiences of continuity and rupture' (p. 118) and offer multiple views of time and history. Her interpretation provides a fascinating counter-reading to previous scholarship on Erpenbeck. Daphne Seemann's analysis of Eva Menasse's *Vienna* (2005) similarly highlights the multiplicity of voices in this Austrian family novel, arguing that the post-memorial perspective is crucial to our understanding of historical experiences which are not standard or unified. Elaine Martin's fine analysis of Kathrin Röggla's documentary novel *wir schlafen nicht* (2004) powerfully conveys the text's critique of neoliberalism. She analyses the complex narrative through a Bakhtinian and Brechtian theoretical lens, thus drawing out both the particularities of the narrative and the force of the text's politics.

Siobhán Donovan's essay focuses on the young Swiss author Lea Gottheil's debut novel *Sommervogel*. Her discussion centres on discourses of illness and the protagonist's search for identity, analysing imagery and metaphors of metamorphosis. Deirdre Byrnes's essay on Katrin Schmidt's *Du stirbst nicht* (2009) similarly discusses the hospital as a liminal and transformative space. The proximity of these essays allows the reader to compare the thematic treatment of memory and identity in these authors' works. The essay by Carrie Smith-Prei and Lars Richter on Juli Zeh's *Spieltrieb* (2004) is one of the most illuminating interpretations of this difficult novel to date. The authors focus on the three main characters and interpret them in terms of their 'embodiment of otherness' (p. 192), thus getting to grips with the text's representation of power, domination, and homosocial desire, linking the 'personal' story of the characters to global politics.

Overall this is a stimulating and important book to be recommended for all interested in contemporary writing and culture. Several essays will become important and foundational interpretations of authors who will continue to interest students and scholars of German literature in the future.

NEWCASTLE UNIVERSITY   TERESA LUDDEN

Ethical Approaches in Contemporary German-Language Literature and Culture. Ed.
by EMILY JEREMIAH and FRAUKE MATTHES. (Edinburgh German Yearbook,
7) Rochester, NY: Camden House. 2013. vi+184 pp. $75; £50. ISBN 978-1-
57113-880-4.

This is a well-conceived and timely volume. Taking as its starting-point the 'ethical turn' in the arts and humanities registered in recent years by a number of
key theorists, Emily Jeremiah and Frauke Matthes have put together a collection
that frames German-language literary responses to key contemporary issues—the
continued fascination with the Enlightenment even in our supposedly postmodern
era, globalization, universalism and particularism, colonialism and postcolonialism, race, ethnicity, and gender—as primarily *ethical* engagements. The volume
covers a range of writers and film-makers, including Uwe Timm, Christian Petzold,
Angelika Overath and Angela Krauß, Julia Schoch, Stefan Moster, Antje Rávic
Strubel, Judith Schalansky, Robert Schneider, Sybille Berg, Annette Pehnt, Tink
Diaz, Hans Christoph Buch, Nicole Vosseler, Zafer Şenocak, Navid Kermani, and
Yoko Tawada. Indeed, one of the book's greatest strengths is that, despite its com-
pactness, it manages to cover a great number and a large variety of both familiar
and less-known voices.

The editors' introduction, which perhaps errs on the side of brevity, sets out the
book's remit with admirable precision: 'the relationship between self and other;
the connection between particular and general; the personal and the political consequences of individuals' actions; and the potential, and danger, of representation
itself' (p. 1). The volume's focus on 'the ethical turn' is contextualized with reference to a variety of contemporary (and not so contemporary) thinkers, beginning
with Kant and continuing to Judith Butler and Eve Kosofsky Sedgwick, via Levinas,
Derrida, and Agamben. At the same time, and again with a refreshing directness,
the relevance of the particular focus in each chapter on the interplay between ethics
and aesthetics is conceptualized and justified.

Nine substantive chapters follow. Monika Albrecht's essay on Uwe Timm explores *Rot* (2001) through the lens of French philosopher Alain Badiou's critique
of our contemporary interest in 'the ethical' as a mode of reconciling ourselves to
actual injustice rather than seeking to challenge it and change the world. Albrecht's
chapter is one of the less original in volume—her argument that the novel sets itself
against the depoliticization of the present day thirty years after '68 is not particularly new—but it is well written and engaging. Alasdair King follows with an essay
on Petzold's TV films *Toter Mann* (2001) and *Wolfsburg* (2003), which addresses
the same issue, while drawing on Jacques Rancière rather than Badiou. This subtle
reading of Petzold's output—framed within the (by now) conventional critique of
the Berlin School as 'consensual' rather than challenging—precedes Gillian Pye's
highly original and demanding (in the best sense of the word) reading of narratives
by Overath and Krauß as explorations of our ethical (or more often unethical)
engagement with objects—that is, with the *materiality* of the world we inhabit,
beyond discourse, speech, and text. Jeremiah's contribution is no less challenging,

and no less original. She continues the focus on writers from the 'old' East Germany and asks 'what is at stake, ethically, in writings of the GDR past' (p. 65), linking this question to the issue of shame ('Giving an account of oneself', to cite Judith Butler, quoted on p. 70), and specifically the shame that East German writers may feel in relation to their background. Angelika Baier follows with a discussion of Robert Schneider's *Die Luftgängerin* (1998) and Sybille Berg's *Vielen Dank für das Leben* (2012) in relation to contemporary theories of 'affect' as an ethical response. This too is an extremely sophisticated chapter, though some may feel that here theory sometimes threatens to overwhelm the (very good) close readings of literary texts.

Anna Ertel and Tilmann Köppe shift the focus back towards a more conventional literary interest in representation, and the ethics of representation, here in relation to age and ageing in Annette Pehnt's *Haus der Schildkröten* (2001). This chapter raises the important question of the ethical 'utility' of a literary text dealing with a pressing social concern such as ageing for readers, but it is perhaps one of the less provocative essays in the volume. Kate Roy's chapter on the different ways in which Emily Reute's *Memorien einer arabischen Prinzessin* (1886) has been rewritten by contemporary authors and film-makers similarly understands 'ethical' as a measure of how 'fairly'/'unfairly' a particular group or person is represented and thereby perhaps risks becoming overly 'normative' herself, but her reading of Diaz's film *Die Prinzessin von Sansibar* (2007), Buch's *Sansibar Blues* (2008), and Vosseler's *Sterne über Sansibar* (2010) is thoughtful, well researched, and theoretically informed in its application of a Deleuzian framework. David Courey reads Zafer Şenocak and Navid Kermani in relation to contemporary German debates on multiculturalism and Enlightenment: the context is set out very well, but the readings of texts are somewhat cursory. Finally, Áine McMurtry offers a detailed and compelling interpretation of bilingualism as a form of ethical engagement in the work of Yoko Tawada, framing this author's working across languages as a form of ethical nomadism in the sense elaborated by (among others) Rosi Braidotti.

This short volume is a useful, and for the most part inspirational, opening to an important (and as yet under-researched) dimension in our understanding of contemporary German-language literature and film. It would have benefited from an index and perhaps even a select bibliography, but it is well edited, tightly focused, and a credit to the Edinburgh German Yearbook series in which it appears.

UNIVERSITY OF LEEDS STUART TABERNER

Polemical Austria: The Rhetorics of National Identity. From Empire to the Second Republic. By ANTHONY BUSHELL. Cardiff: University of Wales Press. 2013. 314 pp. £75. ISBN 978-0-7083-2604-6.

In 2013 the Austrian author Robert Menasse's essay *Der Europäische Landbote: Die Wut der Bürger und der Friede Europas; oder Warum die geschenkte Demokratie einer erkämpften weichen muss* (Vienna: Zsolnay, 2012) won the accolade of 'Political Book of the Year'. In it, Menasse proposes the denationalization of the European Union—an argument that also touches on his wider sense that contemporary

Austria lacks a coherent national identity. Published against this provocative background, Anthony Bushell's study *Polemical Austria* is thus particularly timely in its attempt to refocus our attention on the question of Austrian identity formation not simply as a political phenomenon, but as a rhetorical and linguistic one.

In his preface Bushell notes how what became such a wide-ranging volume (spanning Austrian identity over three centuries) began as a more localized study of contemporary Austrian self-perception. Yet, Bushell notes, his original time-frame proved to be limiting, since 'contemporary Austrian identity is the product of a long and involved process, one over which Austrians themselves have had little influence' (p. 5). His study thus considers a long view of the many 'rhetorical traditions employed to express the often nebulous concept of Austria' (p. 6) from the age of empire onwards, while also relating these traditions back to Austrian society after 1945. This is a rich and nuanced approach, which allows Bushell to highlight always interesting—and often surprising—correspondences between multiple eras of Austrian history.

Structurally, the work is divided into three sections, but these avoid a strictly chronological framework, allowing each section to be read as a stand-alone piece. The first, 'Towards a Theory of Austria', questions why 'the notion of Austria proved such a difficult concept to maintain or assert' (p. 24). Over three chapters, Bushell explores contemporary Austrian identity and the relation of that identity to multiple historical contexts (including Metternich and the First and Second World Wars), and a range of socio-political settings (such as the European Union, the Church, the 'German Question'). Throughout, cultural sources are also used, from Schiller to Menasse, and although the material presented is necessarily selective, it is always varied. This opening section clearly sets out both Austria's need for self-definition and the challenges and pitfalls facing those tasked with defining that identity. Flitting across centuries and contexts, Bushell expertly shows how Austria grew to be an entirely 'negotiable product' (p. 74).

The two chapters of the second section, 'Writing Austria', are distinctly more historical in focus, tracing the story of Austria's shift from a military and political power to an intellectual and cultural construction—a process that Bushell argues went hand in hand with the growth of Vienna and the dominating role of this capital city in the construction of Austrian consciousness. The 'writing' referred to in the section title is predominantly that of the feuilleton, though more conventional literary figures are considered, particularly in the context of state censorship. Especially penetrating is Bushell's discussion of the Jewish community's impact on the rhetoric of national identity, not least through a substantial role in the Viennese press.

In 'Austria: Revived, Reviled, Revised', the third and largest section of the study, Bushell returns to the present, tracing over four chapters the development of Austrian identity after 1918, and in particular expanding the Vienna-centric discussion of the previous section to include the significance of the provinces. Here the well-trod story of the *Anschluss* and the 'rhetorics of forgetfulness' (p. 178) after the Second World War are expertly summarized, before the study moves into its perhaps most interesting discussion, of contemporary Austria from Waldheim to Haider. In a densely researched section, Bushell notes how in many respects Austrian identity has become 'an act of performance' (p. 242)—a notion that might fruitfully have been pursued even further throughout the entire study. When read as whole, then, Bushell's exploration of Austrian identity begins and ends in the present, with the past not deployed simply to explain the current state of affairs, but rather to reveal the echoes and parallels that have underpinned Austrian identity over centuries.

Inevitably, not all elements of Austrian identity culture can be covered in such a volume (and as Bushell himself notes, for example, sport surely also plays a significant role). Those already well versed in Austrian Studies might sometimes wish to hear more from Bushell about each of the texts, contexts, and case studies he uses to illuminate his argument. Nevertheless, his skill in balancing detail with overview is considerable, and the work will surely appeal to an unusually wide range of readers. For undergraduates and postgraduates, the study offers a clearly argued, well-focused overview of Austrian identity politics, and the use of English translation throughout opens this work up to those outside of Germanic Studies. Meanwhile, established scholars will still discover much of use here, not least in the unusual range of sources (from Grillparzer and Kraus to political slogans and chocolate-box designs).

Bushell's study traces the momentous manner in which Austria 'went from a large continental empire to a small Alpine republic more or less overnight' (p. 6). Read as a whole, it provides an engaging and deeply readable narrative of the struggle for Austrian identity. Its breadth of focus is a genuine strength, with a great deal of material presented quickly and concisely, yet generally avoiding the impression of incompleteness or breathlessness. The historical context is pertinent, and the study is genuinely innovative in its discussion of the post-1945 period and, in particular, the legacy of past rhetoric for Austrian identity today. *Polemical Austria* clearly has the makings of a standard reference work, both for those coming new to the study of Austria and for those looking to refresh or deepen their existing understanding.

King's College London   Benedict Schofield

On Becoming God: Late Medieval Mysticism and the Modern Western Self. By Ben Morgan. New York: Fordham University Press. 2013. xi+301 pp. $55. ISBN 978-0-8232-3992-4.

On Becoming God traces the transition in the early fourteenth century from the concept of 'becoming God' (which Ben Morgan reads as an orientation of personal spiritual development towards the relinquishing of individual control and the erasing of the distinction between self and God) to a modern sense of identity that sets store by its own sovereignty and in which self-policing precisely excludes such a forfeiting of agency.

The book is structured in three parts. In the first section it assesses attempts by Jacques Lacan, Luce Irigaray, and Amy Hollywood to appropriate historical texts associated with mysticism, attempts in which a 'different way of living in the world' (p. 11) is sought but in the context of conceptualizations of identity that are ultimately modern: autonomous, self-contained, and sovereign. The limitations of this kind of approach to subjectivity are indicated in the light of selected recent neuroscientific research on human coexistence and identity. The second section presents fourteenth-century mystical texts and their medieval contexts in more detail, with Meister Eckhart taking centre stage as the thinker who does most to explore ideas of identity in which sovereignty is relinquished. Albeit within a model of self-development, Eckhart aims for 'a mode of being beyond self-orientation' (p. 135). Even ritual or ascetic regimes are seen as potentially self-centred, what Eckhart calls an 'attachment [. . .] that involves the loss of freedom to wait on God' (p. 92). From this point, Morgan focuses on the change of climate in the 1320s in which self-policing starts to replace self-abandonment, whereby the 'freedom to wait on God' (p. 92) transforms into the freedom to impose control on one's self. He asserts that this is constitutive of modern selfhood, only in the light of which the idea of 'becoming God' seems so other-worldly. The final section seeks to trace the continuities between the fourteenth and twentieth centuries in how identity functions as a 'policing of spiritual growth'. In particular, it compares the medieval relationships between female mystics and their male confessors and early psychoanalytic relationships between (often female) patients and (exclusively male) therapists. Psychoanalysis is thus understood as a means for integrating 'troublesome emotions', and as such—in fourteenth-century parlance—as a way of controlling the aspiration of 'becoming God'.

For Morgan the fact that many mystics and psychoanalytic subjects are female is not incidental. Gender represents an obvious way in which we inhabit pre-existing socially prescribed roles, as well as being an important prism for his examination of the ways in which modern habits of selfhood have been challenged in the fourteenth century and after. Morgan laments a widespread neglect of gender difference in theoretical contributions on identity beyond sovereign selfhood: Charles Taylor's otherwise commended reflections on selfhood are seen as being unable to accommodate female identity, and Peter Bürger's contribution is identified as a cul-de-sac for female identity, which is either marginalized or 'absorbed into male identity' (p. 73). Female theorists are not immune: Irigaray is taken to task for a binary view of identity, where male is rational, systematic, and above bodily impulse, and all that is excluded by this is affirmed in the female subject. The strong focus on gender begs the question of whether this dimension of identity is more significant than any other aspect (such as class or ethnography), and there are steps in this direction in that Morgan makes a link between visionary status and social exclusion, but he does not explore it further.

Another dimension of existence that is seen to take us beyond the conventional model of sovereign subjectivity is the social norms, shared habits and discourse, that Morgan identifies as 'forms of connectedness that go beyond individual identity' (p. 66) and which provide evidence for an ontology of 'human togetherness' (p. 219). This connectedness or togetherness is seen to precede identity and make it possible, rather than merely modifying it. Morgan draws attention to the tension between this interpersonal dimension and the seemingly individual, inward 'phenomenological stream that gives our life its tenor' and fosters the '"mineness" of identity' (pp. 69 and 76). However, because of the ontological priority given to togetherness, what is never fully explored is how this inward stream of experience relates to structures, norms, and power relations. This deficiency is compounded by the lack of a sense of what the status of this togetherness is: it is presented as a fact of existence, but also as something with value (that is, it makes us relate to ourselves and others in a better way). Presumably, however, if this togetherness is a fact of existence, then it must contain within it both the possibility of taking care of, or empathizing with, others, but also of exploiting and instrumentalizing them. There is a similar problem with Eckhart's notion of seeking a mode of identity that avoids reliance on autonomous selfhood: presumably there is always and inevitably something paradoxical (and dialectical) in the avoidance of the attachments of habit and ritual, which is in some sense also a way of returning to the self.

However, these reservations do not detract from the merit of a very interesting account of a particular vein of thinking about identity and a convincing analysis of key parallels between otherwise disparate periods. The book is a valuable contribution to what Morgan calls the 'longer development of modern practices of selfhood' (p. 153). It is impeccably written and well researched—one only occasionally wants more support in the use of secondary sources, for instance in the discussion of the relational and situational aspects of identity in Freud's writings, on which much of value has been written already.

University of Nottingham   Jerome Carroll

Popular History and Fiction: The Myth of August the Strong in German Literature, Art and Media. By Madeleine Brook. (Cultural Identity Studies, 28) Oxford: Peter Lang. 2013. x+260 pp. £42. ISBN 978-3-0343-0842-7.

This study of the reception of August the Strong (1670–1733), Elector of Saxony and King of Poland, charts the establishment of the myth surrounding the man, and developments in the retelling of this myth in various historical and cultural contexts within the German-speaking lands from the early eighteenth century up until almost the present day (2010). This in turn provides a springboard for two other major concerns of the book: an examination of Saxon history (particularly the history of Dresden) and its place in a cultural and national consciousness that generally viewed Saxony as Prussia's inferior; and, most ambitiously, an assessment of the practices of historical narrative, its limitations, and the mutual influences of history, popular fiction, and other media, including visual art. In this way, the book moves beyond August the Strong's legacy and offers food for thought to historians and literary critics alike regarding the practice of their disciplines.

The first two chapters set up the critical discussion for the broad chronological sweep that follows. Chapter 1 presents a discourse about the reliability of historical narratives that privilege certain sources, and more generally about modes of historical narration. Madeleine Brook's later concise explanation of the seventeenth-century concepts *Gedichtgeschichte*—which 'contained the main elements of factual history with additional, invented fictions to elaborate the story'—and *Geschichtgedichte*—'with a didactic purpose, cither hid the events of a true history under a veil of fiction and added probable events or was an entirely invented story' (p. 69)—is an additional useful marker for when she proceeds to examine the potential value of fiction as offering new insights into August's myth (e.g. pp. 70–90 and pp. 132–33). In Chapter 2 the reader learns how 'August the Strong was the first architect of his own myth' (p. 33). That August forged an image of himself as 'a man of universal interests and abilities' (p. 60) via the promotion of the arts at court, alongside self-conscious participation in the visual spectacle of power, means that the reduction of this myth to the popular perception that 'his reign was marked by failure' and that he was 'oversexed' (p. 19) is all the more striking. The remaining chapters reveal how this latter version of the story came to dominate popular opinion, while also uncovering pockets of resistance to a hegemonic interpretation in fiction or art which, as Brook suggests, might yet be exploited by historians to reveal a more rounded image of August's lasting impact.

The book impresses for its chronological breadth, but also for the author's range of sources: in her quest to encourage further historical assessment of August's legacy, Brook evaluates film, extracts from TV series, and art exhibition guides alongside drama, epic poetry, literature, biography, and official histories. Despite this vast scope, there is no trace of superficiality in her analysis—on the contrary, the fluctuating fortunes of August's myth are tightly bound to a concise and clear explanation of the changing nature of German regional and national identities through the centuries in what is overall an immensely readable account. The outstanding chapters, for this reader, are Chapters 4 and 6, about the nineteenth-century and the GDR reception of August the Strong respectively. On the national stage, August's legend is sidelined by the nineteenth-century Prussian concept of German identity, which stood in opposition to August's perceived 'French' morals and his all too easy conversion to Catholicism in a (successful) bid to win the Polish crown. August's rejection on the grounds of his unsuitability as a national hero was partially reversed in the GDR, however. There, despite his unwelcome royal status, August represents an alternative historical figure via which to review the Saxon/East German past in a culture keen to reject the imperialist narrative that privileged Prussia's Friedrich Wilhelm. These 'official' interpretations are contrasted interestingly with more nuanced or critical narratives, often found, as the author is keen to stress, outside the traditional historical account. Elsewhere, August's reputation as a *galant* becomes the focus for a discussion of female perspectives on the period of his reign, including the *histoires à clef* written by one of his many mistresses, Maria Aurora von Königsmarck (1662–1728).

The breadth of the study necessarily means that detailed analysis has to be sacrificed in some cases, but the author provides compelling reasons for other scholars to turn to less well-known or overlooked sources, and thereby to question the pre-eminence of accepted historical accounts. It is to be hoped that this challenge will be taken up.

THE QUEEN'S COLLEGE, OXFORD   JOANNA NEILLY

Aspects of Dostoevskii: Art, Ethics and Faith. Ed. by ROBERT REID and JOE AN-
    DREW. (Studies in Slavic Literature and Poetics, 57) Amsterdam and New York:
    Rodopi. 2012. xiv+306 pp. €66. ISBN 978–90–420–3514–0.

Dostoevskii's 'Overcoat': Influence, Comparison, and Transposition. Ed. by JOE
    ANDREW and ROBERT REID. (Studies in Slavic Literature and Poetics, 58)
    Amsterdam and New York: Rodopi. 2013. vi+354 pp. €75. ISBN 978–90–
    420–3793–9.

These two volumes of essays on Fedor Dostoevskii, published in Rodopi's Studies in Slavic Literature and Poetics series, have their origins in the 2008 'Aspects of Dostoevskii' conference organized by the Neo-Formalist Circle, which is led by Joe Andrew and Robert Reid, who served as co-editors in each case. However, they are not conference proceedings. Rather, the two thematic volumes constitute essays that have been carefully curated. Together they showcase the breadth and vibrancy of Dostoevskii scholarship today.

The first volume, *Aspects of Dostoevskii: Art, Ethics and Faith*, includes an in-troduction by Reid and fourteen essays by Dostoevskii specialists: Katalin Kroó, Audun J. Mørch, Sarah Hudspith, Hristo Manolakev, Olga Soboleva, Diane Oen-ning Thompson, Robin Milner-Gulland, Leon Burnett, Robin Aizlewood, Andrew, Katherine Jane Briggs, Robin Feuer Miller, Richard Peace, and Cleo Protokhristova. The essays cover a broad range of Dostoevskii's works, including his major novels (*Crime and Punishment, The Idiot, Demons*, and *The Brothers Karamazov*) as well as a selection of his shorter works (*White Nights, Notes from the House of the Dead, Notes from Underground, Bobok, The Meek One*, and *The Dream of a Ridiculous Man*). There is one essay focused on each work, aside from *The Idiot*, which is the focus of two chapters, and *The Brothers Karamazov*, which looms large in the second half of the volume. The essays by Andrew, Briggs, Miller, Peace, and Protokhristova all examine aspects of Dostoevskii's last novel.

The volume's subtitle—'Art, Ethics and Faith'—reveals its emphasis. In his ex-cellent introduction to the collection Reid shows how these three major thematic areas unite Dostoevskii's œuvre, existing Dostoevskii scholarship, and, indeed, the essays in this volume. In Reid's (and the volume's) view, 'Each is at the mercy of the other: the ethics cannot break free from the religious content; the religious content is often found wanting ethically and Dostoevskii's art ensures that what we are reading is but a small narrative fragment embedded in a vastly greater structure—into which, however, he thought it worthwhile to embed it' (p. 20). It is this 'system of checks and balances', as Reid terms it (ibid.), that resists unilateral interpretations and continuously invites new readings.

All the essays in this volume provide innovative readings, but unfortunately limitations of space prevent me from mentioning them all. However, several stood out. Thompson's contribution explores references to Muhammad's *Night Journey* in *The Idiot* and *Demons*, in particular its relationship to the moment of epiphany by Myshkin and Kirillov, respectively. Her reading of this Islamic motif results in a fresh conclusion about the binary of transcendence and nothingness. Two essays examining visual arts in different works resonate well together, shedding new light on Dostoevskii's literary interaction with and philosophical understanding of the image. These are Soboleva's essay on photography and painting in *The Idiot* and Burnett's essay on the icon in *The Meek One*. Lastly, a small but intriguing point: there is disagreement between Miller's reading of the 'Onion' parable in *The Brothers Karamazov* and Peace's examination of the same, but both use their respective readings of the parable to productive ends in their essays. Such moments of critical debate point to the collection's richness; its essays provide multiple insights into the interaction of art, ethics, and faith in Dostoevskii's works.

While the first volume focuses on Dostoevskii's œuvre, the second, *Dostoevskii's 'Overcoat': Influence, Comparison, and Transposition*, delves into the enormous body of works that influenced or were influenced by it in Russia and beyond. Where the first volume is tightly themed, the second is by necessity less cohesive. Introducing the collection, Andrew states the volume's aim: 'To turn the oft-quoted apocryphal comment [that 'We have all come out from underneath Gogol's *Overcoat*'] on its head as it were, [. . .] to see the profound influence Dostoevskii has had, both within his own lifetime and since, on the lives, work and thought of his contemporaries and successors' (p. 1).

While Dostoevskii remains central in these essays, the volume's broad remit allows for the exploration of his works in productive new contexts. Strikingly, the majority of the contributors here specialize in areas of Russian literature and culture other than Dostoevskii: poetry, other nineteenth-century writers, twentieth-century literature, genre fiction, as well as other media, including theatre, film, and comic books. The list of contributors includes Radosvet Kolarov, Michael Pursglove, Eric de Haard, Richard Freeborn, Claire Whitehead, Alexandra Smith, Michael Basker, Henrietta Mondry, Andrzej Dudek, Neil Cornwell, Cynthia Marsh, Deborah A. Martinsen, Reid, Andrea Hacker, Olga Peters Hasty, and Irina Makoveeva.

Arranged chronologically, the first four essays stretch back into the early nineteenth century, while the last thirteen spread beyond Dostoevskii's works and era, bringing in materials from the nineteenth, twentieth, and even twenty-first centuries. The first three essays look for Dostoevskii's influences and find them in, for example, the work of writers with whom he collaborated, such as Apollon Grigorovich, poetry such as that by Iakov Polonskii, and the work of rivals such as Ivan Turgenev. The fourth essay examines how Dostoevskii used his later work to revise and recast his own earlier material. As the following five essays demonstrate, Dostoevskii's influence on later Russian literature and culture was broad, including crime fiction by Aleksandr Shkliarevskii, the cult of Pushkin, Andrei Belyi's Symbolist novel *Silver Dove*, Vasilii Rozanov's relationships and art, and even Dmitrii Merezhkovskii's interpretations of Dostoevskii's works.

The final seven essays examine Dostoevskii's reach beyond his native culture. Contributions explore the following topics: the debt of writers such as Orhan Pamuk and Vladimir Nabokov to Dostoevskii; Russian theatrical adaptations of his novels on the British stage; works by authors ranging from Italo Svevo and Albert Camus to Iain Pears and Aravind Adiga that echo the narrator from *Notes from Underground*; 'The Grand Inquisitor' and dystopian novels and films; Akira Kurosawa's film adaptation of *The Idiot*; Robert Bresson's film *The Pickpocket*; and contemporary comic-book and graphic-novel adaptations of *Crime and Punishment*. These essays constitute one of the first collections of research on Dostoevskii's reach outside of Russia by scholars of Russian literature and culture.

The two volumes demonstrate the breadth of anglophone Dostoevskii scholarship. The strength of the first volume's new readings of Dostoevskii's works is enhanced by the second volume, which emphasizes the relevance of his writing beyond Russian literature and culture and beyond the nineteenth century. Together, the volumes constitute a significant contribution to Dostoevskii studies as they showcase both new readings of Dostoevskii's work and new research on his broader cultural influence, providing a multifaceted overview of the state of the field today.

UNIVERSITY OF BRITISH COLUMBIA   KATHERINE BOWERS

The Prose of Sasha Sokolov: Reflections on/of the Real. By ELENA KRAVCHENKO. (MHRA Texts and Dissertations, 86) London: Modern Humanities Research Association. 2013. 156 pp. £19.99. ISBN 978–1–907322–52–5.

While the number of essays and scholarly articles devoted to the works of Sasha Sokolov grows steadily every year, Elena Kravchenko's book, based on her doctoral dissertation at University College London, is the first ever monograph exploring his three acclaimed novels: *A School for Fools*, *Between Dog and Wolf*, and *Palisandriia*.

Approaching the novels in the order in which they were written, Kravchenko explores Sokolov's elusive concept of reality and, in particular, the relationship between art and reality. In the first chapter, 'Metaphor of Origin: Narcissism as a Constructive Principle in *School for Fools*', she uses the myth of Narcissus as a metaphor for the dynamics between the 'real' and the 'constructed', and shows 'how memory, instead of retrieving the past, signifies it, and how language, instead of expressing reality, engenders it' (p. 12), that is, becomes 'the only element that constitutes and controls reality' (p. 129).

In the second chapter, 'A Realized Metaphor: The Eucharist Miracles in *Between Dog and Wolf*', Kravchenko presents her reading of the novel as a re-enactment of the Eucharist. 'In this re-enactment representation of reality becomes represented reality, in which language does not so much communicate as embody what is absent' (p. 12). As Kravchenko aptly explains, '*Between Dog and Wolf* is a twilight zone in which the gap between fiction and reality, between times and spaces is transcended through language. The lost context emerges from the text, reduced to the materiality of the letter, to the surface of the page, and to the very moment of reading' (p. 90). This allows the scholar to conclude: 'As sound becomes yeast, language becomes wine, text becomes the body, and the act of reading turns into a communion' (p. 129).

In the third chapter, 'A Lie that Tells the Truth: Mediation of Reality in *Palisandriia*', Kravchenko analyses the novel by applying to it Julia Kristeva's notion of the 'abject' and exploring such aesthetic sensibilities as Camp and Kitsch. Showing Palisandriia's 'deconstruction' of common historical clichés as well as the author's playful attempt to end the novel as a genre, Kravchenko concludes that 'the real has to be mediated in order to be appreciated or even experienced' because 'historical reality is discursive reality: we receive and know it already as a text' (p. 13).

Among the most enlightening and interesting parts of Kravchenko's scholarly discourse are detailed, probing discussions of the three novels, constituting a stimulating and often surprising and profound *explication de texte*. For instance, besides just explaining that the name Vitia Pliaskin is used in the dedication to *A School for Fools* as a hidden reference to chorea (St Vitus's dance), Kravchenko goes further, providing numerous details from the life of the saint and finding in them elements significant to our better understanding of the other parts of the text (pp. 22–24). Discussing the appearance of Leonardo da Vinci in the novel, she finds intriguing bits of information about the Renaissance master in Giorgio Vasari and connects the Mona Lisa portrait to the novel's heroine, Veta Akatova (pp. 40–41). Equally important are, for example, Kravchenko's discussions of schizophrenic glossomania (p. 25), of paronomasia (pp. 26–28), of the importance of lists (pp. 29–32), of the use of texts in texts (pp. 32–34), of ekphrasis (pp. 60–64), and of the poetics of recycling (pp. 69–71). All of them enhance and deepen our understanding of Sokolov's novels and help us navigate their complex labyrinths.

The depth and breadth of Kravchenko's scholarly analysis posits a fascinating paradox: while readers will be easily convinced that Sokolov always questions reality and asserts the dominant role of language in literature, the study may seem to imply that he read scores of scholarly works, ranging from Mikhail Bakhtin to Jacques Derrida, and used their scholarly discourses to construct his complex prose. This is, of course, not true. On the contrary, Sokolov always denied reading or being influenced by scholarship (with the sole exception of works related to schizophrenia, when he was simulating mental illness in order to be dismissed from the army). In other words, Sokolov's literary solutions are visceral, perhaps often subconscious. Following his idea of 'proetry'—prose elevated to the level of poetry—Sokolov arranges his narrative space 'in such a way that the reader won't doubt even for a second that existence is precisely what is happening here and now, on the given page' (Sasha Sokolov, *In the House of the Hanged: Essays and Vers Libres*, trans. by Alexander Boguslawski (Toronto: University of Toronto Press, 2012), p. 76). What the author does naturally, what he hears and feels with his 'melodic guts' (*In the House of the Hanged*, p. 44), can, as Kravchenko aptly demonstrates, be explained, justified, or clarified by using the works of many scholars and researchers. These explanations, revealing Sokolov's intricate intertextual links and his erudition, prove again and again that he is one of the world's most important living authors of the last four decades.

Notwithstanding the overall merits of Kravchenko's work, and its importance for Sokolov's scholars and critics, a few minor flaws need to be mentioned here. They can be divided into two groups: (*a*) typographical and editorial errors, and (*b*) slight misinterpretations, mistranslations, and misreadings that crept into the book. In addition, although it is not due to Kravchenko's negligence but rather to publishing schedules and deadlines, it is necessary to point out that the book's notes and bibliography include neither the 2012 English translation of Sokolov's *In the House of the Hanged* mentioned above nor the Japanese translation of *Between Dog and Wolf* (Tokyo: Kawade Shobo Shinsha, 2012). Since Kravchenko acknowledges the importance of the essays in the introduction, but quotes them (in their Russian version) only once, a more appropriate title for the book would be *The Novels of Sasha Sokolov*. Readers interested in Sokolov's shorter works will find in the essays many vivid examples confirming, strengthening, and elucidating Kravchenko's excellent research.

ROLLINS COLLEGE   ALEXANDER BOGUSLAWSKI

Vladimir Sorokin's Languages. Ed. by TINE ROESEN and DIRK UFFELMANN. (Slavica Bergensia, 11) Bergen: Department of Foreign Languages, University of Bergen. 2013. 381 pp. £16. ISBN 978–82–90249–37–8.

This volume, edited by Tine Roesen and Dirk Uffelmann, represents the proceedings of a conference which took place at Aarhus University in 2012. It includes sixteen individual contributions by Sorokin scholars from Europe, Russia, and America, thereby offering an international collection of the latest research on Sorokin's most recent works and his œuvre more generally, focusing on the significance of language in Sorokin's poetics. As such it makes a very important, English-language, and multifaceted contribution to our understanding of a central feature of Sorokin's writings. Even though Vladimir Sorokin is unquestionably one of the most important, most prolific, most debated, and much-translated Russian writers, especially of the post-Soviet period, the study of his works remains nevertheless a comparatively narrow field. The reasons for this may be associated with the fact that his writings, often labelled postmodernist, pose considerable challenges to aesthetic expectations, analysis, and interpretation. The problem of Sorokin scholarship, which the present book tries to address, is language 'as one of the main focal points, if not *the* main focal point, of Sorokin's œuvre, which possesses metalinguistic, metarhetorical, metastylistic, metadiscursive, and metapragmatic dimensions' (p. 10, emphasis original).

In the introduction, Roesen and Uffelmann identify five 'nodes' around which existing scholarship on the importance and role of language(s) in Sorokin's works revolves: (1) the author's preference for borrowing from specific literary styles over employing his 'own' distinct language, and the concomitant questioning of the concept of authorship; (2) the postmodernist metalingual nature of Sorokin's works, aimed at laying bare certain functions and mechanisms of language; (3) the relationship between plot and language, exemplified, for instance, in the materialization of metaphors; (4) the dominance of foreign languages, most prevalently Chinese and German; (5) issues that pertain to dealing with translated works by Sorokin.

The sixteen very readable articles which follow the introduction are organized according to their analytical focus into five sections: 'Discourse and Narration'; 'Ideal Languages'; 'Bad Words, Bad Writing?'; 'Bodies in and beyond the Text'; and 'The Languages of the Retrofuture'. The first two sections concentrate on Sorokin's earlier works, and the last three deal with his latest publications. At the same time, the sections also fall into a chronological progression. The approaches adopted by these highly engaging discussions range, among others, from Mark Lipovetsky's suggestion of viewing carnalization—the turning of discourse into flesh—as Sorokin's master trope, to Peter Deutschmann's discussion of narration and speech, which suggests a relationship between text and consciousness, from Maxim Marusenkov's typologically Romanticist reading of Sorokin and Nadezhda Grigoryeva's discussion of cardiocentrism to Manuela Kovalev's analysis of obscenities in Sorokin's fiction and Dirk Uffelmann's examination of the incomprehensibility effects of Sorokin's use of Chinese words and passages, from Martin Paulsen's discussion of the significance of the Latin script to José Alaniz's fascinating application of disability and stuttering studies, to analyses of subjecthood (Lisa Ryoko Wakamiya), of implied authorial judgement (Brigitte Obermayr), and of the relationship between the collective and the individual (Tine Roesen).

As the topics addressed by these contributions suggest, none of them approaches questions of language and style in isolation from other aspects of Sorokin's writings; on the contrary, Sorokin's language(s) are viewed as part and parcel of his works' semantic make-up, in spite of the fact that at first sight his language often seems to mock the very idea that his texts might have a recognizable meaning. This is well illustrated in the penultimate section, in which Marina Aptekman, Ingunn Lunde, and Ilya Kukulin show in great detail in their respective articles the extent to which analysis of Sorokin's style and language is central to discerning the implied authorial intention. In the cases of the texts which they examine, implied semantic intention may be discovered at the levels of psychological, social, or historical commentary, for example.

The sixth section contains the transcription of a round-table discussion entitled 'Translation Sorokin/Translated Sorokin', involving Vladimir Sorokin himself and the translators of his works, Jamey Gambrell (English), Tine Roesen (Danish), Andreas Tretner (German), and other contributors to the volume. The discussion between Sorokin and his translators provides rare insight into Sorokin's experience with translations and translators of his texts. It also offers a glimpse of the multifaceted challenges which his translators face. These include the lack of a clear authorial voice in Sorokin's works as much as the question of the translatability of both intonation and historical, specifically ideological terms bound to a precise time and culture. Further questions which they deal with are how to represent in translation the use of foreign languages in the original text and the ever-present intertextual layers, viz. the cultural and social context. The many different approaches represented in this volume make it a rewarding read for anyone interested in Vladimir Sorokin and post-Soviet literature and culture more generally.

HAMBURG   NICOLAS DREYER

ABSTRACTS

Satirical Journals and Neutrality in the Franco-Prussian War   by William Webster

With the outbreak of the **Franco-Prussian War, humorous and satirical journals** in the major European states were for the first time confronted by an event of truly international dimensions. This article explores how the major organs in **France, Prussia, the United Kingdom**, and **Austria** viewed the conduct of **neutral states** in the conflict. It demonstrates how journals in the combatant nations reacted to the conduct of their detached neighbours; and it examines how influential periodicals in the neutral states responded to the events and controversies of the war as well as to the policies of their own governments.

Influence Revisited: Irène Némirovsky's Creative Reading of English Literature   by Angela Kershaw

This article offers a comparative reading of **Irène Némirovsky**'s fiction, drawing on approaches to national literary history that are sensitive to border crossings. Considering Némirovsky's engagement with English literature in the light of her broad interest in foreign literature, **influence** emerges as a multiple and creative interaction. The article examines the mediation of Némirovsky's reading of Tolstoy through **E. M. Forster** and **Percy Lubbock** and compares the depiction of the younger generation between the two world wars in novels by Némirovsky and **Evelyn Waugh**. It argues that interpreting Némirovsky's creative reading as literary hospitality is both ethically and aesthetically productive.

Under the Magnifying Glass: Investigating the First World War in Recent Crime Novels by Ben Elton, and Jan Eik and Horst Bosetzky   by Nóra de Buiteléir

This article compares **representations of the First World War** in two **crime novels** recently published in Britain and Germany. Reflecting both a Europe-wide boom in **historical crime fiction** and popular fascination, in Britain at least, with **WWI memory**, both novels complicate the surface crime plot with deeper narratives of detectives struggling to maintain integrity in a time of chaos. I examine how the conventions of the **procedural** and the **whodunnit** package the experiences of the wartime detective in different ways, and consider the implications of this for the position negotiated by the texts towards the crisis of war more generally.

Embedded Extempore Verse in the Intimate Letters of John, Lord Hervey (1696–1743)   by Bill Overton

Embedded extempore verse is verse occurring in a prose letter that has been composed during the process of writing. While the **eighteenth century** was the heyday of the **verse epistle**, and while it is not uncommon to find verse quoted in prose letters, embedded extempore verse is extremely rare. After introducing the concept and distinguishing it from other kinds of verse that occur in prose letters, this article provides analysis of the thirty-odd examples in the surviving letters of Lord Hervey, focusing on those he wrote to his most intimate correspondents, **Stephen Fox, Francesco Algarotti**, and **Lady Mary Wortley Montagu**.

Transcending Time and Space: Barry MacSweeney's Experimental Odes of the 1970s   by Oliver Bevington

During the 1970s, the **British poet Barry MacSweeney** carried out a series of poetic experiments with the **ode form**. With reference to MacSweeney's 1978 collection *Odes: 1971–1978*, and a poetry poster entitled *Ode to Coal*, which MacSweeney designed in collaboration with the visual artist **Michael Chaplin**, this article situates MacSweeney's experimental poems in relation to the history of the ode form. It also suggests that the experimental impetus of MacSweeney's odes is indebted to a **twentieth-century** shift in the nature of poetic form that has sought to align poetry with **visual art** rather than with **music**.

Plotting and the Novel: The Duplicity of Espionage in Balzac's *Une ténébreuse affaire* by Michael Tilby

Une ténébreuse affaire has been seen as a novel in which **plot** is especially prominent. Yet plot in this disconcerting work is undermined by both its plurality and its elliptical nature. **Balzac**'s focus on espionage, which derives from his reading of **Fenimore Cooper**, is but one strand in a universal emphasis on mutual observation that leads to stasis. While susceptible of a political interpretation, this also represents Balzac's concern to detach the novel from the adventure-story model. The doubling of characters and the network of restricted thematic reference-points produce a **self-reflexive** composition admired by **Gide**, **Valéry**, and arguably **Claudel**.

Queering Photography: Race, Death, and Sexuality in Roland Barthes's *La Chambre claire* and *Fragments d'un discours amoureux* by Benjamin Hiramatsu Ireland

This study examines, through intertextual and intratextual readings of *La Chambre claire* and *Fragments d'un discours amoureux*, Roland **Barthes**'s queer illuminations of the **photograph**'s function towards homoerotic desire, suicidal propensities, and French **colonialism**. Barthes's desired Object is an epistemological construct, constituting not only the semiotician's mother but also a virtualized homosexual figure, both of whom are racialized as 'coloured'. The **racialization** of Barthes's desired Object, concurrently his deceased mother and an imagined male homosexual, prompts a critical re-evaluation of Barthesian sexuality's relationship with **queer** desire, textual/visual mediation, **necrophilia**, and the **Maternal**.

Exemplarity in and around the *Novelas ejemplares* by Barry Taylor

We may never know what the 'mystery' is that according to **Cervantes** lies in his *Novelas ejemplares*. His teasing combination of **novella** and **exemplum** belongs in the tradition of brief narrative works which display or obscure the **promythium** and **epimythium**. This article traces these elements in works before his time which Cervantes knew, probably knew, and almost certainly did not know; and in works inspired by the *Novelas ejemplares* and the *Decameron* after his time.

Modernity and the Cultural Memory Crisis in Gustavo Adolfo Bécquer's *La cruz del diablo* and *El monte de las ánimas* by Sarah Sierra

Gustavo Adolfo Bécquer's *leyendas La cruz del diablo* and *El monte de las ánimas* document an interstitial cultural moment in which **oral memory rituals** were disappearing in favour of new ways of managing cultural knowledge such as archive and print culture. This analysis considers Bécquer's emphasis on **orality** and **memory** in the guise of ritual storytelling within these two legends. It demonstrates an increasing anxiety experienced during this transitional period, in which human behaviour was radically transformed by the transference from ritual memory traditions to external memory storage in the practice of recollecting the cultural past.

Zurich Dada's Forgotten Music Master: Hans Heusser by Peter Dayan

Hans Heusser was the only person apart from **Tristan Tzara** to have an entire **Zurich Dada** soiree devoted to his work. Heusser's music was played at almost all the Zurich Dada soirees, and the **Cabaret Voltaire**. But it has since been ignored. Heusser has been erased from the history and legacy of Dada. Why? This article suggests two answers. One: **music** in general, for the Zurich Dadaists, is that of which one must not speak; therefore, they did not speak of Heusser's music. Two: reassessing Heusser's contribution would radically challenge our stereoptype of Dada as a movement of noise and provocation.

CPSIA information can be obtained
at www.ICGtesting.com
Printed in the USA
FFOW01n1619140415
12611FF